The Air Racer

Charles A. Mendenhall

SPECIALTY PRESS

To Diane—my ever patient wife, always ready to encourage
when this project seemed hopeless.

Copyright 1971 by Diane Publishing Company
1975 and 1976 by Pylon Publications
1979 by Charles A. Mendenhall
All rights reserved. Printed in the United States of America

First printing—March 1979
Revised—October 1994

ISBN 0-933424-01-9
LC # 79-4715

Library of Congress Cataloging in Publication Data

Mendenhall, Charles A.
  The air racer.

"Material in this book was previously published in three volumes by Pylon Publications under
the titles: The early air racers in three views, 1909-29; The national air racers in three views,
1929-49; and The modern air racers in three views, 1949-1975."
  Bibliography: p. 184
  1. Airplanes, Racing—Drawings.   I. Title.
TL685.6. M44   629.133 '343   79-4715
ISBN 0-933424-01-9

Published by: Specialty Press Publishers and Wholesalers
North Branch, MN 55056

INTRODUCTION

Rheims, France situated in the middle of Europe's champagne country is widely known for its beautiful cathedral. For the air racing enthusiast, this city has an added significance for it was here in 1909 that Glenn Curtiss fluttered around a race course at 47.65 miles per hour in his "Golden Flyer" to win the world's first air race. That race, for the James Gordon Bennett Cup, was to herald the coming of a motor sport that would eventually evolve into the fastest and most demanding competition in history.

The Rheims event, less than six years after the Wright's first heavier than air flight at Kitty Hawk, was inevitable as history shows whenever man invents a new transportation contrivance, it is soon thereafter that his competitive spirit demands that he engage in a test of speed with others of the same bent. Thus, aircraft racing, auto racing, clipper ship racing, chariot racing, and undoubtedly dug-out canoe racing, has occurred. This is all to the good because air racing, aside from the exciting and thrill charged atmosphere of the races themselves, has served an important purpose in the development of the airplane as we know it today. As one settles into a comfortable seat to be whisked across oceans at supersonic speed or marvels at the agility and performance of first line fighter planes, it is well to remember that a great deal of the evolution of today's fine aircraft lies vested in those racing machines of yesteryear.

Before World War I, the quest for greater speed and reliability in racing aircraft brought forth the monoplane Deperdussin and Nieuport racers which, for example, were significant advances over the stick and wire "Baby Wright" and Curtiss "Golden Flyer" machines. These aircraft could, in fact, be considered prototypes of the early fighters of World War I. While major aeronautical advances occurred during World War I and World War II, equally great achievements also occurred during peacetime because of air racing.

After Rheims the Gordon Bennett races continued as an annual event thru 1920 with the exception of the war years. While the Bennett race was only for land planes another event, the Schneider Trophy Race, began in 1913 for seaplanes and this series continued thru 1931 with speeds of racers developed solely for the contest exceeding four hundred miles per hour.

The military became enamoured of air racing in the twenties and competed in a series of Pulitzer Trophy Races with the Curtiss design team fielding the greatest number of winners. Their efforts culminated eventually in the beautiful P-6E Hawk fighters.

By 1929, the races again became the domain of civilians as Doug Davis expertly piloted the Travel Air "Mystery Ship" around the pylons in the Thompson Cup Race to win out over the best equipment the military people could field. With this, the Army and Navy gave up racing and the time of the ingenious, gutsy little guy began — the Golden Age of air racing. As the most colorful and dramatic period of air racing history, the time span between 1929 and 1939 shows the greatest amount of aeronautical ingenuity on the part of individuals of any era. Racing aircraft of these years still stand as monuments to such greats as the Granville Brothers, Ben Howard, Matty Laird, Gordon Israel, Clayton Folkerts and Jimmy Wedell, to name a few of many. The designer/flyers of the thirties came up with such then spectacular items as retractable landing gears, landing flaps and controllable pitch propellers as well as new lighter and stronger methods of airframe construction.

With the advent of World War II all racing activity was suspended and the airplane, based on the secrets learned in racing, leaped ahead a quantum jump in performance under the input of thousands of people and millions of dollars. By 1946, however, with the War behind us, air racing once more returned to Cleveland where modified fighter planes soldiered on in the pylon contests till 1949. Since fielding a modified fighter was extremely expensive, the Goodyear Trophy race was created to allow those of less means to compete. This race, of course, centered around home built midget racers that later became the Formula Ones raced today. Perhaps the public had become jaded for the post war races never equalled the ones of the Golden Age in entertainment and thrills. With the tragic crash of round the world flyer Bill Odom's "Beguine" into a Cleveland apartment house in 1949 the sport of air racing seemingly had come to an end.

True, the Continental Motors Race was carried on in Miami and Detroit but this was a rather half-hearted effort when compared to the mighty Bendix and Thompson Trophy Races of earlier years. Under the auspices of the Professional Race Pilots Association the midgets continued to dust the pylons at such places as Dansville, Niagara Falls, Fort Wayne, Oshkosh and Springfield during the fifties. These turned out to be mostly local interest events, however, with little if any coverage by the national press.

In 1964 the Reno National Air Races was established. These races featured not only the midgets but marked the return of the mighty unlimiteds to the racing scene. As this is written, still another year of Reno racing has transpired, the fourteenth, and no end is yet in sight.

The book, is an effort to draw together, under one cover, the intriguing story of the air racer by means of plan-type illustrations. The drawings contain information on over two hundred of the most interesting of these specialty aircraft. It was surprising to learn during research for this book that in some cases, no formal plans had ever been drawn. A few of the older planes continue to exist in museums around the world but most have been reduced to rubble either in accidents or by the ravages of time.

The drawings in this book, perhaps arbitrarily, cover the

air racers from 1909 thru 1975. 1975 was chosen as a cut-off date, for the period 1909-1975 seems to realistically encompass all the major developments of these colorful, fascinating aircraft. To continue past that date simply means another "Mustang" drawing with a different paint scheme or another "Formula I" with a slightly different shaped wing or fuselage.

Scale squares are provided on the illustrations for ease of scaling up for model aircraft plans. It is hoped that as much enjoyment is encountered by the reader in studying the advancement of aircraft design, as presented here, as was obtained by the author in preparing this book.

Rochester, New York
December, 1978

TABLE OF CONTENTS

Curtiss "Golden Flyer" 10
Wright 11
Latham "Antoinette" 12
Bleriot XI 13
Baby Wright 14
Hanriot 15
Nieuport 16
Nieuport Floatplane 17
Deperdussin 18
Deperdussin Floatplane 19
Sopwith "Tabloid" 20
Ponnier 21
Dayton-Wright 22
Verville-Packard R-1 23
Curtiss-Cox "Texas Wildcat" Monoplane 24
Curtiss-Cox "Texas Wildcat" Biplane 25
Curtiss-Cox "Cactus Kitten" Triplane 26
Nieuport Sesquiplane 27
Curtiss CR-1 28
Curtiss CR-2 29
Navy-Wright NW-1 30
Navy-Wright NW-2 31
Navy "Bee Line" BR-1 and BR-2 32
Curtiss CR-3 33
Curtiss R-6 34
Verville-Sperry R-3 35
Curtiss R2C-1 & -2 36
Wright F2W-1 37
Wright F2W-2 38
Curtiss R3C-1 & -2 39
Supermarine S-4 40
Gloster III 41
Macchi M-39 42
Gloster IV B 43
Short Crusader 44
Kirkham-Williams 45
Supermarine S-5 46
Macchi M-52 47
Gloster VI 48
Navy Curtiss F6C-3 Hawk 49
Fiat C-29 50
Supermarine S-6 51
Macchi M-67 52
Savoia S-65 53
American Mercury 54
Supermarine S-6B 55
Travel Air Model R 56
Page-Curtiss XF6C-6 57
Laird "Solution" LC-DW-300 58
Laird "Super Solution" LC-DW-500 59

Howard "Pete" DGA-3 60
Israel "Redhead" 61
Gee Bee Model Y 62
Gee Bee Model Z 63
Gee Bee R-1 64
Gee Bee R-2 and I.F. (R-1/R-2) 65
Hall "Bulldog" 66
Wedell-Williams "44" and "92" 67
Wedell-Williams "57" 68
Howard "Mike" DGA-4 and "Ike" DGA-5 69
Rider R-1 — "San Francisco I" — "Suzy" 70
Rider R-2 — "San Francisco II" — "Bumblebee"-
    Bushey-McGrew B7M1 71
Chester "Jeep" 72
Cessna CR-2 and CR-3 73
Miles and Atwood Special 74
DeHavilland "Comet" 75
Macchi-Castoldi M-72 76
Gee Bee "Q.E.D." R6H 77
Howard "Mr. Mulligan" DGA-6 78
Percival "Mew Gull" 79
Miles Racer 80
Wittman "Chief Oshkosh" 81
Brown B-1 82
Brown B-2 "Miss Los Angeles" 83
Wittman "Bonzo" D-12 84
Caudron C-460 85
Folkert SK-2 "Toots" 86
Hughes H-1 87
Crosby Special CR-3 and CR-4 88
Rider R-4 "Firecracker", R-5 "Jackrabbit",
    Elmendorf Special 89
Rider R-3 and Marcoux-Bromberg Special 90
Folkerts SK-3 "Jupiter" and SK-4 91
Laird-Turner LTR-14 "Meteor" 92
Military Aircraft HM-1 and "Time Flies" 93
Rider R-6 "8-Ball" 94
Bellanca Tri-Motor 28-92 95
Chester "Goon" 96
Chambers "Chambermaid" 97
Pearson-Williams "Mr. Smoothie" 98
Heinkel He 100 V-8 99
Messerschmitt ME209 V-1 (Bf109R) 100
High Speed Spitfire 101
Heston Racer 102
Bell P-39Q "Aircobra" 103
North American P-51 "Mustang" 104
Goodyear F2G-1 "Corsair" 105
Hawker "Sea Fury" #0, "Miss Merced" 106
Lockheed P-38L "Lightning"; #38 107

North American P-51D "Mustang"; "Miss America"   108
North American P-51D "Mustang"; "Miss
  Van Nuys" 109
North American P-51D "Mustang"; "Miss R.J." &
  "Roto Finish" 110
North American P-51D "Mustang"; "RB-51 Red
  Baron", "Miss Foxy Lady" 111
Grumman F8F-2 "Bearcat"; "Smirnoff"; "Conquest
  I", "American Jet" #1 112
Grumman F8F-2 "Bearcat"; "Able Cat", U.S.
  Thrift" 113
Chester "Swee Pea I & II" — "Skybaby" 114
Wittman "Buster" — "Bonzo" 115
Cosmic Wind "Minnow", "Ballerina", "Little Toni" . . 116
Long "Midget Mustang" LA-1 117
Wittman "Bonzo" 118
Foss "Jinny" and "Little Mike" 119
Cosmic Wind "Little Toni", "Ballerina" 120
Loving-Wayne WR-1 "Lovings Love" 121
Cassutt Model 2 122
Cassutt "Boo Ray" 123
"Idjets Midget" and "Moonshiner" 124
Mace R-1 "Mr. B" 125
"Shushonic" and "Deja Vu" 126
001 Baker Special "Aquarius" 127
"Frenzer Special" and "El Bandito" 128
Minges Special M-30 "Ol Blue" 129

Miller "Little Gem" 130
"Little Gem" and "Ole Tiger" 131
Owl OR-65-2 "Pogo" 132
Owl OR-70-1 "Fang" 133
Owl OR-71-1 "Lil Quickie" 134
Falck's Special "Rivets" 135
Williams W-17 "Stinger" 136
Mace R-2 "Shark" 137
Rollason "Beta"; "Blue Chip", "Forerunner" 138
WH-1 "Thunderchicken" and "Sump'n Else" 139
"Shoestring" 140
"Yellow Jacket", "Rickey Rat" 141
Miller JM-2 "Texas Gem" 142
North American AT-6 (SNJ) "Texan"; #7, #25 143
Pitts Special #21 144
Pitts Special; "Sulu", "Chance IV" 145
Starduster; #0, #1 146
Imperial Knight Twister #5 147
Smith DSA "Miniplane"; "Flighty", #4 148
Forbes Special (DSA) "Olympia Swallow" 149
Speed F8F "Beercat" 150
Warwick W-4 "Hot Canary" 151
Christian "Mongster" 152
Boland "Gone Mong" 153
Mahoney "Sorceress" 154
WC-1 "Sundancer" 155

APPENDICES

I   Wedell-Williams "22" 156
     Wedell-Williams "45"
     Livingston Monocoupe
     Heath "Baby Bullet"

II   Alden-Brown Racer 157
     Folkerts SK-1 (Whittenbeck Special)
     Delgado "Maid"
     Delgado "Flash"

III Lockheed Vega "Winnie Mae" 158
     Lockheed "Air Express"
     Lockheed "Altair"
     Lockheed "Orion"

IV   Northrup "Gamma" 159
     Beechcraft C-17
     Seversky SEV-S2
     Sundorph A-1

V   Tilbury-Fundy "Flash" 160
     Hostler "Fury"
     Pobjoy Flaggship
     Haines "Mystery" H-3

VI   Lockheed P-38L-5 "Lightning" 161
     Bell P-63F "Kingcobra"
     Lockheed P-80A-1 "Shooting Star"
     North American F-86A "Sabre"

VII   Howard DGA-3 "Pete" (1947) 162
            "Cosmic Wind" Minnow (1949)
            Falck "Rivets" (1949)
            "Shoestring" (1949)

VIII   North American SNJ-5 "Texan" 163
            "Gotcha"
            North American AT-6C "Texan"
            "Miss Behavin"
            North American SNJ-4 "Texan"
            North American "Harvard Mk.II"

IX   North American P-51D "Mustang" 164
            "Rockwell International"
            North American P-51D "Mustang"
            "Miss Suzie Q"
            North American P-51D "Mustang"
            "Miss Candace"
            North American P-51D "Mustang"
            "Bardahl II"

X   Bell P-39Q "Airacobra" 165
            "Mr. Mennon"
            Bell P-63C "King Cobra"
            "Tipsy Miss"
            Republic P-47D "Thunderbolt"
            Vought F4U-7 "Corsair"
            "Blue Max"

XI   Canadair T-33 "Silver Star" 166
            Canadair CL-13B (F-86) "Sabre"
            Hawker "Sea Fury II"
            Grumman F8F-2 "Bearcat"
            "Miss Priss"

XII   Fischer "Super Mong" 167
            Nagel "Mong Goose"
            RK-3 Jungster III "Jonathan Livingston Seagull"
            Hoffman "Suzie Bee"

XIII   Owl OR-65 "Yellow Peril" 168
            "Shoestring IV", "Wagner Solution"
            "Shoestring V", "Nobigthing"
            Prosch "Loki"

XIV   Cassutt "Scarab" 169
            Cassutt "Mother Holliday"
            Cassutt "Snoopy", ("Dixie Rebel")
            Cassutt "Plum Crazy"

Field Layout — 1932 National Air Races — Cleveland 170

Racing Flags & Their Meaning & 1975 Reno Race Course 171

Table of Major Air Race Entries and Results 172

Bibliography 179

Table of World Speed Records for Aircraft 180

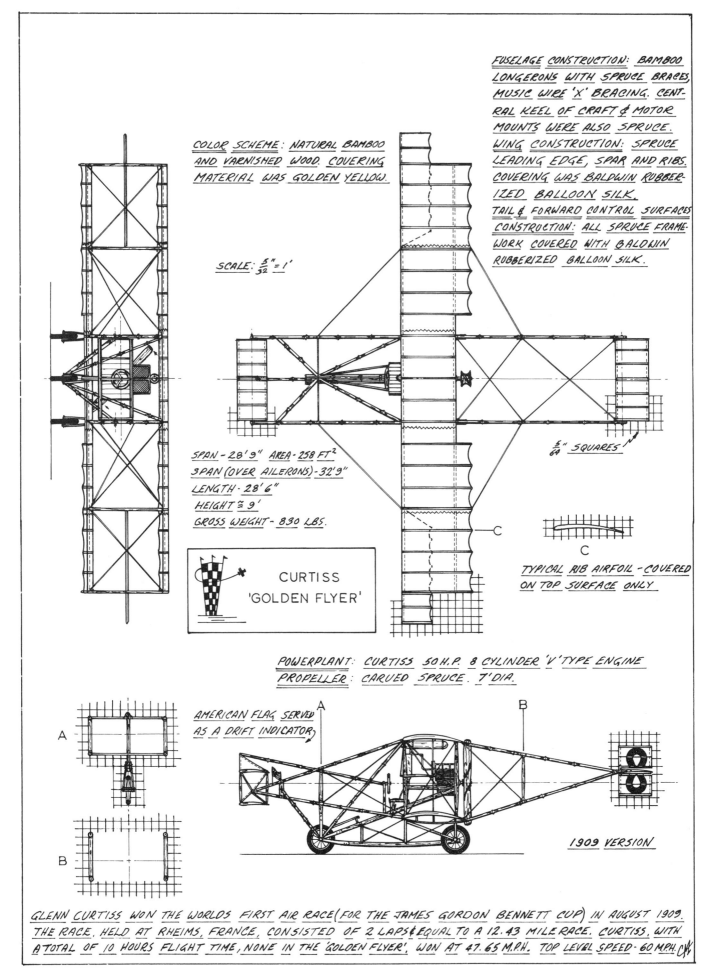

COLOR SCHEME: NATURAL BAMBOO AND VARNISHED WOOD. COVERING MATERIAL WAS GOLDEN YELLOW.

SCALE: $\frac{5}{32}" = 1'$

FUSELAGE CONSTRUCTION: BAMBOO LONGERONS WITH SPRUCE BRACES, MUSIC WIRE 'X' BRACING. CENTRAL KEEL OF CRAFT & MOTOR MOUNTS WERE ALSO SPRUCE.
WING CONSTRUCTION: SPRUCE LEADING EDGE, SPAR AND RIBS. COVERING WAS BALDWIN RUBBERIZED BALLOON SILK.
TAIL & FORWARD CONTROL SURFACES CONSTRUCTION: ALL SPRUCE FRAMEWORK COVERED WITH BALDWIN RUBBERIZED BALLOON SILK.

$\frac{5}{64}"$ SQUARES

SPAN - 28' 9"   AREA - 258 FT²
SPAN (OVER AILERONS) - 32' 9"
LENGTH - 28' 6"
HEIGHT ≅ 9'
GROSS WEIGHT - 830 LBS.

CURTISS 'GOLDEN FLYER'

C

TYPICAL RIB AIRFOIL - COVERED ON TOP SURFACE ONLY

POWERPLANT: CURTISS 50 H.P. 8 CYLINDER 'V' TYPE ENGINE
PROPELLER: CARVED SPRUCE. 7' DIA.

AMERICAN FLAG SERVED AS A DRIFT INDICATOR)

A

B

1909 VERSION

GLENN CURTISS WON THE WORLDS FIRST AIR RACE (FOR THE JAMES GORDON BENNETT CUP) IN AUGUST 1909. THE RACE, HELD AT RHEIMS, FRANCE, CONSISTED OF 2 LAPS & EQUAL TO A 12.43 MILE RACE. CURTISS, WITH A TOTAL OF 10 HOURS FLIGHT TIME, NONE IN THE 'GOLDEN FLYER', WON AT 47.65 M.P.H. TOP LEVEL SPEED - 60 M.P.H.

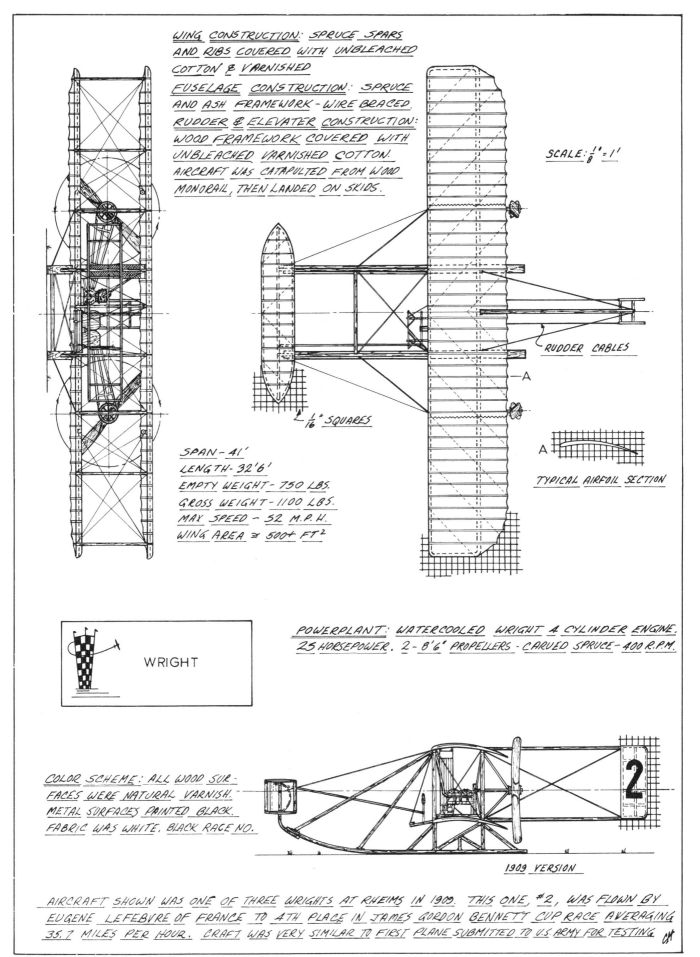

WING CONSTRUCTION: SPRUCE SPARS AND RIBS COVERED WITH UNBLEACHED COTTON & VARNISHED

FUSELAGE CONSTRUCTION: SPRUCE AND ASH FRAMEWORK - WIRE BRACED.

RUDDER & ELEVATER CONSTRUCTION: WOOD FRAMEWORK COVERED WITH UNBLEACHED VARNISHED COTTON. AIRCRAFT WAS CATAPULTED FROM WOOD MONORAIL, THEN LANDED ON SKIDS.

SCALE: $\frac{1}{8}" = 1'$

RUDDER CABLES

—A

$\frac{1}{16}"$ SQUARES

SPAN - 41'
LENGTH - 32'6'
EMPTY WEIGHT - 750 LBS.
GROSS WEIGHT - 1100 LBS.
MAX SPEED - 52 M.P.H.
WING AREA ≅ 500+ FT²

A

TYPICAL AIRFOIL SECTION

WRIGHT

POWERPLANT: WATERCOOLED WRIGHT 4 CYLINDER ENGINE. 25 HORSEPOWER. 2 - 8'6" PROPELLERS - CARVED SPRUCE - 400 R.P.M.

COLOR SCHEME: ALL WOOD SURFACES WERE NATURAL VARNISH. METAL SURFACES PAINTED BLACK. FABRIC WAS WHITE, BLACK RACE NO.

2

1909 VERSION

AIRCRAFT SHOWN WAS ONE OF THREE WRIGHTS AT RHEIMS IN 1909. THIS ONE, #2, WAS FLOWN BY EUGENE LEFEBVRE OF FRANCE TO 4TH PLACE IN JAMES GORDON BENNETT CUP RACE AVERAGING 35.7 MILES PER HOUR. CRAFT WAS VERY SIMILAR TO FIRST PLANE SUBMITTED TO U.S. ARMY FOR TESTING

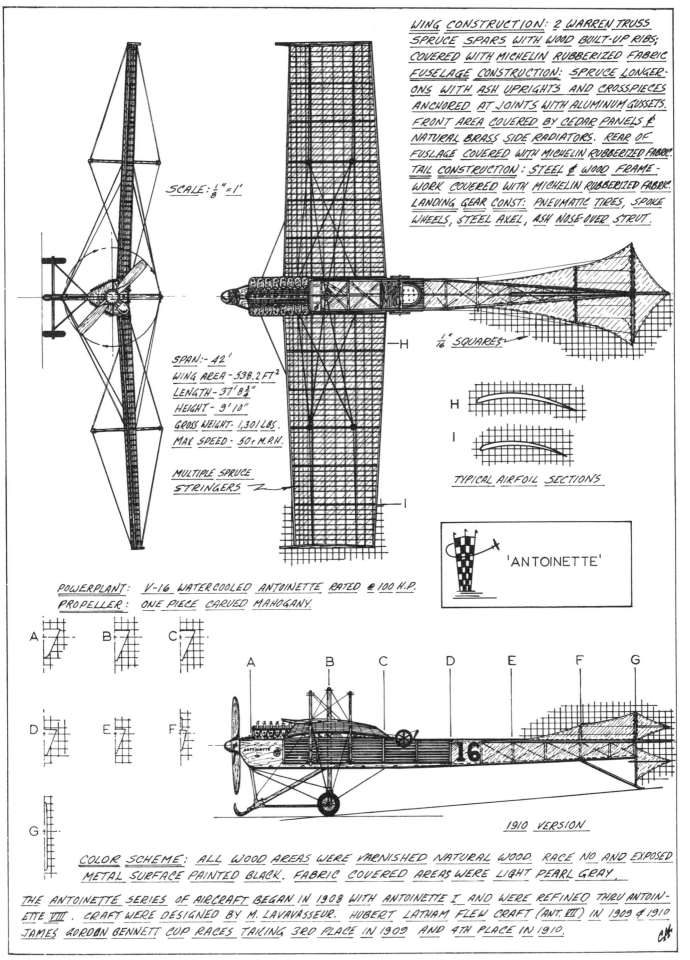

SCALE: $\frac{1}{8}" = 1'$

WING CONSTRUCTION: 2 WARREN TRUSS SPRUCE SPARS WITH WOOD BUILT-UP RIBS; COVERED WITH MICHELIN RUBBERIZED FABRIC. FUSELAGE CONSTRUCTION: SPRUCE LONGERONS WITH ASH UPRIGHTS AND CROSSPIECES ANCHORED AT JOINTS WITH ALUMINUM GUSSETS. FRONT AREA COVERED BY CEDAR PANELS & NATURAL BRASS SIDE RADIATORS. REAR OF FUSLAGE COVERED WITH MICHELIN RUBBERIZED FABRIC. TAIL CONSTRUCTION: STEEL & WOOD FRAMEWORK COVERED WITH MICHELIN RUBBERIZED FABRIC. LANDING GEAR CONST: PNEUMATIC TIRES, SPOKE WHEELS, STEEL AXEL, ASH NOSE-OVER STRUT.

$\frac{1}{16}"$ SQUARES

SPAN:- 42'
WING AREA - 538.2 FT^2
LENGTH - 37' 8$\frac{3}{4}$"
HEIGHT - 9' 10"
GROSS WEIGHT - 1,301 LBS.
MAX SPEED - 50+ M.P.H.

MULTIPLE SPRUCE STRINGERS

H

I

TYPICAL AIRFOIL SECTIONS

'ANTOINETTE'

POWERPLANT: V-16 WATERCOOLED ANTOINETTE RATED @ 100 H.P.
PROPELLER: ONE PIECE CARVED MAHOGANY.

A B C
D E F
G

A B C D E F G

16

1910 VERSION

COLOR SCHEME: ALL WOOD AREAS WERE VARNISHED NATURAL WOOD. RACE NO AND EXPOSED METAL SURFACE PAINTED BLACK. FABRIC COVERED AREAS WERE LIGHT PEARL GRAY.

THE ANTOINETTE SERIES OF AIRCRAFT BEGAN IN 1908 WITH ANTOINETTE I AND WERE REFINED THRU ANTOINETTE VIII. CRAFT WERE DESIGNED BY M. LAVAVASSEUR. HUBERT LATHAM FLEW CRAFT (ANT. VII) IN 1909 & 1910 JAMES GORDON BENNETT CUP RACES TAKING 3RD PLACE IN 1909 AND 4TH PLACE IN 1910.

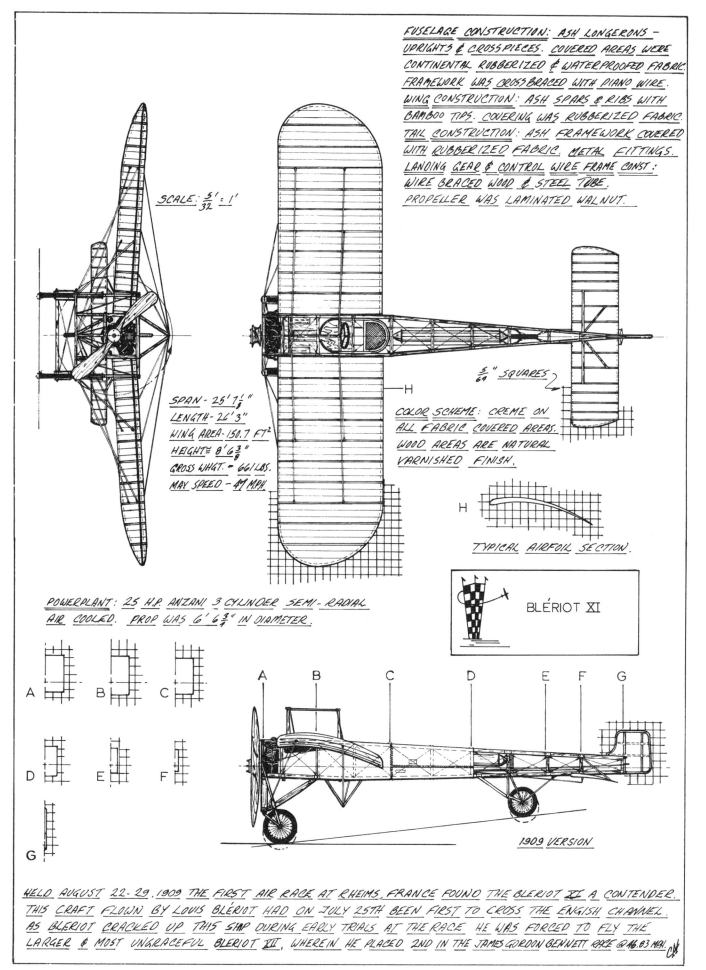

FUSELAGE CONSTRUCTION: ASH LONGERONS – UPRIGHTS & CROSSPIECES. COVERED AREAS WERE CONTINENTAL RUBBERIZED & WATERPROOFED FABRIC. FRAMEWORK WAS CROSSBRACED WITH PIANO WIRE. WING CONSTRUCTION: ASH SPARS & RIBS WITH BAMBOO TIPS. COVERING WAS RUBBERIZED FABRIC. TAIL CONSTRUCTION: ASH FRAMEWORK COVERED WITH RUBBERIZED FABRIC. METAL FITTINGS. LANDING GEAR & CONTROL WIRE FRAME CONST: WIRE BRACED WOOD & STEEL TUBE. PROPELLER WAS LAMINATED WALNUT.

SCALE: $\frac{5}{32}' = 1"$

SPAN – 25' 7$\frac{1}{8}$"
LENGTH – 26' 3"
WING AREA – 150.7 FT²
HEIGHT ≅ 8' 6$\frac{3}{8}$"
GROSS WHGT. – 661 LBS.
MAX SPEED – 47 M.P.H.

$\frac{5}{64}"$ SQUARES

COLOR SCHEME: CREME ON ALL FABRIC COVERED AREAS. WOOD AREAS ARE NATURAL VARNISHED FINISH.

H

TYPICAL AIRFOIL SECTION.

POWERPLANT: 25 H.P. ANZANI 3 CYLINDER SEMI-RADIAL AIR COOLED. PROP WAS 6' 6$\frac{3}{4}$" IN DIAMETER.

BLÉRIOT XI

A   B   C

D   E   F

G

A   B   C   D   E   F   G

1909 VERSION

HELD AUGUST 22-29, 1909 THE FIRST AIR RACE AT RHEIMS, FRANCE FOUND THE BLERIOT XI A CONTENDER. THIS CRAFT FLOWN BY LOUIS BLÉRIOT HAD ON JULY 25TH BEEN FIRST TO CROSS THE ENGISH CHANNEL. AS BLÉRIOT CRACKED UP THIS SHIP DURING EARLY TRIALS AT THE RACE HE WAS FORCED TO FLY THE LARGER & MOST UNGRACEFUL BLÉRIOT XII. WHEREIN HE PLACED 2ND IN THE JAMES GORDON BENNETT RACE @ 46.03 M.P.H.

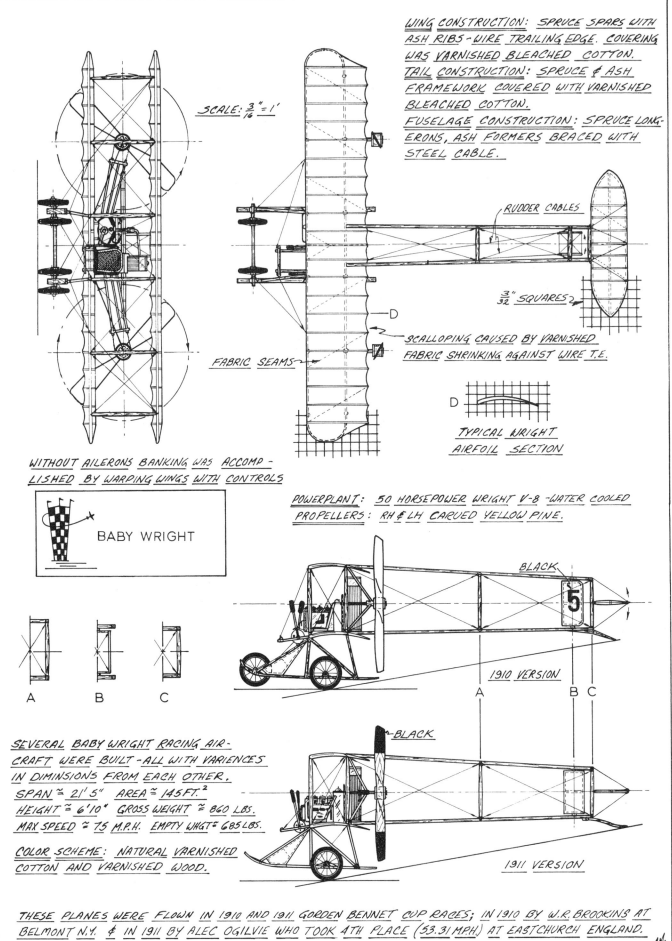

SCALE: $\frac{3}{16}"=1'$

WING CONSTRUCTION: SPRUCE SPARS WITH
ASH RIBS - WIRE TRAILING EDGE. COVERING
WAS VARNISHED BLEACHED COTTON.
TAIL CONSTRUCTION: SPRUCE & ASH
FRAMEWORK COVERED WITH VARNISHED
BLEACHED COTTON.
FUSELAGE CONSTRUCTION: SPRUCE LONG-
ERONS, ASH FORMERS BRACED WITH
STEEL CABLE.

RUDDER CABLES

$\frac{3}{32}"$ SQUARES

SCALLOPING CAUSED BY VARNISHED
FABRIC SHRINKING AGAINST WIRE T.E.

FABRIC SEAMS

D

TYPICAL WRIGHT
AIRFOIL SECTION

WITHOUT AILERONS BANKING WAS ACCOMP-
LISHED BY WARPING WINGS WITH CONTROLS

BABY WRIGHT

POWERPLANT: 50 HORSEPOWER WRIGHT V-8 -WATER COOLED
PROPELLERS: RH & LH CARVED YELLOW PINE.

BLACK

5

1910 VERSION

A   B   C

A   B C

BLACK

SEVERAL BABY WRIGHT RACING AIR-
CRAFT WERE BUILT - ALL WITH VARIENCES
IN DIMINSIONS FROM EACH OTHER.
SPAN ≈ 21' 5"   AREA ≈ 145 FT.²
HEIGHT ≈ 6'10"   GROSS WEIGHT ≈ 860 LBS.
MAX SPEED ≈ 75 M.P.H.   EMPTY WHGT ≈ 685 LBS.

COLOR SCHEME: NATURAL VARNISHED
COTTON AND VARNISHED WOOD.

1911 VERSION

THESE PLANES WERE FLOWN IN 1910 AND 1911 GORDEN BENNET CUP RACES; IN 1910 BY W.R. BROOKINS AT
BELMONT N.Y. & IN 1911 BY ALEC OGILVIE WHO TOOK 4TH PLACE (53.31 MPH.) AT EASTCHURCH ENGLAND.

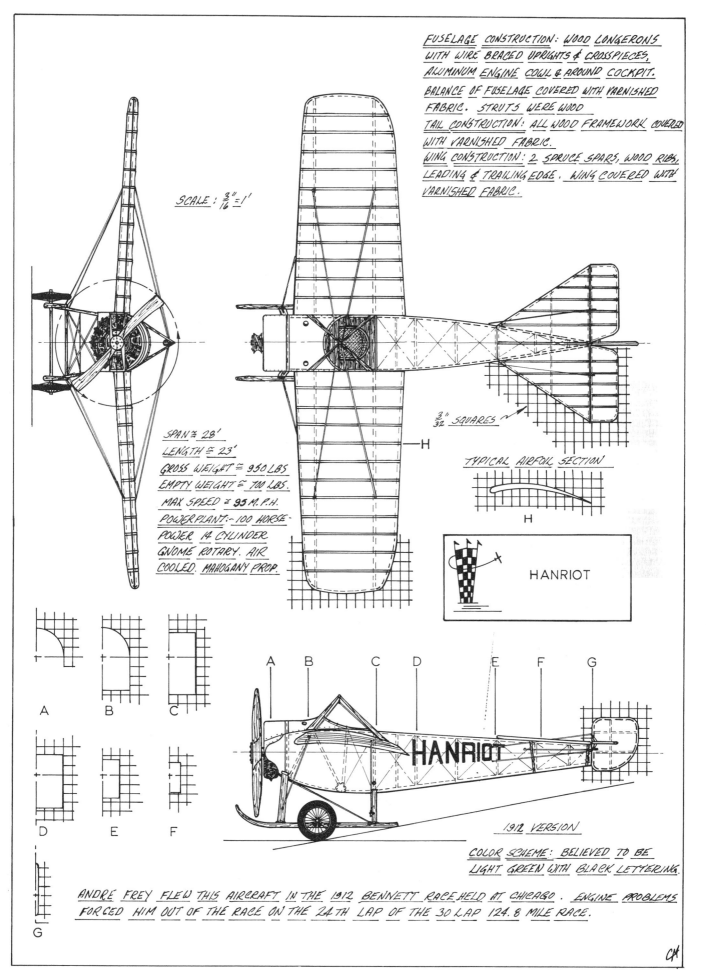

FUSELAGE CONSTRUCTION: WOOD LONGERONS
WITH WIRE BRACED UPRIGHTS & CROSSPIECES,
ALUMINUM ENGINE COWL & AROUND COCKPIT.
BALANCE OF FUSELAGE COVERED WITH VARNISHED
FABRIC. STRUTS WERE WOOD
TAIL CONSTRUCTION: ALL WOOD FRAMEWORK COVERED
WITH VARNISHED FABRIC.
WING CONSTRUCTION: 2 SPRUCE SPARS, WOOD RIBS,
LEADING & TRAILING EDGE. WING COVERED WITH
VARNISHED FABRIC.

SCALE: $\frac{3}{16}" = 1'$

SPAN ≅ 28'
LENGTH ≅ 23'
GROSS WEIGHT ≅ 950 LBS
EMPTY WEIGHT ≅ 700 LBS.
MAX SPEED ≅ 95 M.P.H.
POWERPLANT:- 100 HORSE-
POWER 14 CYLINDER
GNOME ROTARY. AIR
COOLED. MAHOGANY PROP.

$\frac{3}{32}"$ SQUARES

TYPICAL AIRFOIL SECTION

H

— H

A   B   C

D   E   F

G

HANRIOT

A   B   C   D   E   F   G

HANRIOT

1912 VERSION

COLOR SCHEME: BELIEVED TO BE
LIGHT GREEN WITH BLACK LETTERING.

ANDRÉ FREY FLEW THIS AIRCRAFT IN THE 1912 BENNETT RACE HELD AT CHICAGO. ENGINE PROBLEMS
FORCED HIM OUT OF THE RACE ON THE 24TH LAP OF THE 30 LAP 124.8 MILE RACE.

CA

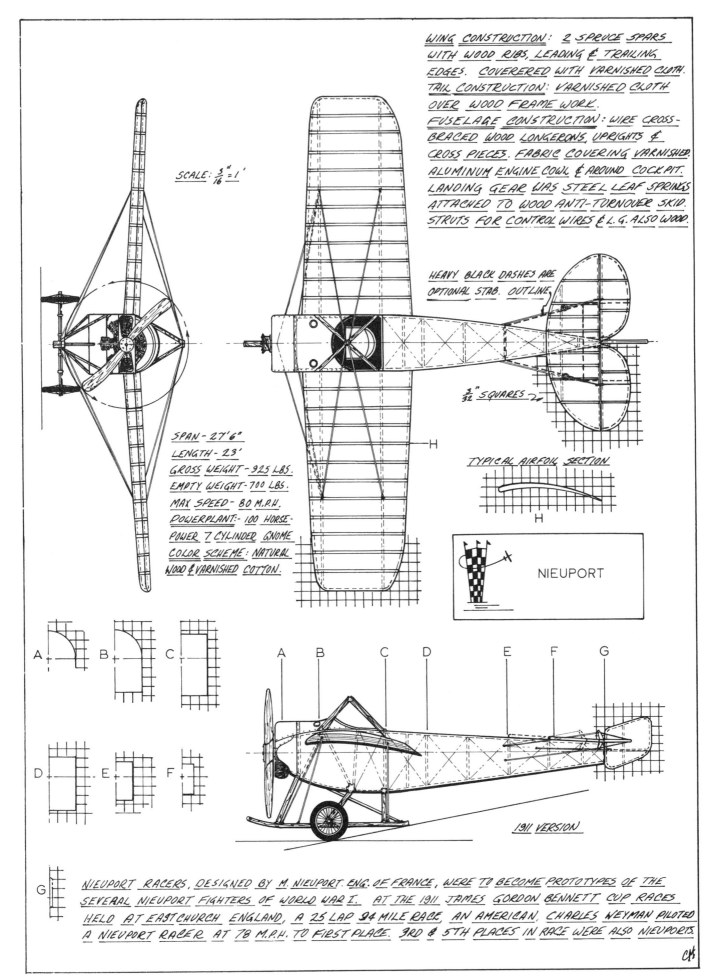

SCALE: $\frac{3}{16}$" = 1'

WING CONSTRUCTION: 2 SPRUCE SPARS WITH WOOD RIBS, LEADING & TRAILING EDGES. COVERERED WITH VARNISHED CLOTH. TAIL CONSTRUCTION: VARNISHED CLOTH OVER WOOD FRAME WORK. FUSELAGE CONSTRUCTION: WIRE CROSS-BRACED WOOD LONGERONS, UPRIGHTS & CROSS PIECES. FABRIC COVERING VARNISHED. ALUMINUM ENGINE COWL & AROUND COCKPIT. LANDING GEAR WAS STEEL LEAF SPRINGS ATTACHED TO WOOD ANTI-TURNOVER SKID. STRUTS FOR CONTROL WIRES & L.G. ALSO WOOD.

HEAVY BLACK DASHES ARE OPTIONAL STAB. OUTLINE

$\frac{3}{32}$" SQUARES

TYPICAL AIRFOIL SECTION

H

SPAN - 27' 6"
LENGTH - 23'
GROSS WEIGHT - 925 LBS.
EMPTY WEIGHT - 700 LBS.
MAX SPEED - 80 M.P.H.
POWERPLANT: - 100 HORSE-POWER 7 CYLINDER GNOME
COLOR SCHEME: NATURAL WOOD & VARNISHED COTTON.

H

NIEUPORT

1911 VERSION

NIEUPORT RACERS, DESIGNED BY M. NIEUPORT. ENG. OF FRANCE, WERE TO BECOME PROTOTYPES OF THE SEVERAL NIEUPORT FIGHTERS OF WORLD WAR I. AT THE 1911 JAMES GORDON BENNETT CUP RACES HELD AT EASTCHURCH ENGLAND, A 25 LAP 94 MILE RACE, AN AMERICAN, CHARLES WEYMAN PILOTED A NIEUPORT RACER AT 78 M.P.H. TO FIRST PLACE. 3RD & 5TH PLACES IN RACE WERE ALSO NIEUPORTS.

CM

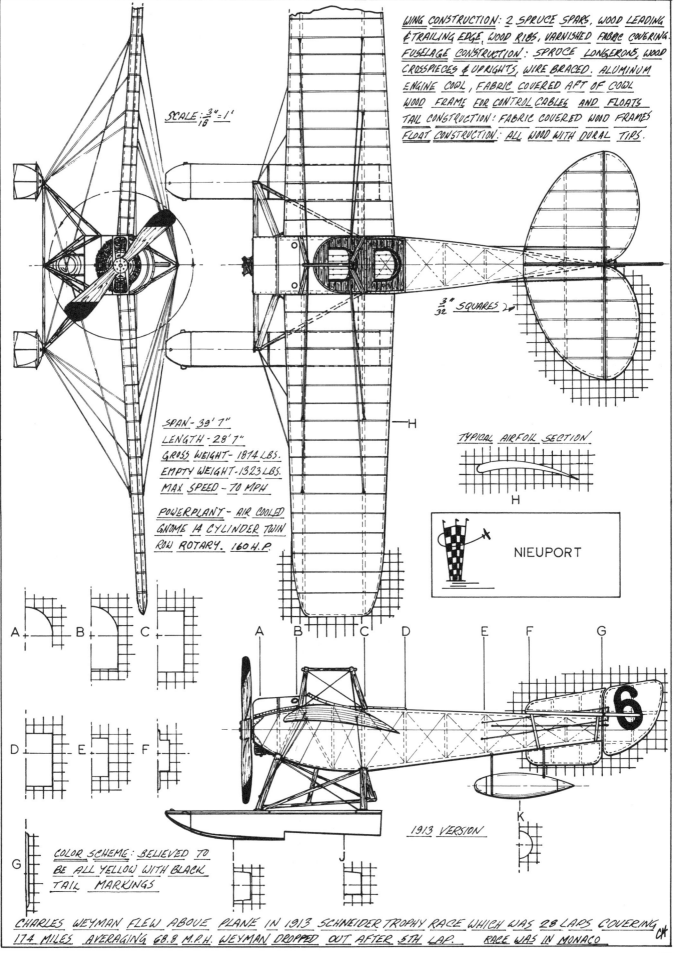

SCALE: $\frac{3}{16}'' = 1'$

WING CONSTRUCTION: 2 SPRUCE SPARS, WOOD LEADING & TRAILING EDGE, WOOD RIBS, VARNISHED FABRIC COVERING. FUSELAGE CONSTRUCTION: SPRUCE LONGERONS, WOOD CROSSPIECES & UPRIGHTS, WIRE BRACED. ALUMINUM ENGINE COWL, FABRIC COVERED AFT OF COWL WOOD FRAME FOR CONTROL CABLES AND FLOATS TAIL CONSTRUCTION: FABRIC COVERED WOOD FRAMES FLOAT CONSTRUCTION: ALL WOOD WITH DURAL TIPS.

$\frac{3}{32}''$ SQUARES

SPAN - 39' 7"
LENGTH - 28' 7"
GROSS WEIGHT - 1814 LBS.
EMPTY WEIGHT - 1323 LBS.
MAX SPEED - 70 MPH

POWERPLANT - AIR COOLED GNOME 14 CYLINDER TWIN ROW ROTARY. 160 H.P.

TYPICAL AIRFOIL SECTION

H

NIEUPORT

A   B   C

D   E   F

G

COLOR SCHEME: BELIEVED TO BE ALL YELLOW WITH BLACK TAIL MARKINGS

A   B   C   D   E   F   G

6

1913 VERSION

K

J

CHARLES WEYMAN FLEW ABOVE PLANE IN 1913 SCHNEIDER TROPHY RACE WHICH WAS 28 LAPS COVERING 174 MILES. AVERAGING 68.8 M.P.H. WEYMAN DROPPED OUT AFTER 5TH LAP.   RACE WAS IN MONACO.

CM

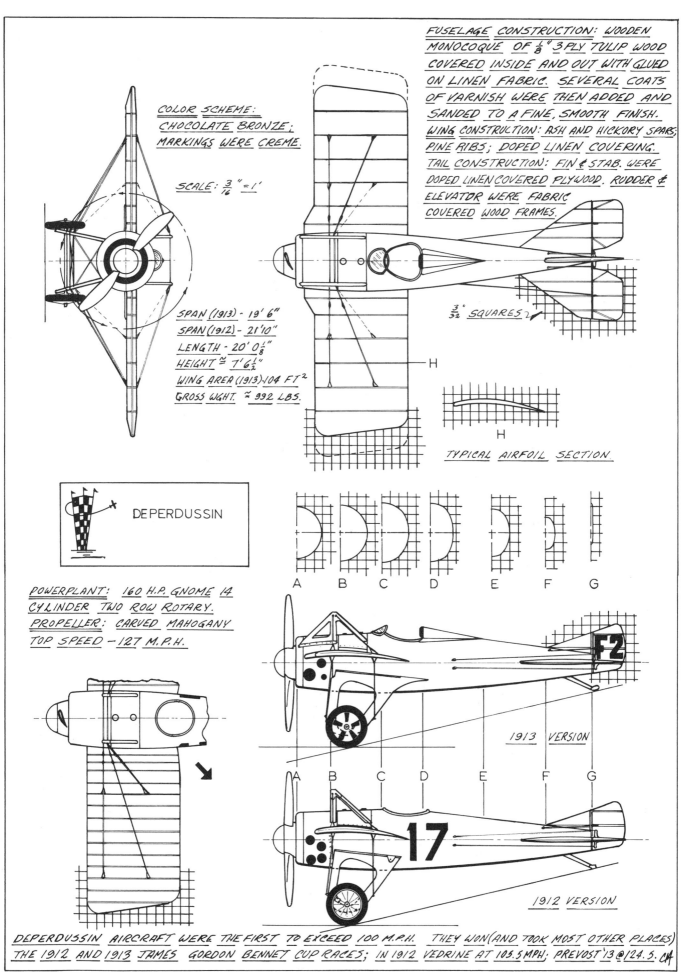

COLOR SCHEME:
CHOCOLATE BRONZE;
MARKINGS WERE CREME.

SCALE: $\frac{3}{16}$" = 1'

FUSELAGE CONSTRUCTION: WOODEN MONOCOQUE OF $\frac{1}{8}$" 3 PLY TULIP WOOD COVERED INSIDE AND OUT WITH GLUED ON LINEN FABRIC. SEVERAL COATS OF VARNISH WERE THEN ADDED AND SANDED TO A FINE, SMOOTH FINISH. WING CONSTRUCTION: ASH AND HICKORY SPARS; PINE RIBS; DOPED LINEN COVERING. TAIL CONSTRUCTION: FIN & STAB. WERE DOPED LINEN COVERED PLYWOOD. RUDDER & ELEVATOR WERE FABRIC COVERED WOOD FRAMES.

SPAN (1913) - 19' 6"
SPAN (1912) - 21' 10"
LENGTH - 20' 0$\frac{1}{8}$"
HEIGHT $\cong$ 7' 6$\frac{1}{2}$"
WING AREA (1913) -104 FT^2
GROSS WGHT. $\cong$ 992 LBS.

$\frac{3}{32}$" SQUARES

H

TYPICAL AIRFOIL SECTION.

DEPERDUSSIN

POWERPLANT: 160 H.P. GNOME 14 CYLINDER TWO ROW ROTARY.
PROPELLER: CARVED MAHOGANY
TOP SPEED - 127 M.P.H.

A B C D E F G

F·2

1913 VERSION

A B C D E F G

17

1912 VERSION

DEPERDUSSIN AIRCRAFT WERE THE FIRST TO EXCEED 100 M.P.H. THEY WON (AND TOOK MOST OTHER PLACES) THE 1912 AND 1913 JAMES GORDON BENNET CUP RACES; IN 1912 VEDRINE AT 105.5 MPH, PREVOST '13 @ 124.5. CA

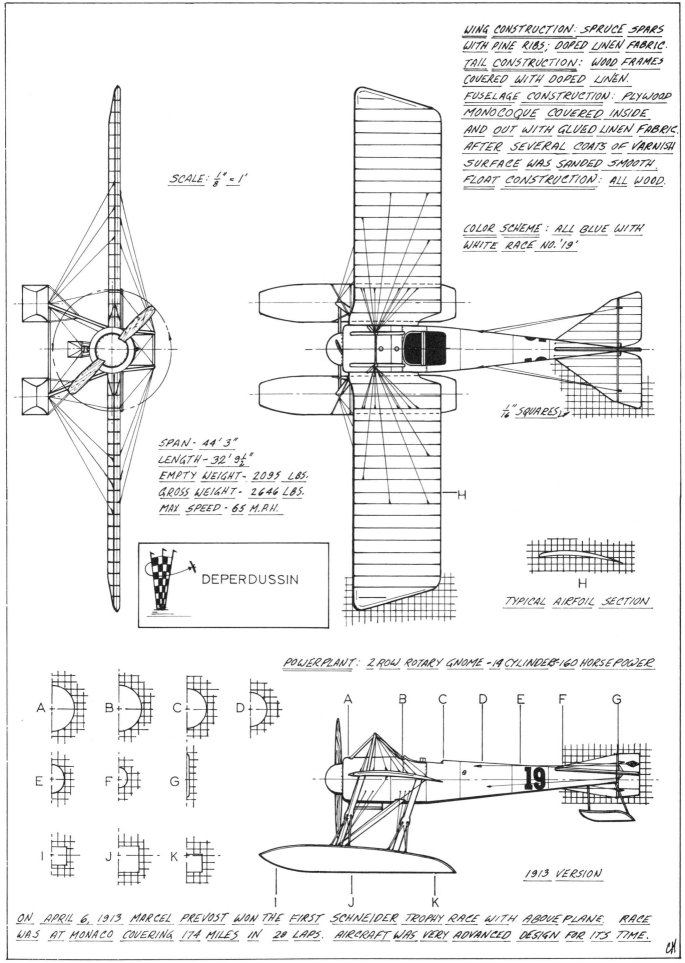

SCALE: $\frac{1}{8}" = 1'$

WING CONSTRUCTION: SPRUCE SPARS
WITH PINE RIBS; DOPED LINEN FABRIC.
TAIL CONSTRUCTION: WOOD FRAMES
COVERED WITH DOPED LINEN.
FUSELAGE CONSTRUCTION: PLYWOOD
MONOCOQUE COVERED INSIDE
AND OUT WITH GLUED LINEN FABRIC.
AFTER SEVERAL COATS OF VARNISH
SURFACE WAS SANDED SMOOTH.
FLOAT CONSTRUCTION: ALL WOOD.

COLOR SCHEME: ALL BLUE WITH
WHITE RACE NO. '19'

$\frac{1}{16}"$ SQUARES

SPAN - 44' 3"
LENGTH - 32' $9\frac{1}{2}"$
EMPTY WEIGHT - 2095 LBS.
GROSS WEIGHT - 2646 LBS.
MAX SPEED - 65 M.P.H.

DEPERDUSSIN

H

TYPICAL AIRFOIL SECTION

POWERPLANT: 2 ROW ROTARY GNOME - 14 CYLINDERS - 160 HORSEPOWER

1913 VERSION

ON APRIL 6, 1913 MARCEL PREVOST WON THE FIRST SCHNEIDER TROPHY RACE WITH ABOVE PLANE. RACE
WAS AT MONACO COVERING 174 MILES IN 28 LAPS. AIRCRAFT WAS VERY ADVANCED DESIGN FOR ITS TIME.

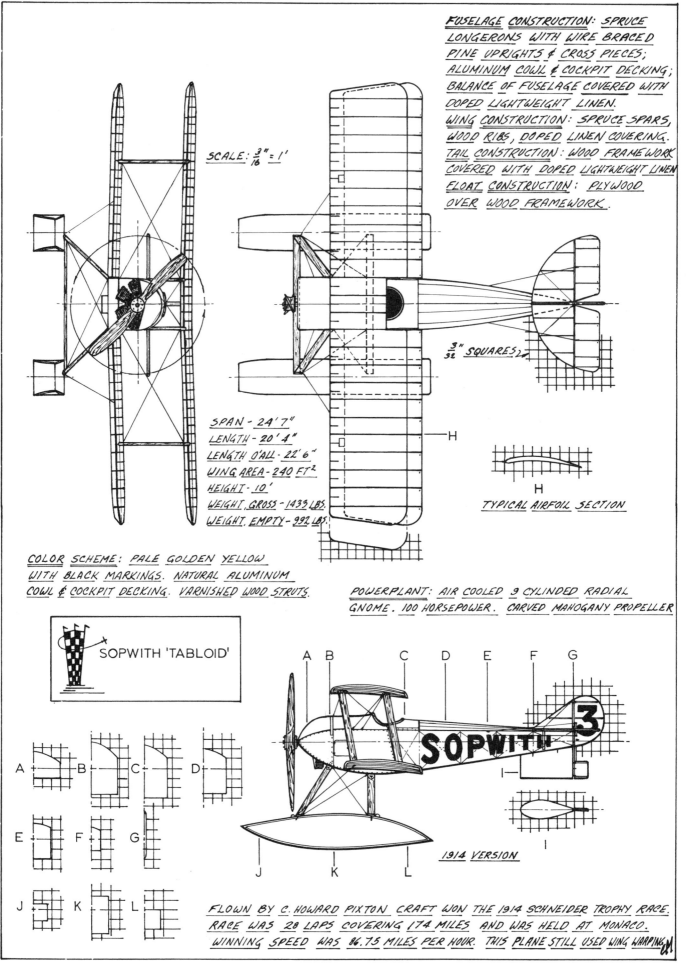

SCALE: $\frac{3}{16}$" = 1'

FUSELAGE CONSTRUCTION: SPRUCE LONGERONS WITH WIRE BRACED PINE UPRIGHTS & CROSS PIECES; ALUMINUM COWL & COCKPIT DECKING; BALANCE OF FUSELAGE COVERED WITH DOPED LIGHTWEIGHT LINEN.
WING CONSTRUCTION: SPRUCE SPARS, WOOD RIBS, DOPED LINEN COVERING.
TAIL CONSTRUCTION: WOOD FRAMEWORK COVERED WITH DOPED LIGHTWEIGHT LINEN
FLOAT CONSTRUCTION: PLYWOOD OVER WOOD FRAMEWORK.

$\frac{3}{32}$" SQUARES

SPAN - 24' 7"
LENGTH - 20' 4"
LENGTH O'ALL - 22' 6"
WING AREA - 240 FT²
HEIGHT - 10'
WEIGHT, GROSS - 1433 LBS.
WEIGHT, EMPTY - 992 LBS.

H

TYPICAL AIRFOIL SECTION

COLOR SCHEME: PALE GOLDEN YELLOW WITH BLACK MARKINGS. NATURAL ALUMINUM COWL & COCKPIT DECKING. VARNISHED WOOD STRUTS.

POWERPLANT: AIR COOLED 9 CYLINDER RADIAL GNOME. 100 HORSEPOWER. CARVED MAHOGANY PROPELLER

SOPWITH 'TABLOID'

A   B   C   D   E   F   G

SOPWITH 3

I

A   B   C   D
E   F   G
J   K   L

J   K   L

1914 VERSION

FLOWN BY C. HOWARD PIXTON. CRAFT WON THE 1914 SCHNEIDER TROPHY RACE. RACE WAS 28 LAPS COVERING 174 MILES AND WAS HELD AT MONACO. WINNING SPEED WAS 86.75 MILES PER HOUR. THIS PLANE STILL USED WING WARPING.

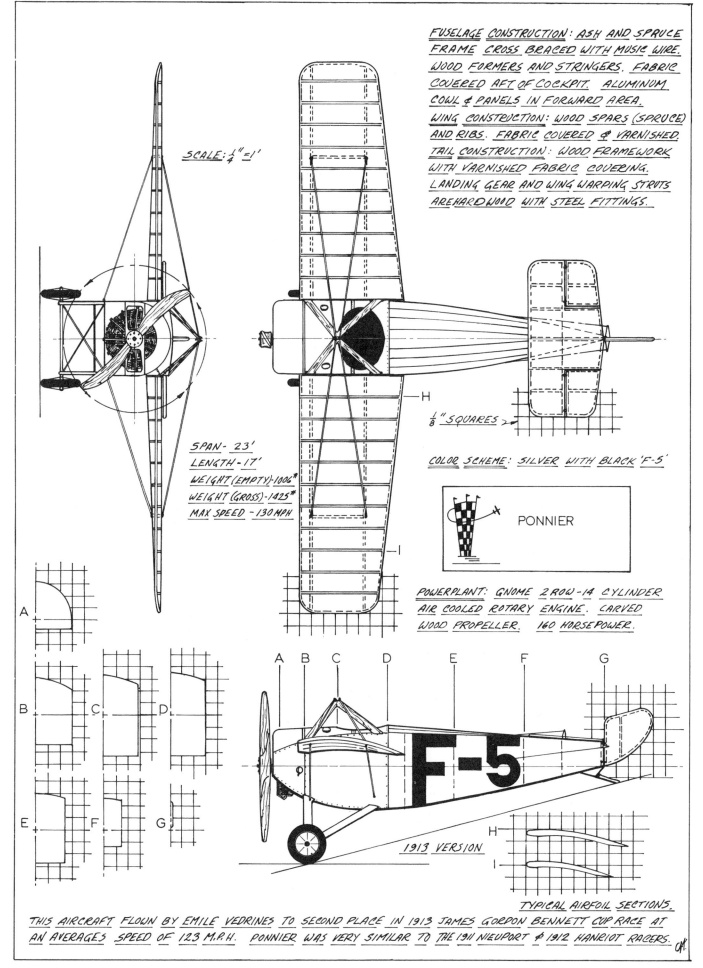

SCALE: $\frac{1}{4}$" = 1'

FUSELAGE CONSTRUCTION: ASH AND SPRUCE FRAME CROSS BRACED WITH MUSIC WIRE. WOOD FORMERS AND STRINGERS. FABRIC COVERED AFT OF COCKPIT. ALUMINUM COWL & PANELS IN FORWARD AREA.
WING CONSTRUCTION: WOOD SPARS (SPRUCE) AND RIBS. FABRIC COVERED & VARNISHED.
TAIL CONSTRUCTION: WOOD FRAMEWORK WITH VARNISHED FABRIC COVERING.
LANDING GEAR AND WING WARPING STRUTS ARE HARD WOOD WITH STEEL FITTINGS.

SPAN - 23'
LENGTH - 17'
WEIGHT (EMPTY) - 1006#
WEIGHT (GROSS) - 1425#
MAX SPEED - 130 MPH

$\frac{1}{8}$" SQUARES

COLOR SCHEME: SILVER WITH BLACK 'F-5'

PONNIER

POWERPLANT: GNOME 2 ROW - 14 CYLINDER AIR COOLED ROTARY ENGINE. CARVED WOOD PROPELLER. 160 HORSEPOWER.

A B C D E F G

F-5

1913 VERSION

A B C D E F G H I

H
I

TYPICAL AIRFOIL SECTIONS.

THIS AIRCRAFT FLOWN BY EMILE VEDRINES TO SECOND PLACE IN 1913 JAMES GORDON BENNETT CUP RACE AT AN AVERAGE SPEED OF 123 M.P.H. PONNIER WAS VERY SIMILAR TO THE 1911 NIEUPORT & 1912 HANRIOT RACERS.

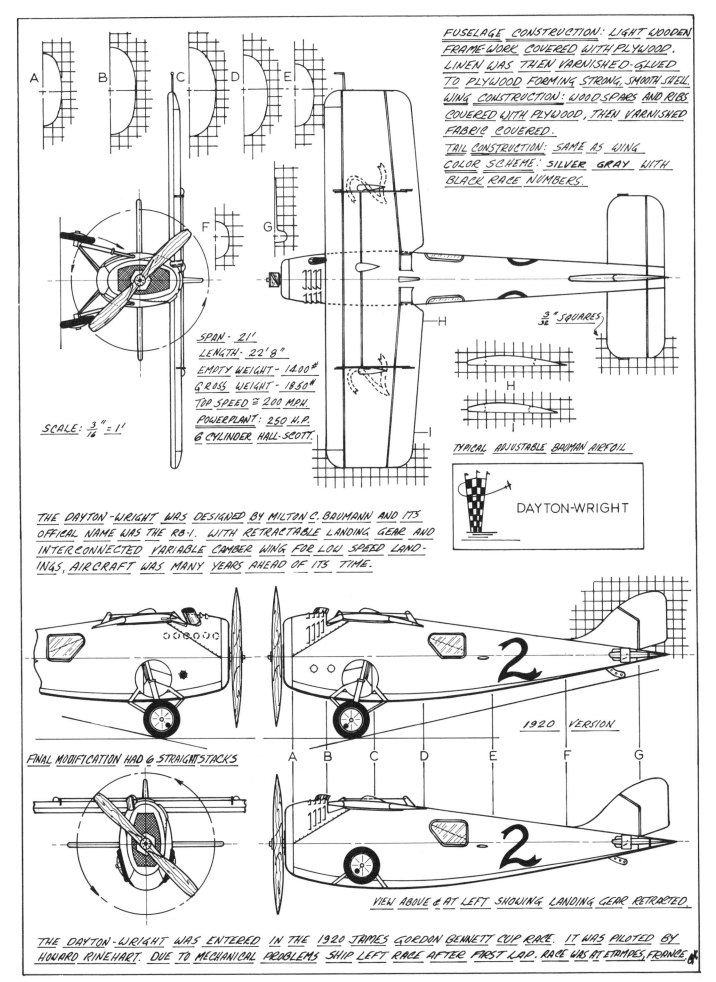

FUSELAGE CONSTRUCTION: LIGHT WOODEN FRAME-WORK COVERED WITH PLYWOOD. LINEN WAS THEN VARNISHED-GLUED TO PLYWOOD FORMING STRONG, SMOOTH SHELL.
WING CONSTRUCTION: WOOD SPARS AND RIBS COVERED WITH PLYWOOD, THEN VARNISHED FABRIC COVERED.
TAIL CONSTRUCTION: SAME AS WING
COLOR SCHEME: SILVER GRAY WITH BLACK RACE NUMBERS.

SPAN - 21'
LENGTH - 22'8"
EMPTY WEIGHT - 1400#
GROSS WEIGHT - 1850#
TOP SPEED ≅ 200 M.P.H.
POWERPLANT: 250 H.P.
6 CYLINDER HALL-SCOTT.

SCALE: 3/16" = 1'

3/32" SQUARES

TYPICAL ADJUSTABLE BAUMAN AIRFOIL

DAYTON-WRIGHT

THE DAYTON-WRIGHT WAS DESIGNED BY MILTON C. BAUMANN AND ITS OFFICAL NAME WAS THE RB-1. WITH RETRACTABLE LANDING GEAR AND INTERCONNECTED VARIABLE CAMBER WING FOR LOW SPEED LANDINGS, AIRCRAFT WAS MANY YEARS AHEAD OF ITS TIME.

FINAL MODIFICATION HAD 6 STRAIGHT STACKS

1920 VERSION

A B C D E F G

VIEW ABOVE & AT LEFT SHOWING LANDING GEAR RETRACTED.

THE DAYTON-WRIGHT WAS ENTERED IN THE 1920 JAMES GORDON GENNETT CUP RACE. IT WAS PILOTED BY HOWARD RINEHART. DUE TO MECHANICAL PROBLEMS SHIP LEFT RACE AFTER FIRST LAP. RACE WAS AT ETAMPES, FRANCE.

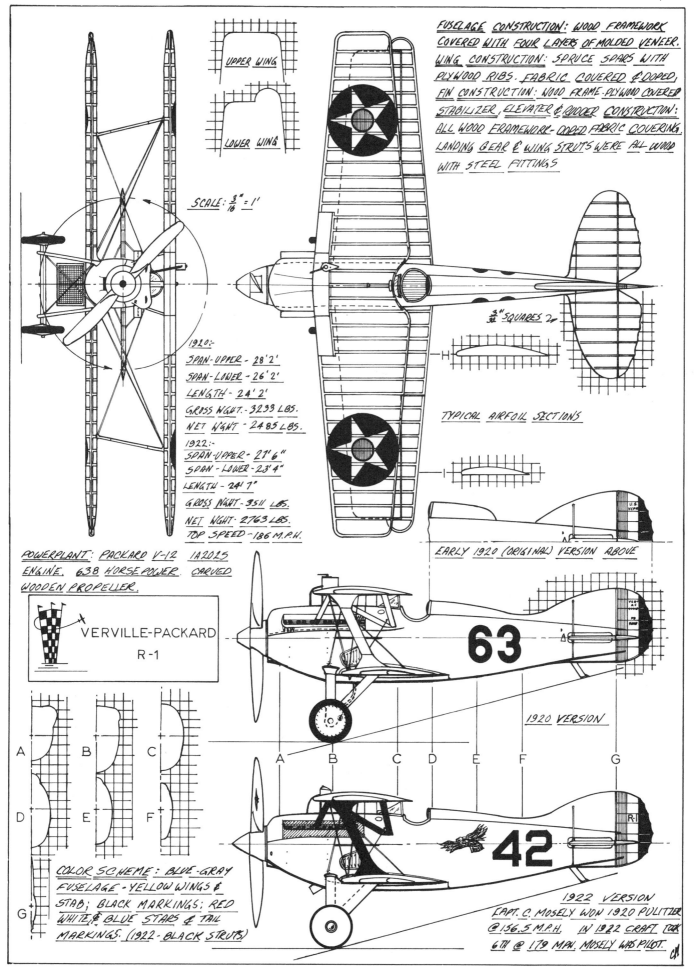

FUSELAGE CONSTRUCTION: WOOD FRAMEWORK COVERED WITH FOUR LAYERS OF MOLDED VENEER. WING CONSTRUCTION: SPRUCE SPARS WITH PLYWOOD RIBS. FABRIC COVERED & DOPED. FIN CONSTRUCTION: WOOD FRAME-PLYWOOD COVERED STABILIZER, ELEVATOR & RUDDER CONSTRUCTION: ALL WOOD FRAMEWORK- DOPED FABRIC COVERING. LANDING GEAR & WING STRUTS WERE ALL WOOD WITH STEEL FITTINGS

UPPER WING

LOWER WING

SCALE: $\frac{3}{16}$" = 1'

$\frac{3}{32}$" SQUARES

TYPICAL AIRFOIL SECTIONS

H

I

1920:-
SPAN-UPPER - 28'2'
SPAN-LOWER - 26'2'
LENGTH - 24'2'
GROSS WGHT.- 3293 LBS.
NET WGHT - 2485 LBS.

1922:-
SPAN-UPPER - 27'6"
SPAN-LOWER - 23'4"
LENGTH - 24'7"
GROSS WGHT - 3511 LBS.
NET WGHT- 2763 LBS.
TOP SPEED -186 M.P.H.

EARLY 1920 (ORIGINAL) VERSION ABOVE

POWERPLANT: PACKARD V-12 1A2025 ENGINE. 638 HORSEPOWER. CARVED WOODEN PROPELLER.

VERVILLE-PACKARD
R-1

63

1920 VERSION

A B C

D E F

G

A B C D E F G

42

R-1

1922 VERSION
CAPT. C. MOSELY WON 1920 PULITZER @156.5 M.P.H. IN 1922 CRAFT TOOK 6TH @ 179 M.P.H. MOSELY WAS PILOT.

COLOR SCHEME: BLUE-GRAY FUSELAGE-YELLOW WINGS & STAB; BLACK MARKINGS; RED WHITE & BLUE STARS & TAIL MARKINGS. (1922-BLACK STRUTS)

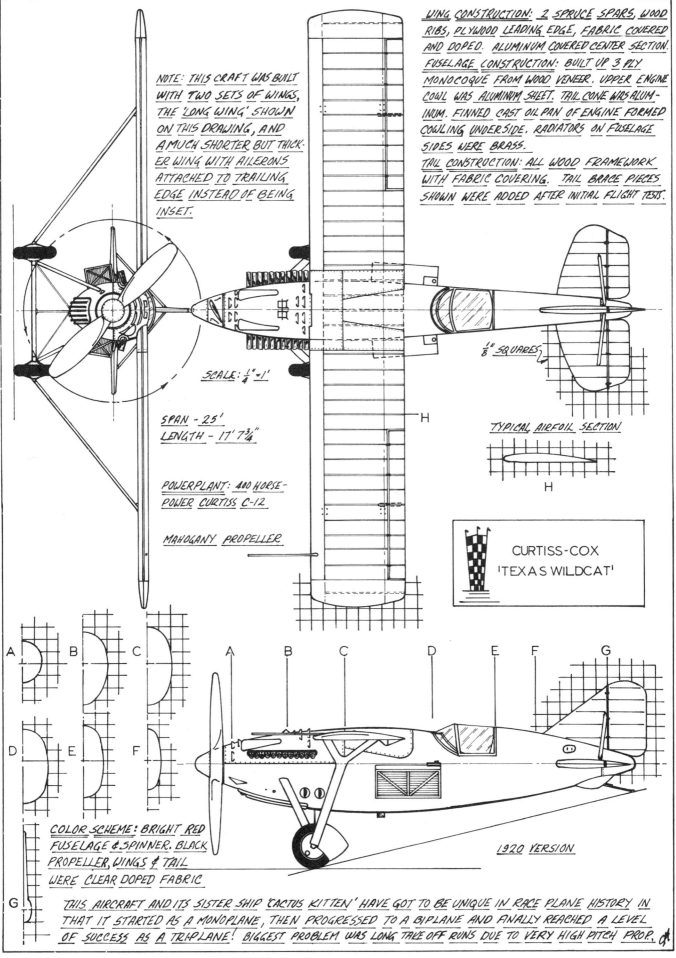

NOTE: THIS CRAFT WAS BUILT WITH TWO SETS OF WINGS, THE 'LONG WING' SHOWN ON THIS DRAWING, AND A MUCH SHORTER BUT THICKER WING WITH AILERONS ATTACHED TO TRAILING EDGE INSTEAD OF BEING INSET.

WING CONSTRUCTION: 2 SPRUCE SPARS, WOOD RIBS, PLYWOOD LEADING EDGE, FABRIC COVERED AND DOPED. ALUMINUM COVERED CENTER SECTION. FUSELAGE CONSTRUCTION: BUILT UP 3 PLY MONOCOQUE FROM WOOD VENEER. UPPER ENGINE COWL WAS ALUMINUM SHEET. TAIL CONE WAS ALUMINUM. FINNED CAST OIL PAN OF ENGINE FORMED COWLING UNDERSIDE. RADIATORS ON FUSELAGE SIDES WERE BRASS.
TAIL CONSTRUCTION: ALL WOOD FRAMEWORK WITH FABRIC COVERING. TAIL BRACE PIECES SHOWN WERE ADDED AFTER INITIAL FLIGHT TESTS.

SCALE: 1/4" = 1'

SPAN - 25'
LENGTH - 17' 7¾"

POWERPLANT: 400 HORSE-POWER CURTISS C-12

MAHOGANY PROPELLER

1/8" SQUARES

TYPICAL AIRFOIL SECTION

H

CURTISS-COX
'TEXAS WILDCAT'

A   B   C
D   E   F

A   B   C   D   E   F   G

COLOR SCHEME: BRIGHT RED FUSELAGE & SPINNER. BLACK PROPELLER. WINGS & TAIL WERE CLEAR DOPED FABRIC

1920 VERSION

G

THIS AIRCRAFT AND ITS SISTER SHIP 'CACTUS KITTEN' HAVE GOT TO BE UNIQUE IN RACE PLANE HISTORY IN THAT IT STARTED AS A MONOPLANE, THEN PROGRESSED TO A BIPLANE AND FINALLY REACHED A LEVEL OF SUCCESS AS A TRIPLANE! BIGGEST PROBLEM WAS LONG TAKE OFF RUNS DUE TO VERY HIGH PITCH PROP.

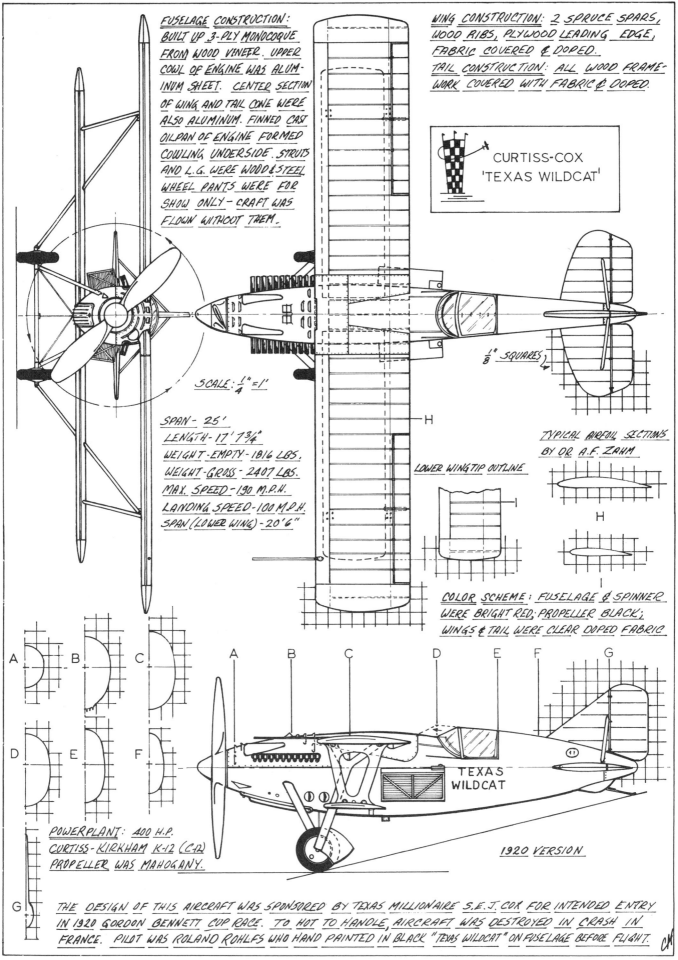

FUSELAGE CONSTRUCTION:
BUILT UP 3-PLY MONOCOQUE
FROM WOOD VENEER. UPPER
COWL OF ENGINE WAS ALUM-
INUM SHEET. CENTER SECTION
OF WING AND TAIL CONE WERE
ALSO ALUMINUM. FINNED CAST
OILPAN OF ENGINE FORMED
COWLING UNDERSIDE. STRUTS
AND L.G. WERE WOOD & STEEL
WHEEL PANTS WERE FOR
SHOW ONLY - CRAFT WAS
FLOWN WITHOUT THEM.

WING CONSTRUCTION: 2 SPRUCE SPARS,
WOOD RIBS, PLYWOOD LEADING EDGE,
FABRIC COVERED & DOPED.
TAIL CONSTRUCTION: ALL WOOD FRAME-
WORK COVERED WITH FABRIC & DOPED.

CURTISS-COX
'TEXAS WILDCAT'

SCALE: 1/4" = 1'

SPAN - 25'
LENGTH - 17' 7¾"
WEIGHT-EMPTY - 1816 LBS.
WEIGHT-GROSS - 2407 LBS.
MAX. SPEED - 190 M.P.H.
LANDING SPEED - 100 M.P.H.
SPAN (LOWER WING) - 20' 6"

1/8" SQUARES

LOWER WINGTIP OUTLINE

TYPICAL AIRFOIL SECTIONS
BY DR. A.F. ZAHM

H

COLOR SCHEME: FUSELAGE & SPINNER
WERE BRIGHT RED; PROPELLER BLACK;
WINGS & TAIL WERE CLEAR DOPED FABRIC

A   B   C
D   E   F

A   B   C   D   E   F   G

TEXAS
WILDCAT

1920 VERSION

POWERPLANT: 400 H.P.
CURTISS-KIRKHAM K-12 (C-12)
PROPELLER WAS MAHOGANY.

G

THE DESIGN OF THIS AIRCRAFT WAS SPONSORED BY TEXAS MILLIONAIRE S.E.J. COX FOR INTENDED ENTRY
IN 1920 GORDON BENNETT CUP RACE. TO HOT TO HANDLE, AIRCRAFT WAS DESTROYED IN CRASH IN
FRANCE. PILOT WAS ROLAND ROHLFS WHO HAND PAINTED IN BLACK "TEXAS WILDCAT" ON FUSELAGE BEFORE FLIGHT.

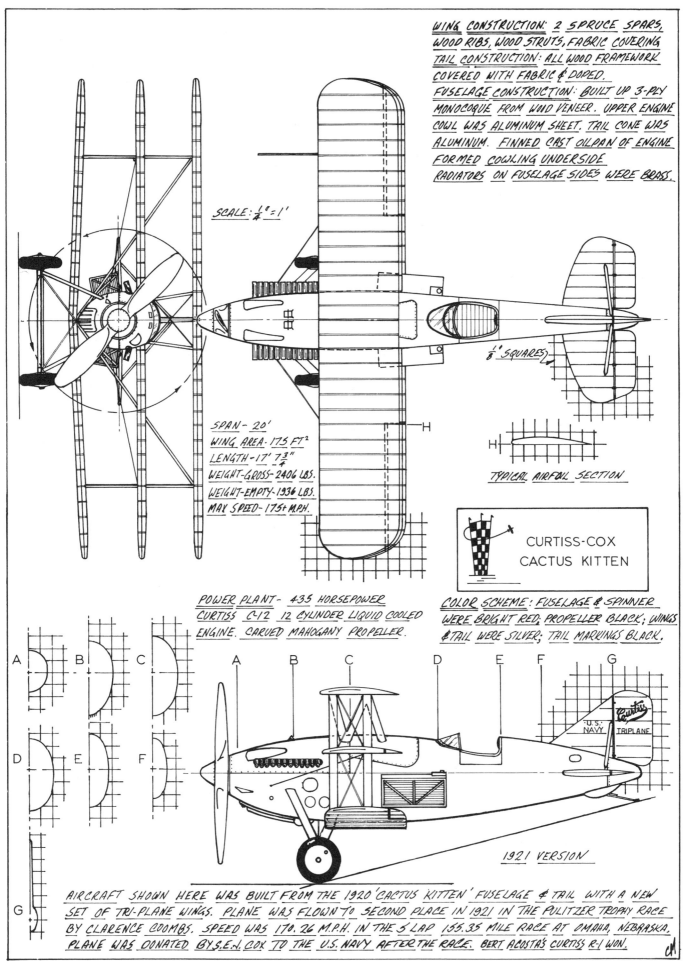

WING CONSTRUCTION: 2 SPRUCE SPARS, WOOD RIBS, WOOD STRUTS, FABRIC COVERING
TAIL CONSTRUCTION: ALL WOOD FRAMEWORK COVERED WITH FABRIC & DOPED.
FUSELAGE CONSTRUCTION: BUILT UP 3-PLY MONOCOQUE FROM WOOD VENEER. UPPER ENGINE COWL WAS ALUMINUM SHEET. TAIL CONE WAS ALUMINUM. FINNED CAST OILPAN OF ENGINE FORMED COWLING UNDERSIDE
RADIATORS ON FUSELAGE SIDES WERE BRASS.

SCALE: 1/4" = 1'

1/8" SQUARES

SPAN - 20'
WING AREA - 175 FT²
LENGTH - 17' 7 3/4"
WEIGHT - GROSS - 2406 LBS.
WEIGHT - EMPTY - 1936 LBS.
MAX SPEED - 175+ M.P.H.

TYPICAL AIRFOIL SECTION

CURTISS-COX
CACTUS KITTEN

POWER PLANT - 435 HORSEPOWER CURTISS C-12 12 CYLINDER LIQUID COOLED ENGINE. CARVED MAHOGANY PROPELLER.

COLOR SCHEME: FUSELAGE & SPINNER WERE BRIGHT RED; PROPELLER BLACK; WINGS & TAIL WERE SILVER; TAIL MARKINGS BLACK.

U.S. NAVY   Curtiss TRIPLANE

1921 VERSION

AIRCRAFT SHOWN HERE WAS BUILT FROM THE 1920 'CACTUS KITTEN' FUSELAGE & TAIL WITH A NEW SET OF TRI-PLANE WINGS. PLANE WAS FLOWN TO SECOND PLACE IN 1921 IN THE PULITZER TROPHY RACE BY CLARENCE COOMBS. SPEED WAS 170.26 M.P.H. IN THE 5 LAP 155.35 MILE RACE AT OMAHA, NEBRASKA. PLANE WAS DONATED BY S.E.J. COX TO THE U.S. NAVY AFTER THE RACE. BERT ACOSTA'S CURTISS R-1 WON.

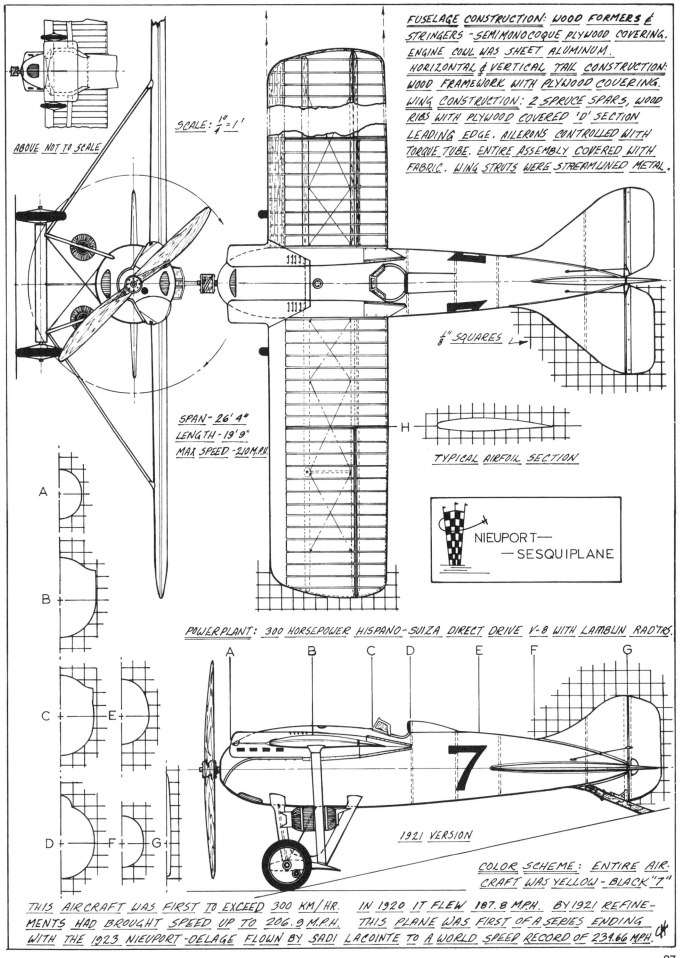

ABOVE NOT TO SCALE

SCALE: $\frac{1"}{4} = 1'$

FUSELAGE CONSTRUCTION: WOOD FORMERS &
STRINGERS - SEMIMONOCOQUE PLYWOOD COVERING.
ENGINE COWL WAS SHEET ALUMINUM.
HORIZONTAL & VERTICAL TAIL CONSTRUCTION:
WOOD FRAMEWORK WITH PLYWOOD COVERING.
WING CONSTRUCTION: 2 SPRUCE SPARS, WOOD
RIBS WITH PLYWOOD COVERED 'D' SECTION
LEADING EDGE. AILERONS CONTROLLED WITH
TORQUE TUBE. ENTIRE ASSEMBLY COVERED WITH
FABRIC. WING STRUTS WERE STREAMLINED METAL.

SPAN - 26' 4"
LENGTH - 19' 9"
MAX SPEED - 210 M.P.H.

$\frac{1"}{8}$ SQUARES

H

TYPICAL AIRFOIL SECTION

NIEUPORT—
—SESQUIPLANE

POWERPLANT: 300 HORSEPOWER HISPANO-SUIZA DIRECT DRIVE V-8 WITH LAMBLIN RADTRS.

A   B   C   D   E   F   G

1921 VERSION

COLOR SCHEME: ENTIRE AIR-
CRAFT WAS YELLOW - BLACK "7"

THIS AIRCRAFT WAS FIRST TO EXCEED 300 KM/HR. IN 1920 IT FLEW 187.8 M.P.H. BY 1921 REFINE-
MENTS HAD BROUGHT SPEED UP TO 206.9 M.P.H. THIS PLANE WAS FIRST OF A SERIES ENDING
WITH THE 1923 NIEUPORT-DELAGE FLOWN BY SADI LACOINTE TO A WORLD SPEED RECORD OF 234.66 M.P.H.

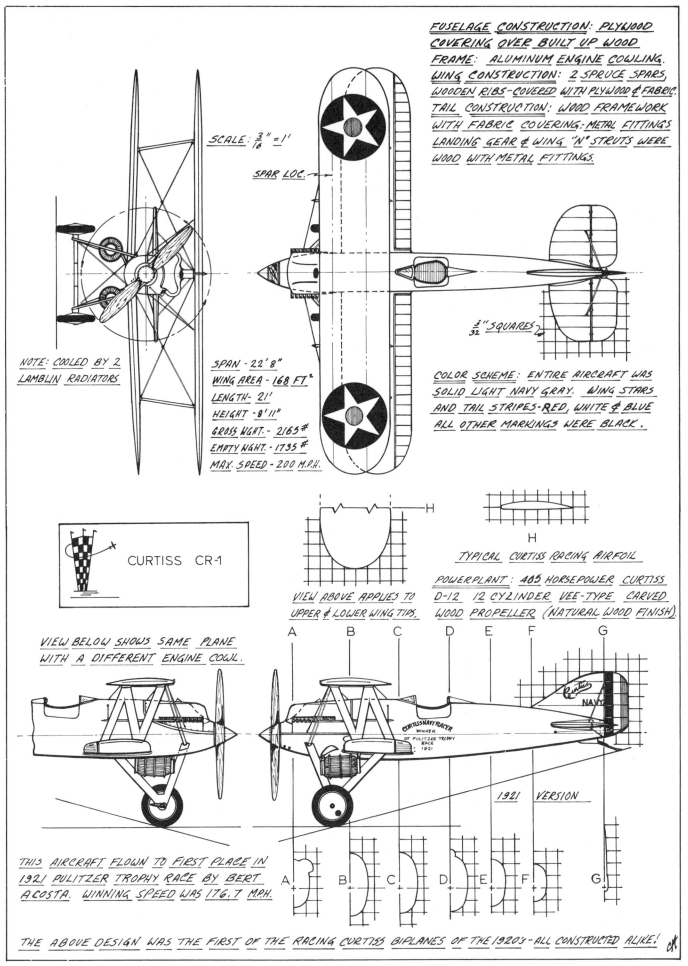

FUSELAGE CONSTRUCTION: PLYWOOD COVERING OVER BUILT UP WOOD FRAME: ALUMINUM ENGINE COWLING. WING CONSTRUCTION: 2 SPRUCE SPARS, WOODEN RIBS-COVERED WITH PLYWOOD & FABRIC. TAIL CONSTRUCTION: WOOD FRAMEWORK WITH FABRIC COVERING-METAL FITTINGS LANDING GEAR & WING "N" STRUTS WERE WOOD WITH METAL FITTINGS.

SCALE: 3/16" = 1'

SPAR LOC.

NOTE: COOLED BY 2 LAMBLIN RADIATORS

SPAN - 22' 8"
WING AREA - 168 FT²
LENGTH - 21'
HEIGHT - 8' 11"
GROSS WGHT. - 2165 #
EMPTY WGHT. - 1755 #
MAX. SPEED - 200 M.P.H.

3/32" SQUARES

COLOR SCHEME: ENTIRE AIRCRAFT WAS SOLID LIGHT NAVY GRAY. WING STARS AND TAIL STRIPES-RED, WHITE & BLUE ALL OTHER MARKINGS WERE BLACK.

CURTISS CR-1

VIEW ABOVE APPLIES TO UPPER & LOWER WING TIPS.

TYPICAL CURTISS RACING AIRFOIL

POWERPLANT: 405 HORSEPOWER CURTISS D-12 12 CYLINDER VEE-TYPE CARVED WOOD PROPELLER (NATURAL WOOD FINISH).

VIEW BELOW SHOWS SAME PLANE WITH A DIFFERENT ENGINE COWL.

CURTISS NAVY RACER
WINNER
OF PULITZER TROPHY
RACE
1921

NAVY

1921 VERSION

THIS AIRCRAFT FLOWN TO FIRST PLACE IN 1921 PULITZER TROPHY RACE BY BERT ACOSTA. WINNING SPEED WAS 176.7 M.P.H.

THE ABOVE DESIGN WAS THE FIRST OF THE RACING CURTISS BIPLANES OF THE 1920's - ALL CONSTRUCTED ALIKE!

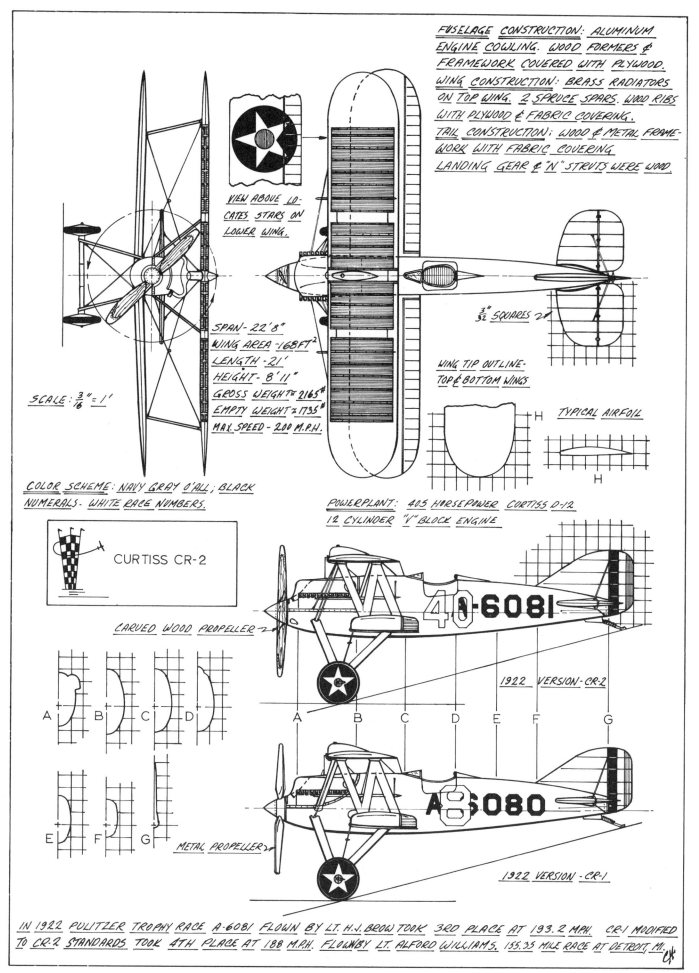

FUSELAGE CONSTRUCTION: ALUMINUM ENGINE COWLING. WOOD FORMERS & FRAMEWORK COVERED WITH PLYWOOD. WING CONSTRUCTION: BRASS RADIATORS ON TOP WING. 2 SPRUCE SPARS. WOOD RIBS WITH PLYWOOD & FABRIC COVERING. TAIL CONSTRUCTION: WOOD & METAL FRAMEWORK WITH FABRIC COVERING LANDING GEAR & "N" STRUTS WERE WOOD.

VIEW ABOVE LOCATES STARS ON LOWER WING.

SPAN - 22' 8"
WING AREA - 168 FT²
LENGTH - 21'
HEIGHT - 8' 11"
GROSS WEIGHT ≈ 2165 #
EMPTY WEIGHT ≈ 1735 #
MAX. SPEED - 200 M.P.H.

SCALE: 3/16" = 1'

$\frac{3}{32}$" SQUARES 2

WING TIP OUTLINE - TOP & BOTTOM WINGS

H

TYPICAL AIRFOIL

H

COLOR SCHEME: NAVY GRAY O'ALL; BLACK NUMERALS - WHITE RACE NUMBERS.

POWERPLANT: 405 HORSEPOWER CURTISS D-12 12 CYLINDER "V" BLOCK ENGINE

CURTISS CR-2

CARVED WOOD PROPELLER

A B C D

A-6081

40

A B C D E F G

1922 VERSION - CR-2

E F G

METAL PROPELLER

A-6080

8

1922 VERSION - CR-1

IN 1922 PULITZER TROPHY RACE A-6081 FLOWN BY LT. H.J. BROW TOOK 3RD PLACE AT 193.2 MPH. CR-1 MODIFIED TO CR-2 STANDARDS TOOK 4TH PLACE AT 188 M.P.H. FLOWN BY LT. ALFORD WILLIAMS. 155.35 MILE RACE AT DETROIT, MI.

29

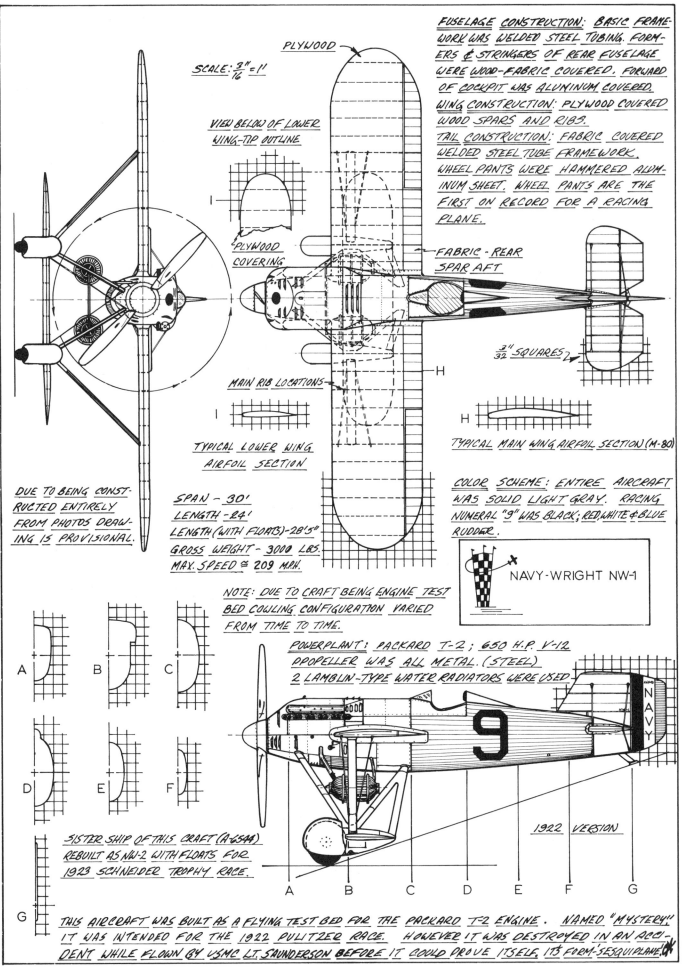

SCALE: $\frac{3}{16}$" = 1'

PLYWOOD

VIEW BELOW OF LOWER WING-TIP OUTLINE

PLYWOOD COVERING

FUSELAGE CONSTRUCTION: BASIC FRAMEWORK WAS WELDED STEEL TUBING. FORMERS & STRINGERS OF REAR FUSELAGE WERE WOOD-FABRIC COVERED. FORWARD OF COCKPIT WAS ALUMINUM COVERED.
WING CONSTRUCTION: PLYWOOD COVERED WOOD SPARS AND RIBS.
TAIL CONSTRUCTION: FABRIC COVERED WELDED STEEL TUBE FRAMEWORK. WHEEL PANTS WERE HAMMERED ALUMINUM SHEET. WHEEL PANTS ARE THE FIRST ON RECORD FOR A RACING PLANE.

FABRIC - REAR SPAR AFT

$\frac{3}{32}$" SQUARES

MAIN RIB LOCATIONS

TYPICAL LOWER WING AIRFOIL SECTION

H TYPICAL MAIN WING AIRFOIL SECTION (M-80)

DUE TO BEING CONSTRUCTED ENTIRELY FROM PHOTOS DRAWING IS PROVISIONAL.

SPAN - 30'
LENGTH - 24'
LENGTH (WITH FLOATS) - 28'5"
GROSS WEIGHT - 3000 LBS.
MAX. SPEED ≅ 209 M.P.H.

COLOR SCHEME: ENTIRE AIRCRAFT WAS SOLID LIGHT GRAY. RACING NUMERAL "9" WAS BLACK; RED, WHITE & BLUE RUDDER.

NAVY-WRIGHT NW-1

NOTE: DUE TO CRAFT BEING ENGINE TEST BED COWLING CONFIGURATION VARIED FROM TIME TO TIME.

POWERPLANT: PACKARD T-2; 650 H.P. V-12
PROPELLER WAS ALL METAL. (STEEL)
2 LAMBLIN-TYPE WATER RADIATORS WERE USED.

A B C

D E F

SISTER SHIP OF THIS CRAFT (A-6544) REBUILT AS NW-2 WITH FLOATS FOR 1923 SCHNEIDER TROPHY RACE.

G

1922 VERSION

A B C D E F G

THIS AIRCRAFT WAS BUILT AS A FLYING TEST BED FOR THE PACKARD T-2 ENGINE. NAMED "MYSTERY" IT WAS INTENDED FOR THE 1922 PULITZER RACE. HOWEVER IT WAS DESTROYED IN AN ACCIDENT WHILE FLOWN BY USMC LT. SAUNDERSON BEFORE IT COULD PROVE ITSELF. IT'S FORM - SESQUIPLANE.

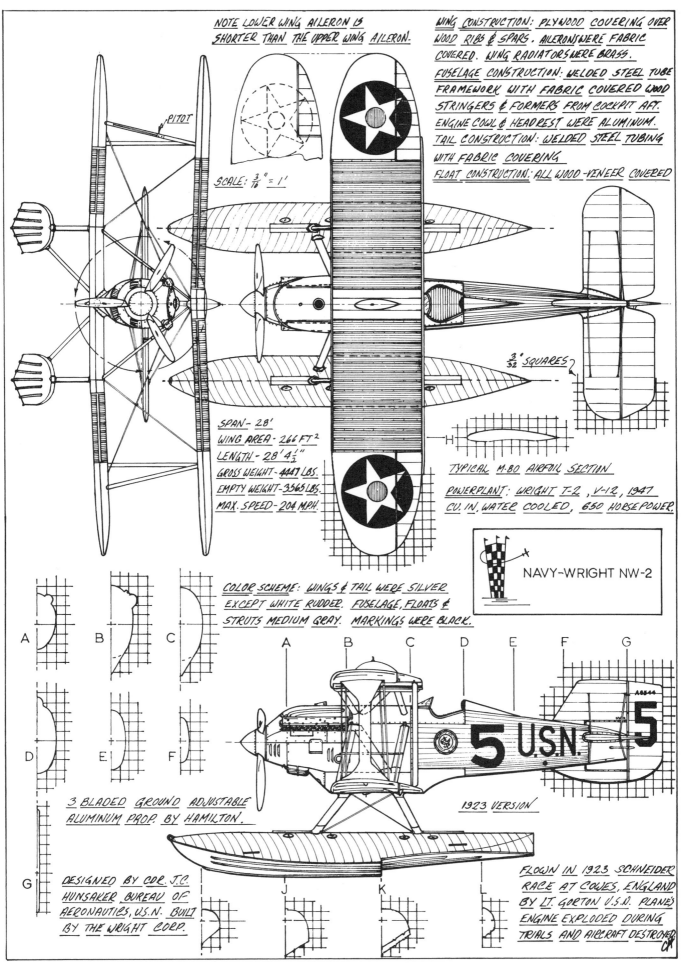

NOTE LOWER WING AILERON IS SHORTER THAN THE UPPER WING AILERON.

WING CONSTRUCTION: PLYWOOD COVERING OVER WOOD RIBS & SPARS. AILERONS WERE FABRIC COVERED. WING RADIATORS WERE BRASS.
FUSELAGE CONSTRUCTION: WELDED STEEL TUBE FRAMEWORK WITH FABRIC COVERED WOOD STRINGERS & FORMERS FROM COCKPIT AFT. ENGINE COWL & HEADREST WERE ALUMINUM.
TAIL CONSTRUCTION: WELDED STEEL TUBING WITH FABRIC COVERING
FLOAT CONSTRUCTION: ALL WOOD-VENEER COVERED

PITOT

SCALE: $\frac{3}{16}'' = 1'$

$\frac{3}{32}''$ SQUARES

SPAN - 28'
WING AREA - 266 FT²
LENGTH - 28' 4½"
GROSS WEIGHT - 4447 LBS.
EMPTY WEIGHT - 3565 LBS.
MAX. SPEED - 204 M.P.H.

H

TYPICAL M-80 AIRFOIL SECTION

POWERPLANT: WRIGHT T-2, V-12, 1947 CU. IN. WATER COOLED, 650 HORSEPOWER.

NAVY-WRIGHT NW-2

A B C

D E F

COLOR SCHEME: WINGS & TAIL WERE SILVER EXCEPT WHITE RUDDER. FUSELAGE, FLOATS & STRUTS MEDIUM GRAY. MARKINGS WERE BLACK.

A B C D E F G

A6544
5 U.S.N. 5

G

3 BLADED GROUND ADJUSTABLE ALUMINUM PROP. BY HAMILTON.

1923 VERSION

J K L

DESIGNED BY CDR. J.C. HUNSAKER BUREAU OF AERONAUTICS, U.S.N. BUILT BY THE WRIGHT CORP.

FLOWN IN 1923 SCHNEIDER RACE AT COWES, ENGLAND BY LT. GORTON U.S.N. PLANE'S ENGINE EXPLODED DURING TRIALS AND AIRCRAFT DESTROYED.

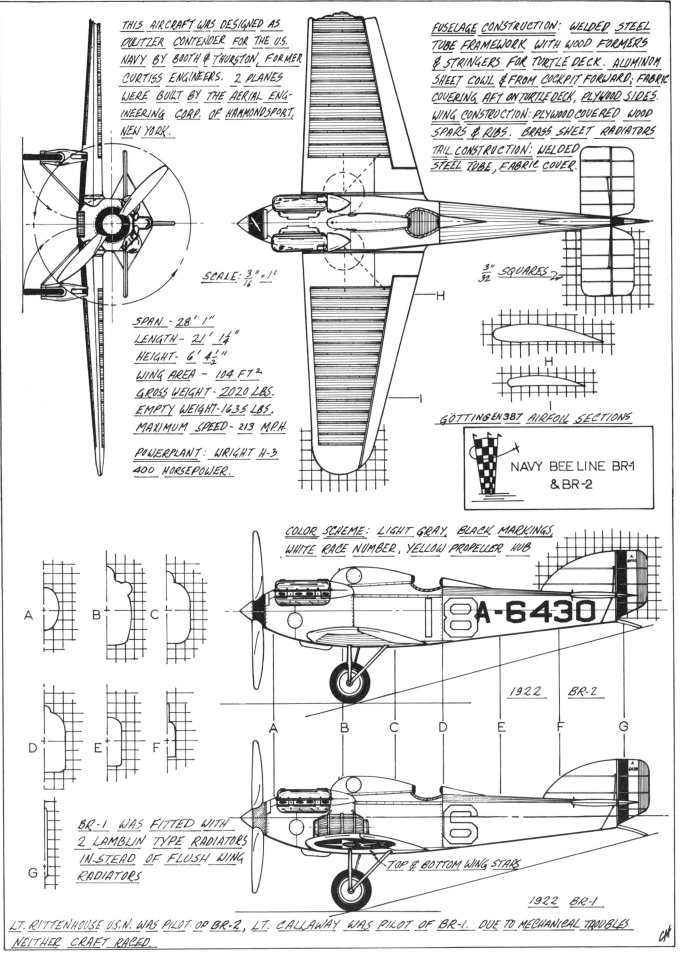

THIS AIRCRAFT WAS DESIGNED AS PULITZER CONTENDER FOR THE U.S. NAVY BY BOOTH & THURSTON, FORMER CURTISS ENGINEERS. 2 PLANES WERE BUILT BY THE AERIAL ENGINEERING CORP. OF HAMMONDSPORT, NEW YORK.

FUSELAGE CONSTRUCTION: WELDED STEEL TUBE FRAMEWORK WITH WOOD FORMERS & STRINGERS FOR TURTLE DECK. ALUMINUM SHEET COWL & FROM COCKPIT FORWARD; FABRIC COVERING AFT ON TURTLE DECK, PLYWOOD SIDES. WING CONSTRUCTION: PLYWOOD COVERED WOOD SPARS & RIBS. BRASS SHEET RADIATORS TAIL CONSTRUCTION: WELDED STEEL TUBE, FABRIC COVER.

SCALE: $\frac{3}{16}$" = 1'

SPAN - 28' 1"
LENGTH - 21' 1$\frac{1}{4}$"
HEIGHT - 6' 4$\frac{1}{2}$"
WING AREA - 104 FT²
GROSS WEIGHT - 2020 LBS.
EMPTY WEIGHT - 1635 LBS.
MAXIMUM SPEED - 213 M.P.H.

POWERPLANT: WRIGHT H-3 400 HORSEPOWER.

$\frac{3}{32}$" SQUARES

H

I

GÖTTINGEN 387 AIRFOIL SECTIONS

NAVY BEE LINE BR-1 & BR-2

COLOR SCHEME: LIGHT GRAY, BLACK MARKINGS, WHITE RACE NUMBER, YELLOW PROPELLER HUB

A B C

D E F

G

A-6430

8

1922 BR-2

A B C D E F G

BR-1 WAS FITTED WITH 2 LAMBLIN TYPE RADIATORS INSTEAD OF FLUSH WING RADIATORS

6

TOP & BOTTOM WING STARS

1922 BR-1

LT. RITTENHOUSE U.S.N. WAS PILOT OF BR-2, LT. CALLAWAY WAS PILOT OF BR-1. DUE TO MECHANICAL TROUBLES NEITHER CRAFT RACED.

CM

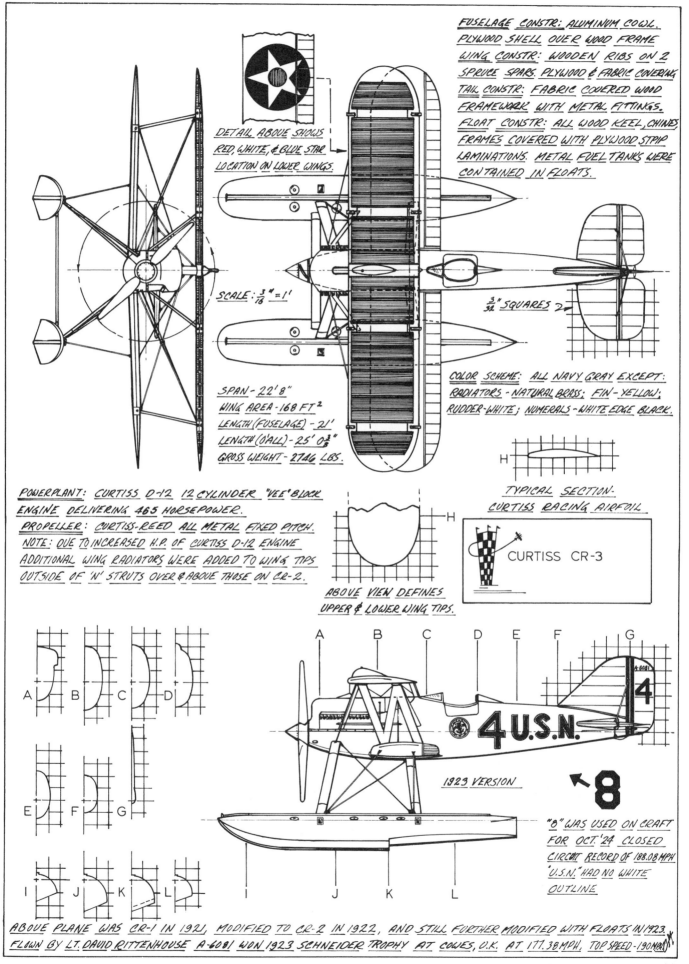

DETAIL ABOVE SHOWS
RED, WHITE, & BLUE STAR
LOCATION ON LOWER WINGS.

FUSELAGE CONSTR: ALUMINUM COWL.
PLYWOOD SHELL OVER WOOD FRAME
WING CONSTR: WOODEN RIBS ON 2
SPRUCE SPARS. PLYWOOD & FABRIC COVERING
TAIL CONSTR: FABRIC COVERED WOOD
FRAMEWORK WITH METAL FITTINGS.
FLOAT CONSTR: ALL WOOD KEEL, CHINES,
FRAMES COVERED WITH PLYWOOD STRIP
LAMINATIONS. METAL FUEL TANKS WERE
CONTAINED IN FLOATS.

SCALE: $\frac{3}{16}$" = 1'

$\frac{3}{32}$" SQUARES

SPAN - 22'8"
WING AREA - 168 FT^2
LENGTH (FUSELAGE) - 21'
LENGTH (O'ALL) - 25' 0 $\frac{3}{8}$"
GROSS WEIGHT - 2746 LBS.

COLOR SCHEME: ALL NAVY GRAY EXCEPT:
RADIATORS - NATURAL BRASS; FIN - YELLOW;
RUDDER - WHITE; NUMERALS - WHITE EDGE BLACK.

POWERPLANT: CURTISS D-12 12 CYLINDER "VEE" BLOCK
ENGINE DELIVERING 465 HORSEPOWER.
PROPELLER: CURTISS-REED ALL METAL FIXED PITCH.
NOTE: DUE TO INCREASED H.P. OF CURTISS D-12 ENGINE
ADDITIONAL WING RADIATORS WERE ADDED TO WING TIPS
OUTSIDE OF 'N' STRUTS OVER & ABOVE THOSE ON CR-2.

H

ABOVE VIEW DEFINES
UPPER & LOWER WING TIPS.

TYPICAL SECTION -
CURTISS RACING AIRFOIL

CURTISS CR-3

1923 VERSION

8

"8" WAS USED ON CRAFT
FOR OCT. '24 CLOSED
CIRCUIT RECORD OF 188.08 MPH.
"U.S.N." HAD NO WHITE
OUTLINE

ABOVE PLANE WAS CR-1 IN 1921, MODIFIED TO CR-2 IN 1922, AND STILL FURTHER MODIFIED WITH FLOATS IN 1923.
FLOWN BY LT. DAVID RITTENHOUSE A-6081 WON 1923 SCHNEIDER TROPHY AT COWES, U.K. AT 177.38 M.P.H., TOP SPEED - 190 M.P.H.

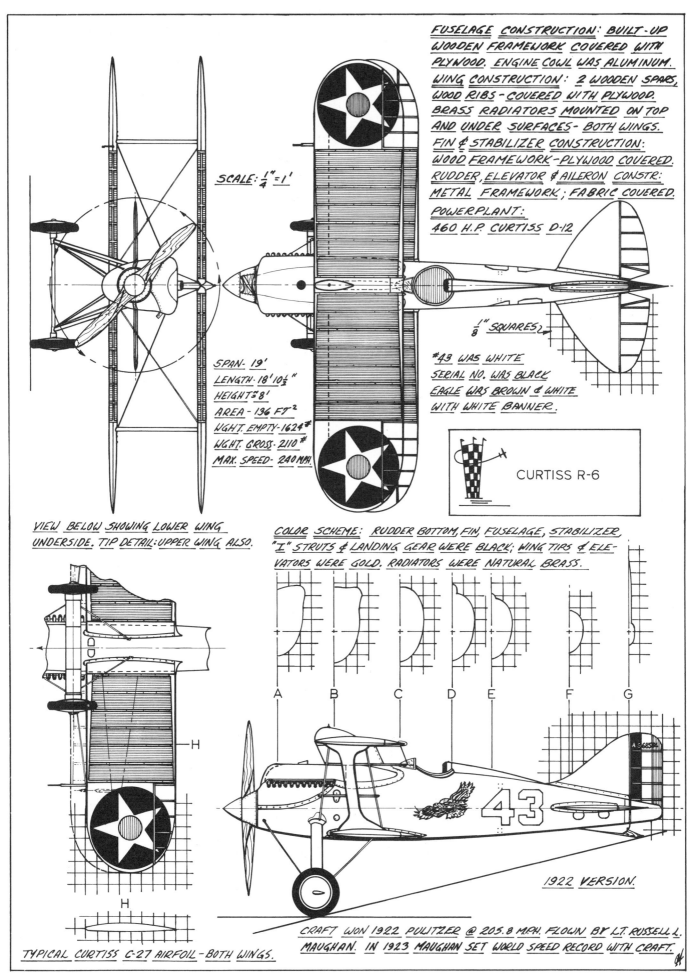

FUSELAGE CONSTRUCTION: BUILT-UP WOODEN FRAMEWORK COVERED WITH PLYWOOD. ENGINE COWL WAS ALUMINUM. WING CONSTRUCTION: 2 WOODEN SPARS, WOOD RIBS - COVERED WITH PLYWOOD. BRASS RADIATORS MOUNTED ON TOP AND UNDER SURFACES - BOTH WINGS. FIN & STABILIZER CONSTRUCTION: WOOD FRAMEWORK - PLYWOOD COVERED. RUDDER, ELEVATOR & AILERON CONSTR: METAL FRAMEWORK; FABRIC COVERED. POWERPLANT: 460 H.P. CURTISS D-12.

SCALE: $\frac{1}{4}" = 1'$

$\frac{1}{8}"$ SQUARES

#43 WAS WHITE SERIAL NO. WAS BLACK EAGLE WAS BROWN & WHITE WITH WHITE BANNER.

SPAN - 19'
LENGTH - 18'10½"
HEIGHT - 8'
AREA - 136 FT²
WGHT. EMPTY - 1624#
WGHT. GROSS - 2110#
MAX. SPEED - 240 M.P.H.

CURTISS R-6

VIEW BELOW SHOWING LOWER WING UNDERSIDE. TIP DETAIL: UPPER WING ALSO.

COLOR SCHEME: RUDDER BOTTOM, FIN, FUSELAGE, STABILIZER, "I" STRUTS & LANDING GEAR WERE BLACK; WING TIPS & ELEVATORS WERE GOLD. RADIATORS WERE NATURAL BRASS.

A   B   C   D   E   F   G

H

H

1922 VERSION.

TYPICAL CURTISS C-27 AIRFOIL - BOTH WINGS.

CRAFT WON 1922 PULITZER @ 205.8 M.P.H. FLOWN BY LT. RUSSELL L. MAUGHAN. IN 1923 MAUGHAN SET WORLD SPEED RECORD WITH CRAFT.

34

A.S.22-328 (1923) & P-362 (1924) ARE SAME AIRCRAFT. PLANE WAS ONE OF THREE R-3S BUILT AND WERE DESIGNED BY ALFRED V. VERVILLE IN 1922. THEY WERE BUILT BY THE SPERRY AIRCRAFT CORP. IN 1922, RACED IN '22, '23 & '24 PULITZER; MODIFIED EACH YEAR

FUSELAGE CONSTRUCTION: WELDED STEEL TUBE FRAMEWORK. FORWARD PORTION & AROUND COCKPIT WAS SHEET ALUMINUM. REAR PORTION WAS FABRIC COVERED. WING CONSTRUCTION: SPRUCE BOX SPARS, PLYWOOD RIBS; PLYWOOD COVERING. TAIL CONSTRUCTION: WELDED STEEL TUBING - FABRIC COVERED.

SCALE: $\frac{3}{16}$" = 1'

SPAN - 30'6"
LENGTH - 23'6"
WING AREA - 146.5 FT²
WEIGHT EMPTY - 2032 LBS.
GROSS WEIGHT - 2503 LBS.
MAX SPEED (1924) - 219 M.P.H.
STALL SPEED - 78 M.P.H.
COLOR SCHEME (1923): OLIVE DRAB WITH WHITE RACE NUMBERS. RED, WHITE & BLUE RUDDER & STARS; BRASS RADIATORS.

$\frac{3}{32}$" SQUARES

H

I

TYPICAL VERVILLE MODIFIED NACA 81 AIRFOIL

VERVILLE-SPERRY R-3

NOTE RETRACTABLE LANDING GEAR.

POWERPLANT: CURTISS D-12 500 H.P. V-12
PROPELLER: CURTISS-REED 92" DURALUMINUM

A   B   C

D   E   F

G

A.S.22-328

48

1923 VERSION

A   B   C   D   E   F   G

COLOR SCHEME (1924): BASIC COLOR OF ENTIRE AIRCRAFT WAS SILVER - RUDDER WAS RED, WHITE, & BLUE WITH BLACK LETTERING; RADIATORS WERE BRASS '70' WAS ALSO UNDER LEFT WING TIP.

70

1924 VERSION

1924 VERSION WON PULITZER RACE FLOWN BY LT. H.H. MILLS AT 215.72 M.P.H. AT DAYTON, OHIO OCTOBER 4TH.

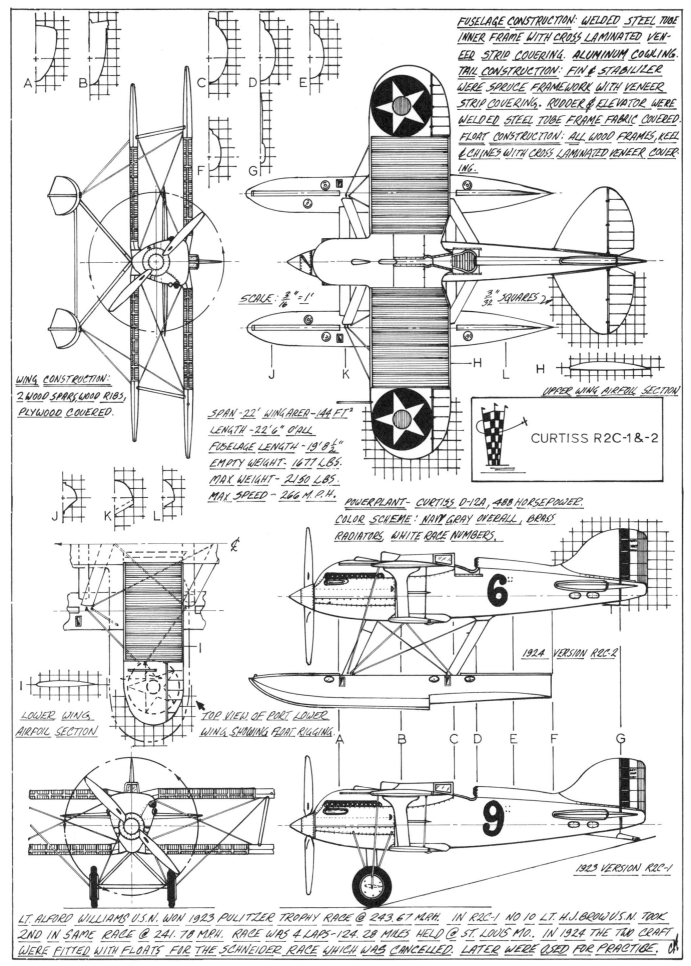

FUSELAGE CONSTRUCTION: WELDED STEEL TUBE INNER FRAME WITH CROSS LAMINATED VENEER STRIP COVERING. ALUMINUM COWLING. TAIL CONSTRUCTION: FIN & STABILIZER WERE SPRUCE FRAMEWORK WITH VENEER STRIP COVERING. RUDDER & ELEVATOR WERE WELDED STEEL TUBE FRAME FABRIC COVERED. FLOAT CONSTRUCTION: ALL WOOD FRAMES, KEEL & CHINES WITH CROSS LAMINATED VENEER COVERING.

SCALE: $\frac{3}{16}$" = 1'

$\frac{3}{32}$" SQUARES

UPPER WING AIRFOIL SECTION

WING CONSTRUCTION: 2 WOOD SPARS, WOOD RIBS, PLYWOOD COVERED.

SPAN - 22' WING AREA - 144 FT²
LENGTH - 22'6" O'ALL
FUSELAGE LENGTH - 19'8½"
EMPTY WEIGHT - 1677 LBS.
MAX WEIGHT - 2150 LBS.
MAX SPEED - 266 M.P.H.

CURTISS R2C-1 & -2

POWERPLANT - CURTISS D-12A, 488 HORSEPOWER.
COLOR SCHEME: NAVY GRAY OVERALL, BRASS RADIATORS, WHITE RACE NUMBERS.

LOWER WING AIRFOIL SECTION

TOP VIEW OF PORT LOWER WING SHOWING FLOAT RIGGING.

1924 VERSION R2C-2

1923 VERSION R2C-1

LT. ALFORD WILLIAMS U.S.N. WON 1923 PULITZER TROPHY RACE @ 243.67 M.P.H. IN R2C-1 NO 10 LT. H.J.BROW U.S.N. TOOK 2ND IN SAME RACE @ 241.78 M.P.H. RACE WAS 4 LAPS - 124.28 MILES HELD @ ST. LOUIS MO. IN 1924 THE TWO CRAFT WERE FITTED WITH FLOATS FOR THE SCHNEIDER RACE WHICH WAS CANCELLED. LATER WERE USED FOR PRACTICE.

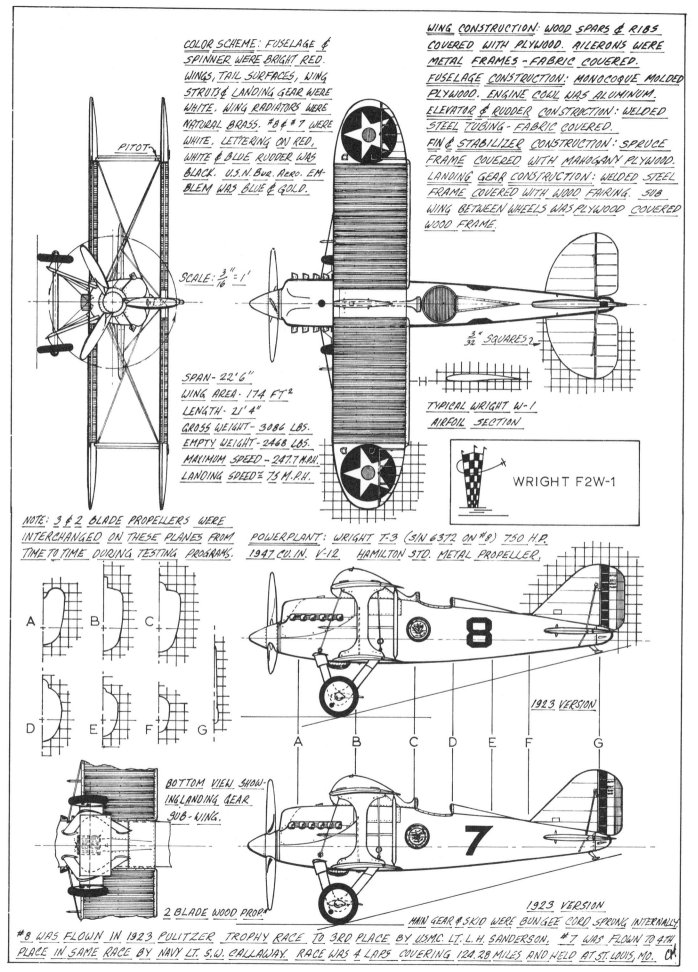

COLOR SCHEME: FUSELAGE & SPINNER WERE BRIGHT RED. WINGS, TAIL SURFACES, WING STRUTS & LANDING GEAR WERE WHITE. WING RADIATORS WERE NATURAL BRASS. #8 & #7 WERE WHITE. LETTERING ON RED, WHITE & BLUE RUDDER WAS BLACK. U.S.N. BUR. AERO. EMBLEM WAS BLUE & GOLD.

WING CONSTRUCTION: WOOD SPARS & RIBS COVERED WITH PLYWOOD. AILERONS WERE METAL FRAMES - FABRIC COVERED. FUSELAGE CONSTRUCTION: MONOCOQUE MOLDED PLYWOOD. ENGINE COWL WAS ALUMINUM. ELEVATOR & RUDDER CONSTRUCTION: WELDED STEEL TUBING - FABRIC COVERED. FIN & STABILIZER CONSTRUCTION: SPRUCE FRAME COVERED WITH MAHOGANY PLYWOOD. LANDING GEAR CONSTRUCTION: WELDED STEEL FRAME COVERED WITH WOOD FAIRING. SUB WING BETWEEN WHEELS WAS PLYWOOD COVERED WOOD FRAME.

PITOT

SCALE: $\frac{3}{16}$" = 1'

SPAN - 22' 6"
WING AREA - 174 FT²
LENGTH - 21' 4"
GROSS WEIGHT - 3086 LBS.
EMPTY WEIGHT - 2468 LBS.
MAXIMUM SPEED - 247.7 M.P.H.
LANDING SPEED ≅ 75 M.P.H.

$\frac{3}{32}$" SQUARES

TYPICAL WRIGHT W-1 AIRFOIL SECTION

WRIGHT F2W-1

NOTE: 3 & 2 BLADE PROPELLERS WERE INTERCHANGED ON THESE PLANES FROM TIME TO TIME DURING TESTING PROGRAMS.

POWERPLANT: WRIGHT T-3 (S/N 6372 ON #8) 750 H.P. 1947 CU. IN. V-12 HAMILTON STD. METAL PROPELLER.

A B C

D E F G

1923 VERSION

A B C D E F G

BOTTOM VIEW SHOWING LANDING GEAR SUB-WING.

2 BLADE WOOD PROP.

1923 VERSION
MAIN GEAR & SKID WERE BUNGEE CORD SPRUNG INTERNALLY

#8 WAS FLOWN IN 1923 PULITZER TROPHY RACE TO 3RD PLACE BY U.S.M.C. LT. L.H. SANDERSON. #7 WAS FLOWN TO 4TH PLACE IN SAME RACE BY NAVY LT. S.W. CALLAWAY. RACE WAS 4 LAPS COVERING 124.28 MILES AND HELD AT ST. LOUIS, MO.

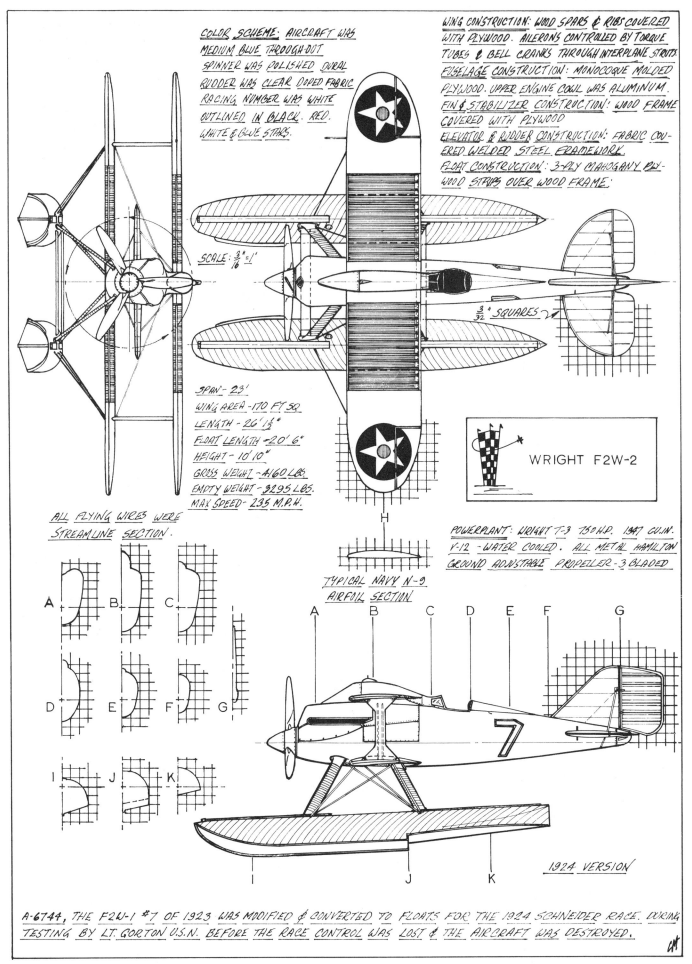

COLOR SCHEME: AIRCRAFT WAS MEDIUM BLUE THROUGH-OUT. SPINNER WAS POLISHED DURAL. RUDDER WAS CLEAR DOPED FABRIC. RACING NUMBER WAS WHITE OUTLINED IN BLACK. RED, WHITE & BLUE STARS.

WING CONSTRUCTION: WOOD SPARS & RIBS COVERED WITH PLYWOOD. AILERONS CONTROLLED BY TORQUE TUBES & BELL CRANKS THROUGH INTERPLANE STRUTS.
FUSELAGE CONSTRUCTION: MONOCOQUE MOLDED PLYWOOD. UPPER ENGINE COWL WAS ALUMINUM.
FIN & STABILIZER CONSTRUCTION: WOOD FRAME COVERED WITH PLYWOOD.
ELEVATOR & RUDDER CONSTRUCTION: FABRIC COVERED WELDED STEEL FRAMEWORK.
FLOAT CONSTRUCTION: 3-PLY MAHOGANY PLYWOOD STRIPS OVER WOOD FRAME.

SCALE: $\frac{3}{16}$" = 1'

$\frac{3}{32}$" SQUARES

SPAN - 23'
WING AREA - 170 FT SQ.
LENGTH - 26' 1½"
FLOAT LENGTH - 20' 6"
HEIGHT - 10' 10"
GROSS WEIGHT - 4160 LBS.
EMPTY WEIGHT - 3295 LBS.
MAX SPEED - 235 M.P.H.

WRIGHT F2W-2

ALL FLYING WIRES WERE STREAMLINE SECTION.

POWERPLANT: WRIGHT T-3 750 H.P. 1347 CU.IN. V-12 - WATER COOLED. ALL METAL HAMILTON GROUND ADJUSTABLE PROPELLER - 3 BLADED.

A   B   C

D   E   F   G

I   J   K

TYPICAL NAVY N-9 AIRFOIL SECTION

A   B   C   D   E   F   G

7

1924 VERSION

I   J   K

A-6744, THE F2W-1 #7 OF 1923 WAS MODIFIED & CONVERTED TO FLOATS FOR THE 1924 SCHNEIDER RACE. DURING TESTING BY LT. GORTON U.S.N. BEFORE THE RACE CONTROL WAS LOST & THE AIRCRAFT WAS DESTROYED.

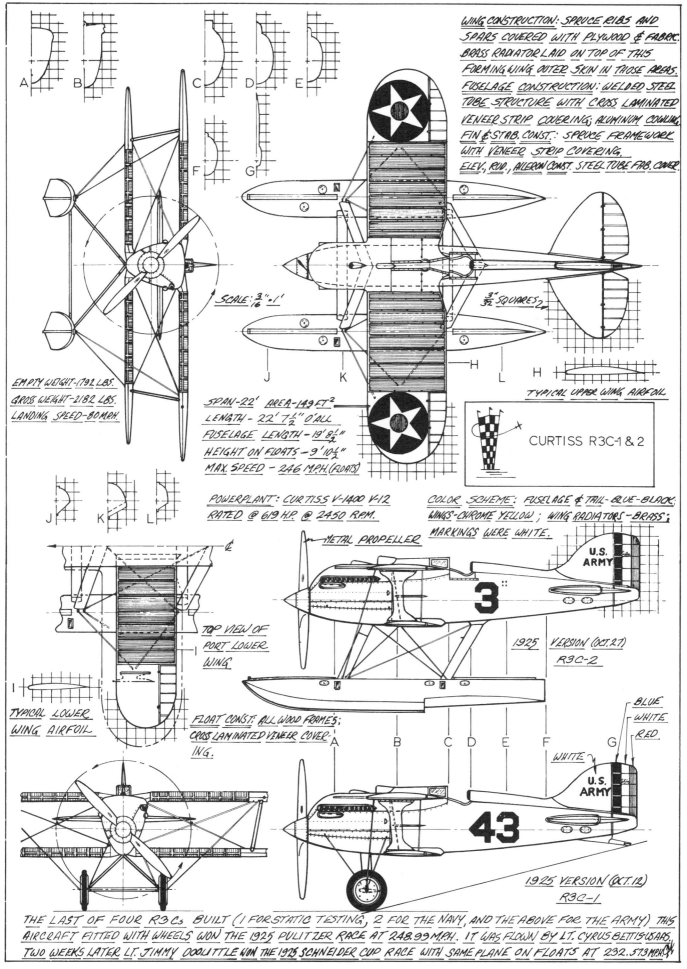

WING CONSTRUCTION: SPRUCE RIBS AND SPARS COVERED WITH PLYWOOD & FABRIC. BRASS RADIATOR LAID ON TOP OF THIS FORMING WING OUTER SKIN IN THOSE AREAS. FUSELAGE CONSTRUCTION: WELDED STEEL TUBE STRUCTURE WITH CROSS LAMINATED VENEER STRIP COVERING; ALUMINUM COWLING. FIN & STAB. CONST.: SPRUCE FRAMEWORK WITH VENEER STRIP COVERING. ELEV., RUD., AILERON CONST. STEEL TUBE FAB. COVER.

A B C D E F G

SCALE: 3/16" = 1'

3"/32 SQUARES

J K H L H

TYPICAL UPPER WING AIRFOIL

EMPTY WEIGHT-1792 LBS.
GROSS WEIGHT-2182 LBS.
LANDING SPEED-80 M.P.H.

SPAN-22' AREA-149 FT²
LENGTH - 22' 7½" O'ALL
FUSELAGE LENGTH - 19'8½"
HEIGHT ON FLOATS - 9'10½"
MAX. SPEED - 246 M.P.H. (FLOATS)

CURTISS R3C-1 & 2

J K L

POWERPLANT: CURTISS V-1400 V-12 RATED @ 619 H.P. @ 2450 R.P.M.

COLOR SCHEME: FUSELAGE & TAIL-BLUE-BLACK; WINGS-CHROME YELLOW; WING RADIATORS-BRASS; MARKINGS WERE WHITE.

TOP VIEW OF PORT LOWER WING

METAL PROPELLER

U.S. ARMY

3

1925 VERSION (OCT. 27)
R3C-2

TYPICAL LOWER WING AIRFOIL

FLOAT CONST.: ALL WOOD FRAMES; CROSS LAMINATED VENEER COVER-ING.

A B C D E F G

BLUE
WHITE
RED
WHITE

U.S. ARMY

43

1925 VERSION (OCT. 12)
R3C-1

THE LAST OF FOUR R3C's BUILT (1 FOR STATIC TESTING, 2 FOR THE NAVY, AND THE ABOVE FOR THE ARMY) THIS AIRCRAFT FITTED WITH WHEELS WON THE 1925 PULITZER RACE AT 248.99 M.P.H. IT WAS FLOWN BY LT. CYRUS BETTIS USAAS. TWO WEEKS LATER LT. JIMMY DOOLITTLE WON THE 1925 SCHNEIDER CUP RACE WITH SAME PLANE ON FLOATS AT 232.573 M.P.H.

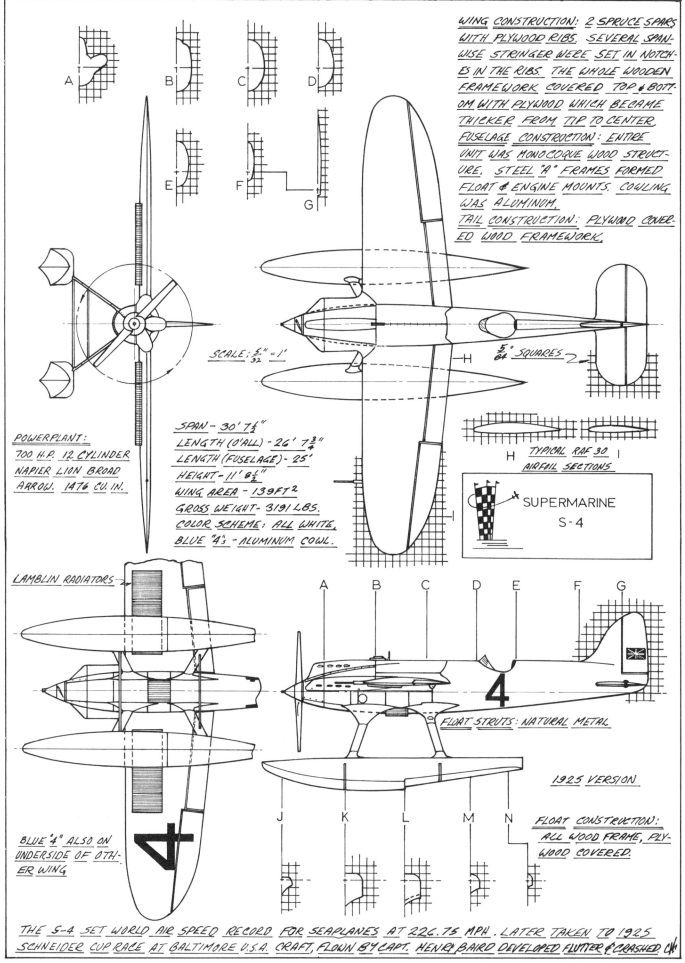

WING CONSTRUCTION: 2 SPRUCE SPARS WITH PLYWOOD RIBS. SEVERAL SPANWISE STRINGER WERE SET IN NOTCHES IN THE RIBS. THE WHOLE WOODEN FRAMEWORK COVERED TOP & BOTTOM WITH PLYWOOD WHICH BECAME THICKER FROM TIP TO CENTER.

FUSELAGE CONSTRUCTION: ENTIRE UNIT WAS MONOCOQUE WOOD STRUCTURE. STEEL "A" FRAMES FORMED FLOAT & ENGINE MOUNTS. COWLING WAS ALUMINUM.

TAIL CONSTRUCTION: PLYWOOD COVERED WOOD FRAMEWORK.

A   B   C   D

E   F   G

SCALE: $\frac{5}{32}$" = 1'

$\frac{5}{64}$" SQUARES

H   TYPICAL RAF 30   I
AIRFOIL SECTIONS

SUPERMARINE S-4

POWERPLANT:
700 H.P. 12 CYLINDER NAPIER LION BROAD ARROW. 1476 CU. IN.

SPAN - 30' 7½"
LENGTH (O'ALL) - 26' 7¾"
LENGTH (FUSELAGE) - 25'
HEIGHT - 11' 8½"
WING AREA - 139 FT²
GROSS WEIGHT - 3191 LBS.
COLOR SCHEME: ALL WHITE,
BLUE "4's - ALUMINUM COWL.

LAMBLIN RADIATORS

A   B   C   D   E   F   G

FLOAT STRUTS: NATURAL METAL

1925 VERSION

BLUE "4" ALSO ON UNDERSIDE OF OTHER WING

J   K   L   M   N

FLOAT CONSTRUCTION: ALL WOOD FRAME, PLYWOOD COVERED.

THE S-4 SET WORLD AIR SPEED RECORD FOR SEAPLANES AT 226.75 MPH. LATER TAKEN TO 1925 SCHNEIDER CUP RACE AT BALTIMORE U.S.A. CRAFT, FLOWN BY CAPT. HENRY BAIRD DEVELOPED FLUTTER & CRASHED.

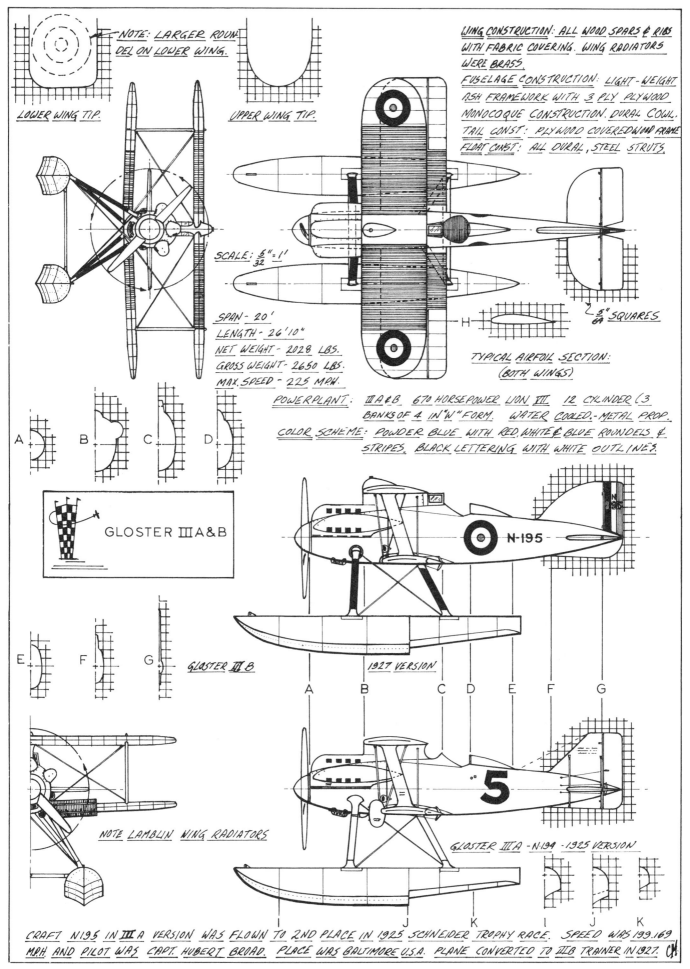

NOTE: LARGER ROUNDEL ON LOWER WING.

LOWER WING TIP.

UPPER WING TIP.

WING CONSTRUCTION: ALL WOOD SPARS & RIBS WITH FABRIC COVERING. WING RADIATORS WERE BRASS.

FUSELAGE CONSTRUCTION: LIGHT-WEIGHT ASH FRAMEWORK WITH 3 PLY PLYWOOD. MONOCOQUE CONSTRUCTION. DURAL COWL.

TAIL CONST: PLYWOOD COVERED WOOD FRAME

FLOAT CONST: ALL DURAL, STEEL STRUTS.

SCALE: 5/32" = 1'

SPAN - 20'
LENGTH - 26'10"
NET WEIGHT - 2028 LBS.
GROSS WEIGHT - 2650 LBS.
MAX. SPEED - 225 MPH.

5/64" SQUARES

TYPICAL AIRFOIL SECTION: (BOTH WINGS)

POWERPLANT: IIIA&B 670 HORSEPOWER LION VII 12 CYLINDER (3 BANKS OF 4 IN "W" FORM. WATER COOLED. - METAL PROP.

COLOR SCHEME: POWDER BLUE WITH RED, WHITE & BLUE ROUNDELS & STRIPES. BLACK LETTERING WITH WHITE OUTLINES.

A   B   C   D

GLOSTER IIIA&B

E   F   G

GLOSTER IIIB

N-195

1927 VERSION

A   B   C   D   E   F   G

NOTE LAMBLIN WING RADIATORS

5

GLOSTER IIIA - N-194 - 1925 VERSION

I   J   K

I   J   K

CRAFT N195 IN IIIA VERSION WAS FLOWN TO 2ND PLACE IN 1925 SCHNEIDER TROPHY RACE. SPEED WAS 199.169 M.P.H. AND PILOT WAS CAPT. HUBERT BROAD. PLACE WAS BALTIMORE U.S.A. PLANE CONVERTED TO IIIB TRAINER IN 1927. CM

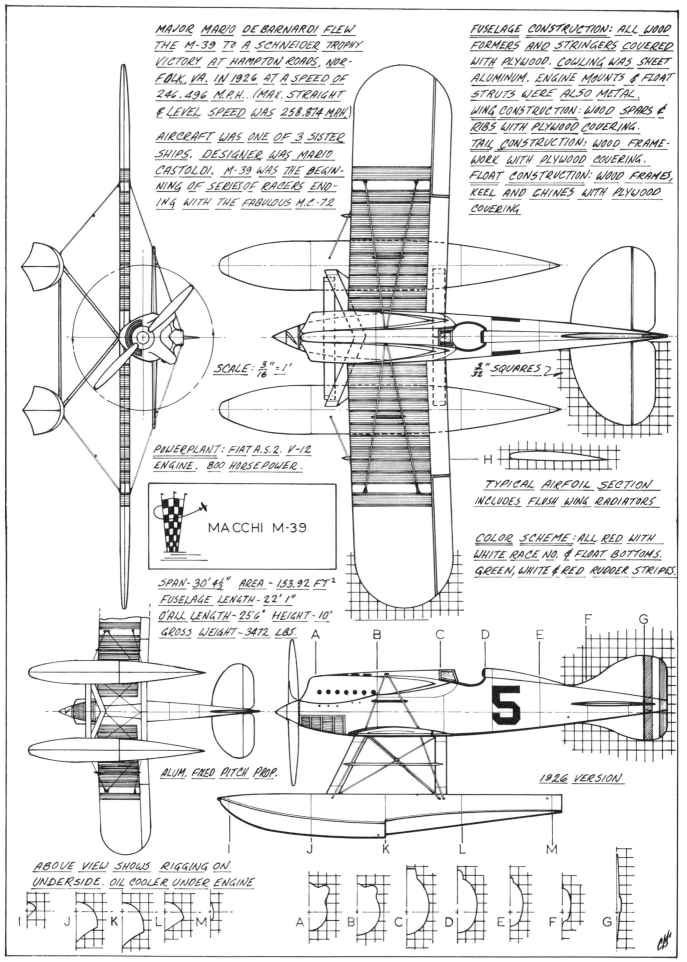

MAJOR MARIO DE BARNARDI FLEW THE M-39 TO A SCHNEIDER TROPHY VICTORY AT HAMPTON ROADS, NORFOLK, VA. IN 1926 AT A SPEED OF 246.496 M.P.H. (MAX. STRAIGHT & LEVEL SPEED WAS 258.874 M.P.H.)

AIRCRAFT WAS ONE OF 3 SISTER SHIPS. DESIGNER WAS MARIO CASTOLDI. M-39 WAS THE BEGINNING OF SERIES OF RACERS ENDING WITH THE FABULOUS M.C.-72.

FUSELAGE CONSTRUCTION: ALL WOOD FORMERS AND STRINGERS COVERED WITH PLYWOOD. COWLING WAS SHEET ALUMINUM. ENGINE MOUNTS & FLOAT STRUTS WERE ALSO METAL.
WING CONSTRUCTION: WOOD SPARS & RIBS WITH PLYWOOD COVERING.
TAIL CONSTRUCTION: WOOD FRAMEWORK WITH PLYWOOD COVERING.
FLOAT CONSTRUCTION: WOOD FRAMES, KEEL AND CHINES WITH PLYWOOD COVERING

SCALE: $\frac{3}{16}'' = 1'$

$\frac{3}{32}''$ SQUARES

POWERPLANT: FIAT A.S.2. V-12 ENGINE. 800 HORSEPOWER.

MACCHI M-39

SPAN - 30' 4½" AREA ~ 153.92 FT²
FUSELAGE LENGTH - 22' 1"
O'ALL LENGTH - 25'6" HEIGHT - 10'
GROSS WEIGHT - 3472 LBS.

H

TYPICAL AIRFOIL SECTION INCLUDES FLUSH WING RADIATORS

COLOR SCHEME: ALL RED WITH WHITE RACE NO. & FLOAT BOTTOMS. GREEN, WHITE & RED RUDDER STRIPES.

ALUM. FIXED PITCH PROP.

5

1926 VERSION

ABOVE VIEW SHOWS RIGGING ON UNDERSIDE. OIL COOLER UNDER ENGINE

I J K L M

A B C D E F G

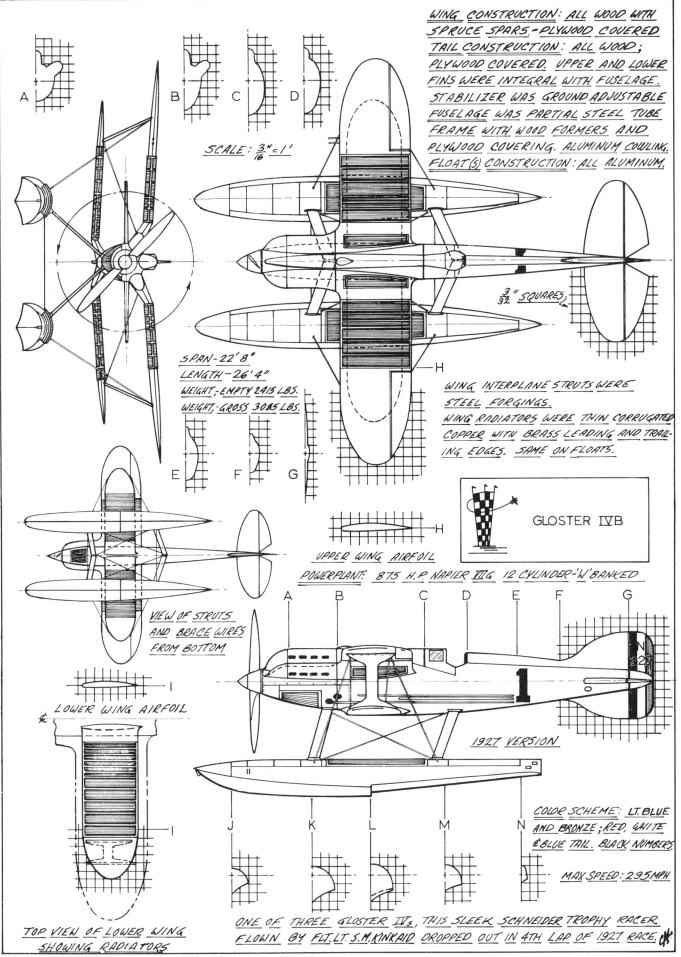

WING CONSTRUCTION: ALL WOOD WITH
SPRUCE SPARS - PLYWOOD COVERED
TAIL CONSTRUCTION: ALL WOOD;
PLYWOOD COVERED. UPPER AND LOWER
FINS WERE INTEGRAL WITH FUSELAGE.
STABILIZER WAS GROUND ADJUSTABLE
FUSELAGE WAS PARTIAL STEEL TUBE
FRAME WITH WOOD FORMERS AND
PLYWOOD COVERING. ALUMINUM COWLING.
FLOAT(S) CONSTRUCTION: ALL ALUMINUM.

SCALE: $\frac{3}{16}$" = 1'

A B C D

$\frac{3}{32}$" SQUARES

H

SPAN - 22' 8"
LENGTH - 26' 4"
WEIGHT - EMPTY 2415 LBS.
WEIGHT - GROSS 3025 LBS.

E F G

WING INTERPLANE STRUTS WERE
STEEL FORGINGS.
WING RADIATORS WERE THIN CORRUGATED
COPPER WITH BRASS LEADING AND TRAIL-
ING EDGES. SAME ON FLOATS.

GLOSTER IVB

H

UPPER WING AIRFOIL

POWERPLANT: 875 H.P. NAPIER VIIG 12 CYLINDER 'W' BANKED

A B C D E F G

VIEW OF STRUTS
AND BRACE WIRES
FROM BOTTOM

1

1927 VERSION

I

LOWER WING AIRFOIL

I

J K L M N

COLOR SCHEME: LT. BLUE
AND BRONZE; RED, WHITE
& BLUE TAIL. BLACK NUMBERS.

MAX SPEED: 295 MPH.

TOP VIEW OF LOWER WING
SHOWING RADIATORS

ONE OF THREE GLOSTER IV3, THIS SLEEK SCHNEIDER TROPHY RACER
FLOWN BY FLT. LT. S.M. KINKAID DROPPED OUT IN 4TH LAP OF 1927 RACE.

THE 'CRUSADER' WAS DESIGNED BY W.G. CARTER AND CONSTRUCTED BY SHORT BROTHERS SEAPLANE WORKS, ROCHESTER, ENGLAND. FIRST FLOWN MAY 4, 1927 BY H.J.L. HINKLER. MAIN DESIGN ADVANTAGE WAS TO BE LOWER WEIGHT OF RADIAL ENGINE & LOWER WEIGHT OF AIRFRAME REQUIRED TO HOLD IT. THIS DID NOT MAKE UP FOR HIGH FRONTAL AREA DRAG, HENCE CRAFT WAS NEVER RACED.

WING CONSTRUCTION: WOOD SPARS & RIBS WITH PLYWOOD COVERING. FUSELAGE CONSTRUCTION: STEEL TUBE FRAMEWORK - ALUMINUM COVERED - FORWARD OF COCKPIT. AFT AREA WAS WOOD FORMERS & STRINGERS - PLY. COVERED. TAIL CONSTRUCTION: WOOD FRAMEWORK COVERED WITH PLYWOOD. FLOAT CONSTRUCTION: ALL DURAL WITH STEEL TUBE STRUTS COVERED WITH ALUMINUM FAIRINGS.

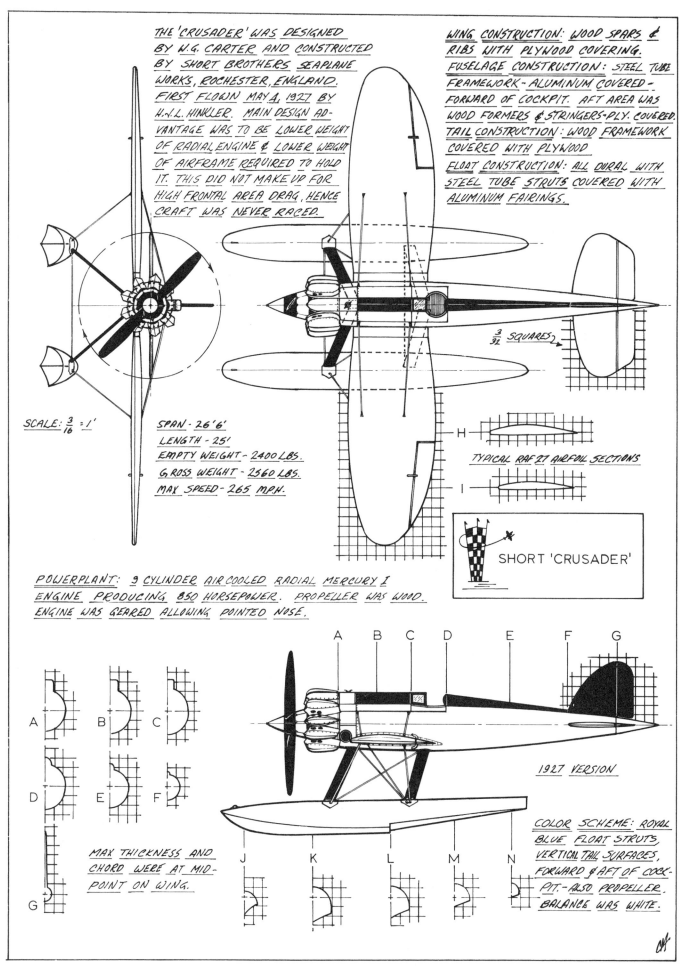

SCALE: $\frac{3}{16}$ = 1'

SPAN - 26' 6'
LENGTH - 25'
EMPTY WEIGHT - 2400 LBS.
GROSS WEIGHT - 2560 LBS.
MAX SPEED - 265 M.P.H.

$\frac{3}{32}$ SQUARES

TYPICAL RAF 27 AIRFOIL SECTIONS

SHORT 'CRUSADER'

POWERPLANT: 9 CYLINDER AIR COOLED RADIAL MERCURY I ENGINE PRODUCING 850 HORSEPOWER. PROPELLER WAS WOOD. ENGINE WAS GEARED ALLOWING POINTED NOSE.

MAX THICKNESS AND CHORD WERE AT MID-POINT ON WING.

1927 VERSION

COLOR SCHEME: ROYAL BLUE FLOAT STRUTS, VERTICAL TAIL SURFACES, FORWARD & AFT OF COCKPIT. - ALSO PROPELLER. BALANCE WAS WHITE.

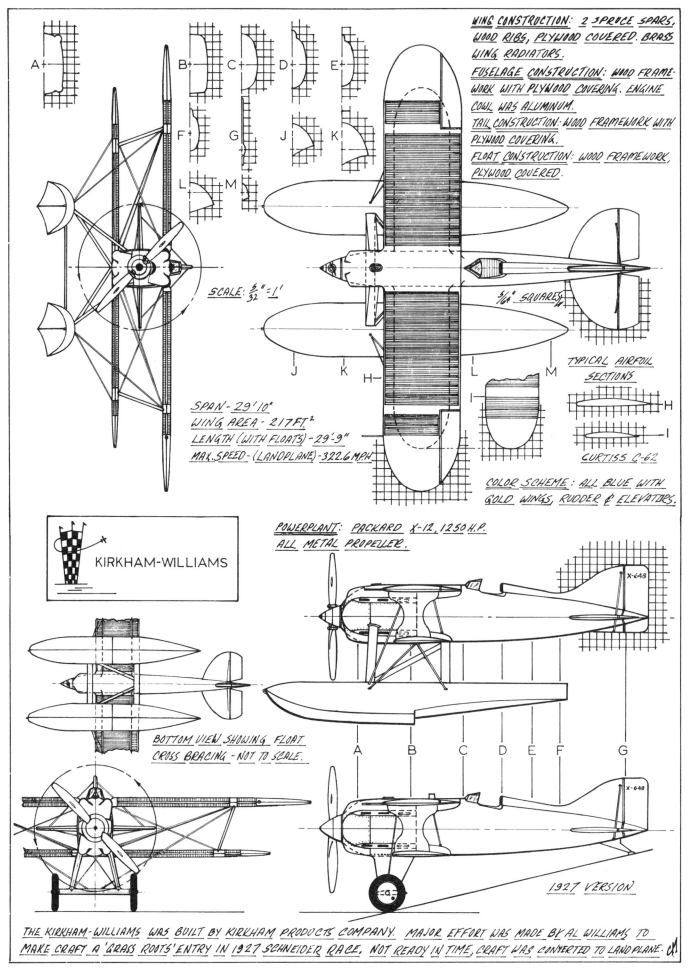

WING CONSTRUCTION: 2 SPRUCE SPARS, WOOD RIBS, PLYWOOD COVERED. BRASS WING RADIATORS.

FUSELAGE CONSTRUCTION: WOOD FRAMEWORK WITH PLYWOOD COVERING. ENGINE COWL WAS ALUMINUM.

TAIL CONSTRUCTION: WOOD FRAMEWORK WITH PLYWOOD COVERING.

FLOAT CONSTRUCTION: WOOD FRAMEWORK, PLYWOOD COVERED.

SCALE: $\frac{3}{32}$" = 1'

5/64" SQUARES

SPAN - 29'10"
WING AREA - 217 FT.^{2}
LENGTH (WITH FLOATS) - 29'-9"
MAX. SPEED - (LANDPLANE) - 322.6 M.P.H.

TYPICAL AIRFOIL SECTIONS

CURTISS C-62

COLOR SCHEME: ALL BLUE WITH GOLD WINGS, RUDDER & ELEVATORS.

POWERPLANT: PACKARD X-12, 1250 H.P. ALL METAL PROPELLER.

KIRKHAM-WILLIAMS

X-648

A B C D E F G

BOTTOM VIEW SHOWING FLOAT CROSS BRACING - NOT TO SCALE.

X-648

1927 VERSION

THE KIRKHAM-WILLIAMS WAS BUILT BY KIRKHAM PRODUCTS COMPANY. MAJOR EFFORT WAS MADE BY AL WILLIAMS TO MAKE CRAFT A 'GRASS ROOTS' ENTRY IN 1927 SCHNEIDER RACE. NOT READY IN TIME, CRAFT WAS CONVERTED TO LANDPLANE.

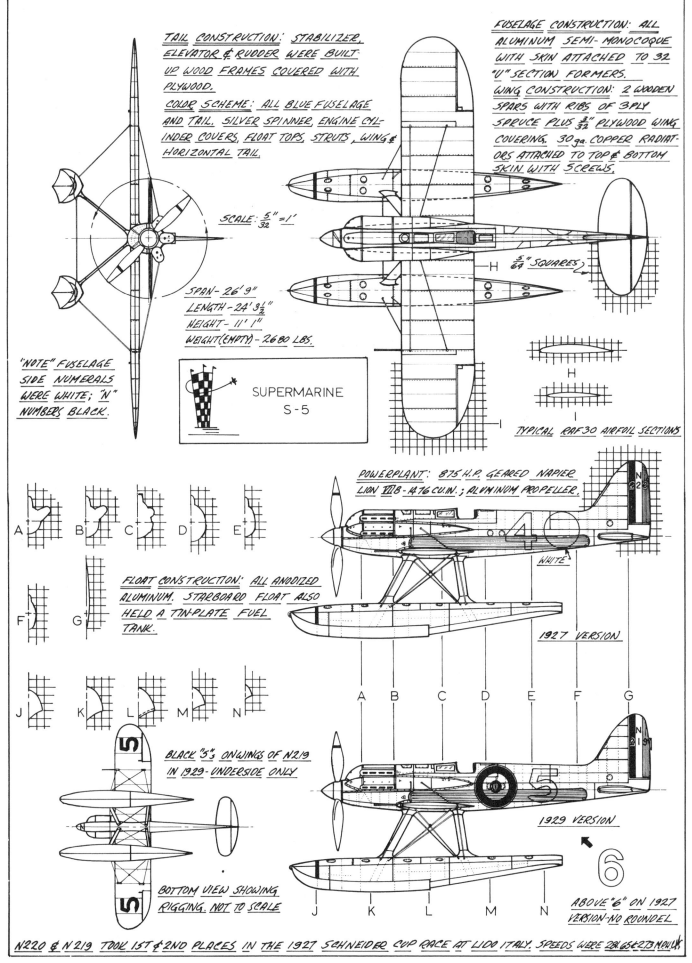

TAIL CONSTRUCTION: STABILIZER, ELEVATOR & RUDDER WERE BUILT-UP WOOD FRAMES COVERED WITH PLYWOOD.

COLOR SCHEME: ALL BLUE FUSELAGE AND TAIL. SILVER SPINNER, ENGINE CYLINDER COVERS, FLOAT TOPS, STRUTS, WING & HORIZONTAL TAIL.

FUSELAGE CONSTRUCTION: ALL ALUMINUM SEMI-MONOCOQUE WITH SKIN ATTACHED TO 32 "U" SECTION FORMERS.

WING CONSTRUCTION: 2 WOODEN SPARS WITH RIBS OF 3 PLY SPRUCE PLUS $\frac{3}{32}$" PLYWOOD WING COVERING. 30 ga. COPPER RADIATORS ATTACHED TO TOP & BOTTOM SKIN WITH SCREWS.

SCALE: $\frac{5}{32}$" = 1'

SPAN - 26' 9"
LENGTH - 24' 3½"
HEIGHT - 11' 1"
WEIGHT (EMPTY) - 2680 LBS.

$\frac{5}{64}$" SQUARES

"NOTE" FUSELAGE SIDE NUMERALS WERE WHITE; "N" NUMBERS BLACK.

SUPERMARINE S-5

H

I

TYPICAL RAF30 AIRFOIL SECTIONS

POWERPLANT: 875 H.P. GEARED NAPIER LION VIIB - 14.76 CU.IN.; ALUMINUM PROPELLER.

A B C D E

F G

FLOAT CONSTRUCTION: ALL ANODIZED ALUMINUM. STARBOARD FLOAT ALSO HELD A TIN-PLATE FUEL TANK.

WHITE

1927 VERSION

A B C D E F G

J K L M N

BLACK "5"s ON WINGS OF N219 IN 1929 - UNDERSIDE ONLY

1929 VERSION

6

BOTTOM VIEW SHOWING RIGGING. NOT TO SCALE

J K L M N

ABOVE "6" ON 1927 VERSION - NO ROUNDEL

N220 & N219 TOOK 1ST & 2ND PLACES IN THE 1927 SCHNEIDER CUP RACE AT LIDO ITALY. SPEEDS WERE 281.65 & 273 M.P.H. U.S.

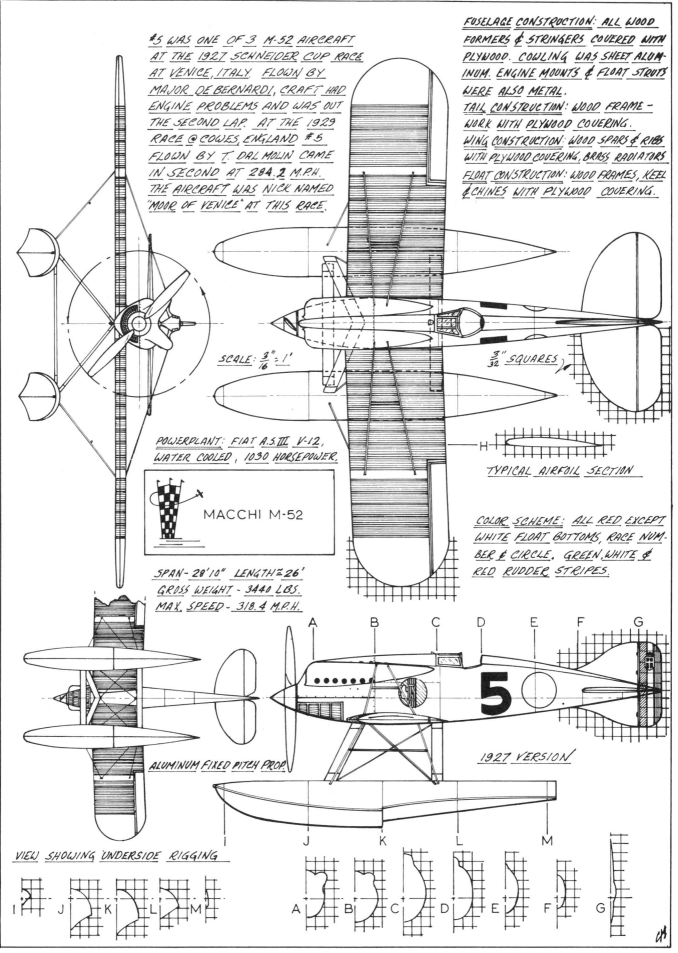

#5 WAS ONE OF 3 M-52 AIRCRAFT AT THE 1927 SCHNEIDER CUP RACE AT VENICE, ITALY. FLOWN BY MAJOR DE BERNARDI, CRAFT HAD ENGINE PROBLEMS AND WAS OUT THE SECOND LAP. AT THE 1929 RACE @ COWES, ENGLAND #5 FLOWN BY T. DAL MOLIN CAME IN SECOND AT 284.2 M.P.H. THE AIRCRAFT WAS NICK NAMED "MOOR OF VENICE" AT THIS RACE.

FUSELAGE CONSTRUCTION: ALL WOOD FORMERS & STRINGERS COVERED WITH PLYWOOD. COWLING WAS SHEET ALUMINUM. ENGINE MOUNTS & FLOAT STRUTS WERE ALSO METAL.
TAIL CONSTRUCTION: WOOD FRAMEWORK WITH PLYWOOD COVERING.
WING CONSTRUCTION: WOOD SPARS & RIBS WITH PLYWOOD COVERING, BRASS RADIATORS
FLOAT CONSTRUCTION: WOOD FRAMES, KEEL & CHINES WITH PLYWOOD COVERING.

SCALE: 3/16" = 1'

3/32" SQUARES

POWERPLANT: FIAT A.S. III V-12, WATER COOLED, 1030 HORSEPOWER.

H ——— TYPICAL AIRFOIL SECTION

MACCHI M-52

SPAN - 28'10" LENGTH ≅ 26'
GROSS WEIGHT - 3440 LBS.
MAX. SPEED - 318.4 M.P.H.

COLOR SCHEME: ALL RED EXCEPT WHITE FLOAT BOTTOMS, RACE NUMBER & CIRCLE. GREEN, WHITE & RED RUDDER STRIPES.

ALUMINUM FIXED PITCH PROP.

5

1927 VERSION

VIEW SHOWING UNDERSIDE RIGGING

I   J   K   L   M

A   B   C   D   E   F   G

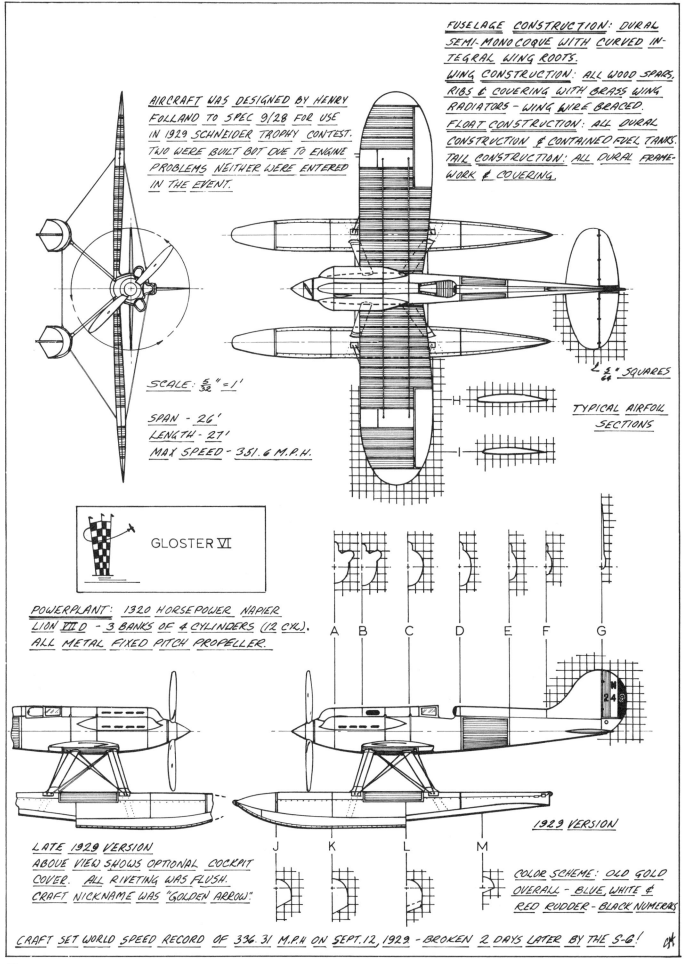

AIRCRAFT WAS DESIGNED BY HENRY
FOLLAND TO SPEC 9/28 FOR USE
IN 1929 SCHNEIDER TROPHY CONTEST.
TWO WERE BUILT BUT DUE TO ENGINE
PROBLEMS NEITHER WERE ENTERED
IN THE EVENT.

FUSELAGE CONSTRUCTION: DURAL
SEMI-MONOCOQUE WITH CURVED IN-
TEGRAL WING ROOTS.
WING CONSTRUCTION: ALL WOOD SPARS,
RIBS & COVERING WITH BRASS WING
RADIATORS - WING WIRE BRACED.
FLOAT CONSTRUCTION: ALL DURAL
CONSTRUCTION & CONTAINED FUEL TANKS.
TAIL CONSTRUCTION: ALL DURAL FRAME-
WORK & COVERING.

SCALE: 5/32" = 1'

SPAN - 26'
LENGTH - 27'
MAX SPEED - 351.6 M.P.H.

5/64" SQUARES

TYPICAL AIRFOIL
SECTIONS

GLOSTER VI

POWERPLANT: 1320 HORSEPOWER NAPIER
LION VII D - 3 BANKS OF 4 CYLINDERS (12 CYL).
ALL METAL FIXED PITCH PROPELLER.

A   B   C   D   E   F   G

N
249

1929 VERSION

LATE 1929 VERSION
ABOVE VIEW SHOWS OPTIONAL COCKPIT
COVER. ALL RIVETING WAS FLUSH.
CRAFT NICKNAME WAS "GOLDEN ARROW".

J   K   L   M

COLOR SCHEME: OLD GOLD
OVERALL - BLUE, WHITE &
RED RUDDER - BLACK NUMERALS

CRAFT SET WORLD SPEED RECORD OF 336.31 M.P.H ON SEPT. 12, 1929 - BROKEN 2 DAYS LATER BY THE S-6!

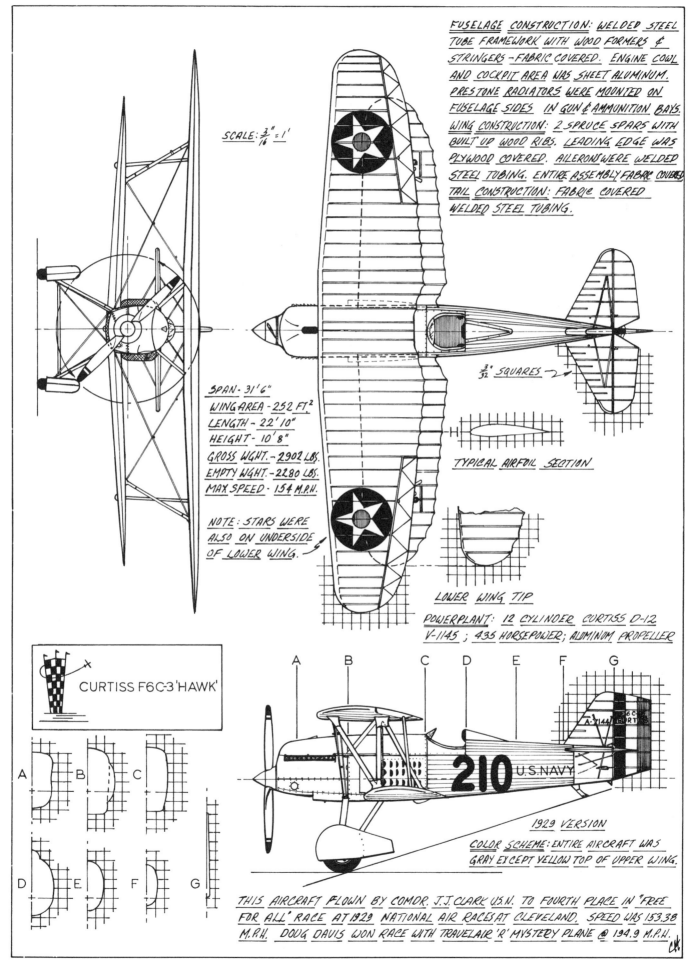

SCALE: $\frac{3}{16}$" = 1'

FUSELAGE CONSTRUCTION: WELDED STEEL TUBE FRAMEWORK WITH WOOD FORMERS & STRINGERS - FABRIC COVERED. ENGINE COWL AND COCKPIT AREA WAS SHEET ALUMINUM. PRESTONE RADIATORS WERE MOUNTED ON FUSELAGE SIDES IN GUN & AMMUNITION BAYS. WING CONSTRUCTION: 2 SPRUCE SPARS WITH BUILT UP WOOD RIBS. LEADING EDGE WAS PLYWOOD COVERED. AILERONS WERE WELDED STEEL TUBING. ENTIRE ASSEMBLY FABRIC COVERED TAIL CONSTRUCTION: FABRIC COVERED WELDED STEEL TUBING.

SPAN - 31'6"
WING AREA - 252 FT²
LENGTH - 22'10"
HEIGHT - 10'8"
GROSS WGHT. - 2902 LBS.
EMPTY WGHT. - 2280 LBS.
MAX SPEED - 154 M.P.H.

NOTE: STARS WERE ALSO ON UNDERSIDE OF LOWER WING.

$\frac{3}{32}$" SQUARES

TYPICAL AIRFOIL SECTION

LOWER WING TIP

POWERPLANT: 12 CYLINDER CURTISS D-12 V-1145 ; 435 HORSEPOWER; ALUMINUM PROPELLER

CURTISS F6C-3 'HAWK'

210 U.S. NAVY

A B C D E F G

1929 VERSION

COLOR SCHEME: ENTIRE AIRCRAFT WAS GRAY EXCEPT YELLOW TOP OF UPPER WING.

THIS AIRCRAFT FLOWN BY COMDR. J.J. CLARK U.S.N. TO FOURTH PLACE IN 'FREE FOR ALL' RACE AT 1929 NATIONAL AIR RACES AT CLEVELAND. SPEED WAS 153.38 M.P.H. DOUG DAVIS WON RACE WITH TRAVELAIR 'R' MYSTERY PLANE @ 194.9 M.P.H.

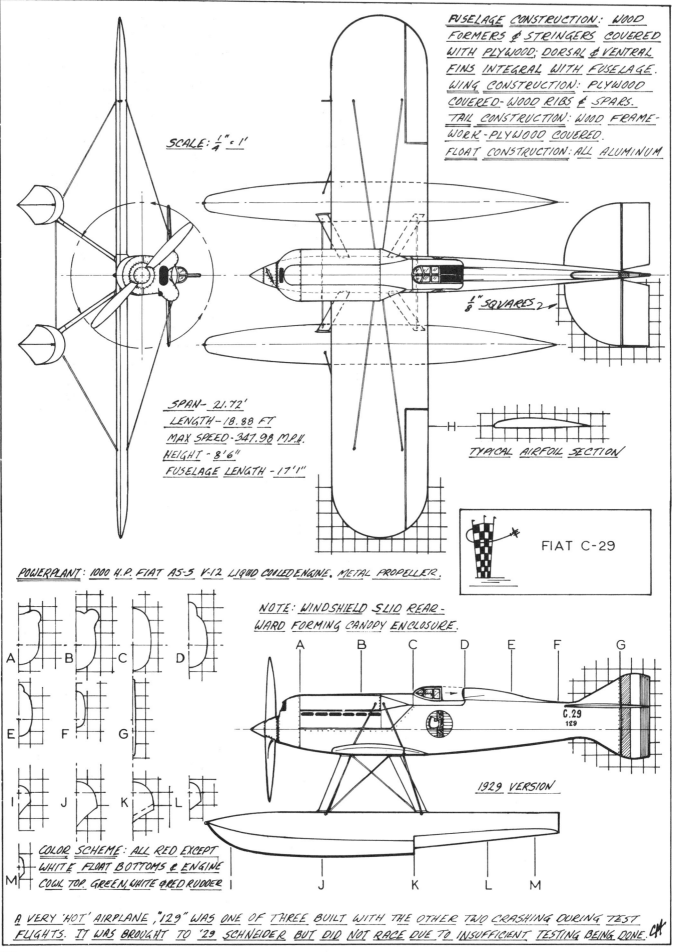

SCALE: $\frac{1}{4}'' = 1'$

FUSELAGE CONSTRUCTION: WOOD FORMERS & STRINGERS COVERED WITH PLYWOOD; DORSAL & VENTRAL FINS INTEGRAL WITH FUSELAGE. WING CONSTRUCTION: PLYWOOD COVERED-WOOD RIBS & SPARS. TAIL CONSTRUCTION: WOOD FRAME-WORK-PLYWOOD COVERED. FLOAT CONSTRUCTION: ALL ALUMINUM

$\frac{1}{8}''$ SQUARES

SPAN- 21.72'
LENGTH - 18.88 FT
MAX SPEED - 347.98 M.P.H.
HEIGHT - 8'6"
FUSELAGE LENGTH - 17'1"

TYPICAL AIRFOIL SECTION

FIAT C-29

POWERPLANT: 1000 H.P. FIAT AS-5 V-12 LIQUID COOLED ENGINE. METAL PROPELLER.

NOTE: WINDSHIELD SLID REAR-WARD FORMING CANOPY ENCLOSURE.

COLOR SCHEME: ALL RED EXCEPT WHITE FLOAT BOTTOMS & ENGINE COWL TOP. GREEN, WHITE & RED RUDDER

1929 VERSION

A VERY 'HOT' AIRPLANE, "129" WAS ONE OF THREE BUILT WITH THE OTHER TWO CRASHING DURING TEST FLIGHTS. IT WAS BROUGHT TO '29 SCHNEIDER BUT DID NOT RACE DUE TO INSUFFICIENT TESTING BEING DONE.

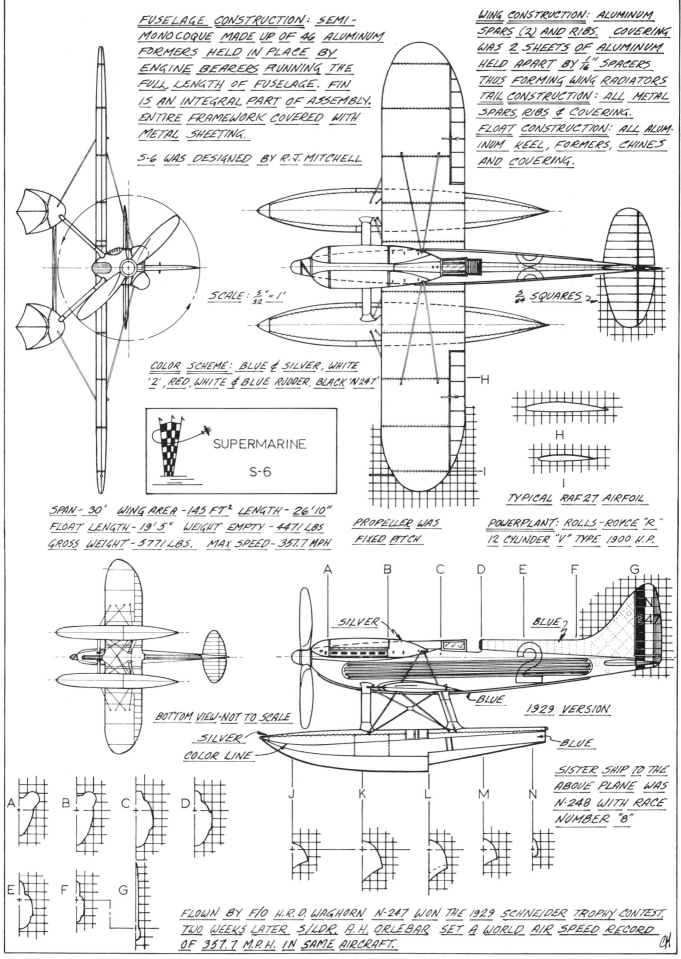

FUSELAGE CONSTRUCTION: SEMI-MONOCOQUE MADE UP OF 46 ALUMINUM FORMERS HELD IN PLACE BY ENGINE BEARERS RUNNING THE FULL LENGTH OF FUSELAGE. FIN IS AN INTEGRAL PART OF ASSEMBLY. ENTIRE FRAMEWORK COVERED WITH METAL SHEETING.

S-6 WAS DESIGNED BY R.J. MITCHELL

WING CONSTRUCTION: ALUMINUM SPARS (2) AND RIBS. COVERING WAS 2 SHEETS OF ALUMINUM HELD APART BY 1/16" SPACERS THUS FORMING WING RADIATORS TAIL CONSTRUCTION: ALL METAL SPARS, RIBS & COVERING. FLOAT CONSTRUCTION: ALL ALUMINUM KEEL, FORMERS, CHINES AND COVERING.

SCALE: 3/32" = 1'

3/64 SQUARES

COLOR SCHEME: BLUE & SILVER, WHITE '2', RED, WHITE & BLUE RUDDER, BLACK 'N247'

SUPERMARINE
S-6

H

I

TYPICAL RAF 27 AIRFOIL

SPAN - 30' WING AREA - 145 FT² LENGTH - 26'10"
FLOAT LENGTH - 19'5" WEIGHT EMPTY - 4471 LBS
GROSS WEIGHT - 5771 LBS. MAX SPEED - 357.7 MPH

PROPELLER WAS FIXED PITCH

POWERPLANT: ROLLS-ROYCE "R" 12 CYLINDER "V" TYPE 1900 H.P.

A B C D E F G

SILVER

BLUE

BLUE

2

1929 VERSION

BOTTOM VIEW - NOT TO SCALE

SILVER

BLUE

SILVER
COLOR LINE

SISTER SHIP TO THE ABOVE PLANE WAS N-248 WITH RACE NUMBER "8"

J K L M N

A B C D

E F G

FLOWN BY F/O H.R.D. WAGHORN N-247 WON THE 1929 SCHNEIDER TROPHY CONTEST. TWO WEEKS LATER S/LDR. A.H. ORLEBAR SET A WORLD AIR SPEED RECORD OF 357.7 M.P.H. IN SAME AIRCRAFT.

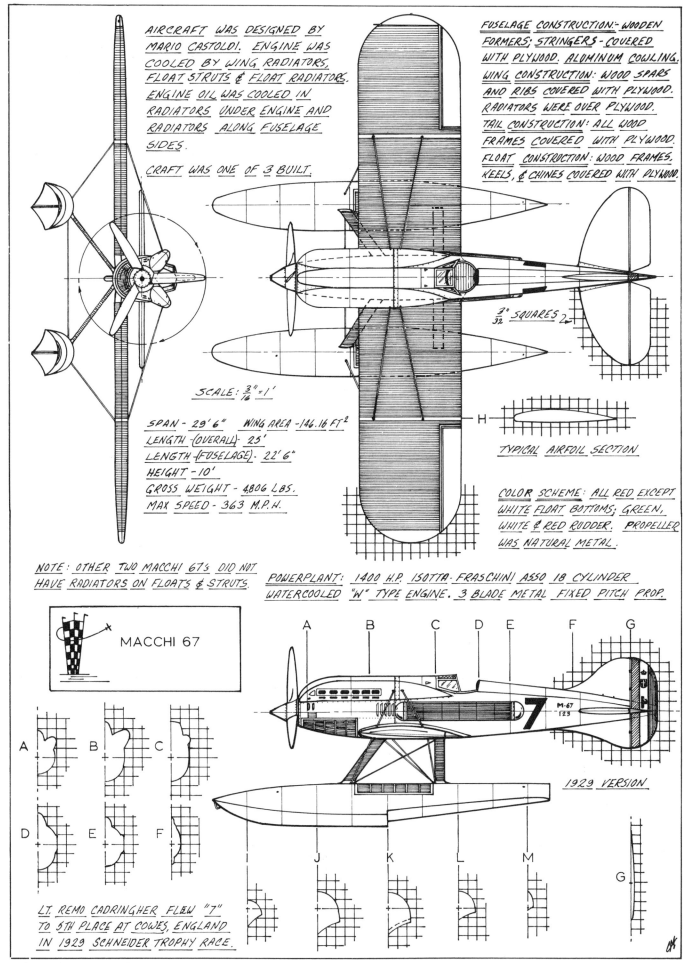

AIRCRAFT WAS DESIGNED BY MARIO CASTOLDI. ENGINE WAS COOLED BY WING RADIATORS, FLOAT STRUTS & FLOAT RADIATORS. ENGINE OIL WAS COOLED IN RADIATORS UNDER ENGINE AND RADIATORS ALONG FUSELAGE SIDES.

CRAFT WAS ONE OF 3 BUILT.

FUSELAGE CONSTRUCTION:- WOODEN FORMERS; STRINGERS- COVERED WITH PLYWOOD. ALUMINUM COWLING. WING CONSTRUCTION: WOOD SPARS AND RIBS COVERED WITH PLYWOOD. RADIATORS WERE OVER PLYWOOD. TAIL CONSTRUCTION: ALL WOOD FRAMES COVERED WITH PLYWOOD. FLOAT CONSTRUCTION: WOOD FRAMES, KEELS, & CHINES COVERED WITH PLYWOOD.

SCALE: $\frac{3}{16}$" = 1'

SPAN - 29'6"   WING AREA - 146.16 FT^2
LENGTH (OVERALL) - 25'
LENGTH (FUSELAGE) - 22'6"
HEIGHT - 10'
GROSS WEIGHT - 4,806 LBS.
MAX SPEED - 363 M.P.H.

$\frac{3}{32}$" SQUARES

H

TYPICAL AIRFOIL SECTION

COLOR SCHEME: ALL RED EXCEPT WHITE FLOAT BOTTOMS; GREEN, WHITE & RED RUDDER. PROPELLER WAS NATURAL METAL.

NOTE: OTHER TWO MACCHI 67's DID NOT HAVE RADIATORS ON FLOATS & STRUTS.

POWERPLANT: 1400 H.P. ISOTTA-FRASCHINI ASSO 18 CYLINDER WATERCOOLED "W" TYPE ENGINE. 3 BLADE METAL FIXED PITCH PROP.

MACCHI 67

A   B   C   D   E   F   G

M-67
123

7

1929 VERSION

A   B   C

D   E   F

J   K   L   M

G

LT. REMO CADRINGHER FLEW "7" TO 5TH PLACE AT COWES, ENGLAND IN 1929 SCHNEIDER TROPHY RACE.

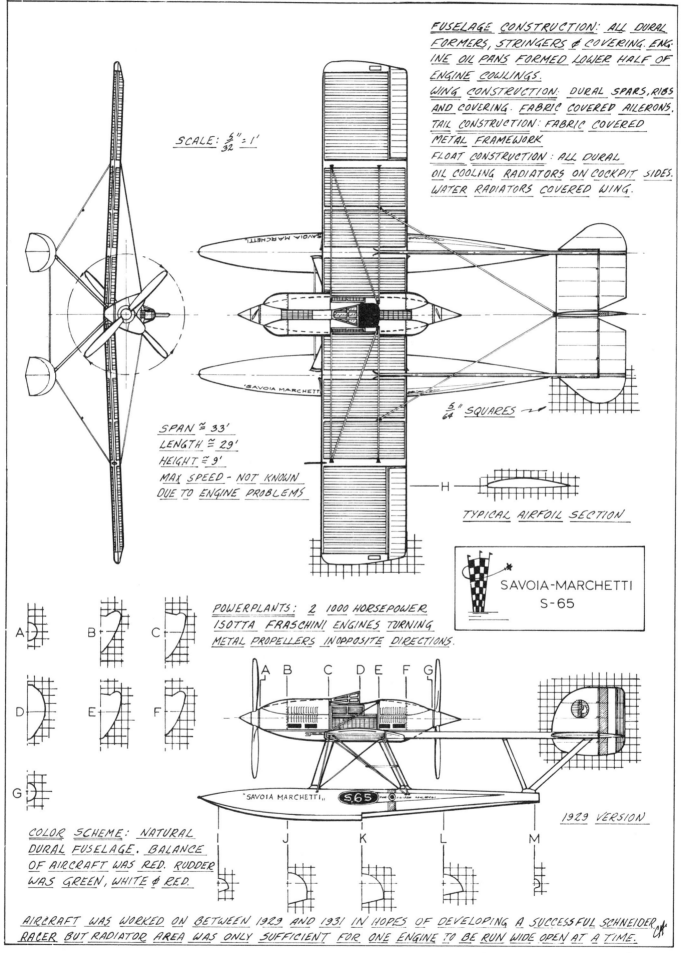

SCALE: $\frac{5}{32}$" = 1'

FUSELAGE CONSTRUCTION: ALL DURAL FORMERS, STRINGERS & COVERING. ENGINE OIL PANS FORMED LOWER HALF OF ENGINE COWLINGS.
WING CONSTRUCTION: DURAL SPARS, RIBS AND COVERING. FABRIC COVERED AILERONS.
TAIL CONSTRUCTION: FABRIC COVERED METAL FRAMEWORK
FLOAT CONSTRUCTION: ALL DURAL
OIL COOLING RADIATORS ON COCKPIT SIDES. WATER RADIATORS COVERED WING.

SPAN ≅ 33'
LENGTH ≅ 29'
HEIGHT ≅ 9'
MAX SPEED - NOT KNOWN DUE TO ENGINE PROBLEMS

$\frac{5}{64}$" SQUARES

TYPICAL AIRFOIL SECTION

SAVOIA-MARCHETTI S-65

POWERPLANTS: 2 1000 HORSEPOWER ISOTTA FRASCHINI ENGINES TURNING METAL PROPELLERS IN OPPOSITE DIRECTIONS.

1929 VERSION

COLOR SCHEME: NATURAL DURAL FUSELAGE. BALANCE OF AIRCRAFT WAS RED. RUDDER WAS GREEN, WHITE & RED.

AIRCRAFT WAS WORKED ON BETWEEN 1929 AND 1931 IN HOPES OF DEVELOPING A SUCCESSFUL SCHNEIDER RACER BUT RADIATOR AREA WAS ONLY SUFFICIENT FOR ONE ENGINE TO BE RUN WIDE OPEN AT A TIME.

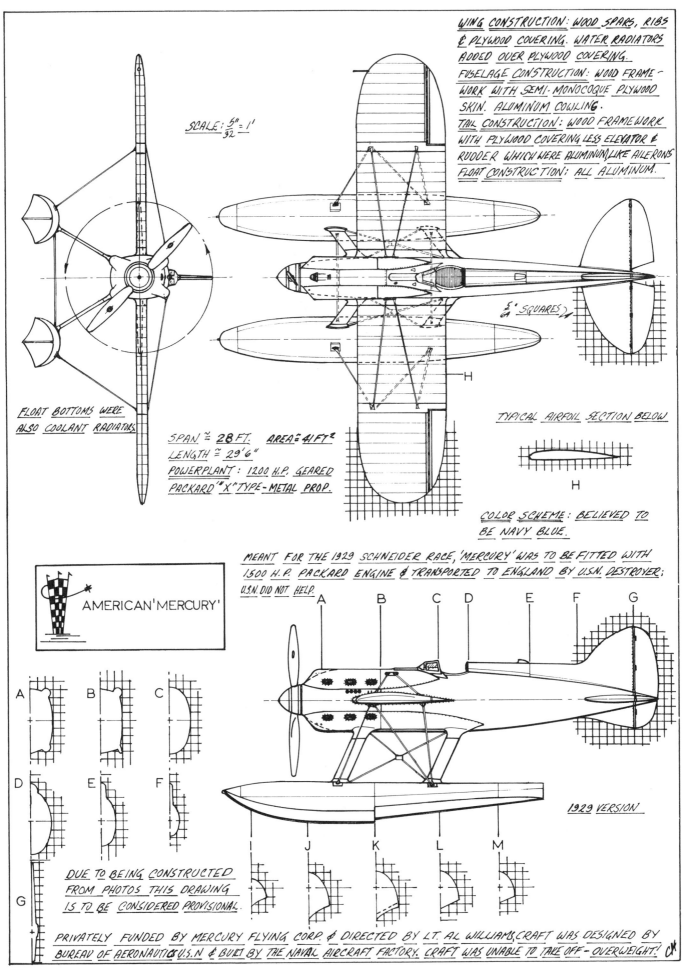

WING CONSTRUCTION: WOOD SPARS, RIBS & PLYWOOD COVERING. WATER RADIATORS ADDED OVER PLYWOOD COVERING.
FUSELAGE CONSTRUCTION: WOOD FRAMEWORK WITH SEMI-MONOCOQUE PLYWOOD SKIN. ALUMINUM COWLING.
TAIL CONSTRUCTION: WOOD FRAMEWORK WITH PLYWOOD COVERING LESS ELEVATOR & RUDDER WHICH WERE ALUMINUM, LIKE AILERONS
FLOAT CONSTRUCTION: ALL ALUMINUM.

SCALE: 5"/32 = 1'

⅛" SQUARES

FLOAT BOTTOMS WERE ALSO COOLANT RADIATORS

SPAN ≈ 28 FT.   AREA ≈ 41 FT²
LENGTH ≈ 29'6"
POWERPLANT: 1200 H.P. GEARED PACKARD "X" TYPE - METAL PROP.

TYPICAL AIRFOIL SECTION BELOW

H

COLOR SCHEME: BELIEVED TO BE NAVY BLUE.

AMERICAN 'MERCURY'

MEANT FOR THE 1929 SCHNEIDER RACE, 'MERCURY' WAS TO BE FITTED WITH 1,500 H.P. PACKARD ENGINE & TRANSPORTED TO ENGLAND BY U.S.N. DESTROYER; U.S.N. DID NOT HELP.

A   B   C   D   E   F   G

1929 VERSION

DUE TO BEING CONSTRUCTED FROM PHOTOS THIS DRAWING IS TO BE CONSIDERED PROVISIONAL.

PRIVATELY FUNDED BY MERCURY FLYING CORP & DIRECTED BY LT. AL WILLIAMS, CRAFT WAS DESIGNED BY BUREAU OF AERONAUTICS U.S.N & BUILT BY THE NAVAL AIRCRAFT FACTORY. CRAFT WAS UNABLE TO TAKE OFF - OVERWEIGHT!

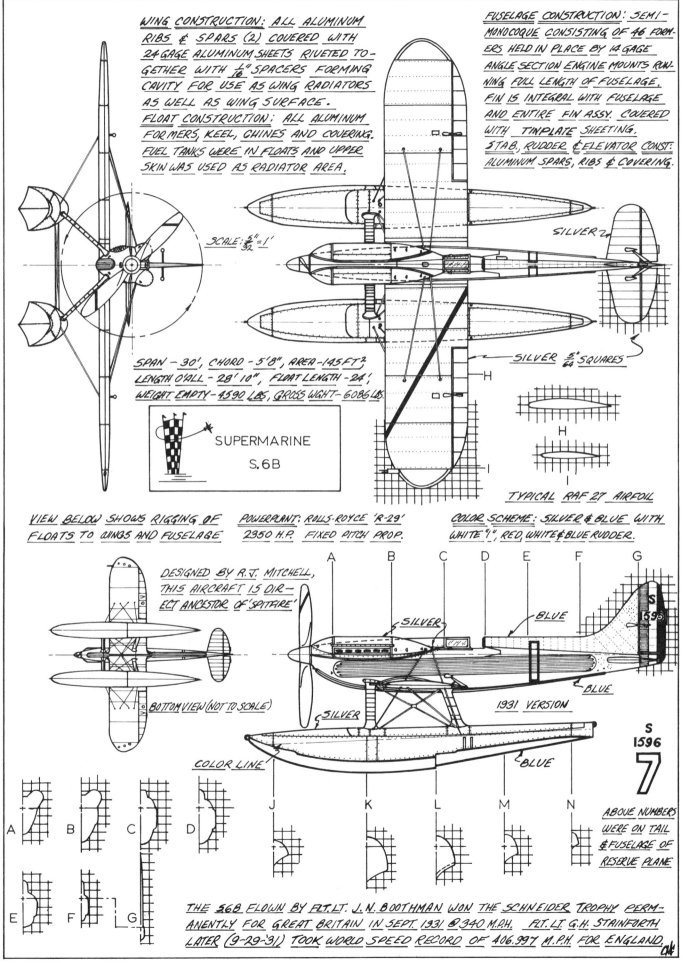

WING CONSTRUCTION: ALL ALUMINUM RIBS & SPARS (2) COVERED WITH 24 GAGE ALUMINUM SHEETS RIVETED TOGETHER WITH $\frac{1}{16}$" SPACERS FORMING CAVITY FOR USE AS WING RADIATORS AS WELL AS WING SURFACE.
FLOAT CONSTRUCTION: ALL ALUMINUM FORMERS, KEEL, CHINES AND COVERING. FUEL TANKS WERE IN FLOATS AND UPPER SKIN WAS USED AS RADIATOR AREA.

FUSELAGE CONSTRUCTION: SEMI-MONOCOQUE CONSISTING OF 46 FORMERS HELD IN PLACE BY 14 GAGE ANGLE SECTION ENGINE MOUNTS RUNNING FULL LENGTH OF FUSELAGE. FIN IS INTEGRAL WITH FUSELAGE AND ENTIRE FIN ASSY. COVERED WITH TINPLATE SHEETING.
STAB, RUDDER & ELEVATOR CONST: ALUMINUM SPARS, RIBS & COVERING.

SCALE: $\frac{5}{32}$" = 1'

SILVER

SILVER $\frac{5}{64}$" SQUARES

SPAN - 30', CHORD - 5' 8", AREA - 145 FT²
LENGTH O'ALL - 28' 10", FLOAT LENGTH - 24',
WEIGHT EMPTY - 4590 LBS, GROSS WGHT - 6086 LBS.

H

H

I

SUPERMARINE S.6B

TYPICAL RAF 27 AIRFOIL

VIEW BELOW SHOWS RIGGING OF FLOATS TO WINGS AND FUSELAGE

POWERPLANT: ROLLS-ROYCE 'R-29' 2350 H.P. FIXED PITCH PROP.

COLOR SCHEME: SILVER & BLUE WITH WHITE "1", RED, WHITE & BLUE RUDDER.

DESIGNED BY R.J. MITCHELL, THIS AIRCRAFT IS DIRECT ANCESTOR OF 'SPITFIRE'

A   B   C   D   E   F   G

SILVER

BLUE

S 1595

BLUE

BOTTOM VIEW (NOT TO SCALE)

SILVER

1931 VERSION

COLOR LINE

BLUE

S 1596

7

J   K   L   M   N

A   B   C   D

ABOVE NUMBERS WERE ON TAIL & FUSELAGE OF RESERVE PLANE

E   F   G

THE S6B FLOWN BY FLT. LT. J. N. BOOTHMAN WON THE SCHNEIDER TROPHY PERMANENTLY FOR GREAT BRITAIN IN SEPT. 1931 @ 340 M.P.H. FLT. LT. G.H. STAINFORTH LATER (9-29-'31) TOOK WORLD SPEED RECORD OF 406.997 M.P.H. FOR ENGLAND.

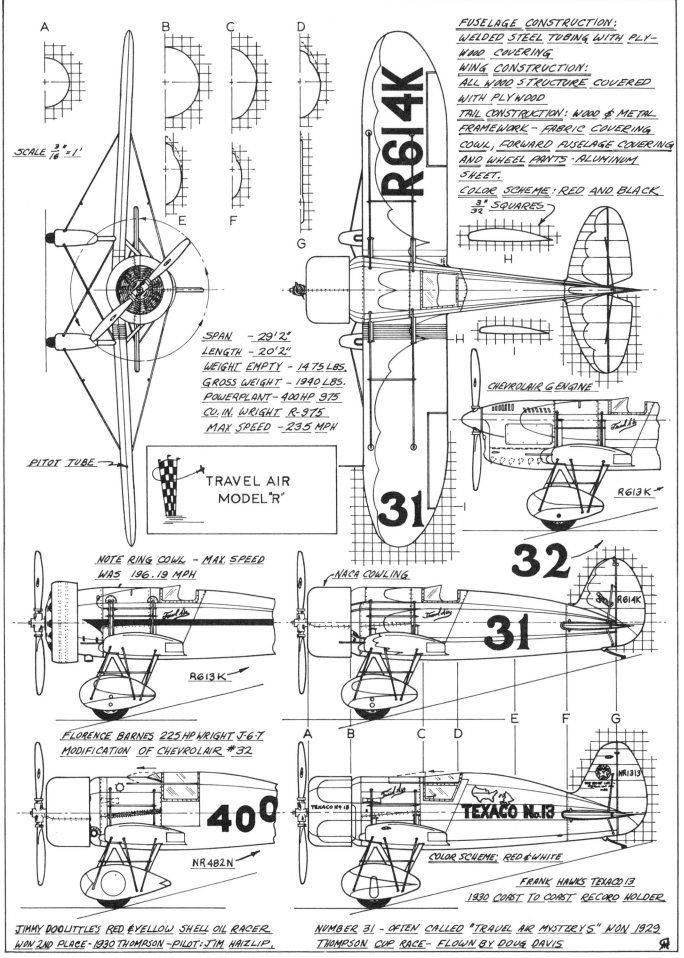

A B C D

SCALE $\frac{3}{16}$" = 1'

E F

G

FUSELAGE CONSTRUCTION:
WELDED STEEL TUBING WITH PLY-
WOOD COVERING
WING CONSTRUCTION:
ALL WOOD STRUCTURE COVERED
WITH PLYWOOD
TAIL CONSTRUCTION: WOOD & METAL
FRAMEWORK - FABRIC COVERING
COWL, FORWARD FUSELAGE COVERING
AND WHEEL PANTS - ALUMINUM
SHEET.
COLOR SCHEME: RED AND BLACK
$\frac{3}{32}$" SQUARES

H

R614K

31

SPAN - 29'2"
LENGTH - 20'2"
WEIGHT EMPTY - 1475 LBS.
GROSS WEIGHT - 1940 LBS.
POWERPLANT - 400 HP 975
CU. IN. WRIGHT R-975
MAX SPEED - 235 MPH

PITOT TUBE

TRAVEL AIR
MODEL "R"

H

CHEVROLAIR G ENGINE

R613K

32

NOTE RING COWL - MAX. SPEED
WAS 196.19 MPH

R613K

NACA COWLING

R614K

31

A B C D

E F G

FLORENCE BARNES 225 HP WRIGHT J-6-7
MODIFICATION OF CHEVROLAIR #32

400

NR482N

JIMMY DOOLITTLE'S RED & YELLOW SHELL OIL RACER
WON 2ND PLACE - 1930 THOMPSON - PILOT: JIM HAIZLIP.

NR1313

TEXACO No.13

TEXACO No 13

COLOR SCHEME: RED & WHITE

FRANK HAWKS TEXACO 13
1930 COAST TO COAST RECORD HOLDER

NUMBER 31 - OFTEN CALLED "TRAVEL AIR MYSTERY S" WON 1929
THOMPSON CUP RACE - FLOWN BY DOUG DAVIS

56

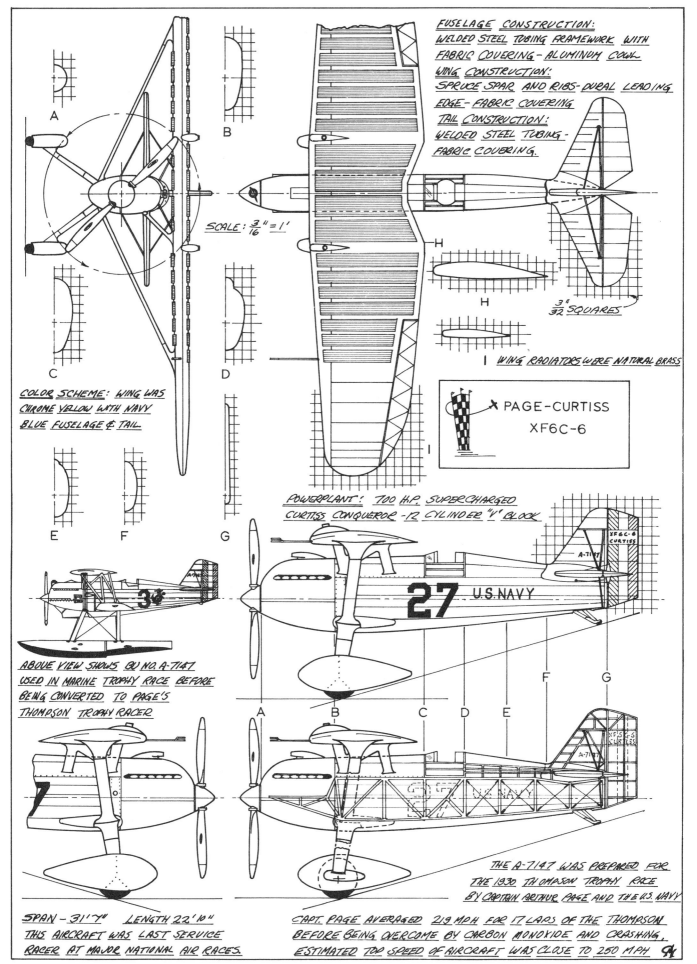

FUSELAGE CONSTRUCTION:
WELDED STEEL TUBING FRAMEWORK WITH
FABRIC COVERING - ALUMINUM COWL
WING CONSTRUCTION:
SPRUCE SPAR AND RIBS - DURAL LEADING
EDGE - FABRIC COVERING
TAIL CONSTRUCTION:
WELDED STEEL TUBING -
FABRIC COVERING.

SCALE: 3/16" = 1'

A

B

$\frac{3}{32}$" SQUARES

H

H

I   WING RADIATORS WERE NATURAL BRASS

COLOR SCHEME: WING WAS
CHROME YELLOW WITH NAVY
BLUE FUSELAGE & TAIL

PAGE-CURTISS
XF6C-6

C

D

I

E   F   G

POWERPLANT: 700 H.P. SUPERCHARGED
CURTISS CONQUEROR - 12 CYLINDER "V" BLOCK

27 U.S.NAVY

ABOVE VIEW SHOWS BU NO. A-7147
USED IN MARINE TROPHY RACE BEFORE
BEING CONVERTED TO PAGE'S
THOMPSON TROPHY RACER.

A   B   C   D   E   F   G

THE A-7147 WAS PREPARED FOR
THE 1930 THOMPSON TROPHY RACE
BY CAPTAIN ARTHUR PAGE AND THE U.S. NAVY

SPAN - 31'7" LENGTH 22'10"
THIS AIRCRAFT WAS LAST SERVICE
RACER AT MAJOR NATIONAL AIR RACES.

CAPT. PAGE AVERAGED 219 MPH FOR 17 LAPS OF THE THOMPSON
BEFORE BEING OVERCOME BY CARBON MONOXIDE AND CRASHING,
ESTIMATED TOP SPEED OF AIRCRAFT WAS CLOSE TO 250 MPH.

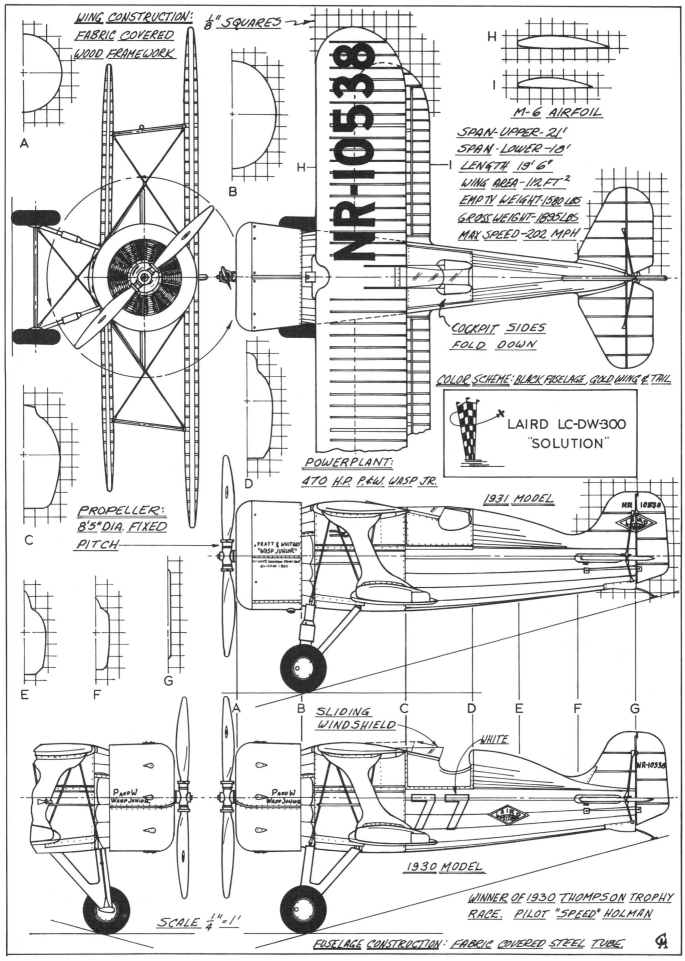

WING CONSTRUCTION: FABRIC COVERED WOOD FRAMEWORK

$\frac{1}{8}"$ SQUARES

NR-10538

H

I

M-6 AIRFOIL

SPAN-UPPER-21'
SPAN-LOWER-18'
LENGTH 19'6"
WING AREA-112.FT²
EMPTY WEIGHT-1580 LBS
GROSS WEIGHT-1895 LBS
MAX SPEED-202 MPH

A

B

C

D

E

F

G

COCKPIT SIDES FOLD DOWN

COLOR SCHEME: BLACK FUSELAGE, GOLD WING & TAIL

LAIRD LC-DW-300 "SOLUTION"

POWERPLANT: 470 H.P. P.&W. WASP JR.

PROPELLER: 8'5" DIA. FIXED PITCH

1931 MODEL

NR 10538

"PRATT & WHITNEY WASP JUNIOR"

SLIDING WINDSHIELD

WHITE

NR-10538

77

LAIRD

1930 MODEL

P and W WASP JUNIOR

SCALE $\frac{1}{4}" = 1'$

WINNER OF 1930 THOMPSON TROPHY RACE. PILOT "SPEED" HOLMAN

FUSELAGE CONSTRUCTION: FABRIC COVERED STEEL TUBE.

58

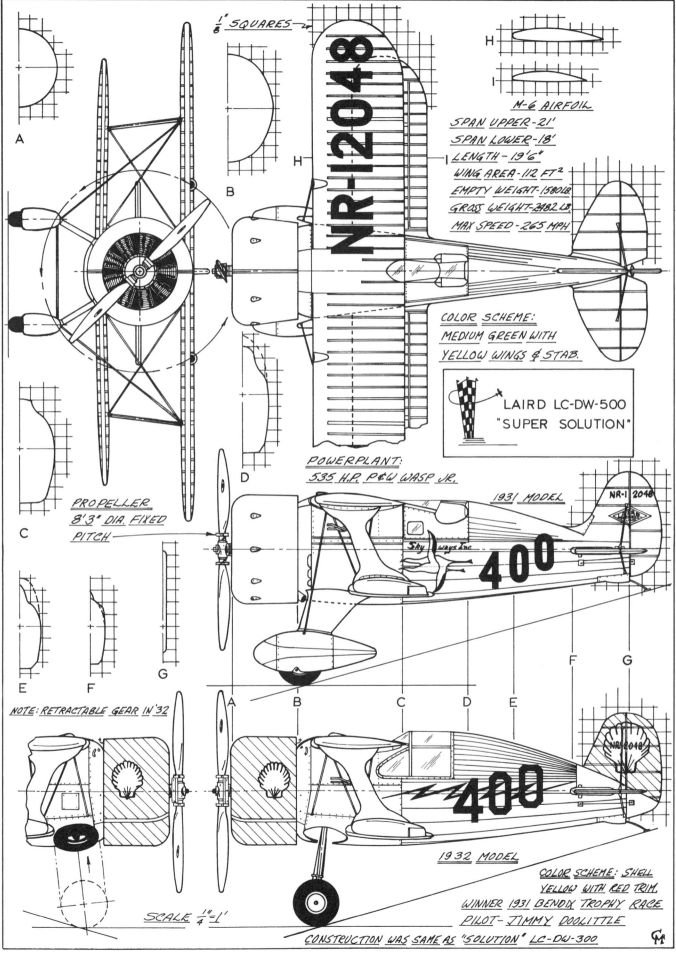

⅛" SQUARES

NR-12048

H

I

M-6 AIRFOIL

SPAN UPPER - 21'
SPAN LOWER - 18'
LENGTH - 19'6"
WING AREA - 112 FT²
EMPTY WEIGHT - 1580 LB.
GROSS WEIGHT - 2982 LB.
MAX SPEED - 265 MPH

COLOR SCHEME:
MEDIUM GREEN WITH
YELLOW WINGS & STAB.

LAIRD LC-DW-500
"SUPER SOLUTION"

POWERPLANT:
535 H.P. P&W WASP JR.

1931 MODEL

NR-1 2048

Sky Ways Inc

400

PROPELLER
8'3" DIA. FIXED
PITCH

A

B

C

D

E

F

G

E   F   G

A   B   C   D   E   F   G

NOTE: RETRACTABLE GEAR IN '32

400

1932 MODEL

NR-12048

COLOR SCHEME: SHELL
YELLOW WITH RED TRIM.
WINNER 1931 BENDIX TROPHY RACE
PILOT - JIMMY DOOLITTLE

SCALE ¼"=1'

CONSTRUCTION WAS SAME AS "SOLUTION" LC-DW-300

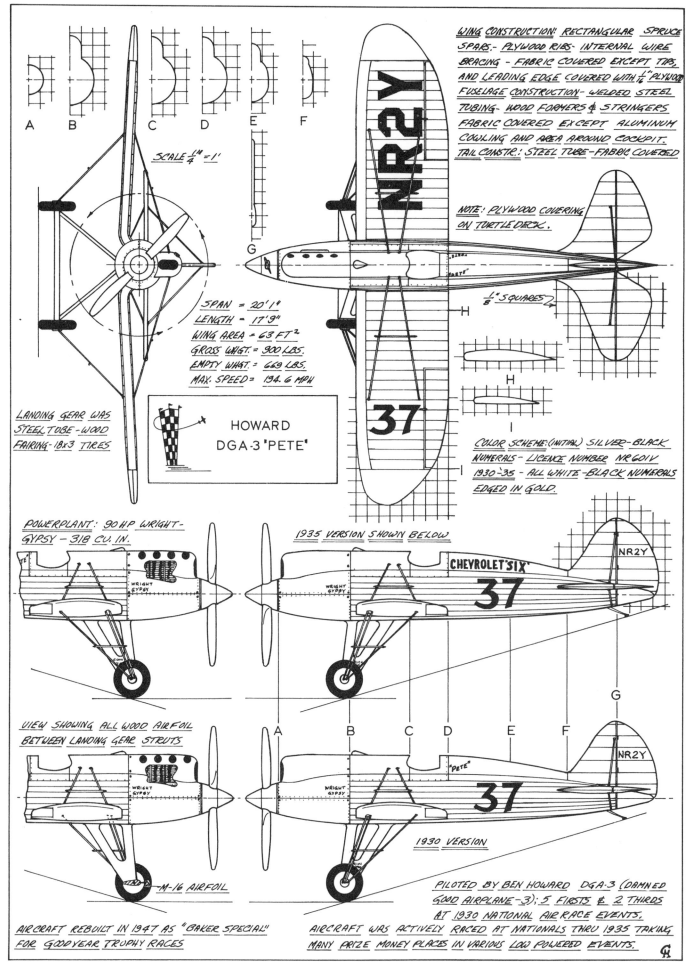

WING CONSTRUCTION: RECTANGULAR SPRUCE SPARS - PLYWOOD RIBS - INTERNAL WIRE BRACING - FABRIC COVERED EXCEPT TIPS, AND LEADING EDGE COVERED WITH 1/16" PLYWOOD FUSELAGE CONSTRUCTION - WELDED STEEL TUBING - WOOD FORMERS & STRINGERS FABRIC COVERED EXCEPT ALUMINUM COWLING AND AREA AROUND COCKPIT. TAIL CONSTR.: STEEL TUBE - FABRIC COVERED

NOTE: PLYWOOD COVERING ON TURTLE DECK.

1/8" SQUARES

COLOR SCHEME: (INITIAL) SILVER - BLACK NUMERALS - LICENCE NUMBER NR601V 1930 -'35 - ALL WHITE - BLACK NUMERALS EDGED IN GOLD.

SCALE 1/4" = 1'

SPAN = 20'1"
LENGTH = 17'9"
WING AREA = 63 FT²
GROSS WHGT. = 900 LBS.
EMPTY WHGT. = 669 LBS.
MAX. SPEED = 194.6 MPH

LANDING GEAR WAS STEEL TUBE - WOOD FAIRING - 18x3 TIRES

HOWARD DGA-3 "PETE"

POWERPLANT: 90 HP WRIGHT-GYPSY - 318 CU. IN.

1935 VERSION SHOWN BELOW

CHEVROLET "SIX"

VIEW SHOWING ALL WOOD AIRFOIL BETWEEN LANDING GEAR STRUTS

M-16 AIRFOIL

1930 VERSION

AIRCRAFT REBUILT IN 1947 AS "BAKER SPECIAL" FOR GOODYEAR TROPHY RACES

PILOTED BY BEN HOWARD DGA-3 (DAMNED GOOD AIRPLANE -3); 5 FIRSTS & 2 THIRDS AT 1930 NATIONAL AIR RACE EVENTS. AIRCRAFT WAS ACTIVELY RACED AT NATIONALS THRU 1935 TAKING MANY PRIZE MONEY PLACES IN VARIOUS LOW POWERED EVENTS.

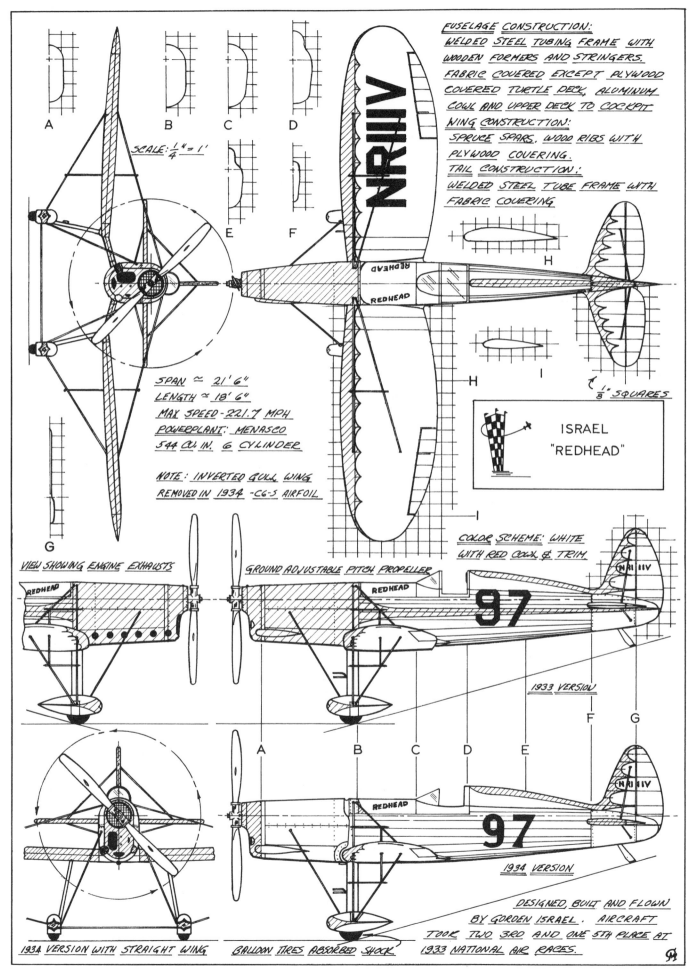

FUSELAGE CONSTRUCTION:
WELDED STEEL TUBING FRAME WITH WOODEN FORMERS AND STRINGERS. FABRIC COVERED EXCEPT PLYWOOD COVERED TURTLE DECK, ALUMINUM COWL AND UPPER DECK TO COCKPIT

WING CONSTRUCTION:
SPRUCE SPARS, WOOD RIBS WITH PLYWOOD COVERING.

TAIL CONSTRUCTION:
WELDED STEEL TUBE FRAME WITH FABRIC COVERING.

SCALE: $\frac{1}{4}'' = 1'$

NRIIIV

REDHEAD

$\frac{1}{8}''$ SQUARES

SPAN ≃ 21' 6"
LENGTH ≃ 18' 6"
MAX SPEED - 221.7 MPH
POWERPLANT: MENASCO 544 CU. IN. 6 CYLINDER

NOTE: INVERTED GULL WING REMOVED IN 1934 -C6-S AIRFOIL

ISRAEL "REDHEAD"

COLOR SCHEME: WHITE WITH RED COWL & TRIM

VIEW SHOWING ENGINE EXHAUSTS

GROUND ADJUSTABLE PITCH PROPELLER

REDHEAD

97

1933 VERSION

1934 VERSION WITH STRAIGHT WING

BALLOON TIRES ABSORBED SHOCK

REDHEAD

97

1934 VERSION

DESIGNED, BUILT AND FLOWN BY GORDEN ISRAEL. AIRCRAFT TOOK TWO 3RD AND ONE 5TH PLACE AT 1933 NATIONAL AIR RACES.

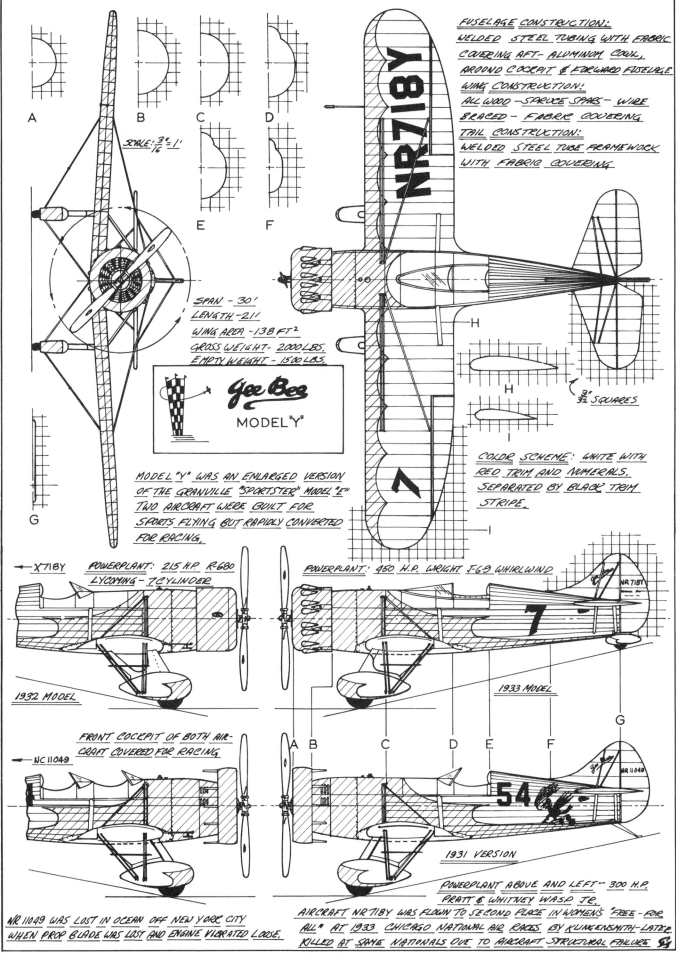

FUSELAGE CONSTRUCTION:
WELDED STEEL TUBING WITH FABRIC
COVERING AFT - ALUMINUM COWL,
AROUND COCKPIT & FORWARD FUSELAGE
WING CONSTRUCTION:
ALL WOOD - SPRUCE SPARS - WIRE
BRACED - FABRIC COVERING
TAIL CONSTRUCTION:
WELDED STEEL TUBE FRAMEWORK
WITH FABRIC COVERING

SCALE: 3/16" = 1'

SPAN - 30'
LENGTH - 21'
WING AREA - 138 FT²
GROSS WEIGHT - 2000 LBS.
EMPTY WEIGHT - 1500 LBS.

Gee Bee
MODEL "Y"

3/32" SQUARES

COLOR SCHEME: WHITE WITH
RED TRIM AND NUMERALS.
SEPARATED BY BLACK TRIM
STRIPE.

MODEL "Y" WAS AN ENLARGED VERSION
OF THE GRANVILLE "SPORTSTER" MODEL "E"
TWO AIRCRAFT WERE BUILT FOR
SPORTS FLYING BUT RAPIDLY CONVERTED
FOR RACING.

← X718Y   POWERPLANT: 215 H.P. R-680
LYCOMING - 7 CYLINDER

POWERPLANT: 450 H.P. WRIGHT J-6-9 WHIRLWIND

1932 MODEL

1933 MODEL

FRONT COCKPIT OF BOTH AIR-
CRAFT COVERED FOR RACING

← NC 11049

1931 VERSION

NR 11049 WAS LOST IN OCEAN OFF NEW YORK CITY
WHEN PROP BLADE WAS LOST AND ENGINE VIBRATED LOOSE.

POWERPLANT ABOVE AND LEFT - 300 H.P.
PRATT & WHITNEY WASP JR.
AIRCRAFT NR718Y WAS FLOWN TO SECOND PLACE IN WOMEN'S "FREE-FOR
ALL" AT 1933 CHICAGO NATIONAL AIR RACES BY KLINGENSMITH-LATER
KILLED AT SAME NATIONALS DUE TO AIRCRAFT STRUCTURAL FAILURE

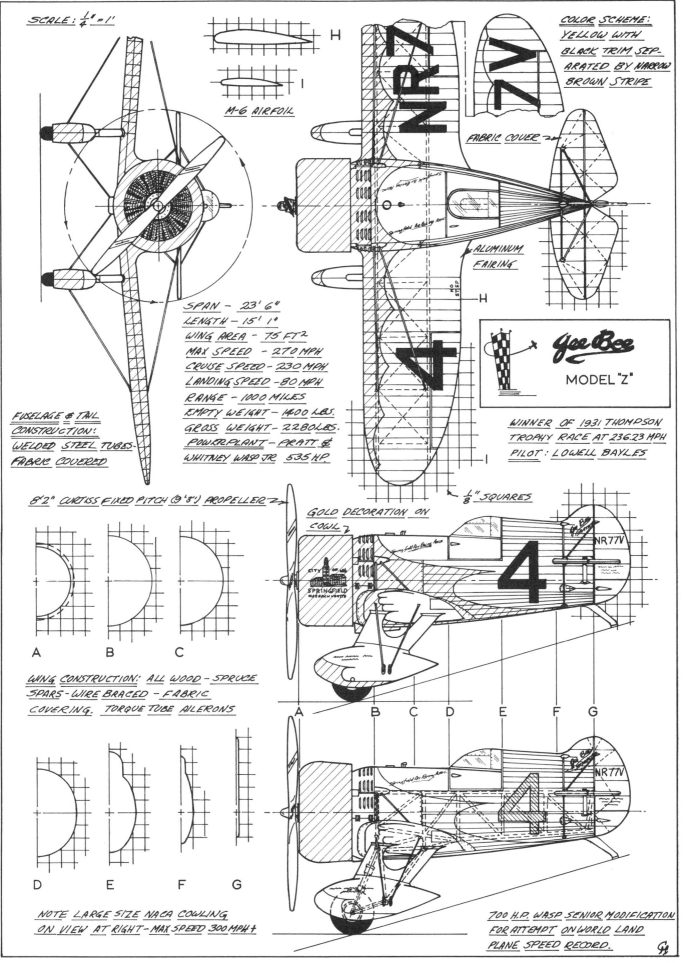

SCALE: $\frac{1}{4}' = 1'$

M-6 AIRFOIL

H

I

COLOR SCHEME:
YELLOW WITH
BLACK TRIM SEP-
ARATED BY NARROW
BROWN STRIPE

FABRIC COVER

ALUMINUM
FAIRING

NR77V

4

SPAN - 23' 6"
LENGTH - 15' 1"
WING AREA - 75 FT²
MAX SPEED - 270 MPH
CRUISE SPEED - 230 MPH
LANDING SPEED - 80 MPH
RANGE - 1000 MILES
EMPTY WEIGHT - 1400 LBS.
GROSS WEIGHT - 2280 LBS.
POWERPLANT - PRATT &
WHITNEY WASP JR. 535 H.P.

FUSELAGE & TAIL
CONSTRUCTION:
WELDED STEEL TUBES-
FABRIC COVERED

Gee Bee
MODEL "Z"

WINNER OF 1931 THOMPSON
TROPHY RACE AT 236.23 MPH
PILOT: LOWELL BAYLES

$\frac{1}{8}$" SQUARES

8'2" CURTISS FIXED PITCH (9'8') PROPELLER

GOLD DECORATION ON
COWL

NR77V

4

A   B   C

WING CONSTRUCTION: ALL WOOD-SPRUCE
SPARS-WIRE BRACED-FABRIC
COVERING. TORQUE TUBE AILERONS

A   B C D   E   F   G

D   E   F   G

NOTE LARGE SIZE NACA COWLING
ON VIEW AT RIGHT-MAX SPEED 300 MPH +

700 H.P. WASP SENIOR MODIFICATION
FOR ATTEMPT ON WORLD LAND
PLANE SPEED RECORD.

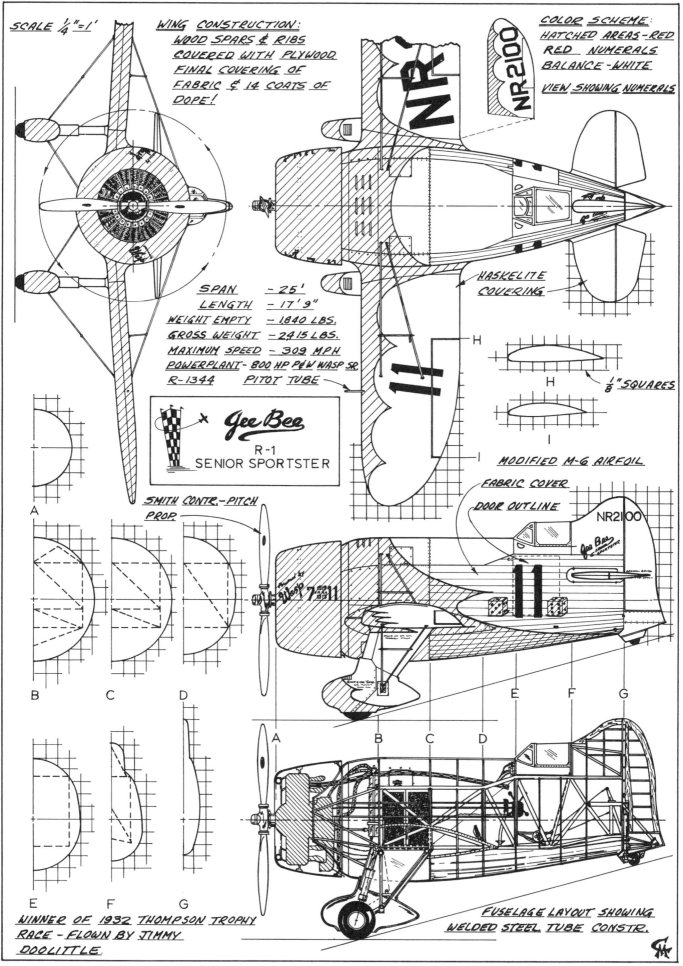

SCALE ¼"=1'

WING CONSTRUCTION: WOOD SPARS & RIBS COVERED WITH PLYWOOD FINAL COVERING OF FABRIC & 14 COATS OF DOPE!

COLOR SCHEME: HATCHED AREAS-RED RED NUMERALS BALANCE-WHITE

VIEW SHOWING NUMERALS

NR2100

NR

11

SPAN — 25'
LENGTH — 17'9"
WEIGHT EMPTY — 1,840 LBS.
GROSS WEIGHT — 2,415 LBS.
MAXIMUM SPEED — 309 MPH
POWERPLANT — 800 HP P&W WASP SR.
R-1344   PITOT TUBE

Gee Bee
R-1
SENIOR SPORTSTER

HASKELITE COVERING

⅛" SQUARES

MODIFIED M-6 AIRFOIL
FABRIC COVER
DOOR OUTLINE

NR2100

SMITH CONTR.-PITCH PROP.

A   B   C   D   E   F   G

11

WINNER OF 1932 THOMPSON TROPHY RACE - FLOWN BY JIMMY DOOLITTLE.

FUSELAGE LAYOUT SHOWING WELDED STEEL TUBE CONSTR.

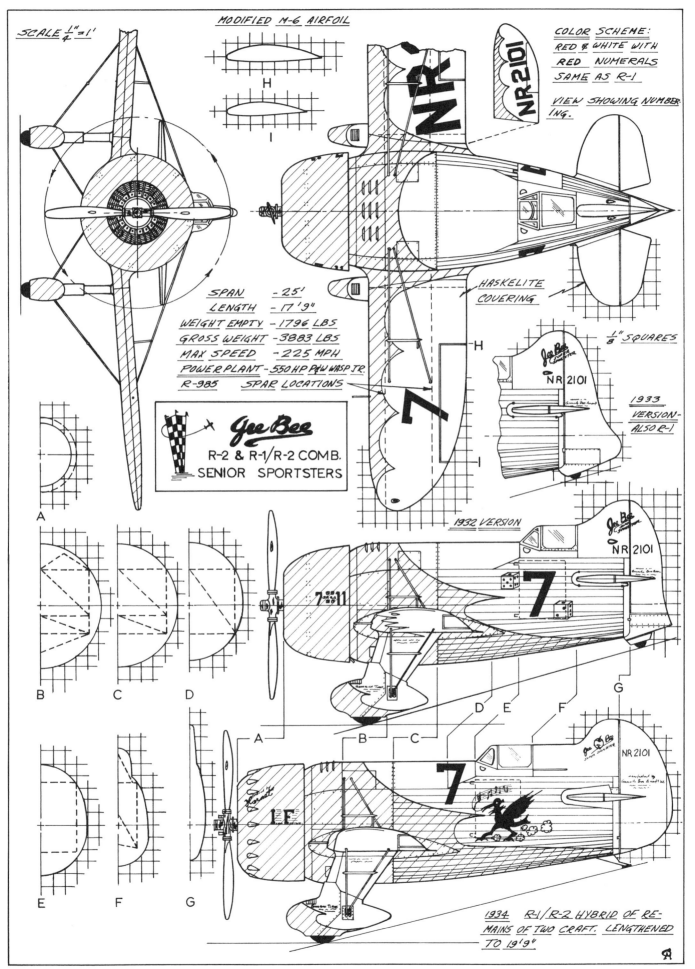

SCALE $\frac{1"}{4}=1'$

MODIFIED M-6 AIRFOIL

H

I

COLOR SCHEME:
RED & WHITE WITH
RED NUMERALS
SAME AS R-1

VIEW SHOWING NUMBER-
ING.

NR2101

NR 2101

SPAN   - 25'
LENGTH   - 17'9"
WEIGHT EMPTY - 1796 LBS
GROSS WEIGHT - 3883 LBS
MAX SPEED   - 225 MPH
POWER PLANT - 550 HP P&W WASP JR.
R-985   SPAR LOCATIONS

HASKELITE
COVERING

H

I

$\frac{L"}{8}$ SQUARES

1933
VERSION-
ALSO R-1

NR 2101

1932 VERSION

Gee Bee
R-2 & R-1/R-2 COMB.
SENIOR SPORTSTERS

A

B   C   D

NR 2101

7

7

A   B   C   D   E   F   G

E   F   G

Hornet

7

IF

NR 2101

1934 R-1/R-2 HYBRID OF RE-
MAINS OF TWO CRAFT. LENGTHENED
TO 19'9"

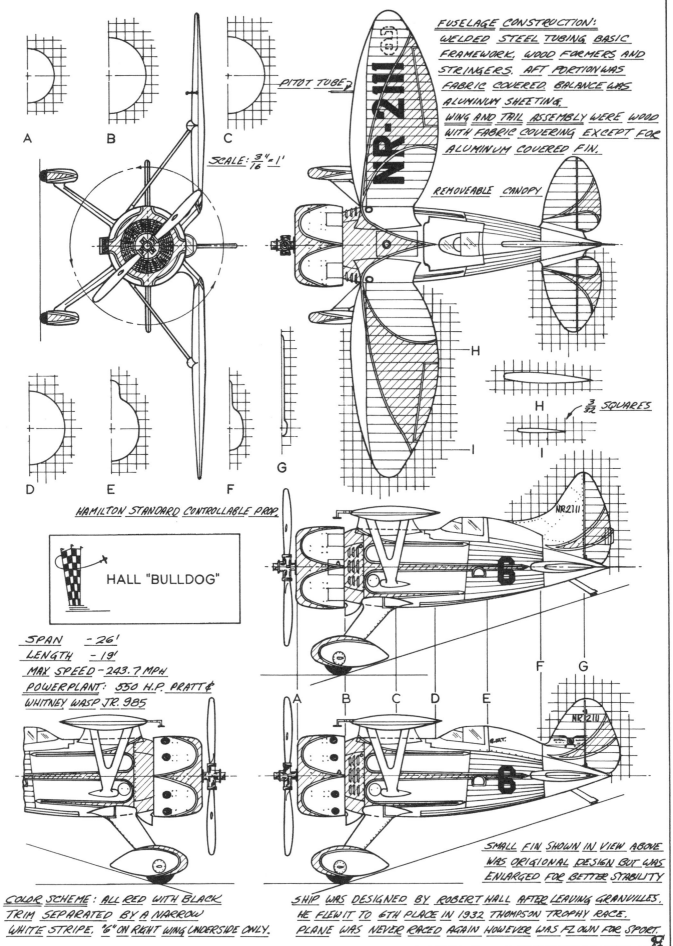

A   B   C

PITOT TUBE

SCALE: $\frac{3"}{16}=1'$

FUSELAGE CONSTRUCTION:
WELDED STEEL TUBING BASIC
FRAMEWORK, WOOD FORMERS AND
STRINGERS. AFT PORTION WAS
FABRIC COVERED. BALANCE WAS
ALUMINUM SHEETING.
WING AND TAIL ASSEMBLY WERE WOOD
WITH FABRIC COVERING EXCEPT FOR
ALUMINUM COVERED FIN.

REMOVEABLE CANOPY

NR-2111

H

$\frac{3}{32}$ SQUARES

D   E   F

G

H

I

HAMILTON STANDARD CONTROLLABLE PROP.

HALL "BULLDOG"

SPAN   - 26'
LENGTH   - 19'
MAX SPEED - 243.7 MPH
POWERPLANT: 550 H.P. PRATT &
WHITNEY WASP JR. 985

NR2111

6

A   B   C   D   E   F   G

NR-2111

6

SMALL FIN SHOWN IN VIEW ABOVE
WAS ORIGIONAL DESIGN BUT WAS
ENLARGED FOR BETTER STABILITY

COLOR SCHEME: ALL RED WITH BLACK
TRIM SEPARATED BY A NARROW
WHITE STRIPE. "6" ON RIGHT WING UNDERSIDE ONLY.

SHIP WAS DESIGNED BY ROBERT HALL AFTER LEAVING GRANVILLES.
HE FLEW IT TO 6TH PLACE IN 1932 THOMPSON TROPHY RACE.
PLANE WAS NEVER RACED AGAIN HOWEVER WAS FLOWN FOR SPORT.

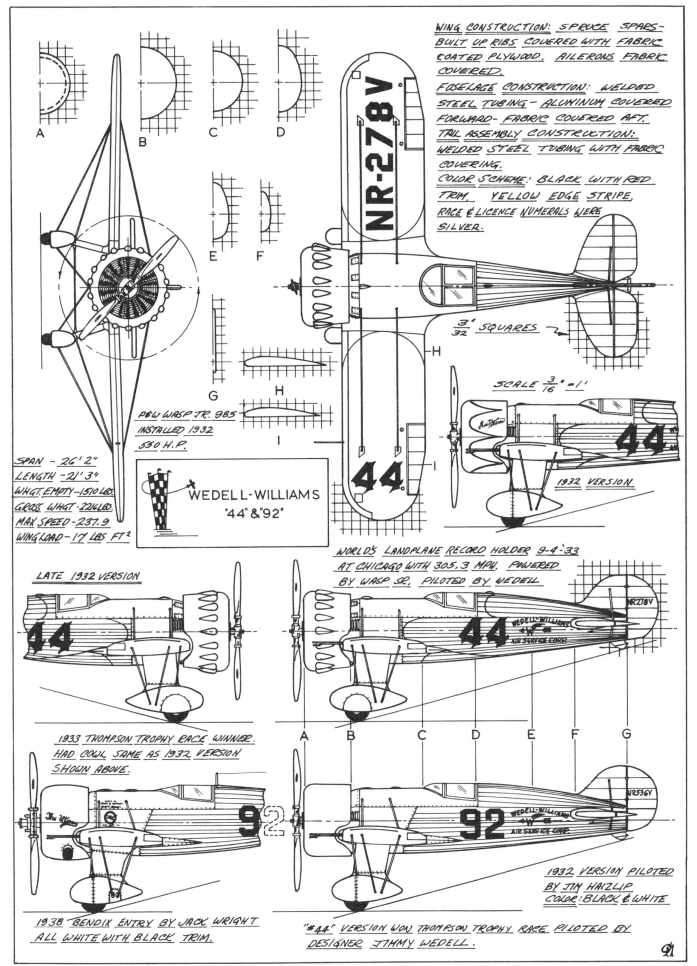

WING CONSTRUCTION: SPRUCE SPARS-
BUILT UP RIBS COVERED WITH FABRIC
COATED PLYWOOD. AILERONS FABRIC
COVERED.
FUSELAGE CONSTRUCTION: WELDED
STEEL TUBING - ALUMINUM COVERED
FORWARD - FABRIC COVERED AFT.
TAIL ASSEMBLY CONSTRUCTION:
WELDED STEEL TUBING WITH FABRIC
COVERING.
COLOR SCHEME: BLACK WITH RED
TRIM. YELLOW EDGE STRIPE.
RACE & LICENCE NUMERALS WERE
SILVER.

A   B   C   D

E   F

G   H

H   I

P&W WASP JR. 985
INSTALLED 1932
550 H.P.

$\frac{3}{32}$' SQUARES

SCALE $\frac{3}{16}$" = 1'

1932 VERSION

SPAN - 26' 2"
LENGTH - 21' 3"
WHGT. EMPTY - 1510 LBS.
GROSS WHGT - 2216 LBS.
MAX SPEED - 237.9
WING LOAD - 17 LBS FT²

WEDELL-WILLIAMS
"44" & "92"

LATE 1932 VERSION

WORLD'S LANDPLANE RECORD HOLDER 9-4-'33
AT CHICAGO WITH 305.3 MPH. POWERED
BY WASP SR. PILOTED BY WEDELL

A   B   C   D   E   F   G

1933 THOMPSON TROPHY RACE WINNER.
HAD COWL SAME AS 1932 VERSION
SHOWN ABOVE.

1938 BENDIX ENTRY BY JACK WRIGHT
ALL WHITE WITH BLACK TRIM.

1932 VERSION PILOTED
BY JIM HAIZLIP
COLOR: BLACK & WHITE

"#44" VERSION WON THOMPSON TROPHY RACE PILOTED BY
DESIGNER JIMMY WEDELL.

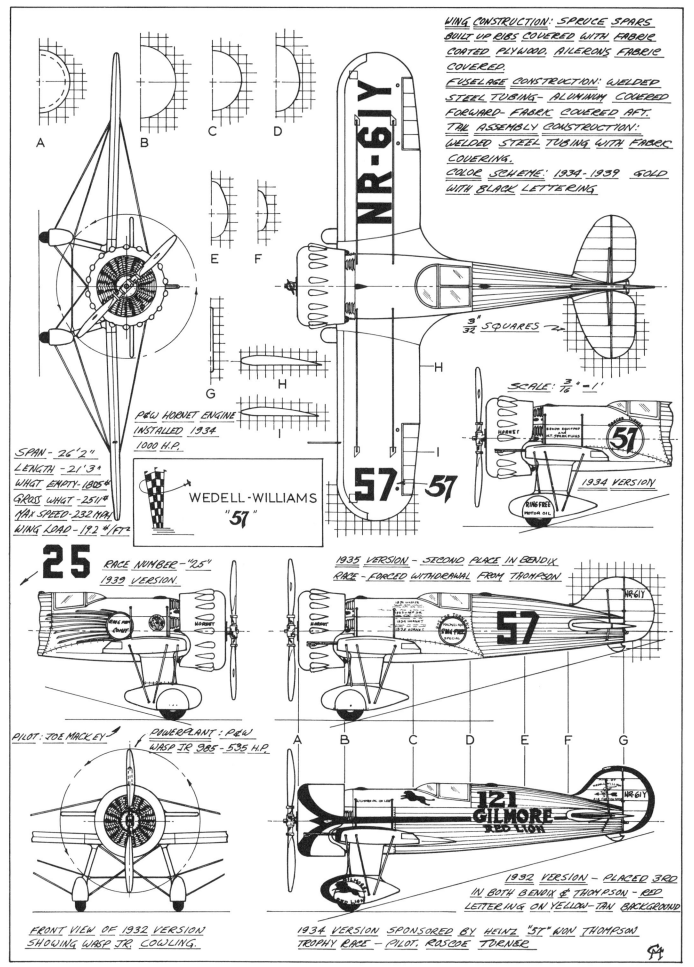

WING CONSTRUCTION: SPRUCE SPARS
BUILT UP RIBS COVERED WITH FABRIC
COATED PLYWOOD. AILERONS FABRIC
COVERED.
FUSELAGE CONSTRUCTION: WELDED
STEEL TUBING - ALUMINUM COVERED
FORWARD - FABRIC COVERED AFT.
TAIL ASSEMBLY CONSTRUCTION:
WELDED STEEL TUBING WITH FABRIC
COVERING.
COLOR SCHEME: 1934-1939 GOLD
WITH BLACK LETTERING

A   B   C   D

E   F

G

H

I

P&W HORNET ENGINE
INSTALLED 1934
1000 H.P.

NR-61Y

$\frac{3}{32}$" SQUARES

H

I

57 · 57

SPAN - 26'2"
LENGTH - 21'3"
WHGT EMPTY - 1805#
GROSS WHGT - 2511#
MAX SPEED - 232 MPH
WING LOAD - 19.2 #/FT²

WEDELL-WILLIAMS
"57"

SCALE: $\frac{3}{16}$" = 1'

HORNET   BENDIX EQUIPPED
AND
M.T. SPARK PLUGS

57

RING FREE
MOTOR OIL

1934 VERSION

25

RACE NUMBER - "25"
1939 VERSION.

RING FREE
COMET   HORNET

1935 VERSION - SECOND PLACE IN BENDIX
RACE - FORCED WITHDRAWAL FROM THOMPSON

HORNET

RING FREE
SPECIAL

57

NR-61Y

PILOT: JOE MACKEY   POWERPLANT: P&W
WASP JR 985 - 535 H.P.

A   B   C   D   E   F   G

121
GILMORE
RED LION

NR-61Y

FRONT VIEW OF 1932 VERSION
SHOWING WASP JR. COWLING.

1932 VERSION - PLACED 3RD
IN BOTH BENDIX & THOMPSON - RED
LETTERING ON YELLOW-TAN BACKGROUND

1934 VERSION SPONSORED BY HEINZ "57" WON THOMPSON
TROPHY RACE - PILOT. ROSCOE TURNER

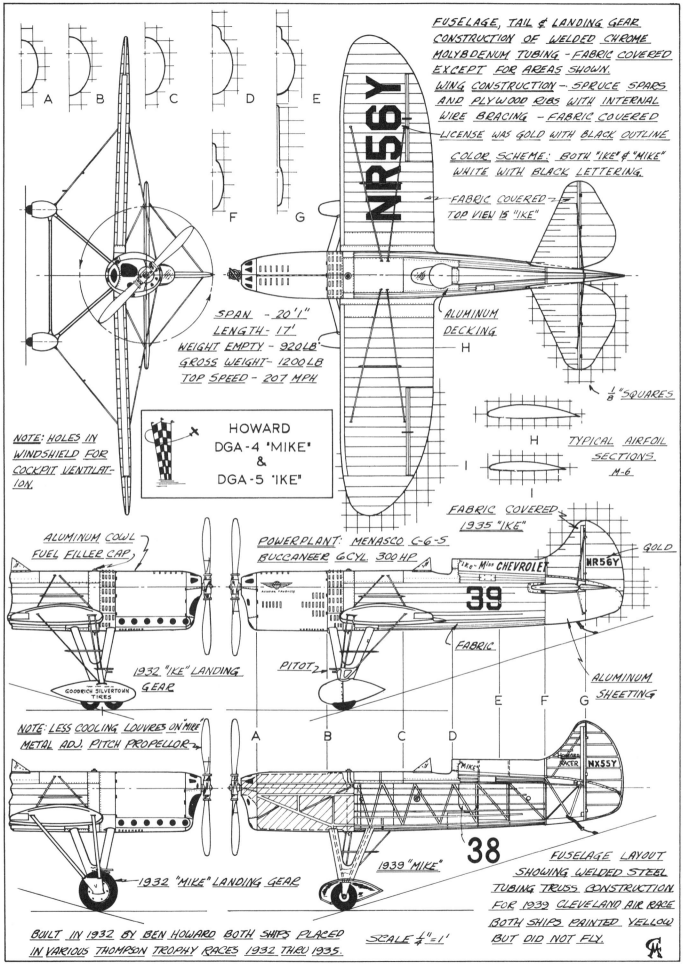

FUSELAGE, TAIL & LANDING GEAR
CONSTRUCTION OF WELDED CHROME
MOLYBDENUM TUBING - FABRIC COVERED
EXCEPT FOR AREAS SHOWN.
WING CONSTRUCTION - SPRUCE SPARS
AND PLYWOOD RIBS WITH INTERNAL
WIRE BRACING - FABRIC COVERED
LICENSE WAS GOLD WITH BLACK OUTLINE

COLOR SCHEME: BOTH "IKE" & "MIKE"
WHITE WITH BLACK LETTERING.

NR56Y

FABRIC COVERED
TOP VIEW IS "IKE"

ALUMINUM
DECKING

H

SPAN - 20'1"
LENGTH - 17'
WEIGHT EMPTY - 920 LB
GROSS WEIGHT - 1200 LB
TOP SPEED - 207 MPH

$\frac{1}{8}$" SQUARES

H

TYPICAL AIRFOIL
SECTIONS
M-6

I

NOTE: HOLES IN
WINDSHIELD FOR
COCKPIT VENTILAT-
ION.

HOWARD
DGA-4 "MIKE"
&
DGA-5 "IKE"

ALUMINUM COWL
FUEL FILLER CAP.

POWERPLANT: MENASCO C-6-S
BUCCANEER 6 CYL. 300 HP

FABRIC COVERED
1935 "IKE"

GOLD

"Ike" Miss CHEVROLET

NR56Y

39

1932 "IKE" LANDING
GEAR

GOODRICH SILVERTOWN
TIRES

PITOT

FABRIC

ALUMINUM
SHEETING

E   F   G

A   B   C   D

NOTE: LESS COOLING LOUVRES ON "MIKE"
METAL ADJ. PITCH PROPELLOR

HOWARD
RACER

"MIKE"

NX55Y

38

1932 "MIKE" LANDING GEAR

1939 "MIKE"

FUSELAGE LAYOUT
SHOWING WELDED STEEL
TUBING TRUSS CONSTRUCTION
FOR 1939 CLEVELAND AIR RACE
BOTH SHIPS PAINTED YELLOW
BUT DID NOT FLY.

BUILT IN 1932 BY BEN HOWARD BOTH SHIPS PLACED
IN VARIOUS THOMPSON TROPHY RACES 1932 THRU 1935.

SCALE $\frac{1}{4}$"=1'

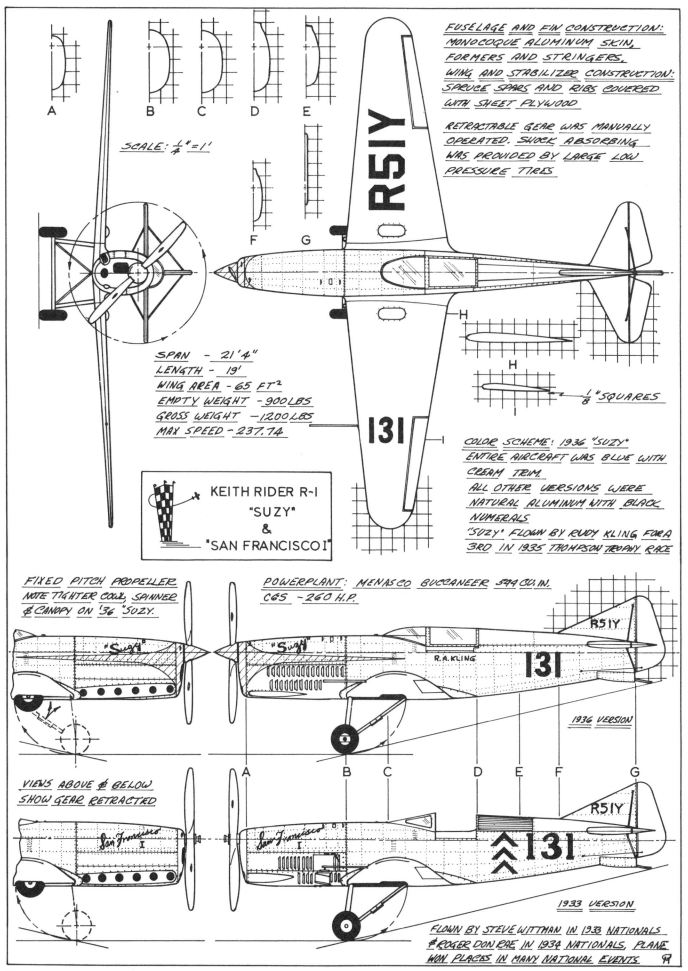

SCALE: $\frac{1''}{4}$ = 1'

FUSELAGE AND FIN CONSTRUCTION:
MONOCOQUE ALUMINUM SKIN,
FORMERS AND STRINGERS.
WING AND STABILIZER CONSTRUCTION:
SPRUCE SPARS AND RIBS COVERED
WITH SHEET PLYWOOD

RETRACTABLE GEAR WAS MANUALLY
OPERATED. SHOCK ABSORBING
WAS PROVIDED BY LARGE LOW
PRESSURE TIRES

SPAN - 21'4"
LENGTH - 19'
WING AREA - 65 FT²
EMPTY WEIGHT - 900 LBS
GROSS WEIGHT - 1200 LBS
MAX SPEED - 237.74

$\frac{1}{8}$" SQUARES

KEITH RIDER R-1
"SUZY"
&
"SAN FRANCISCO I"

COLOR SCHEME: 1936 "SUZY"
ENTIRE AIRCRAFT WAS BLUE WITH
CREAM TRIM.
ALL OTHER VERSIONS WERE
NATURAL ALUMINUM WITH BLACK
NUMERALS
"SUZY" FLOWN BY RUDY KLING FOR A
3RD IN 1935 THOMPSON TROPHY RACE

FIXED PITCH PROPELLER
NOTE TIGHTER COWL, SPINNER
& CANOPY ON '36 "SUZY".

POWERPLANT: MENASCO BUCCANEER 544 CU. IN.
C6S - 260 H.P.

1936 VERSION

VIEWS ABOVE & BELOW
SHOW GEAR RETRACTED

1933 VERSION

FLOWN BY STEVE WITTMAN IN 1933 NATIONALS
& ROGER DON RAE IN 1934 NATIONALS. PLANE
WON PLACES IN MANY NATIONAL EVENTS.

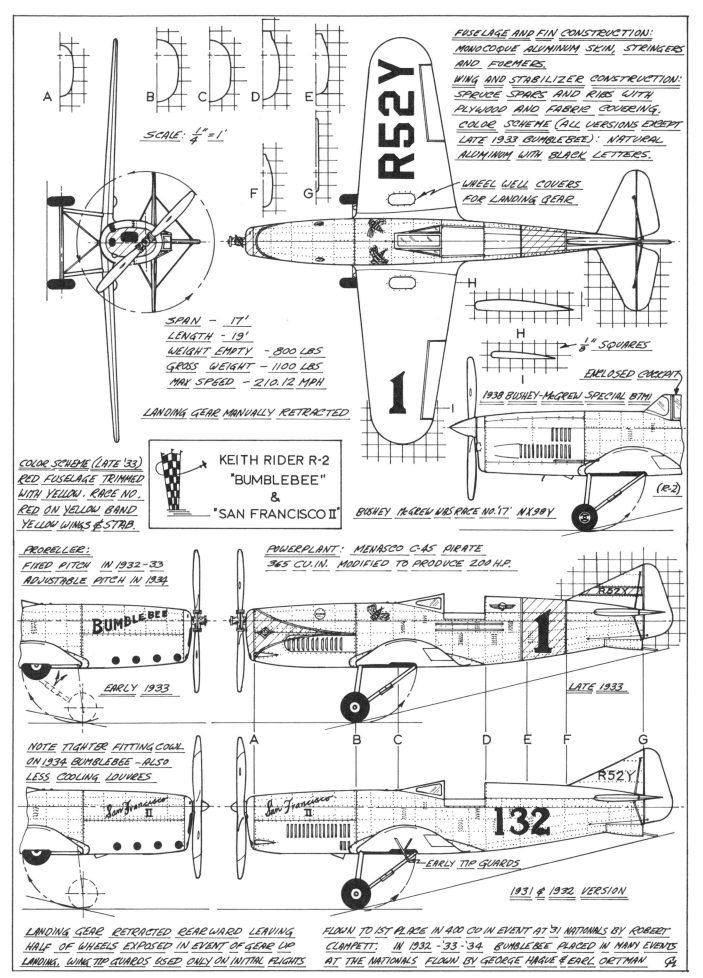

FUSELAGE AND FIN CONSTRUCTION:
MONOCOQUE ALUMINUM SKIN, STRINGERS
AND FORMERS.
WING AND STABILIZER CONSTRUCTION:
SPRUCE SPARS AND RIBS WITH
PLYWOOD AND FABRIC COVERING.
COLOR SCHEME (ALL VERSIONS EXCEPT
LATE 1933 BUMBLEBEE): NATURAL
ALUMINUM WITH BLACK LETTERS.

WHEEL WELL COVERS
FOR LANDING GEAR

SCALE: 1/4" = 1'

A B C D E F G

H

1/8" SQUARES

H

I

ENCLOSED COCKPIT

1938 BUSHEY-McGREW SPECIAL B7M1

(R-2)

BUSHEY McGREW WAS RACE NO. '17' NX98Y

SPAN — 17'
LENGTH — 19'
WEIGHT EMPTY — 800 LBS
GROSS WEIGHT — 1100 LBS
MAX SPEED — 210.12 MPH

LANDING GEAR MANUALLY RETRACTED

COLOR SCHEME (LATE '33)
RED FUSELAGE TRIMMED
WITH YELLOW. RACE NO.
RED ON YELLOW BAND
YELLOW WINGS & STAB.

KEITH RIDER R-2
"BUMBLEBEE"
&
"SAN FRANCISCO II"

PROPELLER:
FIXED PITCH IN 1932-33
ADJUSTABLE PITCH IN 1934

POWERPLANT: MENASCO C-45 PIRATE
365 CU. IN. MODIFIED TO PRODUCE 200 H.P.

BUMBLEBEE

EARLY 1933

R52Y

1

LATE 1933

NOTE TIGHTER FITTING COWL
ON 1934 BUMBLEBEE - ALSO
LESS COOLING LOUVRES

A B C D E F G

San Francisco
II

San Francisco
II

R52Y

132

EARLY TIP GUARDS

1931 & 1932 VERSION

LANDING GEAR RETRACTED REARWARD LEAVING
HALF OF WHEELS EXPOSED IN EVENT OF GEAR UP
LANDING. WING TIP GUARDS USED ONLY ON INITIAL FLIGHTS

FLOWN TO 1ST PLACE IN 400 CU IN EVENT AT '31 NATIONALS BY ROBERT
CLAMPETT. IN 1932-'33-'34 BUMBLEBEE PLACED IN MANY EVENTS
AT THE NATIONALS FLOWN BY GEORGE HAGUE & EARL ORTMAN

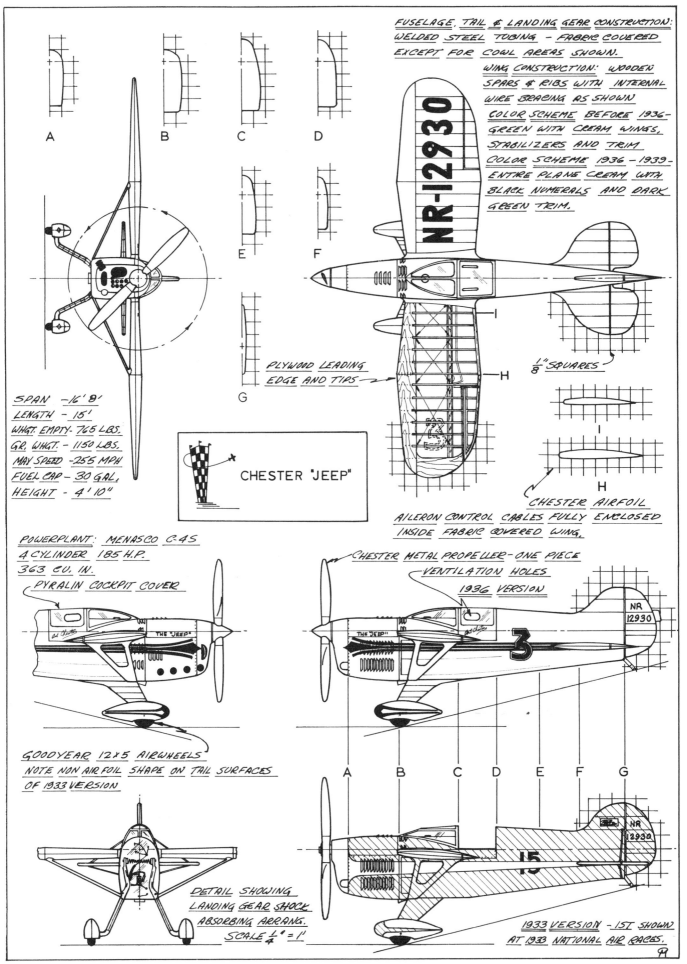

FUSELAGE, TAIL & LANDING GEAR CONSTRUCTION: WELDED STEEL TUBING - FABRIC COVERED EXCEPT FOR COWL AREAS SHOWN.

WING CONSTRUCTION: WOODEN SPARS & RIBS WITH INTERNAL WIRE BRACING AS SHOWN COLOR SCHEME BEFORE 1936- GREEN WITH CREAM WINGS, STABILIZERS AND TRIM COLOR SCHEME 1936 -1939- ENTIRE PLANE CREAM WITH BLACK NUMERALS AND DARK GREEN TRIM.

A   B   C   D

E   F

G

NR-12930

PLYWOOD LEADING EDGE AND TIPS

⅛" SQUARES

I

H

CHESTER AIRFOIL

AILERON CONTROL CABLES FULLY ENCLOSED INSIDE FABRIC COVERED WING.

SPAN - 16' 8'
LENGTH - 15'
WHGT. EMPTY- 765 LBS.
GR. WHGT. - 1150 LBS.
MAX SPEED -255 MPH
FUEL CAP - 30 GAL,
HEIGHT - 4' 10"

CHESTER "JEEP"

POWERPLANT: MENASCO C-4S 4 CYLINDER 185 H.P. 363 CU. IN.

PYRALIN COCKPIT COVER

THE "JEEP"

CHESTER METAL PROPELLER - ONE PIECE

VENTILATION HOLES 1936 VERSION

THE "JEEP"

NR 12930

3

GOODYEAR 12X5 AIRWHEELS

NOTE NON AIR FOIL SHAPE ON TAIL SURFACES OF 1933 VERSION

A   B   C   D   E   F   G

NR 12930

15

DETAIL SHOWING LANDING GEAR SHOCK ABSORBING ARRANG.

SCALE ¼" = 1'

1933 VERSION - 1ST SHOWN AT 1933 NATIONAL AIR RACES.

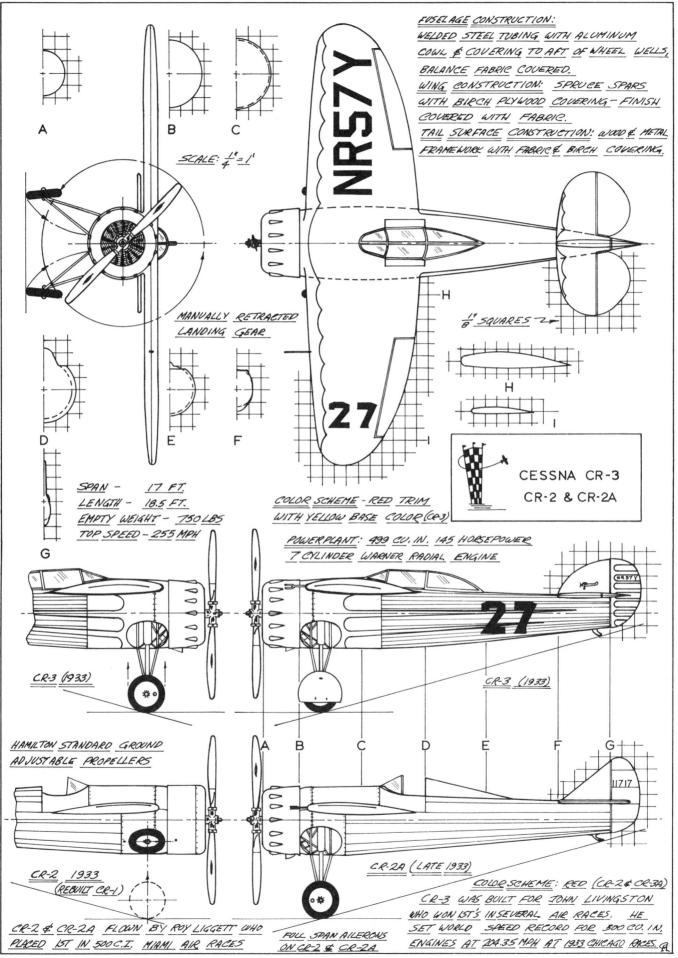

FUSELAGE CONSTRUCTION:
WELDED STEEL TUBING WITH ALUMINUM
COWL & COVERING TO AFT OF WHEEL WELLS,
BALANCE FABRIC COVERED.
WING CONSTRUCTION: SPRUCE SPARS
WITH BIRCH PLYWOOD COVERING – FINISH
COVERED WITH FABRIC.
TAIL SURFACE CONSTRUCTION: WOOD & METAL
FRAMEWORK WITH FABRIC & BIRCH COVERING.

A   B   C

SCALE: $\frac{1"}{4}$ = 1'

MANUALLY RETRACTED
LANDING GEAR

$\frac{1"}{8}$ SQUARES

H

H

I

D   E   F

CESSNA CR-3
CR-2 & CR-2A

G

SPAN - 17 FT.
LENGTH - 18.5 FT.
EMPTY WEIGHT - 750 LBS
TOP SPEED - 255 MPH

COLOR SCHEME - RED TRIM
WITH YELLOW BASE COLOR (CR-3)

POWERPLANT: 499 CU. IN. 145 HORSEPOWER
7 CYLINDER WARNER RADIAL ENGINE

CR-3 (1933)

CR-3 (1933)

HAMILTON STANDARD GROUND
ADJUSTABLE PROPELLERS

A   B   C   D   E   F   G

11717

CR-2 1933
(REBUILT CR-1)

CR-2A (LATE 1933)

COLOR SCHEME: RED (CR-2 & CR-3A)
CR-3 WAS BUILT FOR JOHN LIVINGSTON
WHO WON 1ST'S IN SEVERAL AIR RACES. HE
SET WORLD SPEED RECORD FOR 500 CU. IN.
ENGINES AT 204.35 MPH AT 1933 CHICAGO RACES.

CR-2 & CR-2A FLOWN BY ROY LIGGETT WHO
PLACED 1ST IN 500 C.I. MIAMI AIR RACES

FULL SPAN AILERONS
ON CR-2 & CR-2A

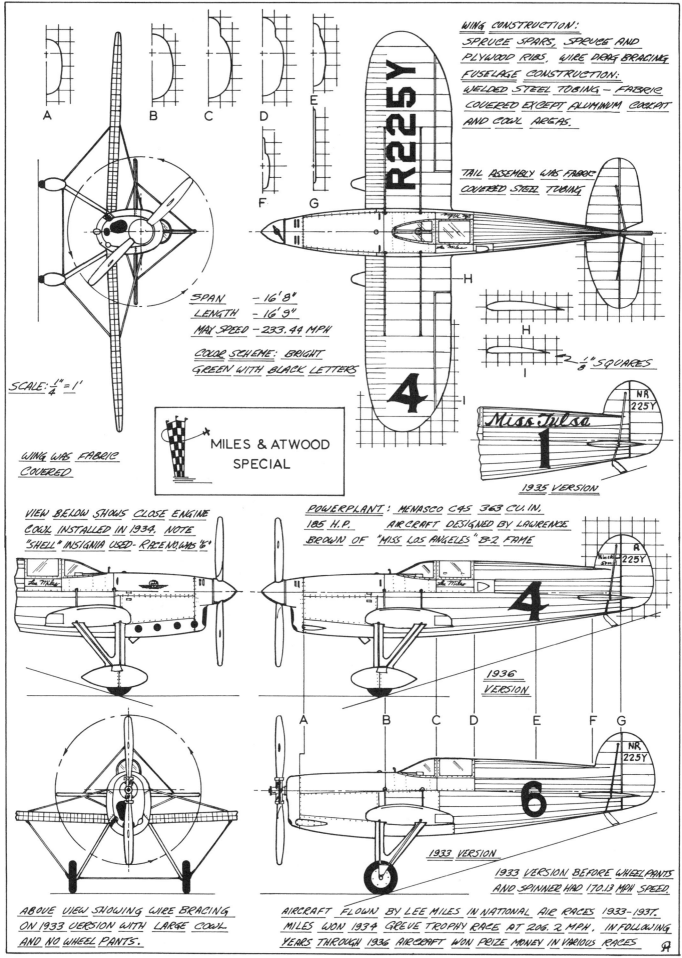

WING CONSTRUCTION:
SPRUCE SPARS, SPRUCE AND PLYWOOD RIBS, WIRE DRAG BRACING

FUSELAGE CONSTRUCTION:
WELDED STEEL TUBING — FABRIC COVERED EXCEPT ALUMINUM COCKPIT AND COWL AREAS.

TAIL ASSEMBLY WAS FABRIC COVERED STEEL TUBING

A   B   C   D   E
F   G

SPAN   – 16' 8"
LENGTH   – 16' 9"
MAX SPEED – 233.44 MPH

COLOR SCHEME: BRIGHT GREEN WITH BLACK LETTERS

R225Y
4

H
H
I   ⅛" SQUARES

SCALE: ¼" = 1'

WING WAS FABRIC COVERED

MILES & ATWOOD SPECIAL

Miss Tulsa
NR 225Y
1
1935 VERSION

VIEW BELOW SHOWS CLOSE ENGINE COWL INSTALLED IN 1934. NOTE "SHELL" INSIGNIA USED - RACE NO. WAS "6"

POWERPLANT: MENASCO C4S 363 CU. IN. 185 H.P.   AIRCRAFT DESIGNED BY LAWRENCE BROWN OF "MISS LOS ANGELES" B-2 FAME

R 225Y
4
1936 VERSION

A   B   C   D   E   F   G

NR 225Y
6
1933 VERSION

1933 VERSION BEFORE WHEEL PANTS AND SPINNER HAD 170.13 MPH SPEED.

ABOVE VIEW SHOWING WIRE BRACING ON 1933 VERSION WITH LARGE COWL AND NO WHEEL PANTS.

AIRCRAFT FLOWN BY LEE MILES IN NATIONAL AIR RACES 1933-1937. MILES WON 1934 GREVE TROPHY RACE AT 206.2 MPH. IN FOLLOWING YEARS THROUGH 1936 AIRCRAFT WON PRIZE MONEY IN VARIOUS RACES

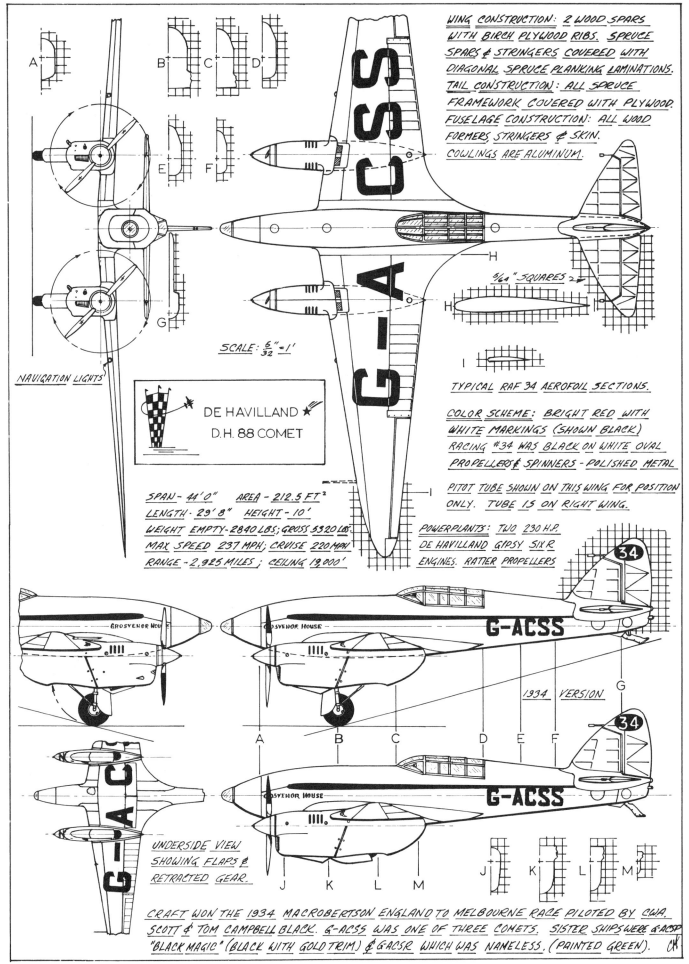

WING CONSTRUCTION: 2 WOOD SPARS WITH BIRCH PLYWOOD RIBS. SPRUCE SPARS & STRINGERS COVERED WITH DIAGONAL SPRUCE PLANKING LAMINATIONS. TAIL CONSTRUCTION: ALL SPRUCE FRAMEWORK COVERED WITH PLYWOOD. FUSELAGE CONSTRUCTION: ALL WOOD FORMERS, STRINGERS & SKIN. COWLINGS ARE ALUMINUM.

NAVIGATION LIGHTS

SCALE: 6/32" = 1'

DE HAVILLAND
D.H. 88 COMET

SPAN - 44' 0"   AREA - 212.5 FT²
LENGTH - 29' 8"   HEIGHT - 10'
WEIGHT EMPTY - 2840 LBS; GROSS 5320 LBS.
MAX SPEED 237 MPH; CRUISE 220 MPH
RANGE - 2,925 MILES ; CEILING 19,000'

5/64" SQUARES

TYPICAL RAF 34 AEROFOIL SECTIONS.

COLOR SCHEME: BRIGHT RED WITH WHITE MARKINGS (SHOWN BLACK) RACING #34 WAS BLACK ON WHITE OVAL PROPELLERS & SPINNERS - POLISHED METAL

PITOT TUBE SHOWN ON THIS WING FOR POSITION ONLY. TUBE IS ON RIGHT WING.

POWERPLANTS: TWO 230 H.P. DE HAVILLAND GIPSY SIX R ENGINES. RATIER PROPELLERS

GROSVENOR HOUSE

G-ACSS

1934 VERSION

UNDERSIDE VIEW SHOWING FLAPS & RETRACTED GEAR.

GROSVENOR HOUSE

G-ACSS

CRAFT WON THE 1934 MACROBERTSON ENGLAND TO MELBOURNE RACE PILOTED BY C.W.A. SCOTT & TOM CAMPBELL BLACK. G-ACSS WAS ONE OF THREE COMETS. SISTER SHIPS WERE G-ACSP "BLACK MAGIC" (BLACK WITH GOLD TRIM) & GACSR WHICH WAS NAMELESS. (PAINTED GREEN).

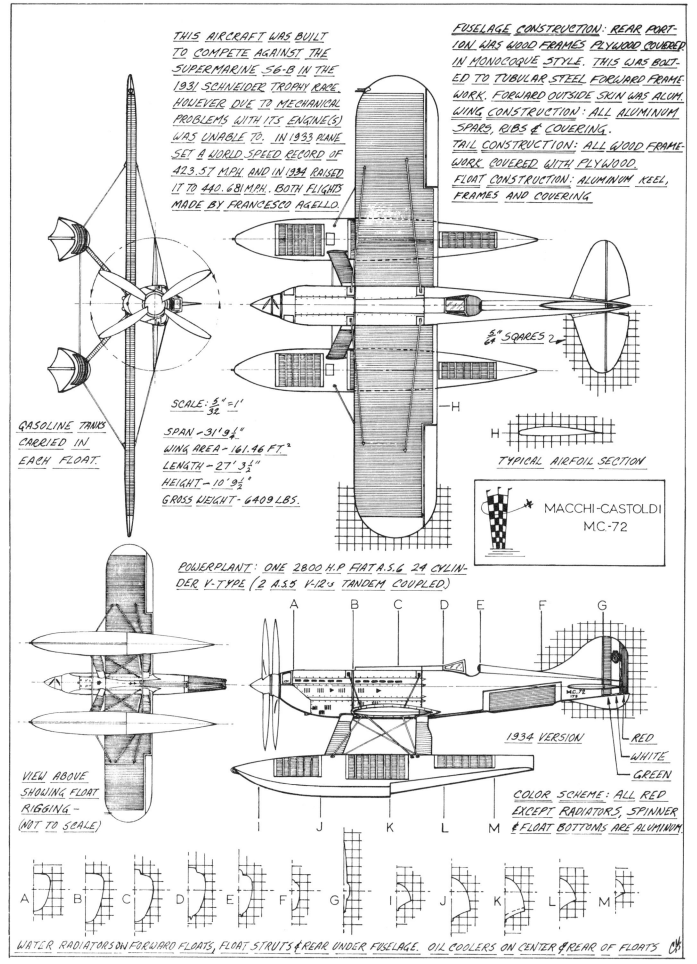

THIS AIRCRAFT WAS BUILT TO COMPETE AGAINST THE SUPERMARINE S6-B IN THE 1931 SCHNEIDER TROPHY RACE. HOWEVER DUE TO MECHANICAL PROBLEMS WITH ITS ENGINE(S) WAS UNABLE TO. IN 1933 PLANE SET A WORLD SPEED RECORD OF 423.57 M.P.H. AND IN 1934 RAISED IT TO 440.681 M.P.H. BOTH FLIGHTS MADE BY FRANCESCO AGELLO.

FUSELAGE CONSTRUCTION: REAR PORTION WAS WOOD FRAMES PLYWOOD COVERED IN MONOCOQUE STYLE. THIS WAS BOLTED TO TUBULAR STEEL FORWARD FRAMEWORK. FORWARD OUTSIDE SKIN WAS ALUM.
WING CONSTRUCTION: ALL ALUMINUM SPARS, RIBS & COVERING.
TAIL CONSTRUCTION: ALL WOOD FRAMEWORK COVERED WITH PLYWOOD.
FLOAT CONSTRUCTION: ALUMINUM KEEL, FRAMES AND COVERING

GASOLINE TANKS CARRIED IN EACH FLOAT.

SCALE: $\frac{5}{32}$" = 1'

SPAN – 31' 9$\frac{1}{4}$"
WING AREA – 161.46 FT.^{2}
LENGTH – 27' 3$\frac{1}{2}$"
HEIGHT – 10' 9$\frac{1}{2}$"
GROSS WEIGHT – 6409 LBS.

$\frac{5}{64}$" SQARES

—H

H

TYPICAL AIRFOIL SECTION

MACCHI-CASTOLDI M.C.-72

POWERPLANT: ONE 2800 H.P. FIAT A.S.6 24 CYLINDER V-TYPE (2 A.S.5 V-12's TANDEM COUPLED.)

A   B   C   D   E   F   G

1934 VERSION

M.C. 72
173

— RED
— WHITE
— GREEN

VIEW ABOVE SHOWING FLOAT RIGGING – (NOT TO SCALE)

I   J   K   L   M

COLOR SCHEME: ALL RED EXCEPT RADIATORS, SPINNER & FLOAT BOTTOMS ARE ALUMINUM.

A   B   C   D   E   F   G   I   J   K   L   M

WATER RADIATORS ON FORWARD FLOATS, FLOAT STRUTS & REAR UNDER FUSELAGE. OIL COOLERS ON CENTER & REAR OF FLOATS

76

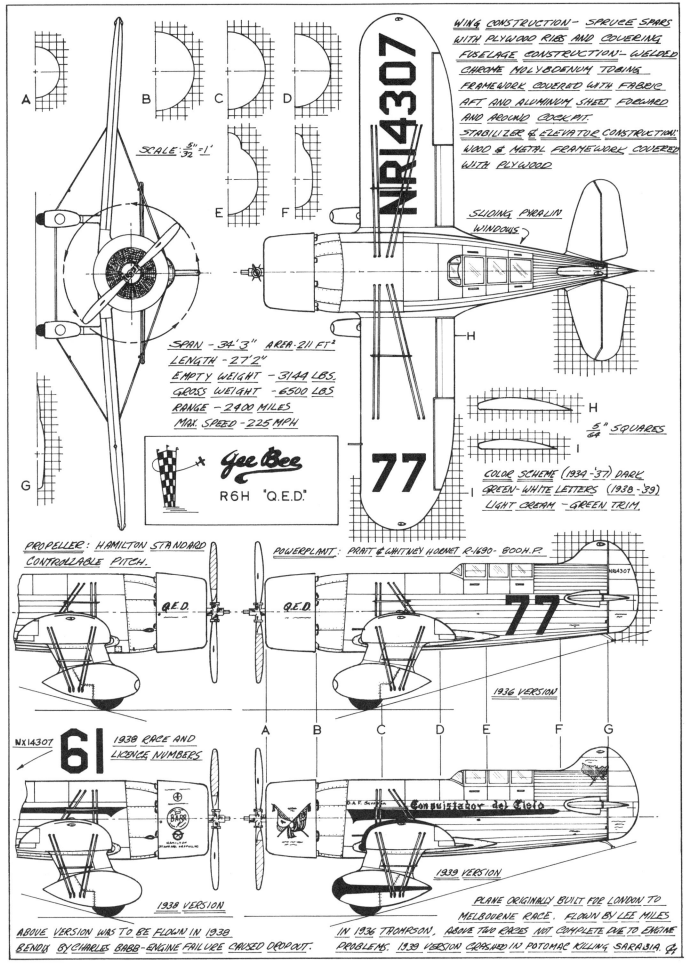

SCALE: $\frac{5}{32}'' = 1'$

WING CONSTRUCTION - SPRUCE SPARS WITH PLYWOOD RIBS AND COVERING FUSELAGE CONSTRUCTION - WELDED CHROME MOLYBDENUM TUBING FRAMEWORK COVERED WITH FABRIC AFT AND ALUMINUM SHEET FORWARD AND AROUND COCKPIT. STABILIZER & ELEVATOR CONSTRUCTION: WOOD & METAL FRAMEWORK COVERED WITH PLYWOOD

NR14307

SLIDING PYRALIN WINDOWS

77

SPAN - 34'3" AREA - 211 FT²
LENGTH - 27'2"
EMPTY WEIGHT - 3144 LBS.
GROSS WEIGHT - 6500 LBS
RANGE - 2400 MILES
MAX. SPEED - 225 MPH

Gee Bee
R6H "Q.E.D."

$\frac{5}{64}''$ SQUARES

COLOR SCHEME (1934 -'37) DARK GREEN - WHITE LETTERS (1938 -'39) LIGHT CREAM - GREEN TRIM.

PROPELLER: HAMILTON STANDARD CONTROLLABLE PITCH.

POWERPLANT: PRATT & WHITNEY HORNET R-1690 - 800 H.P.

Q.E.D.

Q.E.D.

77

NR14307

1936 VERSION

NX14307

61 1938 RACE AND LICENCE NUMBERS

BABB

Conquistador del Cielo

D.A.F. Savedra

1939 VERSION

1938 VERSION

ABOVE VERSION WAS TO BE FLOWN IN 1938 BENDIX BY CHARLES BABB - ENGINE FAILURE CAUSED DROPOUT.

PLANE ORIGINALLY BUILT FOR LONDON TO MELBOURNE RACE. FLOWN BY LEE MILES IN 1936 THOMPSON. ABOVE TWO RACES NOT COMPLETE DUE TO ENGINE PROBLEMS. 1939 VERSION CRASHED IN POTOMAC KILLING SARABIA.

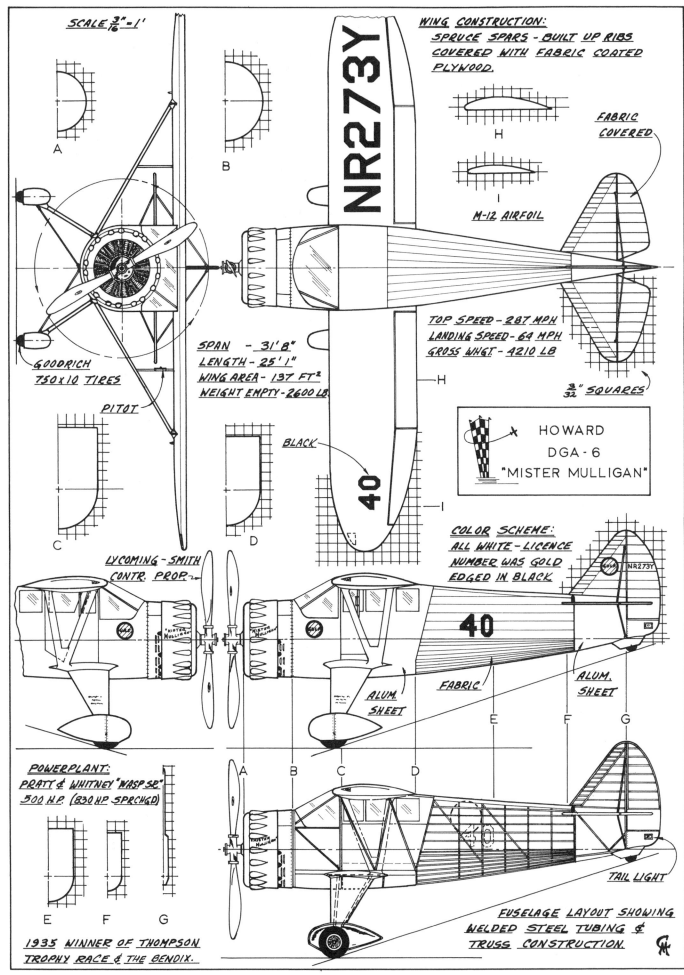

SCALE 3/16" = 1'

NR273Y

WING CONSTRUCTION:
SPRUCE SPARS - BUILT UP RIBS COVERED WITH FABRIC COATED PLYWOOD.

H

I

M-12 AIRFOIL

FABRIC COVERED

A

B

GOODRICH 750x10 TIRES

PITOT

SPAN - 31' 8"
LENGTH - 25' 1"
WING AREA - 137 FT²
WEIGHT EMPTY - 2600 LB.

TOP SPEED - 287 MPH
LANDING SPEED - 64 MPH
GROSS WHGT. - 4210 LB

3/32" SQUARES

BLACK

40

H

I

HOWARD DGA - 6 "MISTER MULLIGAN"

C

D

LYCOMING - SMITH CONTR. PROP.

COLOR SCHEME:
ALL WHITE - LICENCE NUMBER WAS GOLD EDGED IN BLACK

NR273Y

40

FABRIC

ALUM. SHEET

ALUM. SHEET

ALUM. SHEET

E

F

G

POWERPLANT:
PRATT & WHITNEY "WASP SR" 500 H.P. (830 HP SPRCHGD)

A

B

C

D

E

F

G

TAIL LIGHT

1935 WINNER OF THOMPSON TROPHY RACE & THE BENDIX.

FUSELAGE LAYOUT SHOWING WELDED STEEL TUBING & TRUSS CONSTRUCTION.

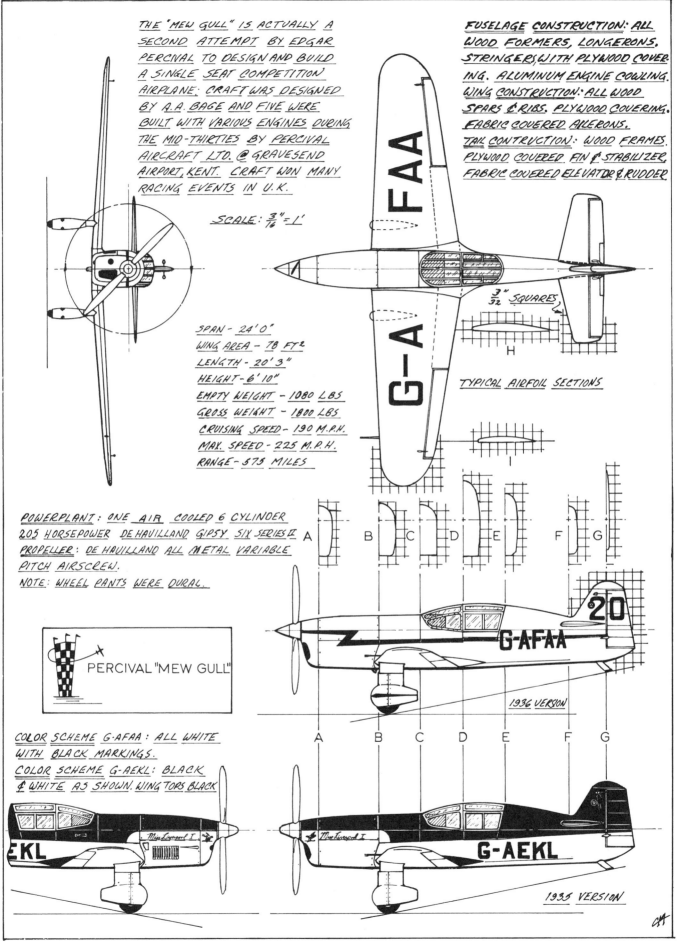

THE "MEW GULL" IS ACTUALLY A SECOND ATTEMPT BY EDGAR PERCIVAL TO DESIGN AND BUILD A SINGLE SEAT COMPETITION AIRPLANE. CRAFT WAS DESIGNED BY A.A. BAGE AND FIVE WERE BUILT WITH VARIOUS ENGINES DURING THE MID-THIRTIES BY PERCIVAL AIRCRAFT LTD. @ GRAVESEND AIRPORT, KENT. CRAFT WON MANY RACING EVENTS IN U.K.

SCALE: 3/16" = 1'

FUSELAGE CONSTRUCTION: ALL WOOD FORMERS, LONGERONS. STRINGERS, WITH PLYWOOD COVERING. ALUMINUM ENGINE COWLING. WING CONSTRUCTION: ALL WOOD SPARS & RIBS. PLYWOOD COVERING. FABRIC COVERED AILERONS. TAIL CONTRUCTION: WOOD FRAMES. PLYWOOD COVERED. FIN & STABILIZER, FABRIC COVERED ELEVATOR & RUDDER

3/32" SQUARES

TYPICAL AIRFOIL SECTIONS

SPAN - 24' 0"
WING AREA - 78 FT²
LENGTH - 20' 3"
HEIGHT - 6' 10"
EMPTY WEIGHT - 1080 LBS
GROSS WEIGHT - 1800 LBS
CRUISING SPEED - 190 M.P.H.
MAX. SPEED - 225 M.P.H.
RANGE - 575 MILES

POWERPLANT: ONE AIR COOLED 6 CYLINDER 205 HORSEPOWER DE HAVILLAND GIPSY SIX SERIES II
PROPELLER: DE HAVILLAND ALL METAL VARIABLE PITCH AIRSCREW.
NOTE: WHEEL PANTS WERE DURAL.

PERCIVAL "MEW GULL"

G-AFAA
1936 VERSION

COLOR SCHEME G·AFAA: ALL WHITE WITH BLACK MARKINGS.
COLOR SCHEME G-AEKL: BLACK & WHITE AS SHOWN. WING TOPS BLACK

G-AEKL
1935 VERSION

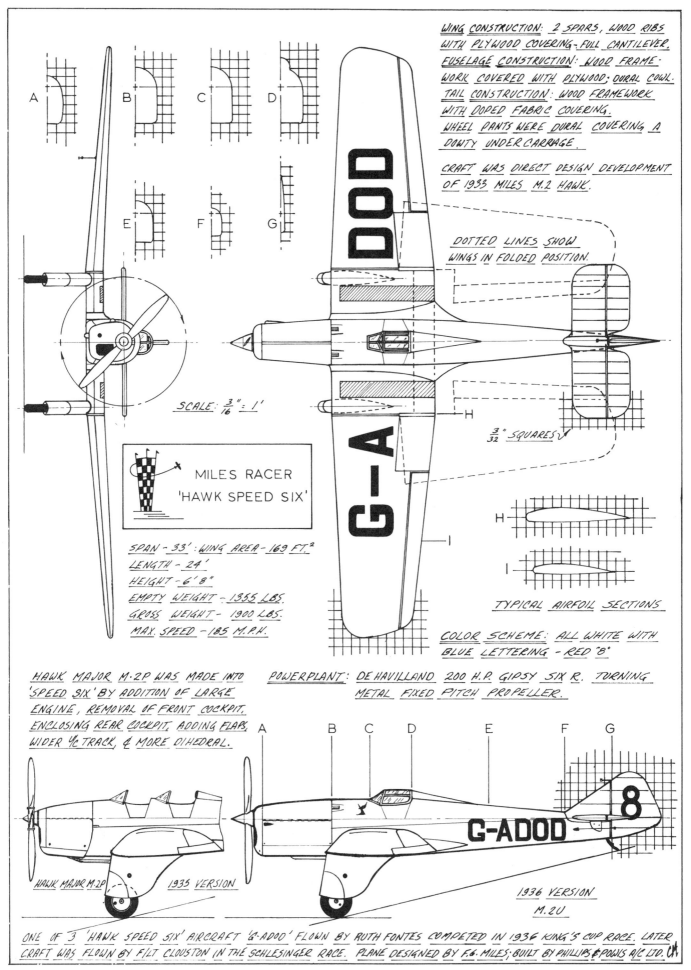

WING CONSTRUCTION: 2 SPARS, WOOD RIBS WITH PLYWOOD COVERING - FULL CANTILEVER. FUSELAGE CONSTRUCTION: WOOD FRAMEWORK COVERED WITH PLYWOOD; DURAL COWL. TAIL CONSTRUCTION: WOOD FRAMEWORK WITH DOPED FABRIC COVERING. WHEEL PANTS WERE DURAL COVERING A DOWTY UNDERCARRIAGE.

CRAFT WAS DIRECT DESIGN DEVELOPMENT OF 1933 MILES M.2 HAWK.

DOTTED LINES SHOW WINGS IN FOLDED POSITION.

$\frac{3}{32}$" SQUARES

SCALE: $\frac{3}{16}$" = 1'

MILES RACER 'HAWK SPEED SIX'

SPAN - 33': WING AREA - 169 FT.²
LENGTH - 24'
HEIGHT - 6'8"
EMPTY WEIGHT - 1355 LBS.
GROSS WEIGHT - 1900 LBS.
MAX. SPEED - 185 M.P.H.

TYPICAL AIRFOIL SECTIONS

COLOR SCHEME: ALL WHITE WITH BLUE LETTERING - RED "8"

HAWK MAJOR M.2P WAS MADE INTO 'SPEED SIX' BY ADDITION OF LARGE ENGINE, REMOVAL OF FRONT COCKPIT, ENCLOSING REAR COCKPIT, ADDING FLAPS, WIDER U/C TRACK, & MORE DIHEDRAL.

POWERPLANT: DE HAVILLAND 200 H.P. GIPSY SIX R. TURNING METAL FIXED PITCH PROPELLER.

HAWK MAJOR M.2P   1935 VERSION

G-ADOD

1936 VERSION M.2U

ONE OF 3 'HAWK SPEED SIX' AIRCRAFT 'G-ADOD' FLOWN BY RUTH FONTES COMPETED IN 1936 KING'S CUP RACE. LATER CRAFT WAS FLOWN BY F/LT CLOUSTON IN THE SCHLESINGER RACE. PLANE DESIGNED BY F.G. MILES; BUILT BY PHILLIPS & POWIS A/C LTD.

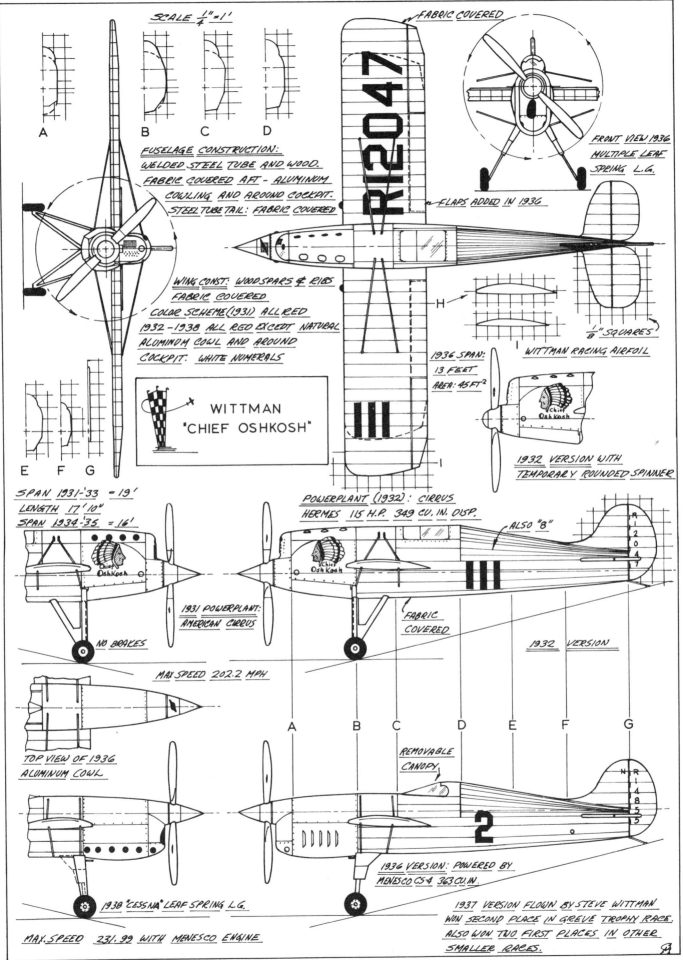

SCALE ¼" = 1'

A B C D

FUSELAGE CONSTRUCTION:
WELDED STEEL TUBE AND WOOD.
FABRIC COVERED AFT - ALUMINUM
COWLING AND AROUND COCKPIT.
STEEL TUBE TAIL: FABRIC COVERED

WING CONST: WOOD SPARS & RIBS
FABRIC COVERED
COLOR SCHEME (1931) ALL RED
1932-1938 ALL RED EXCEPT NATURAL
ALUMINUM COWL AND AROUND
COCKPIT. WHITE NUMERALS

WITTMAN
"CHIEF OSHKOSH"

E F G

SPAN 1931-'33 = 19'
LENGTH 17'10"
SPAN 1934-'35 = 16'

NO BRAKES

MAX SPEED 202.2 MPH

1931 POWERPLANT:
AMERICAN CIRRUS

TOP VIEW OF 1936
ALUMINUM COWL

1938 "CESSNA" LEAF SPRING L.G.

MAX. SPEED 231.99 WITH MENESCO ENGINE

FABRIC COVERED

R12047

FLAPS ADDED IN 1936

FRONT VIEW 1936
MULTIPLE LEAF
SPRING L.G.

1936 SPAN:
13 FEET
AREA: 45 FT²

H

I   ⅛" SQUARES
WITTMAN RACING AIRFOIL

1932 VERSION WITH
TEMPORARY ROUNDED SPINNER

POWERPLANT (1932): CIRRUS
HERMES 115 H.P. 349 CU. IN. DISP.

ALSO "8"

FABRIC
COVERED

1932 VERSION

A B C D E F G

REMOVABLE
CANOPY

2

1936 VERSION: POWERED BY
MENESCO C5A 363 CU.IN.

1937 VERSION FLOWN BY STEVE WITTMAN
WON SECOND PLACE IN GREVE TROPHY RACE.
ALSO WON TWO FIRST PLACES IN OTHER
SMALLER RACES.

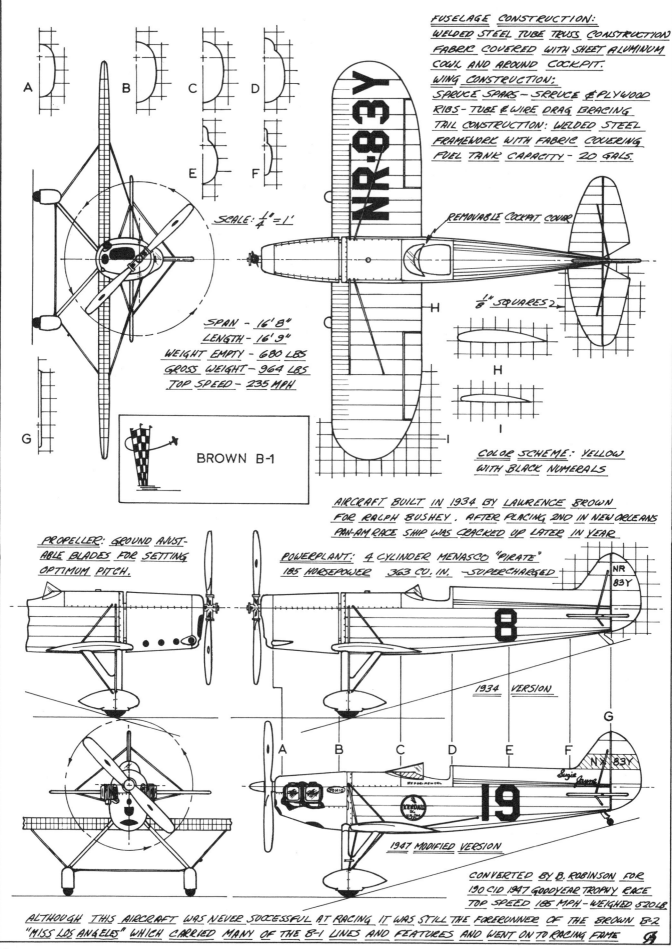

FUSELAGE CONSTRUCTION:
WELDED STEEL TUBE TRUSS CONSTRUCTION
FABRIC COVERED WITH SHEET ALUMINUM
COWL AND AROUND COCKPIT.
WING CONSTRUCTION:
SPRUCE SPARS - SPRUCE & PLYWOOD
RIBS - TUBE & WIRE DRAG BRACING
TAIL CONSTRUCTION: WELDED STEEL
FRAMEWORK WITH FABRIC COVERING
FUEL TANK CAPACITY - 20 GALS.

NR·83Y

A B C D

E F

REMOVABLE COCKPIT COVER

SCALE: 1/4" = 1'

SPAN - 16' 8"
LENGTH - 16' 9"
WEIGHT EMPTY - 680 LBS
GROSS WEIGHT - 964 LBS
TOP SPEED - 235 MPH

1/8" SQUARES

H

H

I

I

G

BROWN B-1

COLOR SCHEME: YELLOW
WITH BLACK NUMERALS

AIRCRAFT BUILT IN 1934 BY LAWRENCE BROWN
FOR RALPH BUSHEY. AFTER PLACING 2ND IN NEW ORLEANS
PAN-AM RACE SHIP WAS CRACKED UP LATER IN YEAR

PROPELLER: GROUND ADJUST-
ABLE BLADES FOR SETTING
OPTIMUM PITCH.

POWERPLANT: 4 CYLINDER MENASCO "PIRATE"
185 HORSEPOWER   363 CU. IN. - SUPERCHARGED

NR
83Y

8

1934 VERSION

A B C D E F G

NR·83Y

Sugie Arras

19

1947 MODIFIED VERSION

CONVERTED BY B. ROBINSON FOR
190 CID 1947 GOODYEAR TROPHY RACE
TOP SPEED 185 MPH - WEIGHED 520 LB

ALTHOUGH THIS AIRCRAFT WAS NEVER SUCCESSFUL AT RACING IT WAS STILL THE FORERUNNER OF THE BROWN B-2
"MISS LOS ANGELES" WHICH CARRIED MANY OF THE B-1 LINES AND FEATURES AND WENT ON TO RACING FAME

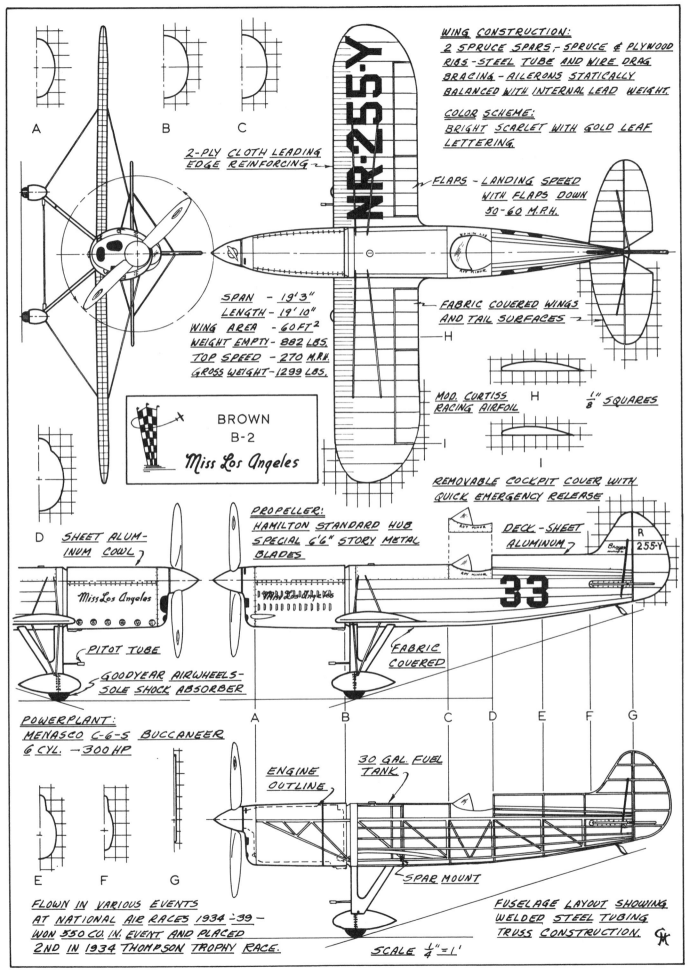

WING CONSTRUCTION:
2 SPRUCE SPARS, SPRUCE & PLYWOOD RIBS, STEEL TUBE AND WIRE DRAG BRACING, AILERONS STATICALLY BALANCED WITH INTERNAL LEAD WEIGHT.

COLOR SCHEME:
BRIGHT SCARLET WITH GOLD LEAF LETTERING.

A   B   C

2-PLY CLOTH LEADING EDGE REINFORCING

FLAPS - LANDING SPEED WITH FLAPS DOWN 50-60 M.P.H.

SPAN - 19'3"
LENGTH - 19'10"
WING AREA - 60 FT²
WEIGHT EMPTY - 882 LBS.
TOP SPEED - 270 M.P.H.
GROSS WEIGHT - 1299 LBS.

FABRIC COVERED WINGS AND TAIL SURFACES

H

BROWN
B-2
Miss Los Angeles

MOD. CURTISS RACING AIRFOIL   H   ⅛" SQUARES

I

REMOVABLE COCKPIT COVER WITH QUICK EMERGENCY RELEASE

D SHEET ALUMINUM COWL

PROPELLER:
HAMILTON STANDARD HUB SPECIAL 6'6" STORY METAL BLADES

DECK - SHEET ALUMINUM

R 255-Y

Miss Los Angeles

33

PITOT TUBE

FABRIC COVERED

GOODYEAR AIRWHEELS - SOLE SHOCK ABSORBER

A   B   C   D   E   F   G

POWERPLANT:
MENASCO C-6-S BUCCANEER 6 CYL. - 300 HP

ENGINE OUTLINE

30 GAL. FUEL TANK

E   F   G

SPAR MOUNT

FLOWN IN VARIOUS EVENTS AT NATIONAL AIR RACES 1934-39 - WON 550 CU. IN. EVENT AND PLACED 2ND IN 1934 THOMPSON TROPHY RACE.

SCALE ¼" = 1'

FUSELAGE LAYOUT SHOWING WELDED STEEL TUBING TRUSS CONSTRUCTION.

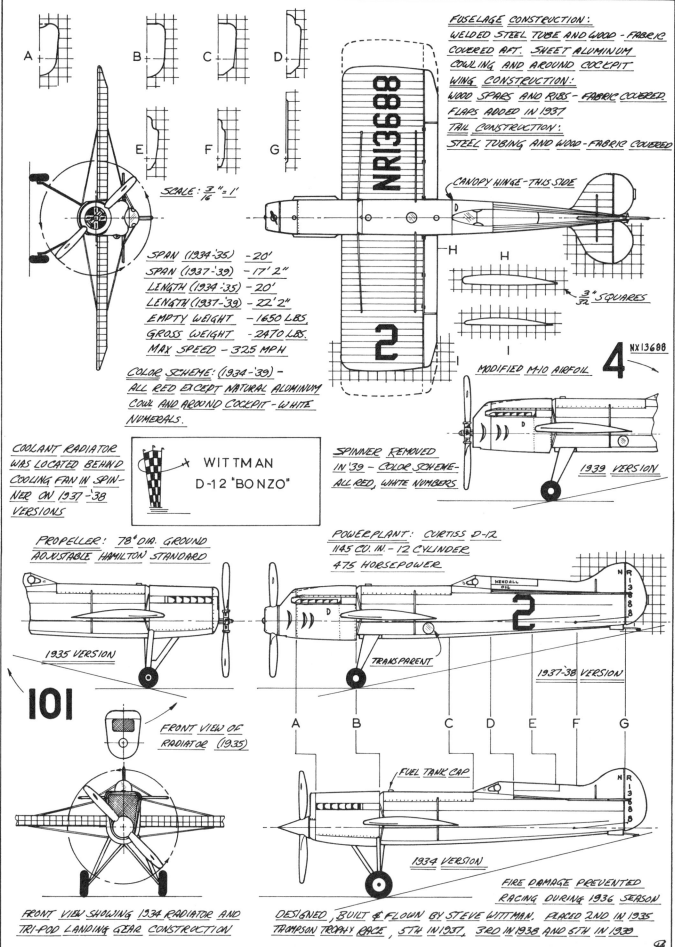

FUSELAGE CONSTRUCTION:
WELDED STEEL TUBE AND WOOD-FABRIC
COVERED AFT. SHEET ALUMINUM
COWLING AND AROUND COCKPIT
WING CONSTRUCTION:
WOOD SPARS AND RIBS - FABRIC COVERED.
FLAPS ADDED IN 1937
TAIL CONSTRUCTION:
STEEL TUBING AND WOOD-FABRIC COVERED

CANOPY HINGE-THIS SIDE

3/32" SQUARES

MODIFIED M-10 AIRFOIL

SCALE: 3/16" = 1'

SPAN (1934-'35) - 20'
SPAN (1937-'39) - 17' 2"
LENGTH (1934-'35) - 20'
LENGTH (1937-'39) - 22' 2"
EMPTY WEIGHT - 1650 LBS.
GROSS WEIGHT - 2470 LBS.
MAX SPEED - 325 MPH

COLOR SCHEME: (1934-'39) -
ALL RED EXCEPT NATURAL ALUMINUM
COWL AND AROUND COCKPIT - WHITE
NUMERALS.

COOLANT RADIATOR
WAS LOCATED BEHIND
COOLING FAN IN SPIN-
NER ON 1937-'38
VERSIONS

WITTMAN
D-12 "BONZO"

SPINNER REMOVED
IN '39 - COLOR SCHEME-
ALL RED, WHITE NUMBERS

NX13688

1939 VERSION

PROPELLER: 78" DIA. GROUND
ADJUSTABLE HAMILTON STANDARD

POWERPLANT: CURTISS D-12
1145 CU. IN. - 12 CYLINDER
475 HORSEPOWER

KENDALL OIL

1935 VERSION

101

TRANSPARENT

1937-'38 VERSION

A   B   C   D   E   F   G

FRONT VIEW OF
RADIATOR (1935)

FUEL TANK CAP

1934 VERSION

FIRE DAMAGE PREVENTED
RACING DURING 1936 SEASON

FRONT VIEW SHOWING 1934 RADIATOR AND
TRI-POD LANDING GEAR CONSTRUCTION

DESIGNED, BUILT & FLOWN BY STEVE WITTMAN. PLACED 2ND IN 1935
THOMPSON TROPHY RACE, 5TH IN 1937, 3RD IN 1938 AND 5TH IN 1939

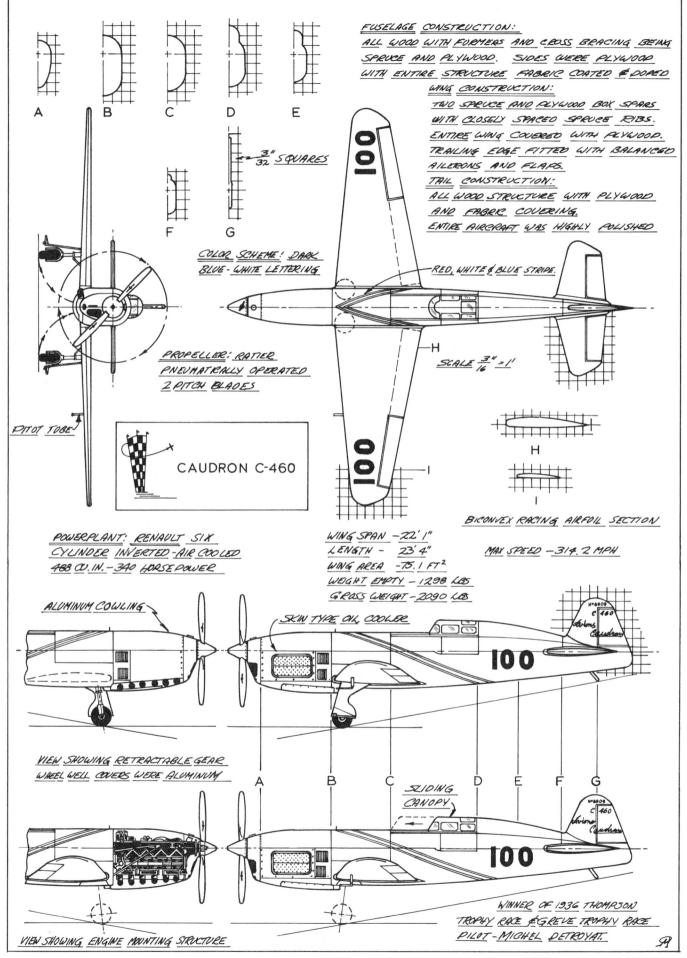

FUSELAGE CONSTRUCTION:
ALL WOOD WITH FORMERS AND CROSS BRACING BEING
SPRUCE AND PLYWOOD. SIDES WERE PLYWOOD
WITH ENTIRE STRUCTURE FABRIC COATED & DOPED

WING CONSTRUCTION:
TWO SPRUCE AND PLYWOOD BOX SPARS
WITH CLOSELY SPACED SPRUCE RIBS.
ENTIRE WING COVERED WITH PLYWOOD.
TRAILING EDGE FITTED WITH BALANCED
AILERONS AND FLAPS.

TAIL CONSTRUCTION:
ALL WOOD STRUCTURE WITH PLYWOOD
AND FABRIC COVERING.
ENTIRE AIRCRAFT WAS HIGHLY POLISHED

A   B   C   D   E

F   G

3/32" SQUARES

COLOR SCHEME: DARK
BLUE- WHITE LETTERING

RED, WHITE & BLUE STRIPE.

100

100

H

SCALE 3/16" = 1'

PROPELLER: RATIER
PNEUMATICALLY OPERATED
2 PITCH BLADES

PITOT TUBE

CAUDRON C-460

H

I

BICONVEX RACING AIRFOIL SECTION

POWERPLANT: RENAULT SIX
CYLINDER INVERTED- AIR COOLED
488 CU. IN. - 340 HORSEPOWER

WING SPAN - 22' 1"
LENGTH - 23' 4"
WING AREA - 75.1 FT²
WEIGHT EMPTY - 1298 LBS
GROSS WEIGHT - 2090 LBS

MAX SPEED - 314.2 MPH

ALUMINUM COWLING

SKIN TYPE OIL COOLER

100

VIEW SHOWING RETRACTABLE GEAR
WHEEL WELL COVERS WERE ALUMINUM

A   B   C   D   E   F   G

SLIDING
CANOPY

100

VIEW SHOWING ENGINE MOUNTING STRUCTURE

WINNER OF 1936 THOMPSON
TROPHY RACE & GREVE TROPHY RACE
PILOT- MICHEL DETROYAT.

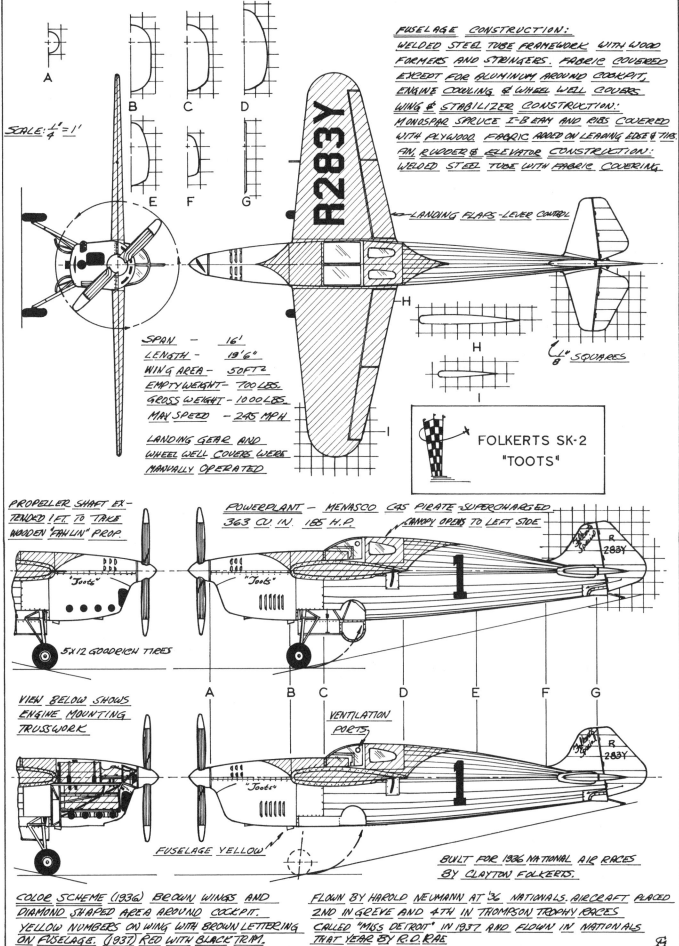

FUSELAGE CONSTRUCTION:
WELDED STEEL TUBE FRAMEWORK WITH WOOD FORMERS AND STRINGERS. FABRIC COVERED EXCEPT FOR ALUMINUM AROUND COCKPIT, ENGINE COWLING & WHEEL WELL COVERS
WING & STABILIZER CONSTRUCTION:
MONOSPAR SPRUCE I-BEAM AND RIBS COVERED WITH PLYWOOD. FABRIC ADDED ON LEADING EDGE & TIPS.
FIN, RUDDER & ELEVATOR CONSTRUCTION:
WELDED STEEL TUBE WITH FABRIC COVERING

SCALE: $\frac{1}{4}$" = 1'

A B C D E F G

LANDING FLAPS-LEVER CONTROL

H

$\frac{1}{8}$" SQUARES

H

I

SPAN — 16'
LENGTH — 19' 6"
WING AREA — 50 FT²
EMPTY WEIGHT — 700 LBS.
GROSS WEIGHT — 1000 LBS.
MAX SPEED — 245 MPH

LANDING GEAR AND WHEEL WELL COVERS WERE MANUALLY OPERATED

FOLKERTS SK-2 "TOOTS"

PROPELLER SHAFT EXTENDED 1 FT. TO TAKE WOODEN "FAHLIN" PROP.

POWERPLANT — MENASCO C4S PIRATE - SUPERCHARGED 363 CU. IN. 185 H.P.

CANOPY OPENS TO LEFT SIDE

"Toots"

"Toots"

1

R 283Y

5×12 GOODRICH TIRES

A B C D E F G

VIEW BELOW SHOWS ENGINE MOUNTING TRUSSWORK

VENTILATION PORTS

"Toots"

1

R 283Y

FUSELAGE YELLOW

BUILT FOR 1936 NATIONAL AIR RACES BY CLAYTON FOLKERTS.

COLOR SCHEME (1936) BROWN WINGS AND DIAMOND SHAPED AREA AROUND COCKPIT. YELLOW NUMBERS ON WING WITH BROWN LETTERING ON FUSELAGE. (1937) RED WITH BLACK TRIM.

FLOWN BY HAROLD NEUMANN AT '36 NATIONALS. AIRCRAFT PLACED 2ND IN GREVE AND 4TH IN THOMPSON TROPHY RACES CALLED "MISS DETROIT" IN 1937 AND FLOWN IN NATIONALS THAT YEAR BY R.O. RAE

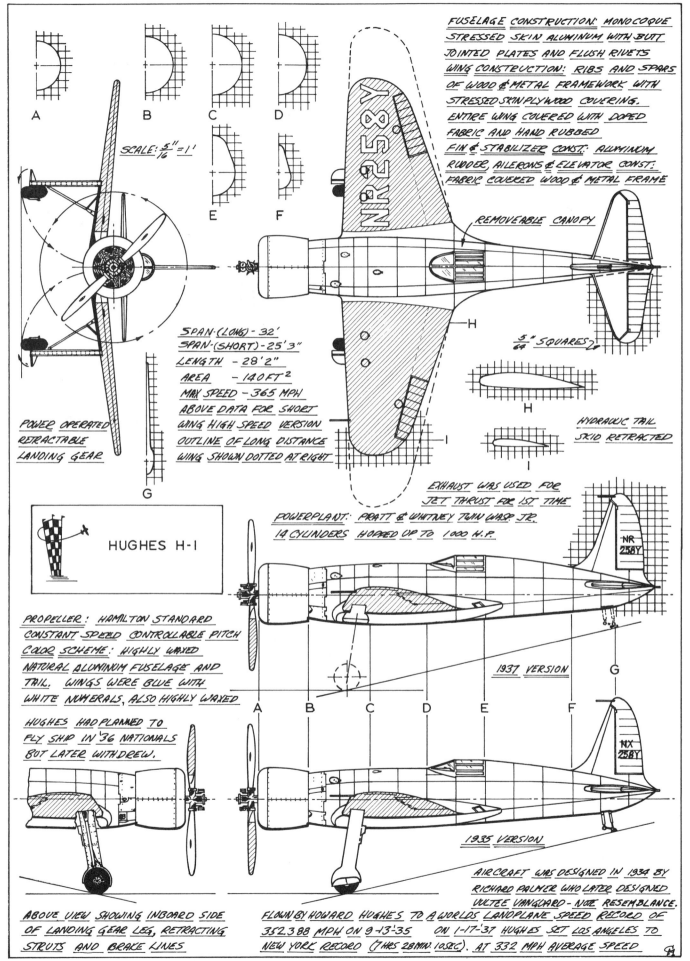

FUSELAGE CONSTRUCTION: MONOCOQUE STRESSED SKIN ALUMINUM WITH BUTT JOINTED PLATES AND FLUSH RIVETS
WING CONSTRUCTION: RIBS AND SPARS OF WOOD & METAL FRAMEWORK WITH STRESSED SKIN PLYWOOD COVERING. ENTIRE WING COVERED WITH DOPED FABRIC AND HAND RUBBED
FIN & STABILIZER CONST: ALUMINUM
RUDDER, AILERONS & ELEVATOR CONST: FABRIC COVERED WOOD & METAL FRAME

REMOVEABLE CANOPY

SCALE: $\frac{5}{16}$" = 1'

A B C D

E F

SPAN·(LONG) - 32'
SPAN·(SHORT) - 25' 3"
LENGTH - 28' 2"
AREA - 140 FT²
MAX SPEED - 365 MPH
ABOVE DATA FOR SHORT WING HIGH SPEED VERSION OUTLINE OF LONG DISTANCE WING SHOWN DOTTED AT RIGHT

POWER OPERATED RETRACTABLE LANDING GEAR

$\frac{5}{64}$" SQUARES

H

HYDRAULIC TAIL SKID RETRACTED

G

HUGHES H-1

EXHAUST WAS USED FOR JET THRUST FOR 1ST TIME

POWERPLANT: PRATT & WHITNEY TWIN WASP JR. 14 CYLINDERS HOPPED UP TO 1000 H.P.

PROPELLER: HAMILTON STANDARD CONSTANT SPEED CONTROLLABLE PITCH
COLOR SCHEME: HIGHLY WAXED NATURAL ALUMINUM FUSELAGE AND TAIL. WINGS WERE BLUE WITH WHITE NUMERALS, ALSO HIGHLY WAXED

HUGHES HAD PLANNED TO FLY SHIP IN '36 NATIONALS BUT LATER WITHDREW.

1937 VERSION

A B C D E F G

1935 VERSION

ABOVE VIEW SHOWING INBOARD SIDE OF LANDING GEAR LEG, RETRACTING STRUTS AND BRAKE LINES

AIRCRAFT WAS DESIGNED IN 1934 BY RICHARD PALMER WHO LATER DESIGNED VULTEE VANGUARD - NOTE RESEMBLANCE.
FLOWN BY HOWARD HUGHES TO A WORLDS LANDPLANE SPEED RECORD OF 352.388 MPH ON 9-13-'35 ON 1-17-'37 HUGHES SET LOS ANGELES TO NEW YORK RECORD (7 HRS 28 MIN. 10 SEC). AT 332 MPH AVERAGE SPEED

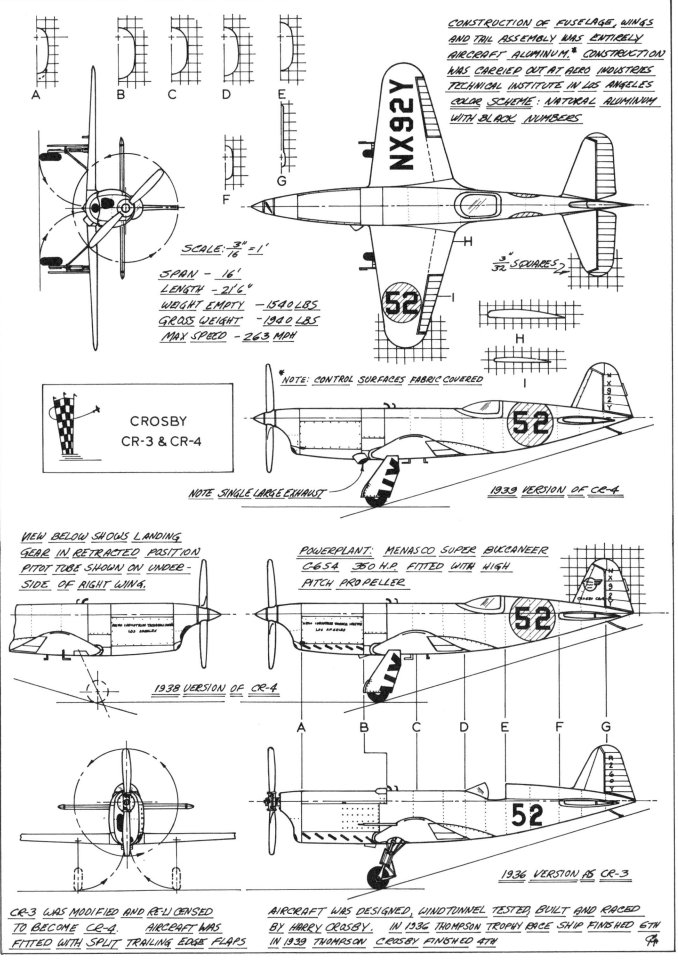

CONSTRUCTION OF FUSELAGE, WINGS AND TAIL ASSEMBLY WAS ENTIRELY AIRCRAFT ALUMINUM.* CONSTRUCTION WAS CARRIED OUT AT AERO INDUSTRIES TECHNICAL INSTITUTE IN LOS ANGELES COLOR SCHEME: NATURAL ALUMINUM WITH BLACK NUMBERS

SCALE: 3/16" = 1'

SPAN - 16'
LENGTH - 21'6"
WEIGHT EMPTY - 1540 LBS
GROSS WEIGHT - 1940 LBS
MAX SPEED - 263 MPH

3/32" SQUARES

*NOTE: CONTROL SURFACES FABRIC COVERED

CROSBY
CR-3 & CR-4

NOTE SINGLE LARGE EXHAUST

1939 VERSION OF CR-4

VIEW BELOW SHOWS LANDING GEAR IN RETRACTED POSITION PITOT TUBE SHOWN ON UNDER-SIDE OF RIGHT WING.

POWERPLANT: MENASCO SUPER BUCCANEER C-6S4 350 H.P. FITTED WITH HIGH PITCH PROPELLER

1938 VERSION OF CR-4

1936 VERSION AS CR-3

CR-3 WAS MODIFIED AND RE-LICENSED TO BECOME CR-4. AIRCRAFT WAS FITTED WITH SPLIT TRAILING EDGE FLAPS

AIRCRAFT WAS DESIGNED, WINDTUNNEL TESTED, BUILT AND RACED BY HARRY CROSBY. IN 1936 THOMPSON TROPHY RACE SHIP FINISHED 6TH IN 1939 THOMPSON CROSBY FINISHED 4TH

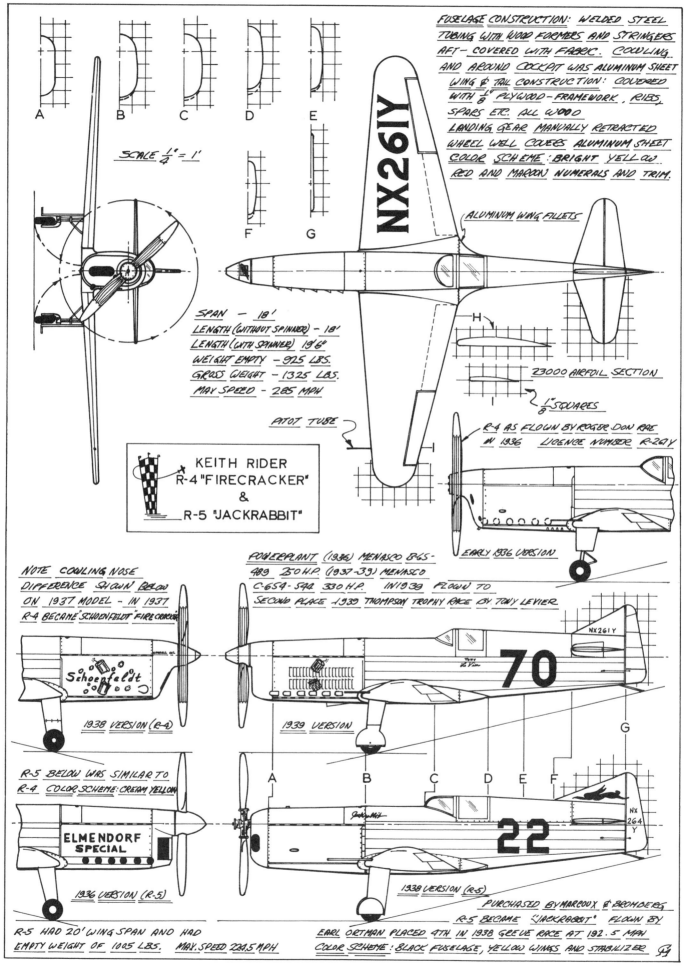

FUSELAGE CONSTRUCTION: WELDED STEEL TUBING WITH WOOD FORMERS AND STRINGERS AFT - COVERED WITH FABRIC. COWLING AND AROUND COCKPIT WAS ALUMINUM SHEET
WING & TAIL CONSTRUCTION: COVERED WITH $\frac{1}{8}$" PLYWOOD - FRAMEWORK, RIBS, SPARS ETC. ALL WOOD
LANDING GEAR MANUALLY RETRACTED
WHEEL WELL COVERS ALUMINUM SHEET
COLOR SCHEME: BRIGHT YELLOW
RED AND MAROON NUMERALS AND TRIM.

A B C D E

F G

SCALE $\frac{1}{4}$" = 1'

NX26IY

ALUMINUM WING FILLETS

SPAN — 18'
LENGTH (WITHOUT SPINNER) — 18'
LENGTH (WITH SPINNER) 19'6"
WEIGHT EMPTY — 925 LBS.
GROSS WEIGHT — 1325 LBS.
MAX SPEED — 285 MPH

H

23000 AIRFOIL SECTION

$\frac{1}{8}$" SQUARES

PITOT TUBE

R-4 AS FLOWN BY ROGER DON RAE IN 1936   LICENCE NUMBER R-26IY

KEITH RIDER
R-4 "FIRECRACKER"
&
R-5 "JACKRABBIT"

EARLY 1936 VERSION

NOTE COWLING NOSE DIFFERENCE SHOWN BELOW ON 1937 MODEL - IN 1937 R-4 BECAME 'SCHOENFELDT' FIRE CRACKER

POWERPLANT (1936) MENASCO B-65-489 250 H.P. (1937-39) MENASCO C-6S4-S4A 330 H.P. IN 1939 FLOWN TO SECOND PLACE 1939 THOMPSON TROPHY RACE BY TONY LEVIER

NX26IY

70

Schoenfeldt

1938 VERSION (R-4)

1939 VERSION

A   B   C   D E F   G

R-5 BELOW WAS SIMILAR TO R-4 COLOR SCHEME: CREAM YELLOW

ELMENDORF SPECIAL

Jackrabbit

22

NX 264 Y

1936 VERSION (R-5)

1938 VERSION (R-5)

R-5 HAD 20' WING SPAN AND HAD EMPTY WEIGHT OF 1005 LBS. MAX. SPEED 224.5 MPH

PURCHASED BY MARCOUX & BROMBERG R-5 BECAME "JACKRABBIT" FLOWN BY EARL ORTMAN PLACED 4TH IN 1938 GREVE RACE AT 192.5 MPH COLOR SCHEME: BLACK FUSELAGE, YELLOW WINGS AND STABILIZER

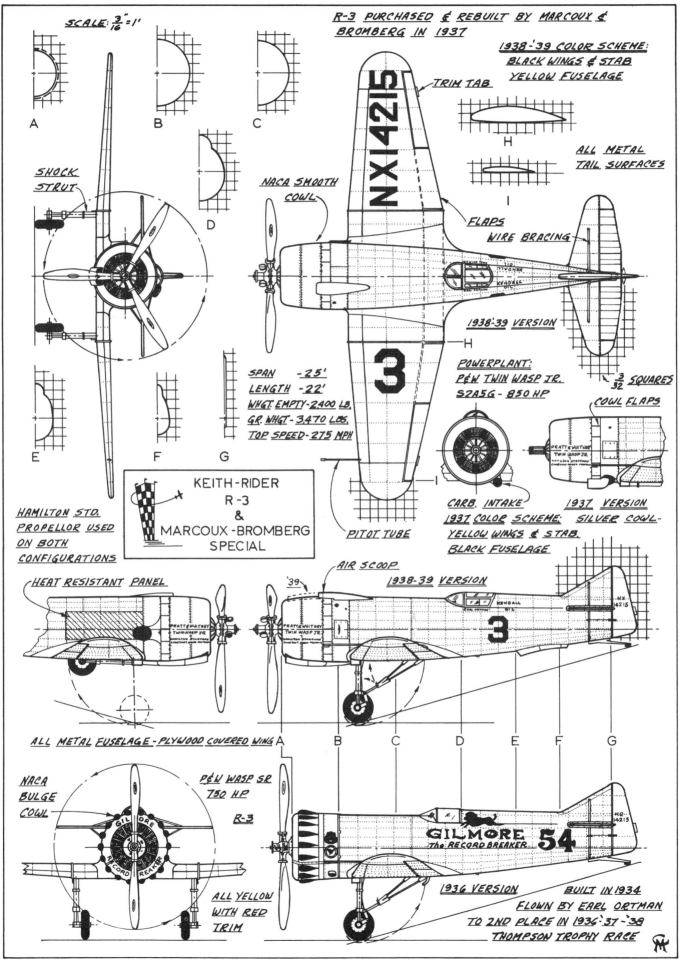

SCALE: $\frac{3}{16}$" = 1'

A   B   C

D

SHOCK STRUT

E   F   G

R-3 PURCHASED & REBUILT BY MARCOUX & BROMBERG IN 1937

1938-'39 COLOR SCHEME:
BLACK WINGS & STAB
YELLOW FUSELAGE

TRIM TAB

NX14215

NACA SMOOTH COWL

H

ALL METAL TAIL SURFACES

I

FLAPS

WIRE BRACING

3

1938-'39 VERSION

H

$\frac{3}{32}$ SQUARES

SPAN - 25'
LENGTH - 22'
WHGT. EMPTY - 2,400 LB.
GR. WHGT. - 3,470 LBS.
TOP SPEED - 275 MPH

POWERPLANT:
P&W TWIN WASP JR.
S2A5G - 850 HP

COWL FLAPS

I

PITOT TUBE

CARB. INTAKE

1937 VERSION

1937 COLOR SCHEME: SILVER COWL-
YELLOW WINGS & STAB.
BLACK FUSELAGE

KEITH-RIDER
R-3
&
MARCOUX-BROMBERG
SPECIAL

HAMILTON STD. PROPELLOR USED ON BOTH CONFIGURATIONS

HEAT RESISTANT PANEL

AIR SCOOP

'39

1938-39 VERSION

3

NX-14215

ALL METAL FUSELAGE - PLYWOOD COVERED WING

A   B   C   D   E   F   G

NACA BULGE COWL

P&W WASP SR. 750 HP

R-3

GILMORE
The RECORD BREAKER
54

NR-14215

ALL YELLOW WITH RED TRIM

1936 VERSION

BUILT IN 1934
FLOWN BY EARL ORTMAN
TO 2ND PLACE IN 1936-37-38
THOMPSON TROPHY RACE

90

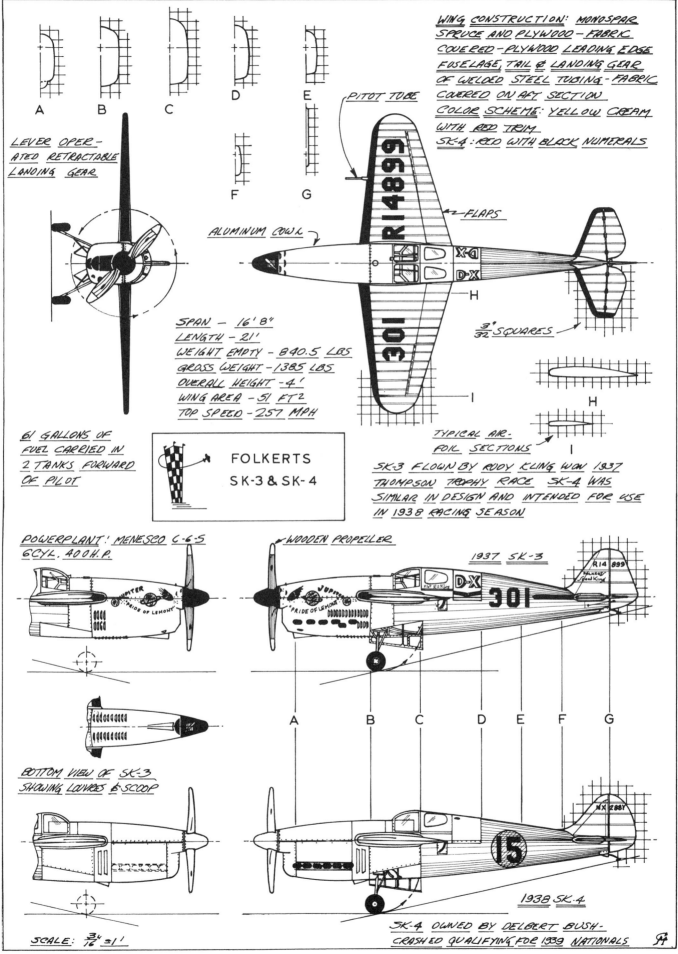

WING CONSTRUCTION: MONOSPAR
SPRUCE AND PLYWOOD - FABRIC
COVERED - PLYWOOD LEADING EDGE
FUSELAGE, TAIL & LANDING GEAR
OF WELDED STEEL TUBING - FABRIC
COVERED ON AFT SECTION
COLOR SCHEME: YELLOW CREAM
WITH RED TRIM
SK-4: RED WITH BLACK NUMERALS

PITOT TUBE

A B C D E
F G

LEVER OPER-
ATED RETRACTABLE
LANDING GEAR

ALUMINUM COWL

R14899

FLAPS

D-X

H

301

I

3/32" SQUARES

SPAN — 16' 8"
LENGTH — 21'
WEIGHT EMPTY — 840.5 LBS
GROSS WEIGHT — 1385 LBS
OVERALL HEIGHT — 4'
WING AREA — 51 FT²
TOP SPEED — 257 MPH

H

TYPICAL AIR-
FOIL SECTIONS

I

61 GALLONS OF
FUEL CARRIED IN
2 TANKS FORWARD
OF PILOT

FOLKERTS
SK-3 & SK-4

SK-3 FLOWN BY RUDY KLING WON 1937
THOMPSON TROPHY RACE SK-4 WAS
SIMILAR IN DESIGN AND INTENDED FOR USE
IN 1938 RACING SEASON

POWERPLANT: MENESCO C-6-S
6 CYL. 400 H.P.

WOODEN PROPELLER

1937 SK-3

R14899

JUPITER
PRIDE OF LEMONT

D-X

301

A B C D E F G

BOTTOM VIEW OF SK-3
SHOWING LOUVRES & SCOOP

NX288Y

15

1938 SK-4

SCALE: 3/16" = 1'

SK-4 OWNED BY DELBERT BUSH-
CRASHED QUALIFYING FOR 1939 NATIONALS

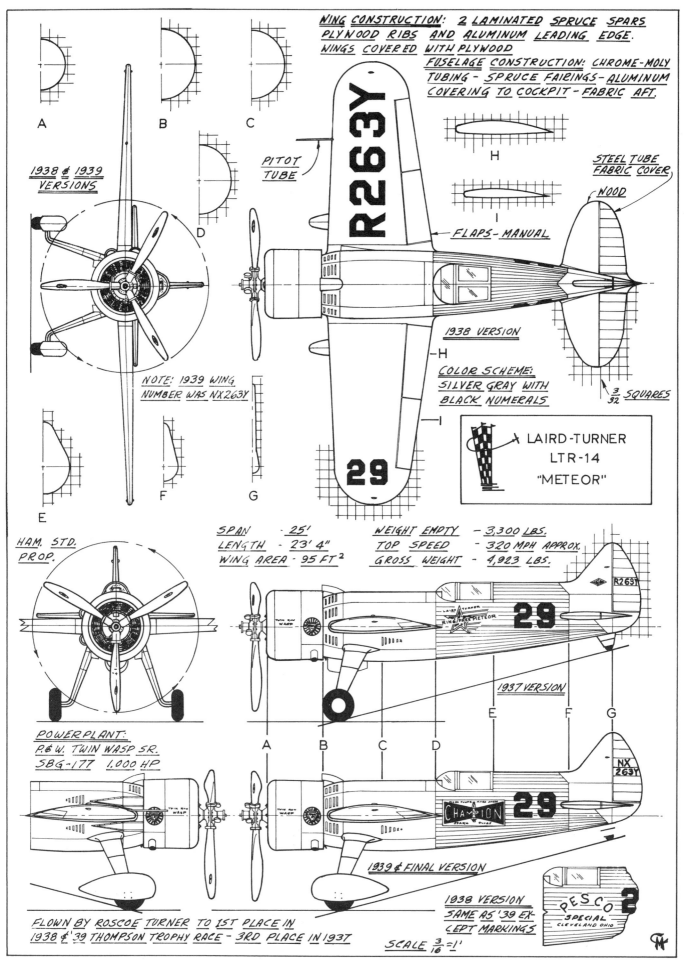

WING CONSTRUCTION: 2 LAMINATED SPRUCE SPARS PLYWOOD RIBS AND ALUMINUM LEADING EDGE. WINGS COVERED WITH PLYWOOD

FUSELAGE CONSTRUCTION: CHROME-MOLY TUBING - SPRUCE FAIRINGS - ALUMINUM COVERING TO COCKPIT - FABRIC AFT.

A

B

C

D

1938 & 1939 VERSIONS

PITOT TUBE

H

I

STEEL TUBE FABRIC COVER

WOOD

FLAPS - MANUAL

1938 VERSION

E

NOTE: 1939 WING NUMBER WAS NX263Y

COLOR SCHEME: SILVER GRAY WITH BLACK NUMERALS

3/32 SQUARES

F

G

LAIRD-TURNER LTR-14 "METEOR"

HAM. STD. PROP.

SPAN - 25'
LENGTH - 23' 4"
WING AREA - 95 FT²

WEIGHT EMPTY - 3,300 LBS.
TOP SPEED - 320 MPH APPROX.
GROSS WEIGHT - 4,923 LBS.

R263Y

29

TWIN ROW WASP

1937 VERSION

A   B   C   D   E   F   G

POWERPLANT: P.& W. TWIN WASP SR. SBG-177 1,000 HP

NX 263Y

CHAMPION

29

1939 & FINAL VERSION

FLOWN BY ROSCOE TURNER TO 1ST PLACE IN 1938 & '39 THOMPSON TROPHY RACE - 3RD PLACE IN 1937

1938 VERSION SAME AS '39 EXCEPT MARKINGS

SCALE 3/16 = 1'

PESCO SPECIAL CLEVELAND OHIO

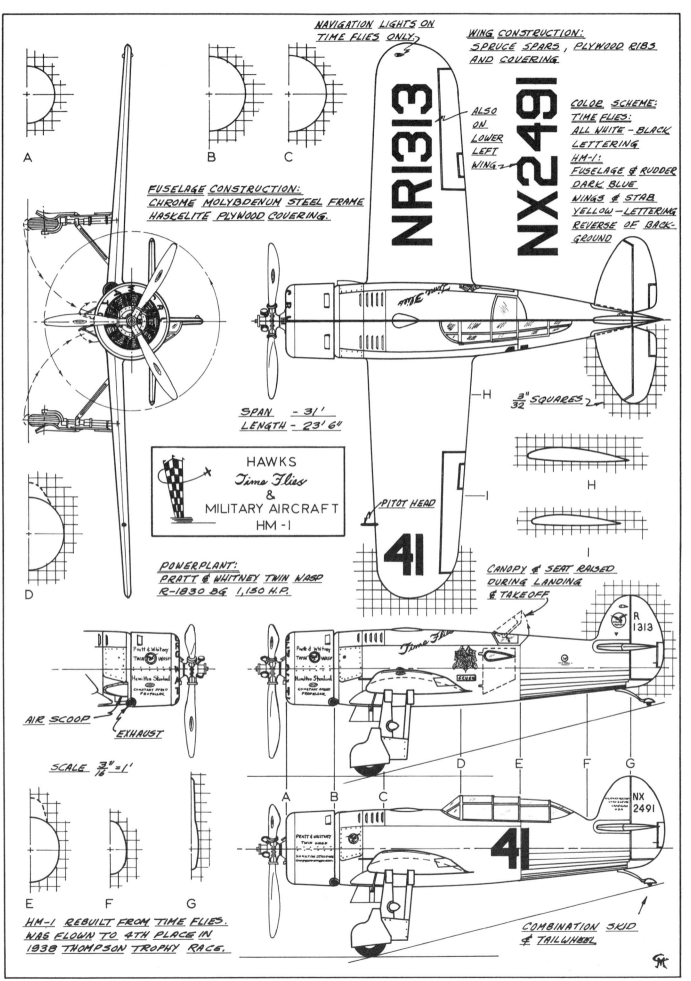

NAVIGATION LIGHTS ON
TIME FLIES ONLY

WING CONSTRUCTION:
SPRUCE SPARS, PLYWOOD RIBS
AND COVERING

NR1313

NX2491

ALSO
ON
LOWER
LEFT
WING

COLOR SCHEME:
TIME FLIES:
ALL WHITE - BLACK
LETTERING
HM-1:
FUSELAGE & RUDDER
DARK BLUE
WINGS & STAB.
YELLOW - LETTERING
REVERSE OF BACK-
GROUND

FUSELAGE CONSTRUCTION:
CHROME MOLYBDENUM STEEL FRAME
HASKELITE PLYWOOD COVERING.

A

B

C

D

SPAN - 31'
LENGTH - 23' 6"

H

3/32" SQUARES

HAWKS
Time Flies
&
MILITARY AIRCRAFT
HM-1

H

I

PITOT HEAD

I

41

POWERPLANT:
PRATT & WHITNEY TWIN WASP
R-1830 BG 1,150 H.P.

CANOPY & SEAT RAISED
DURING LANDING
& TAKEOFF

Pratt & Whitney TWIN WASP
Hamilton Standard CONSTANT SPEED PROPELLER

R
1313

AIR SCOOP

EXHAUST

SCALE 3/16" = 1'

E

F

G

A

B

C

D

E

F

G

NX
2491

41

HM-1 REBUILT FROM TIME FLIES.
WAS FLOWN TO 4TH PLACE IN
1938 THOMPSON TROPHY RACE.

COMBINATION SKID
& TAILWHEEL

GM

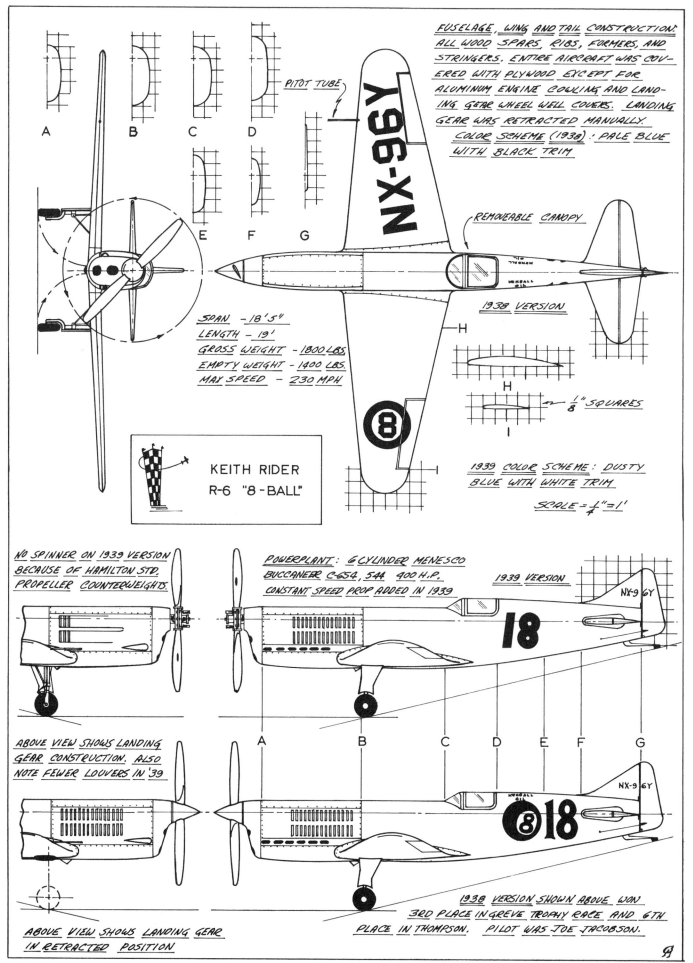

FUSELAGE, WING AND TAIL CONSTRUCTION:
ALL WOOD SPARS, RIBS, FORMERS, AND
STRINGERS. ENTIRE AIRCRAFT WAS COV-
ERED WITH PLYWOOD EXCEPT FOR
ALUMINUM ENGINE COWLING AND LAND-
ING GEAR WHEEL WELL COVERS. LANDING
GEAR WAS RETRACTED MANUALLY.
COLOR SCHEME (1938): PALE BLUE
WITH BLACK TRIM

PITOT TUBE

NX-96Y

REMOVEABLE CANOPY

1938 VERSION

A B C D

E F G

SPAN - 18' 5"
LENGTH - 19'
GROSS WEIGHT - 1800 LBS.
EMPTY WEIGHT - 1400 LBS.
MAX SPEED - 230 MPH

H

H

I ⅛" SQUARES

1939 COLOR SCHEME: DUSTY
BLUE WITH WHITE TRIM

SCALE = ¼" = 1'

KEITH RIDER
R-6 "8-BALL"

NO SPINNER ON 1939 VERSION
BECAUSE OF HAMILTON STD.
PROPELLER COUNTERWEIGHTS.

POWERPLANT: 6 CYLINDER MENESCO
BUCCANEER C-654, 544, 400 H.P.
CONSTANT SPEED PROP ADDED IN 1939

1939 VERSION

NX-96Y

18

ABOVE VIEW SHOWS LANDING
GEAR CONSTRUCTION. ALSO
NOTE FEWER LOUVERS IN '39

A B C D E F G

NX-96Y

8 18

ABOVE VIEW SHOWS LANDING GEAR
IN RETRACTED POSITION

1938 VERSION SHOWN ABOVE WON
3RD PLACE IN GREVE TROPHY RACE AND 6TH
PLACE IN THOMPSON. PILOT WAS JOE JACOBSON.

94

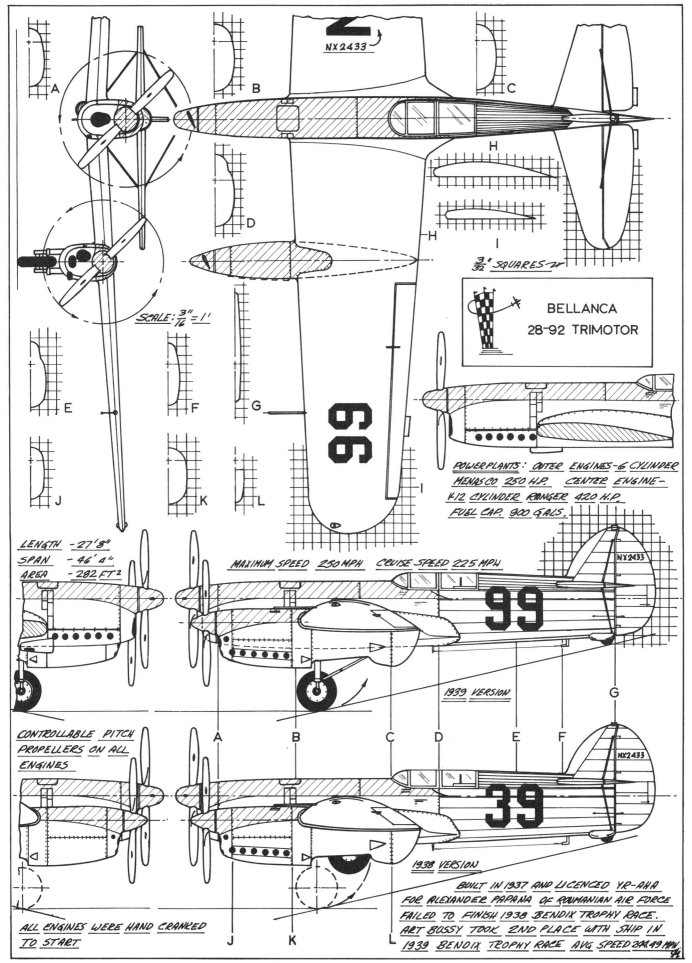

NX2433

$\frac{3}{32}$" SQUARES

SCALE: $\frac{3}{16}$" = 1'

BELLANCA
28-92 TRIMOTOR

POWERPLANTS: OUTER ENGINES-6 CYLINDER MENASCO 250 H.P. CENTER ENGINE-V-12 CYLINDER RANGER 420 H.P. FUEL CAP. 900 GALS.

LENGTH - 27'8"
SPAN - 46'4"
AREA - 282 FT²

MAXIMUM SPEED 250 MPH   CRUISE SPEED 225 MPH

1939 VERSION

CONTROLLABLE PITCH PROPELLERS ON ALL ENGINES

ALL ENGINES WERE HAND CRANKED TO START

1938 VERSION

BUILT IN 1937 AND LICENCED YR-AHA FOR ALEXANDER PAPANA OF ROUMANIAN AIR FORCE. FAILED TO FINISH 1938 BENDIX TROPHY RACE. ART BUSSY TOOK 2ND PLACE WITH SHIP IN 1939 BENDIX TROPHY RACE. AVG SPEED 244.49 MPH.

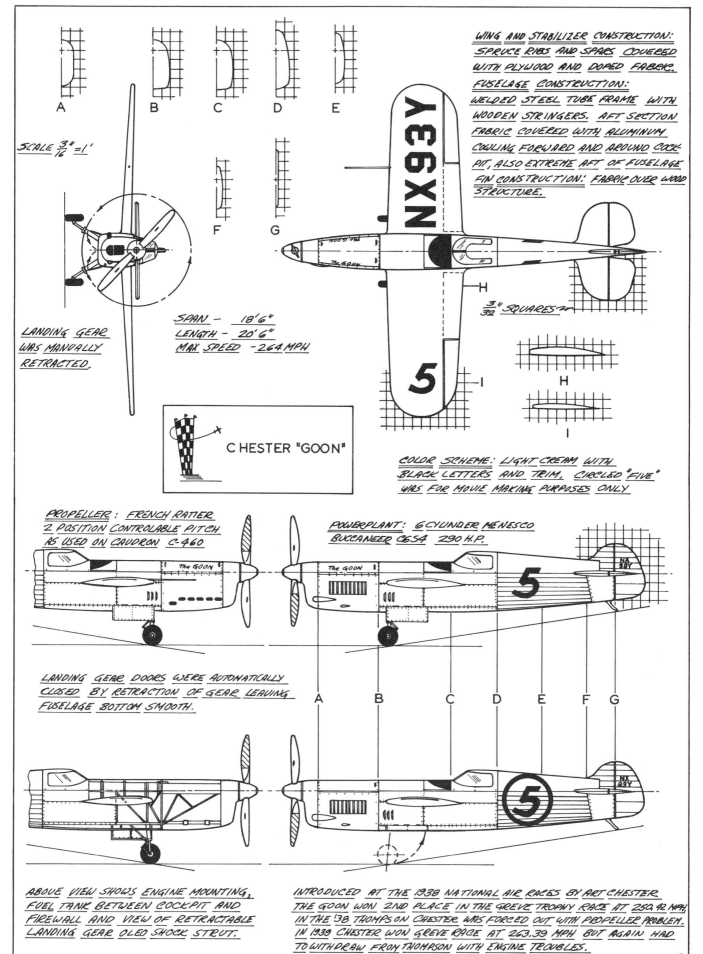

WING AND STABILIZER CONSTRUCTION: SPRUCE RIBS AND SPARS COVERED WITH PLYWOOD AND DOPED FABRIC. FUSELAGE CONSTRUCTION: WELDED STEEL TUBE FRAME WITH WOODEN STRINGERS. AFT SECTION FABRIC COVERED WITH ALUMINUM COWLING FORWARD AND AROUND COCKPIT, ALSO EXTREME AFT OF FUSELAGE FIN CONSTRUCTION: FABRIC OVER WOOD STRUCTURE.

A B C D E

F G

SCALE 3/16" = 1'

LANDING GEAR WAS MANUALLY RETRACTED.

SPAN - 18' 6"
LENGTH - 20' 6"
MAX SPEED - 264 MPH

NX93Y

5

H

3/32 SQUARES

H

I

CHESTER "GOON"

COLOR SCHEME: LIGHT CREAM WITH BLACK LETTERS AND TRIM. CIRCLED "FIVE" WAS FOR MOVIE MAKING PURPOSES ONLY

PROPELLER: FRENCH RATIER 2 POSITION CONTROLABLE PITCH AS USED ON CAUDRON C-460

The GOON

POWERPLANT: 6 CYLINDER MENESCO BUCCANEER C6S4 290 H.P.

The GOON

5

NX 93Y

LANDING GEAR DOORS WERE AUTOMATICALLY CLOSED BY RETRACTION OF GEAR LEAVING FUSELAGE BOTTOM SMOOTH.

A B C D E F G

NX 93Y

5

ABOVE VIEW SHOWS ENGINE MOUNTING, FUEL TANK BETWEEN COCKPIT AND FIREWALL AND VIEW OF RETRACTABLE LANDING GEAR OLEO SHOCK STRUT.

INTRODUCED AT THE 1938 NATIONAL AIR RACES BY ART CHESTER THE GOON WON 2ND PLACE IN THE GREVE TROPHY RACE AT 250.42 MPH. IN THE '38 THOMPSON CHESTER WAS FORCED OUT WITH PROPELLER PROBLEM. IN 1939 CHESTER WON GREVE RACE AT 263.39 MPH BUT AGAIN HAD TO WITHDRAW FROM THOMPSON WITH ENGINE TROUBLES.

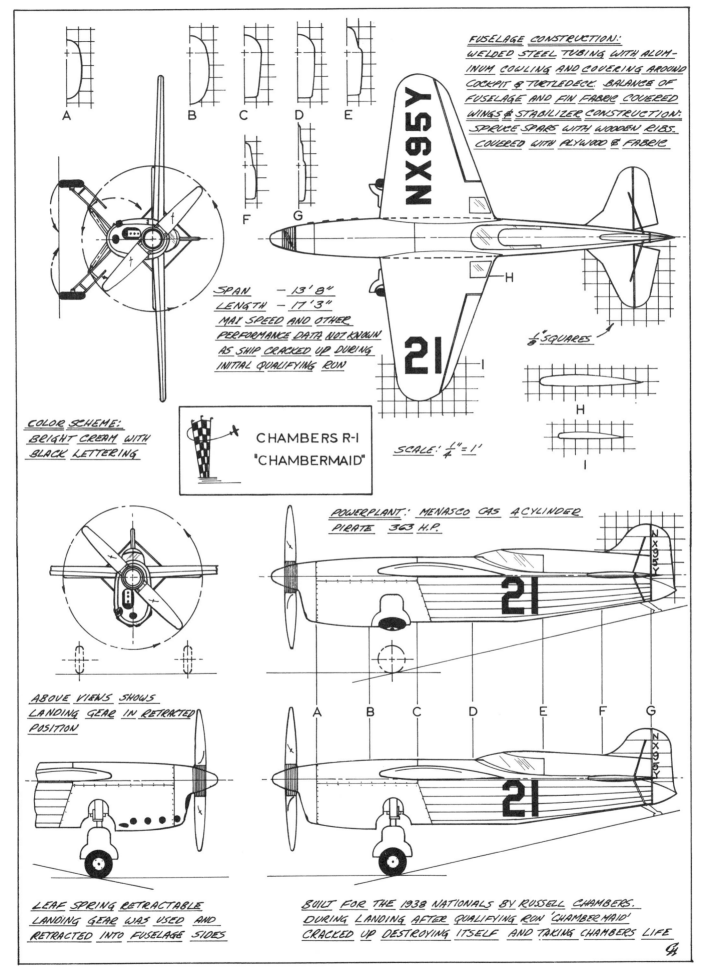

FUSELAGE CONSTRUCTION:
WELDED STEEL TUBING WITH ALUM-
INUM COWLING AND COVERING AROUND
COCKPIT & TURTLEDECK. BALANCE OF
FUSELAGE AND FIN FABRIC COVERED
WINGS & STABILIZER CONSTRUCTION:
SPRUCE SPARS WITH WOODEN RIBS.
COVERED WITH PLYWOOD & FABRIC

A   B   C   D   E

F   G

NX95Y

21

SPAN — 13' 8"
LENGTH — 17' 3"
MAX SPEED AND OTHER
PERFORMANCE DATA NOT KNOWN
AS SHIP CRACKED UP DURING
INITIAL QUALIFYING RUN

1/8" SQUARES

H

H

I

COLOR SCHEME:
BRIGHT CREAM WITH
BLACK LETTERING

CHAMBERS R-I
"CHAMBERMAID"

SCALE: 1/4" = 1'

POWERPLANT: MENASCO C4S 4 CYLINDER
PIRATE 363 H.P.

NX95Y

21

ABOVE VIEWS SHOWS
LANDING GEAR IN RETRACTED
POSITION

A   B   C   D   E   F   G

NX95Y

21

LEAF SPRING RETRACTABLE
LANDING GEAR WAS USED AND
RETRACTED INTO FUSELAGE SIDES

BUILT FOR THE 1938 NATIONALS BY RUSSELL CHAMBERS.
DURING LANDING AFTER QUALIFYING RUN 'CHAMBERMAID'
CRACKED UP DESTROYING ITSELF AND TAKING CHAMBERS LIFE

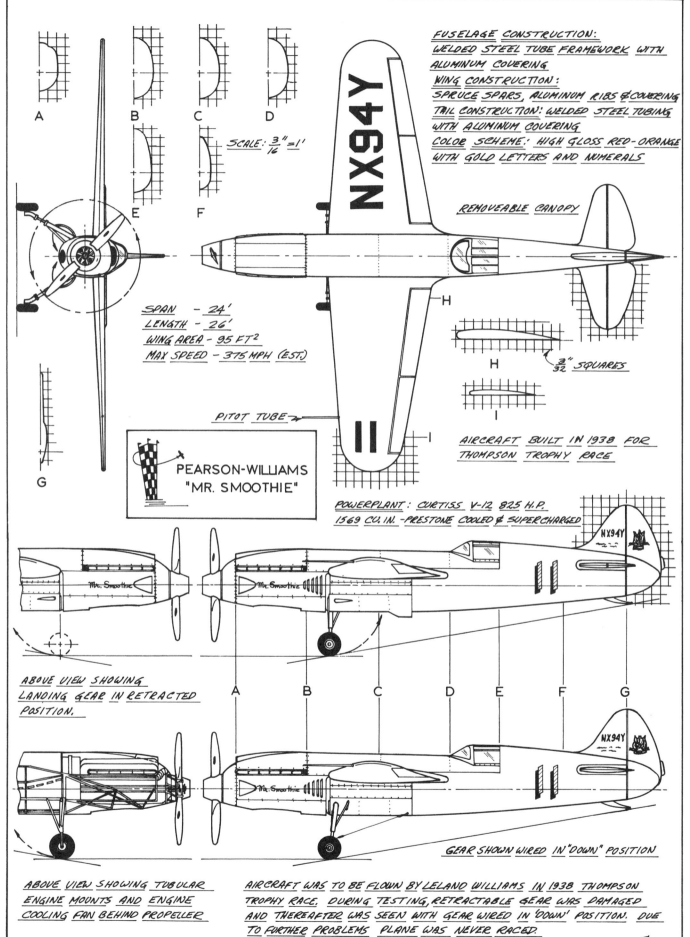

FUSELAGE CONSTRUCTION:
WELDED STEEL TUBE FRAMEWORK WITH
ALUMINUM COVERING
WING CONSTRUCTION:
SPRUCE SPARS, ALUMINUM RIBS & COVERING
TAIL CONSTRUCTION: WELDED STEEL TUBING
WITH ALUMINUM COVERING
COLOR SCHEME: HIGH GLOSS RED-ORANGE
WITH GOLD LETTERS AND NUMERALS

REMOVEABLE CANOPY

A B C D

E F

SCALE: $\frac{3}{16}" = 1'$

SPAN - 24'
LENGTH - 26'
WING AREA - 95 FT²
MAX SPEED - 375 MPH (EST.)

$\frac{3}{32}"$ SQUARES

H H

I

PITOT TUBE

G

PEARSON-WILLIAMS
"MR. SMOOTHIE"

NX94Y

AIRCRAFT BUILT IN 1938 FOR
THOMPSON TROPHY RACE

POWERPLANT: CURTISS V-12 825 H.P.
1569 CU. IN. - PRESTONE COOLED & SUPERCHARGED

Mr. Smoothie

NX94Y

A B C D E F G

ABOVE VIEW SHOWING
LANDING GEAR IN RETRACTED
POSITION.

NX94Y

Mr. Smoothie

GEAR SHOWN WIRED IN "DOWN" POSITION

ABOVE VIEW SHOWING TUBULAR
ENGINE MOUNTS AND ENGINE
COOLING FAN BEHIND PROPELLER

AIRCRAFT WAS TO BE FLOWN BY LELAND WILLIAMS IN 1938 THOMPSON
TROPHY RACE. DURING TESTING, RETRACTABLE GEAR WAS DAMAGED
AND THEREAFTER WAS SEEN WITH GEAR WIRED IN 'DOWN' POSITION. DUE
TO FURTHER PROBLEMS PLANE WAS NEVER RACED.

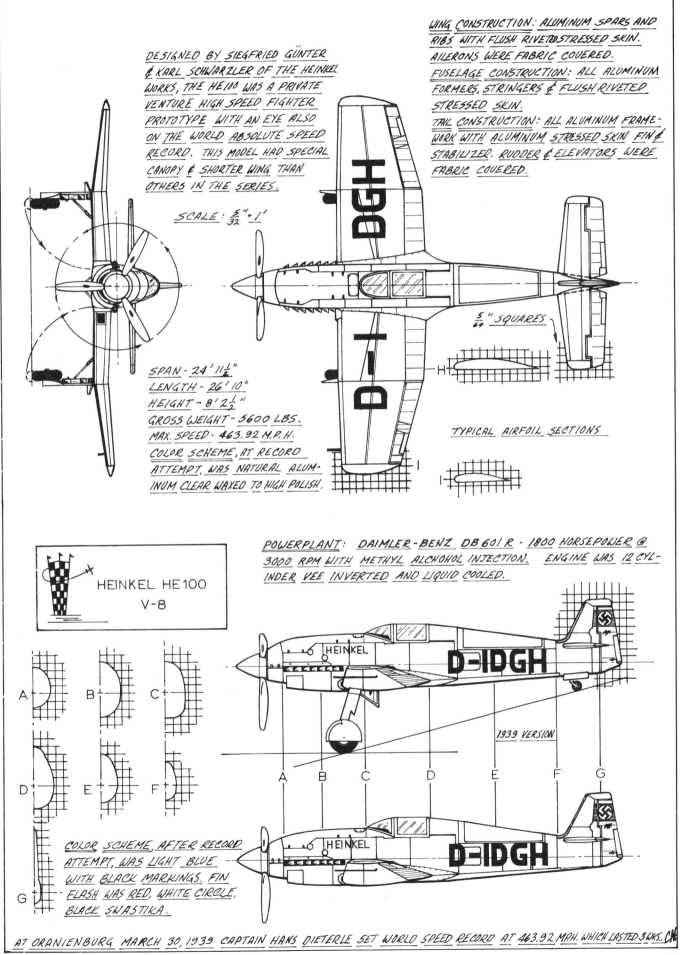

DESIGNED BY SIEGFRIED GÜNTER & KARL SCHWARZLER OF THE HEINKEL WORKS, THE HE100 WAS A PRIVATE VENTURE HIGH SPEED FIGHTER PROTOTYPE WITH AN EYE ALSO ON THE WORLD ABSOLUTE SPEED RECORD. THIS MODEL HAD SPECIAL CANOPY & SHORTER WING THAN OTHERS IN THE SERIES.

SCALE: $\frac{5}{32}$" = 1'

WING CONSTRUCTION: ALUMINUM SPARS AND RIBS WITH FLUSH RIVETED STRESSED SKIN. AILERONS WERE FABRIC COVERED.
FUSELAGE CONSTRUCTION: ALL ALUMINUM FORMERS, STRINGERS & FLUSH RIVETED STRESSED SKIN.
TAIL CONSTRUCTION: ALL ALUMINUM FRAMEWORK WITH ALUMINUM STRESSED SKIN FIN & STABILIZER. RUDDER & ELEVATORS WERE FABRIC COVERED.

$\frac{5}{64}$" SQUARES

SPAN - 24' 11½"
LENGTH - 26' 10"
HEIGHT - 8' 2½"
GROSS WEIGHT - 5600 LBS.
MAX. SPEED - 463.92 M.P.H.
COLOR SCHEME, AT RECORD ATTEMPT, WAS NATURAL ALUMINUM CLEAR WAXED TO HIGH POLISH.

TYPICAL AIRFOIL SECTIONS

HEINKEL HE 100
V-8

POWERPLANT: DAIMLER-BENZ DB 601 R - 1800 HORSEPOWER @ 3000 RPM WITH METHYL ALCHOHOL INJECTION. ENGINE WAS 12 CYLINDER VEE INVERTED AND LIQUID COOLED.

HEINKEL

D-IDGH

1939 VERSION

A   B   C   D   E   F   G

HEINKEL

D-IDGH

COLOR SCHEME, AFTER RECORD ATTEMPT, WAS LIGHT BLUE WITH BLACK MARKINGS. FIN FLASH WAS RED, WHITE CIRCLE, BLACK SWASTIKA.

AT ORANIENBURG MARCH 30, 1939 CAPTAIN HANS DIETERLE SET WORLD SPEED RECORD AT 463.92 M.P.H. WHICH LASTED 3 MOS.

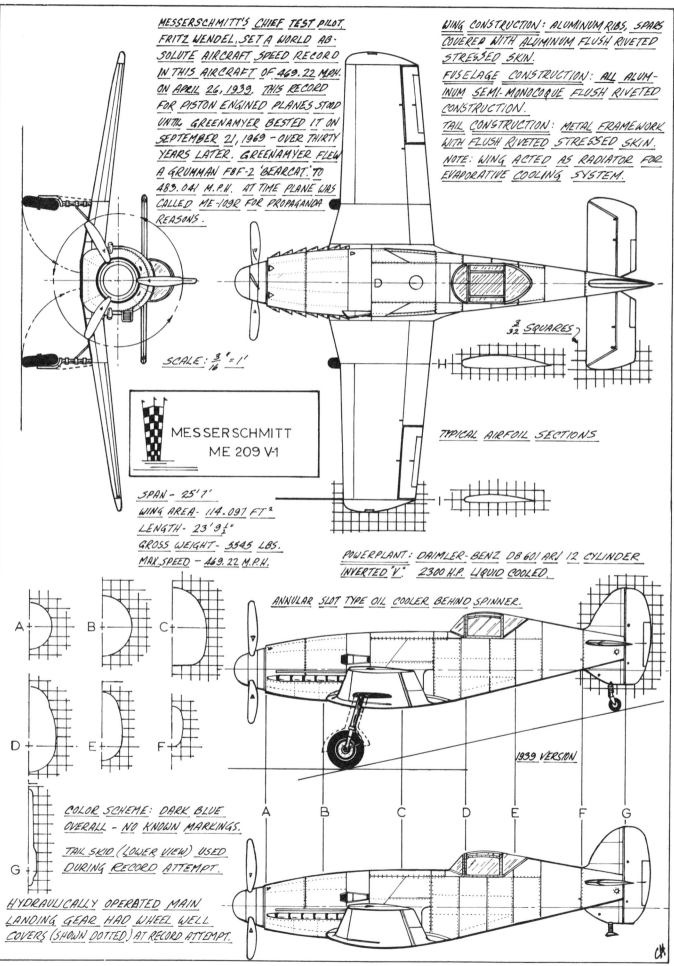

MESSERSCHMITT'S CHIEF TEST PILOT, FRITZ WENDEL, SET A WORLD ABSOLUTE AIRCRAFT SPEED RECORD IN THIS AIRCRAFT OF 469.22 M.P.H. ON APRIL 26, 1939. THIS RECORD FOR PISTON ENGINED PLANES STOOD UNTIL GREENAMYER BESTED IT ON SEPTEMBER 21, 1969 – OVER THIRTY YEARS LATER. GREENAMYER FLEW A GRUMMAN F8F-2 'BEARCAT' TO 483.041 M.P.H. AT TIME PLANE WAS CALLED ME-109R FOR PROPAGANDA REASONS.

WING CONSTRUCTION: ALUMINUM RIBS, SPARS COVERED WITH ALUMINUM FLUSH RIVETED STRESSED SKIN.
FUSELAGE CONSTRUCTION: ALL ALUMINUM SEMI-MONOCOQUE FLUSH RIVETED CONSTRUCTION.
TAIL CONSTRUCTION: METAL FRAMEWORK WITH FLUSH RIVETED STRESSED SKIN.
NOTE: WING ACTED AS RADIATOR FOR EVAPORATIVE COOLING SYSTEM.

SCALE: $\frac{3}{16}$" = 1'

MESSERSCHMITT ME 209 V-1

SPAN – 25' 7'
WING AREA – 114.097 FT²
LENGTH – 23' 9½"
GROSS WEIGHT – 5545 LBS.
MAX. SPEED – 469.22 M.P.H.

$\frac{3}{32}$ SQUARES

TYPICAL AIRFOIL SECTIONS

POWERPLANT: DAIMLER-BENZ DB 601 ARJ 12 CYLINDER INVERTED "V". 2300 H.P. LIQUID COOLED.

ANNULAR SLOT TYPE OIL COOLER BEHIND SPINNER.

1939 VERSION

COLOR SCHEME: DARK BLUE OVERALL – NO KNOWN MARKINGS.

TAIL SKID (LOWER VIEW) USED DURING RECORD ATTEMPT.

HYDRAULICALLY OPERATED MAIN LANDING GEAR HAD WHEEL WELL COVERS (SHOWN DOTTED) AT RECORD ATTEMPT.

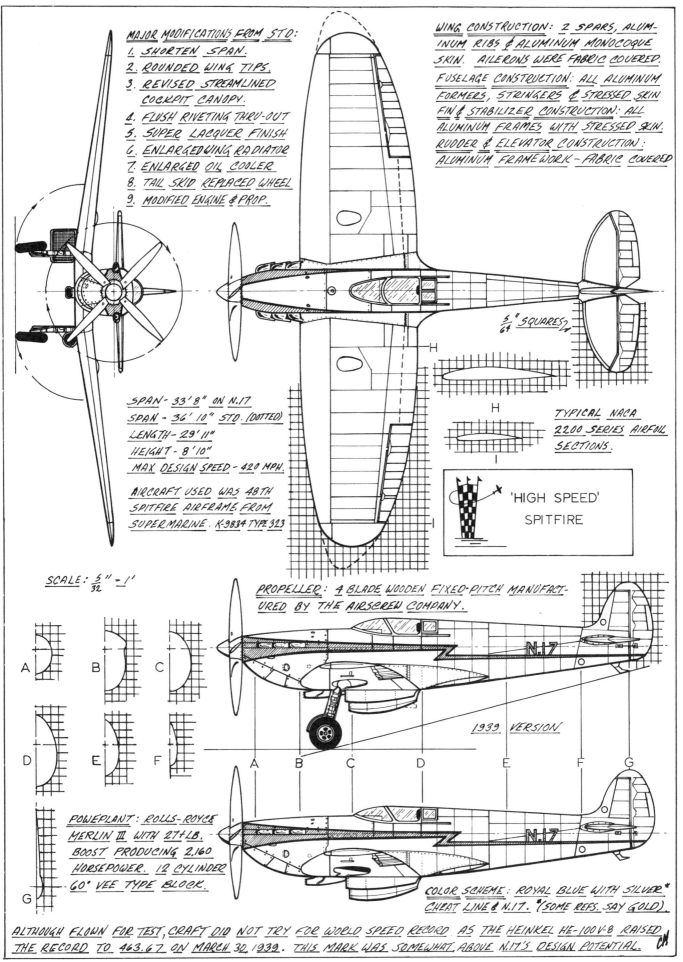

MAJOR MODIFICATIONS FROM STD:
1. SHORTEN SPAN.
2. ROUNDED WING TIPS.
3. REVISED STREAMLINED COCKPIT CANOPY.
4. FLUSH RIVETING THRU-OUT
5. SUPER LACQUER FINISH
6. ENLARGED WING RADIATOR
7. ENLARGED OIL COOLER
8. TAIL SKID REPLACED WHEEL
9. MODIFIED ENGINE & PROP.

WING CONSTRUCTION: 2 SPARS, ALUMINUM RIBS & ALUMINUM MONOCOQUE SKIN. AILERONS WERE FABRIC COVERED.
FUSELAGE CONSTRUCTION: ALL ALUMINUM FORMERS, STRINGERS & STRESSED SKIN
FIN & STABILIZER CONSTRUCTION: ALL ALUMINUM FRAMES WITH STRESSED SKIN.
RUDDER & ELEVATOR CONSTRUCTION: ALUMINUM FRAMEWORK - FABRIC COVERED

SPAN - 33'8" ON N.17
SPAN - 36'10" STD. (DOTTED)
LENGTH - 29'11"
HEIGHT - 8'10"
MAX DESIGN SPEED - 420 M.P.H.

AIRCRAFT USED WAS 48TH SPITFIRE AIRFRAME FROM SUPERMARINE. K-9834 TYPE 323

5/64" SQUARES

TYPICAL NACA 2200 SERIES AIRFOIL SECTIONS.

'HIGH SPEED' SPITFIRE

SCALE: 5/32" = 1'

PROPELLER: 4 BLADE WOODEN FIXED-PITCH MANUFACTURED BY THE AIRSCREW COMPANY.

N.17

1939 VERSION

POWERPLANT: ROLLS-ROYCE MERLIN III WITH 27+LB. BOOST PRODUCING 2,160 HORSEPOWER. 12 CYLINDER 60° VEE TYPE BLOCK.

N.17

COLOR SCHEME: ROYAL BLUE WITH SILVER* CHEAT LINE & N.17. *(SOME REFS. SAY GOLD).

ALTHOUGH FLOWN FOR TEST, CRAFT DID NOT TRY FOR WORLD SPEED RECORD AS THE HEINKEL HE-100V-8 RAISED THE RECORD TO 463.67 ON MARCH 30, 1939. THIS MARK WAS SOMEWHAT ABOVE N.17'S DESIGN POTENTIAL.

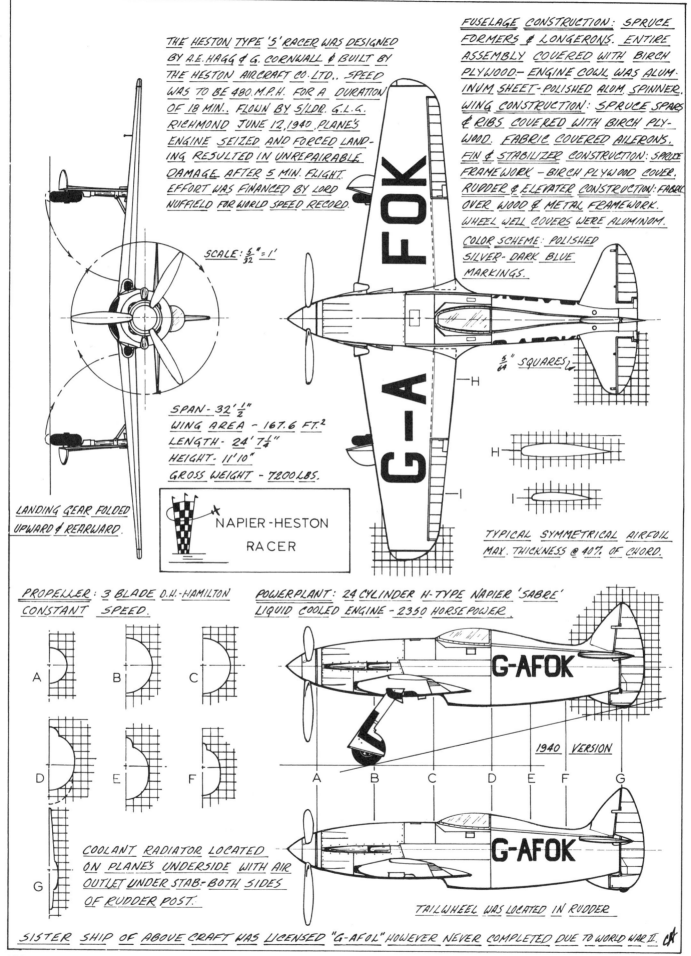

THE HESTON TYPE '5' RACER WAS DESIGNED BY A.E. HAGG & G. CORNWALL & BUILT BY THE HESTON AIRCRAFT CO. LTD.. SPEED WAS TO BE 480 M.P.H. FOR A DURATION OF 18 MIN.. FLOWN BY S/LDR. G.L.G. RICHMOND JUNE 12, 1940, PLANE'S ENGINE SEIZED AND FORCED LANDING RESULTED IN UNREPAIRABLE DAMAGE AFTER 5 MIN. FLIGHT. EFFORT WAS FINANCED BY LORD NUFFIELD FOR WORLD SPEED RECORD.

FUSELAGE CONSTRUCTION: SPRUCE FORMERS & LONGERONS. ENTIRE ASSEMBLY COVERED WITH BIRCH PLYWOOD.- ENGINE COWL WAS ALUMINUM SHEET-POLISHED ALUM. SPINNER. WING CONSTRUCTION: SPRUCE SPARS & RIBS COVERED WITH BIRCH PLYWOOD. FABRIC COVERED AILERONS. FIN & STABILIZER CONSTRUCTION: SPRUCE FRAMEWORK - BIRCH PLYWOOD COVER. RUDDER & ELEVATER CONSTRUCTION: FABRIC OVER WOOD & METAL FRAMEWORK. WHEEL WELL COVERS WERE ALUMINUM.

COLOR SCHEME: POLISHED SILVER- DARK BLUE MARKINGS.

SCALE: $\frac{5}{32}$" = 1'

SPAN - 32' $\frac{1}{2}$"
WING AREA - 167.6 FT.^{2}
LENGTH - 24' 7$\frac{1}{4}$"
HEIGHT - 11' 10"
GROSS WEIGHT - 7200 LBS.

LANDING GEAR FOLDED UPWARD & REARWARD.

NAPIER - HESTON RACER

$\frac{5}{64}$" SQUARES

TYPICAL SYMMETRICAL AIRFOIL MAX. THICKNESS @ 40% OF CHORD.

PROPELLER: 3 BLADE D.H.-HAMILTON CONSTANT SPEED.

POWERPLANT: 24 CYLINDER H-TYPE NAPIER 'SABRE' LIQUID COOLED ENGINE - 2350 HORSEPOWER

G-AFOK

1940 VERSION

COOLANT RADIATOR LOCATED ON PLANE'S UNDERSIDE WITH AIR OUTLET UNDER STAB-BOTH SIDES OF RUDDER POST.

G-AFOK

TAILWHEEL WAS LOCATED IN RUDDER

SISTER SHIP OF ABOVE CRAFT WAS LICENSED "G-AFOL" HOWEVER NEVER COMPLETED DUE TO WORLD WAR II.

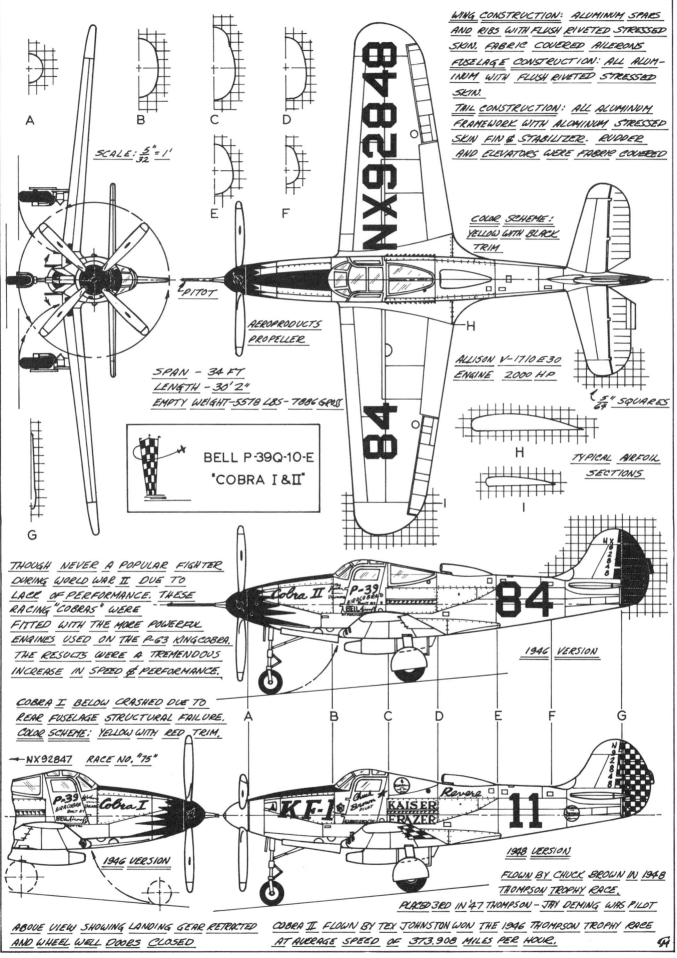

WING CONSTRUCTION: ALUMINUM SPARS AND RIBS WITH FLUSH RIVETED STRESSED SKIN. FABRIC COVERED AILERONS
FUSELAGE CONSTRUCTION: ALL ALUMINUM WITH FLUSH RIVETED STRESSED SKIN.
TAIL CONSTRUCTION: ALL ALUMINUM FRAMEWORK WITH ALUMINUM STRESSED SKIN FIN & STABILIZER. RUDDER AND ELEVATORS WERE FABRIC COVERED

A   B   C   D   E   F

SCALE: $\frac{5}{32}$" = 1'

COLOR SCHEME: YELLOW WITH BLACK TRIM

PITOT

AEROPRODUCTS PROPELLER

NX92848
84

SPAN - 34 FT
LENGTH - 30' 2"
EMPTY WEIGHT - 5578 LBS - 7886 GROSS

ALLISON V-1710 E30 ENGINE 2000 HP

$\frac{5}{64}$" SQUARES

H

TYPICAL AIRFOIL SECTIONS

I   I

BELL P-39Q-10-E "COBRA I & II"

G

THOUGH NEVER A POPULAR FIGHTER DURING WORLD WAR II DUE TO LACK OF PERFORMANCE. THESE RACING "COBRAS" WERE FITTED WITH THE MORE POWERFUL ENGINES USED ON THE P-63 KINGCOBRA. THE RESULTS WERE A TREMENDOUS INCREASE IN SPEED & PERFORMANCE.

Cobra II   P-39 AIRACOBRA BUILT BY BELL   84   NX 92848

1946 VERSION

COBRA I BELOW CRASHED DUE TO REAR FUSELAGE STRUCTURAL FAILURE. COLOR SCHEME: YELLOW WITH RED TRIM.

NX92847   RACE NO. "75"

A   B   C   D   E   F   G

P-39 AIRACOBRA BUILT BY BELL   Cobra I

1946 VERSION

KF-1   Chuck Brown PILOT   KAISER FRAZER   Revere   11   N 92848

1948 VERSION

FLOWN BY CHUCK BROWN IN 1948 THOMPSON TROPHY RACE.
PLACED 3RD IN '47 THOMPSON - JAY DEMING WAS PILOT

ABOVE VIEW SHOWING LANDING GEAR RETRACTED AND WHEEL WELL DOORS CLOSED

COBRA II FLOWN BY TEX JOHNSTON WON THE 1946 THOMPSON TROPHY RACE AT AVERAGE SPEED OF 373.908 MILES PER HOUR.

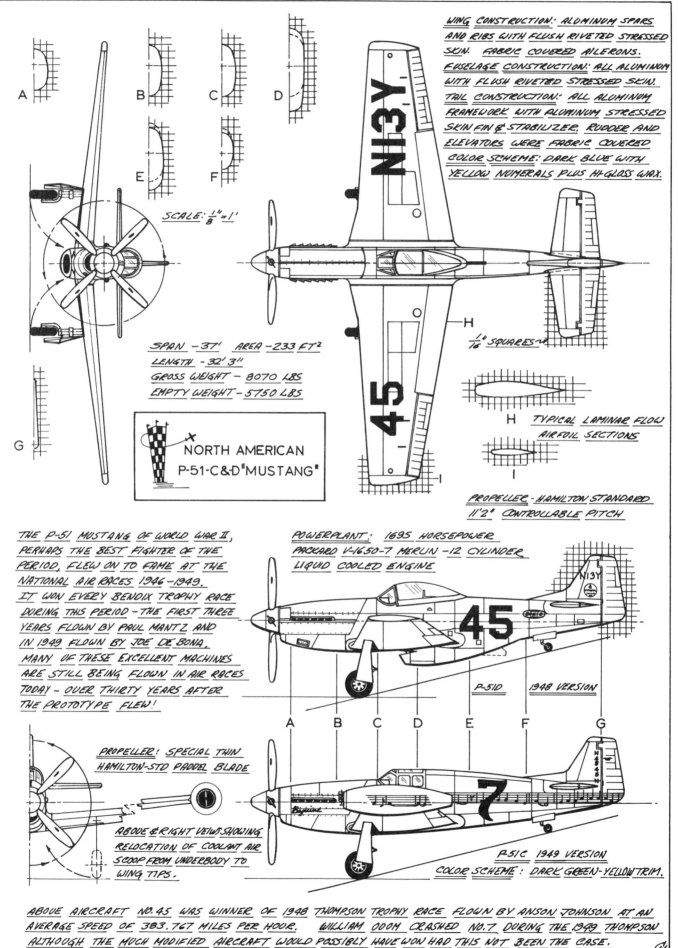

WING CONSTRUCTION: ALUMINUM SPARS AND RIBS WITH FLUSH RIVETED STRESSED SKIN. FABRIC COVERED AILERONS. FUSELAGE CONSTRUCTION: ALL ALUMINUM WITH FLUSH RIVETED STRESSED SKIN. TAIL CONSTRUCTION: ALL ALUMINUM FRAMEWORK WITH ALUMINUM STRESSED SKIN FIN & STABILIZER. RUDDER AND ELEVATORS WERE FABRIC COVERED COLOR SCHEME: DARK BLUE WITH YELLOW NUMERALS PLUS HI-GLOSS WAX.

SCALE: $\frac{1}{8}$" = 1'

SPAN – 37'   AREA – 233 FT²
LENGTH – 32' 3"
GROSS WEIGHT – 8070 LBS
EMPTY WEIGHT – 5750 LBS

NORTH AMERICAN
P-51-C & D "MUSTANG"

$\frac{1}{16}$" SQUARES

H   TYPICAL LAMINAR FLOW AIRFOIL SECTIONS

PROPELLER – HAMILTON STANDARD 11'2" CONTROLLABLE PITCH

THE P-51 MUSTANG OF WORLD WAR II, PERHAPS THE BEST FIGHTER OF THE PERIOD, FLEW ON TO FAME AT THE NATIONAL AIR RACES 1946–1949. IT WON EVERY BENDIX TROPHY RACE DURING THIS PERIOD – THE FIRST THREE YEARS FLOWN BY PAUL MANTZ AND IN 1949 FLOWN BY JOE DE BONA. MANY OF THESE EXCELLENT MACHINES ARE STILL BEING FLOWN IN AIR RACES TODAY – OVER THIRTY YEARS AFTER THE PROTOTYPE FLEW!

POWERPLANT: 1695 HORSEPOWER PACKARD V-1650-7 MERLIN –12 CYLINDER LIQUID COOLED ENGINE

P-51D   1948 VERSION

PROPELLER: SPECIAL THIN HAMILTON-STD PADDEL BLADE

ABOVE & RIGHT VEIWS SHOWING RELOCATION OF COOLANT AIR SCOOP FROM UNDERBODY TO WING TIPS.

P-51C 1949 VERSION
COLOR SCHEME: DARK GREEN-YELLOW TRIM.

ABOVE AIRCRAFT NO.45 WAS WINNER OF 1948 THOMPSON TROPHY RACE FLOWN BY ANSON JOHNSON AT AN AVERAGE SPEED OF 383.767 MILES PER HOUR.   WILLIAM ODOM CRASHED NO.7 DURING THE 1949 THOMPSON ALTHOUGH THE MUCH MODIFIED AIRCRAFT WOULD POSSIBLY HAVE WON HAD THIS NOT BEEN THE CASE.

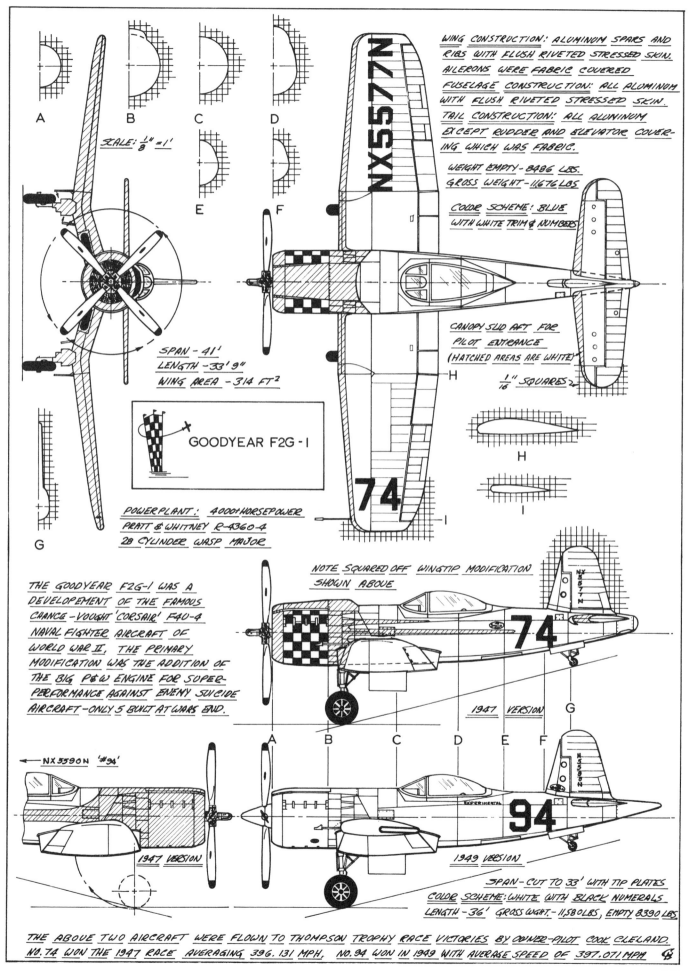

A B C D

E F

SCALE: $\frac{1}{8}$" = 1'

WING CONSTRUCTION: ALUMINUM SPARS AND
RIBS WITH FLUSH RIVETED STRESSED SKIN.
AILERONS WERE FABRIC COVERED
FUSELAGE CONSTRUCTION: ALL ALUMINUM
WITH FLUSH RIVETED STRESSED SKIN.
TAIL CONSTRUCTION: ALL ALUMINUM
EXCEPT RUDDER AND ELEVATOR COVER-
ING WHICH WAS FABRIC.

WEIGHT EMPTY - 8486 LBS.
GROSS WEIGHT - 11676 LBS.

COLOR SCHEME: BLUE
WITH WHITE TRIM & NUMBERS

NX5577N

SPAN - 41'
LENGTH - 33' 9"
WING AREA - 314 FT²

CANOPY SLID AFT FOR
PILOT ENTRANCE
(HATCHED AREAS ARE WHITE)

$\frac{1}{16}$" SQUARES

H

I

GOODYEAR F2G-1

74

POWERPLANT: 4000+ HORSEPOWER
PRATT & WHITNEY R-4360-4
28 CYLINDER WASP MAJOR

G

THE GOODYEAR F2G-1 WAS A
DEVELOPEMENT OF THE FAMOUS
CHANCE-VOUGHT 'CORSAIR' F4U-4
NAVAL FIGHTER AIRCRAFT OF
WORLD WAR II. THE PRIMARY
MODIFICATION WAS THE ADDITION OF
THE BIG P&W ENGINE FOR SUPER-
PERFORMANCE AGAINST ENEMY SUICIDE
AIRCRAFT - ONLY 5 BUILT AT WARS END.

NOTE SQUARED OFF WINGTIP MODIFICATION
SHOWN ABOVE

74

1947 VERSION

A B C D E F G

← NX5590N '#94'

1947 VERSION

EXPERIMENTAL

94

1949 VERSION

SPAN - CUT TO 33' WITH TIP PLATES
COLOR SCHEME: WHITE WITH BLACK NUMERALS
LENGTH - 36' GROSS WGHT. - 11,580 LBS. EMPTY 8390 LBS.

THE ABOVE TWO AIRCRAFT WERE FLOWN TO THOMPSON TROPHY RACE VICTORIES BY OWNER-PILOT, COOK CLELAND.
NO. 74 WON THE 1947 RACE AVERAGING 396.131 MPH. NO. 94 WON IN 1949 WITH AVERAGE SPEED OF 397.071 MPH.

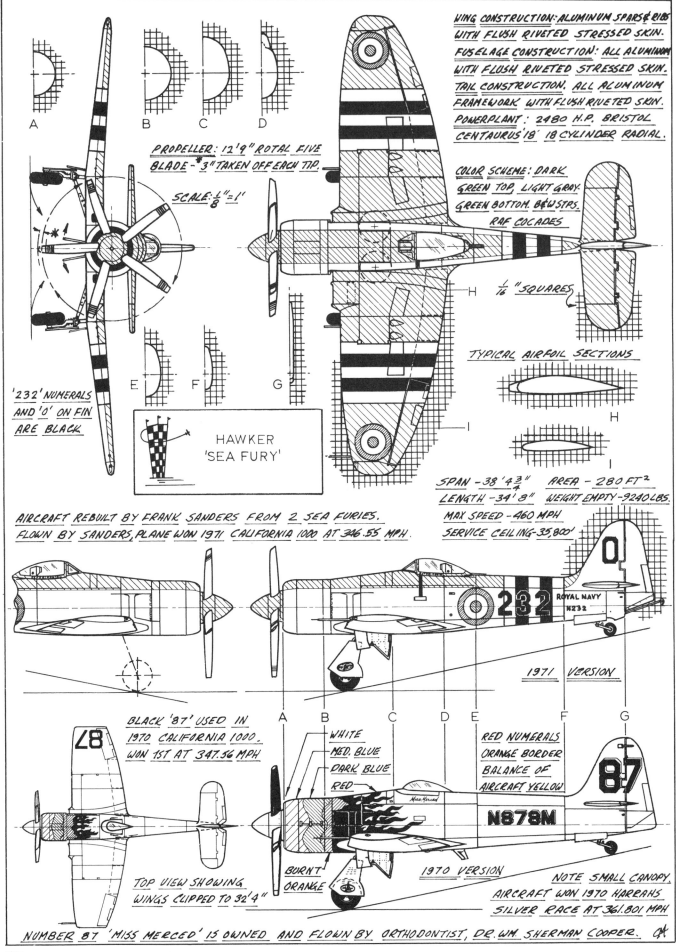

WING CONSTRUCTION: ALUMINUM SPARS & RIBS WITH FLUSH RIVETED STRESSED SKIN. FUSELAGE CONSTRUCTION: ALL ALUMINUM WITH FLUSH RIVETED STRESSED SKIN. TAIL CONSTRUCTION: ALL ALUMINUM FRAMEWORK WITH FLUSH RIVETED SKIN. POWERPLANT: 2480 H.P. BRISTOL CENTAURUS '18' 18 CYLINDER RADIAL.

COLOR SCHEME: DARK GREEN TOP, LIGHT GRAY-GREEN BOTTOM. B&W STRS. RAF COCADES

PROPELLER: 12'9" ROTAL FIVE BLADE - 3" TAKEN OFF EACH TIP.

SCALE: $\frac{1}{8}$" = 1'

$\frac{1}{16}$" SQUARES

TYPICAL AIRFOIL SECTIONS

'232' NUMERALS AND 'O' ON FIN ARE BLACK

HAWKER 'SEA FURY'

SPAN - 38' 4¾"   AREA - 280 FT²
LENGTH - 34' 8"   WEIGHT EMPTY - 9240 LBS.
MAX SPEED - 460 MPH
SERVICE CEILING - 35,800'

AIRCRAFT REBUILT BY FRANK SANDERS FROM 2 SEA FURIES. FLOWN BY SANDERS, PLANE WON 1971 CALIFORNIA 1000 AT 346.55 MPH.

ROYAL NAVY N232

1971 VERSION

BLACK '87' USED IN 1970 CALIFORNIA 1000. WON 1ST AT 347.56 MPH

WHITE
MED. BLUE
DARK BLUE
RED

RED NUMERALS ORANGE BORDER BALANCE OF AIRCRAFT YELLOW

N878M

1970 VERSION

BURNT ORANGE

TOP VIEW SHOWING WINGS CLIPPED TO 32' 4"

NOTE SMALL CANOPY. AIRCRAFT WON 1970 HARRAHS SILVER RACE AT 361.801 MPH

NUMBER 87 'MISS MERCED' IS OWNED AND FLOWN BY ORTHODONTIST, DR. WM. SHERMAN COOPER.

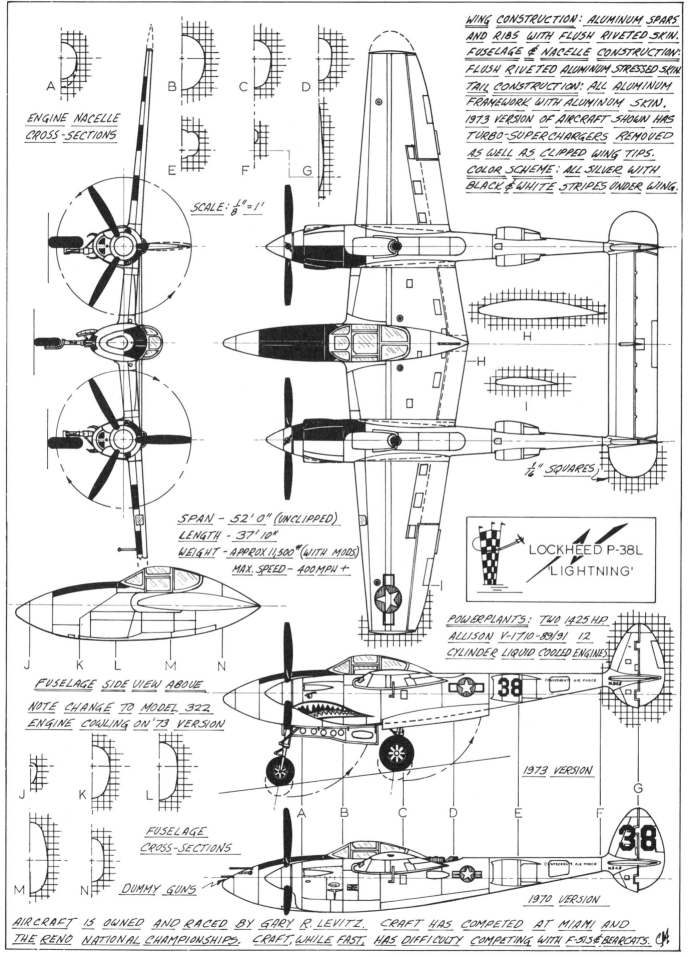

ENGINE NACELLE
CROSS-SECTIONS

A B C D
E F G

WING CONSTRUCTION: ALUMINUM SPARS
AND RIBS WITH FLUSH RIVETED SKIN.
FUSELAGE & NACELLE CONSTRUCTION:
FLUSH RIVETED ALUMINUM STRESSED SKIN.
TAIL CONSTRUCTION: ALL ALUMINUM
FRAMEWORK WITH ALUMINUM SKIN.
1973 VERSION OF AIRCRAFT SHOWN HAS
TURBO-SUPERCHARGERS REMOVED
AS WELL AS CLIPPED WING TIPS.
COLOR SCHEME: ALL SILVER WITH
BLACK & WHITE STRIPES UNDER WING.

SCALE: $\frac{1}{8}'' = 1'$

H
H
I

$\frac{1}{16}''$ SQUARES

SPAN – 52' 0" (UNCLIPPED)
LENGTH – 37' 10"
WEIGHT – APPROX 11,500# (WITH MODS)
MAX. SPEED – 400MPH +

LOCKHEED P-38L
'LIGHTNING'

J K L M N

FUSELAGE SIDE VIEW ABOVE

NOTE CHANGE TO MODEL 322
ENGINE COWLING ON '73 VERSION

POWERPLANTS: TWO 1425 H.P.
ALLISON V-1710-89/91 12
CYLINDER LIQUID COOLED ENGINES.

38

1973 VERSION

J K L
M N

FUSELAGE
CROSS-SECTIONS

DUMMY GUNS

A B C D E F G

38

1970 VERSION

AIRCRAFT IS OWNED AND RACED BY GARY R. LEVITZ. CRAFT HAS COMPETED AT MIAMI AND
THE RENO NATIONAL CHAMPIONSHIPS. CRAFT, WHILE FAST, HAS DIFFICULTY COMPETING WITH F-51S & BEARCATS.

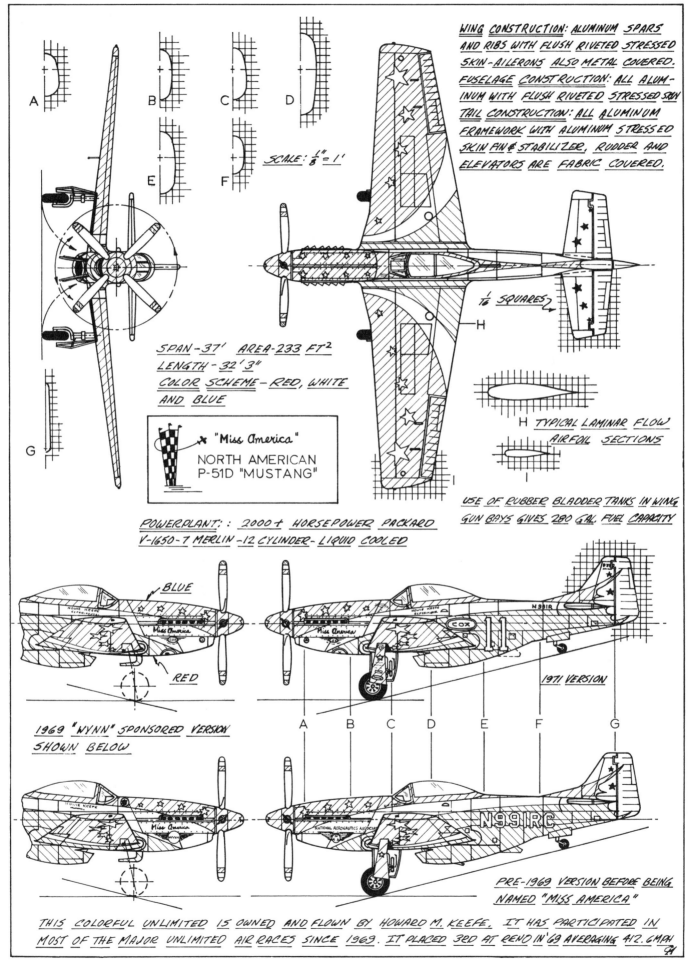

WING CONSTRUCTION: ALUMINUM SPARS AND RIBS WITH FLUSH RIVETED STRESSED SKIN - AILERONS ALSO METAL COVERED. FUSELAGE CONSTRUCTION: ALL ALUMINUM WITH FLUSH RIVETED STRESSED SKIN TAIL CONSTRUCTION: ALL ALUMINUM FRAMEWORK WITH ALUMINUM STRESSED SKIN FIN & STABILIZER, RUDDER AND ELEVATORS ARE FABRIC COVERED.

SCALE: $\frac{1}{8}$" = 1'

$\frac{1}{16}$ SQUARES

SPAN - 37' AREA - 233 FT²
LENGTH - 32' 3"
COLOR SCHEME - RED, WHITE AND BLUE

H TYPICAL LAMINAR FLOW AIRFOIL SECTIONS

"Miss America"
NORTH AMERICAN P-51D "MUSTANG"

USE OF RUBBER BLADDER TANKS IN WING GUN BAYS GIVES 280 GAL. FUEL CAPACITY

POWERPLANT: : 2000+ HORSEPOWER PACKARD V-1650-7 MERLIN -12 CYLINDER- LIQUID COOLED

BLUE

RED

1971 VERSION

1969 "WYNN" SPONSORED VERSION SHOWN BELOW

A B C D E F G

PRE-1969 VERSION BEFORE BEING NAMED "MISS AMERICA"

THIS COLORFUL UNLIMITED IS OWNED AND FLOWN BY HOWARD M. KEEFE. IT HAS PARTICIPATED IN MOST OF THE MAJOR UNLIMITED AIR RACES SINCE 1969. IT PLACED 3RD AT RENO IN '69 AVERAGING 412.6MPH

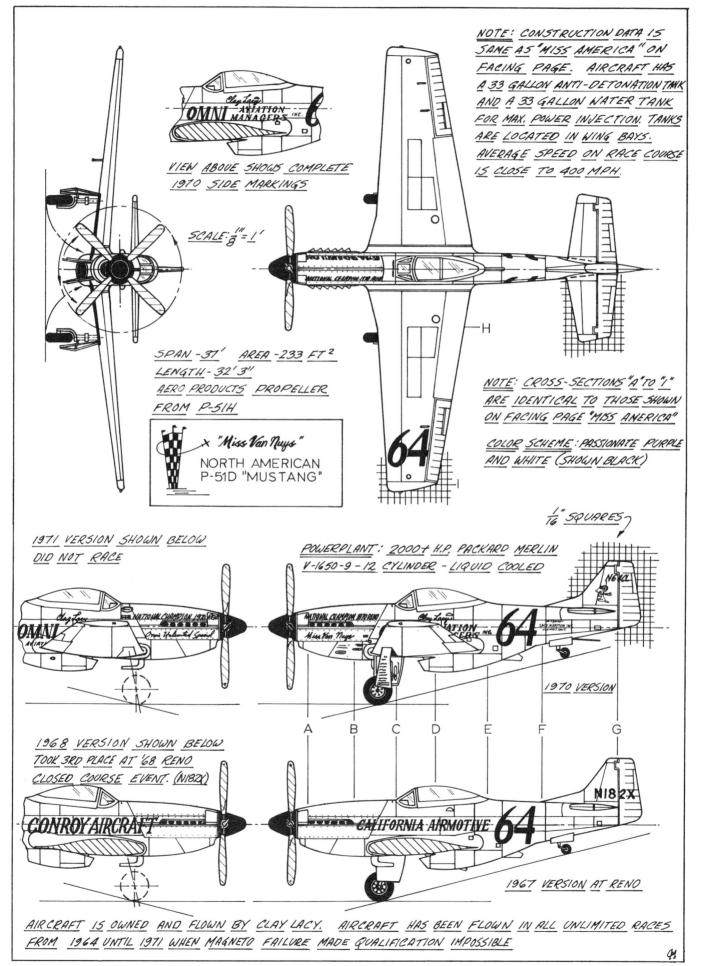

NOTE: CONSTRUCTION DATA IS SAME AS "MISS AMERICA" ON FACING PAGE. AIRCRAFT HAS A 33 GALLON ANTI-DETONATION TANK AND A 33 GALLON WATER TANK FOR MAX. POWER INJECTION. TANKS ARE LOCATED IN WING BAYS. AVERAGE SPEED ON RACE COURSE IS CLOSE TO 400 MPH.

VIEW ABOVE SHOWS COMPLETE 1970 SIDE MARKINGS

SCALE: $\frac{1"}{8} = 1'$

SPAN - 37'   AREA - 233 FT²
LENGTH - 32' 3"
AERO PRODUCTS PROPELLER
FROM P-51H

"Miss Van Nuys"
NORTH AMERICAN
P-51D "MUSTANG"

NOTE: CROSS-SECTIONS "A" TO "I" ARE IDENTICAL TO THOSE SHOWN ON FACING PAGE "MISS AMERICA"

COLOR SCHEME: PASSIONATE PURPLE AND WHITE (SHOWN BLACK)

1971 VERSION SHOWN BELOW DID NOT RACE

$\frac{1}{16}"$ SQUARES

POWERPLANT: 2000+ H.P. PACKARD MERLIN V-1650-9-12 CYLINDER - LIQUID COOLED

1970 VERSION

1968 VERSION SHOWN BELOW TOOK 3RD PLACE AT '68 RENO CLOSED COURSE EVENT. (N182X)

1967 VERSION AT RENO

AIRCRAFT IS OWNED AND FLOWN BY CLAY LACY. AIRCRAFT HAS BEEN FLOWN IN ALL UNLIMITED RACES FROM 1964 UNTIL 1971 WHEN MAGNETO FAILURE MADE QUALIFICATION IMPOSSIBLE

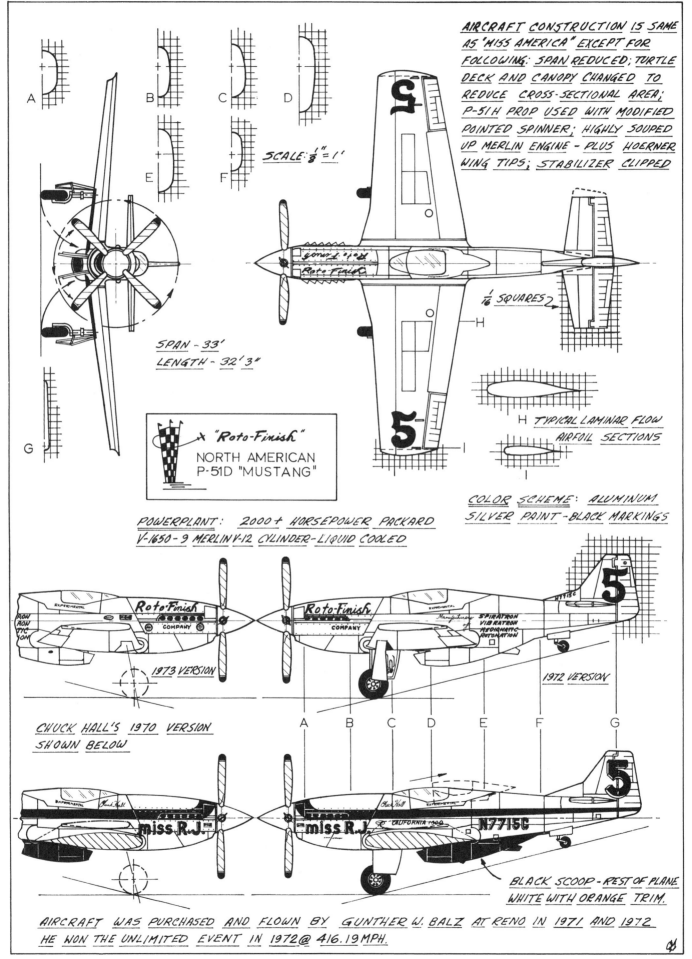

AIRCRAFT CONSTRUCTION IS SAME AS "MISS AMERICA" EXCEPT FOR FOLLOWING: SPAN REDUCED; TURTLE DECK AND CANOPY CHANGED TO REDUCE CROSS-SECTIONAL AREA; P-51H PROP USED WITH MODIFIED POINTED SPINNER; HIGHLY SOUPED UP MERLIN ENGINE - PLUS HOERNER WING TIPS; STABILIZER CLIPPED

SCALE: $\frac{1}{8}$" = 1'

$\frac{1}{16}$ SQUARES

SPAN - 33'
LENGTH - 32' 3"

"Roto-Finish"
NORTH AMERICAN
P-51D "MUSTANG"

H TYPICAL LAMINAR FLOW AIRFOIL SECTIONS

COLOR SCHEME: ALUMINUM SILVER PAINT - BLACK MARKINGS

POWERPLANT: 2000+ HORSEPOWER PACKARD V-1650-9 MERLIN V-12 CYLINDER - LIQUID COOLED

Roto-Finish COMPANY

1973 VERSION

1972 VERSION

CHUCK HALL'S 1970 VERSION SHOWN BELOW

miss R.J.

BLACK SCOOP - REST OF PLANE WHITE WITH ORANGE TRIM.

AIRCRAFT WAS PURCHASED AND FLOWN BY GUNTHER W. BALZ AT RENO IN 1971 AND 1972. HE WON THE UNLIMITED EVENT IN 1972 @ 416.19 MPH.

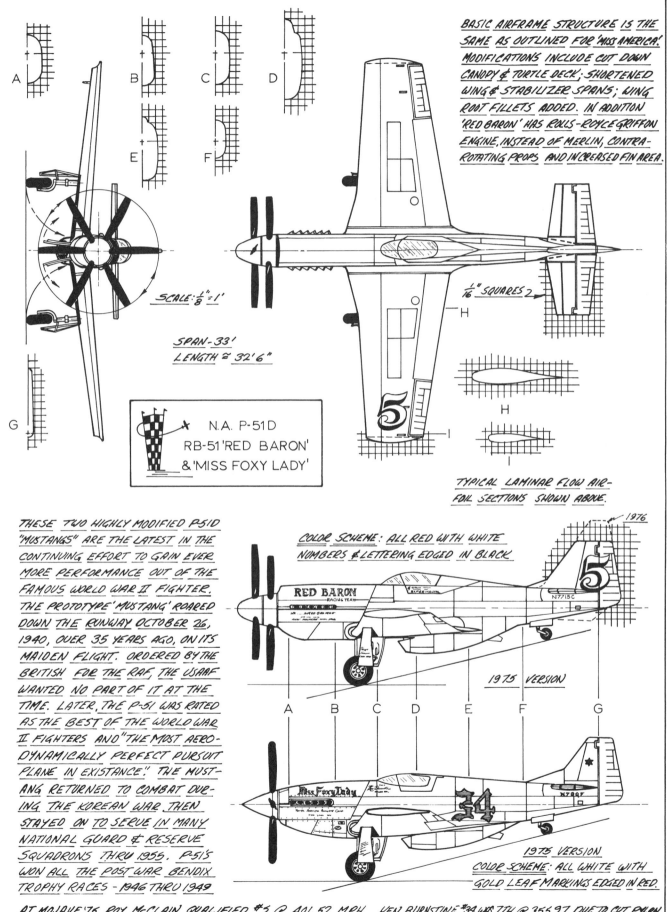

BASIC AIRFRAME STRUCTURE IS THE SAME AS OUTLINED FOR 'MISS AMERICA'. MODIFICATIONS INCLUDE CUT DOWN CANOPY & TURTLE DECK; SHORTENED WING & STABILIZER SPANS; WING ROOT FILLETS ADDED. IN ADDITION 'RED BARON' HAS ROLLS-ROYCE GRIFFON ENGINE, INSTEAD OF MERLIN, CONTRA-ROTATING PROPS AND INCREASED FIN AREA.

SCALE: $\frac{1}{8}$" = 1'

SPAN - 33'
LENGTH ≅ 32' 6"

$\frac{1}{16}$" SQUARES 2

N.A. P-51D
RB-51 'RED BARON'
& 'MISS FOXY LADY'

TYPICAL LAMINAR FLOW AIR-FOIL SECTIONS SHOWN ABOVE.

THESE TWO HIGHLY MODIFIED P-51D "MUSTANGS" ARE THE LATEST IN THE CONTINUING EFFORT TO GAIN EVER MORE PERFORMANCE OUT OF THE FAMOUS WORLD WAR II FIGHTER. THE PROTOTYPE 'MUSTANG' ROARED DOWN THE RUNWAY OCTOBER 26, 1940, OVER 35 YEARS AGO, ON ITS MAIDEN FLIGHT. ORDERED BY THE BRITISH FOR THE RAF, THE USAAF WANTED NO PART OF IT AT THE TIME. LATER, THE P-51 WAS RATED AS THE BEST OF THE WORLD WAR II FIGHTERS AND "THE MOST AERO-DYNAMICALLY PERFECT PURSUIT PLANE IN EXISTANCE." THE MUST-ANG RETURNED TO COMBAT DUR-ING THE KOREAN WAR THEN STAYED ON TO SERVE IN MANY NATIONAL GUARD & RESERVE SQUADRONS THRU 1955. P-51'S WON ALL THE POST WAR BENDIX TROPHY RACES - 1946 THRU 1949

COLOR SCHEME: ALL RED WITH WHITE NUMBERS & LETTERING EDGED IN BLACK

1976

RED BARON
RACING TEAM

N7715C

1975 VERSION

Miss Foxy Lady

N7OOF

1975 VERSION
COLOR SCHEME: ALL WHITE WITH GOLD LEAF MARKINGS EDGED IN RED.

AT MOJAVE '75 ROY McCLAIN QUALIFIED #5 @ 401.52 M.P.H. KEN BURNSTINE, #34, WAS 7TH @ 355.97 DUE TO CUT PYLON. AT RENO 1975 McCLAIN FLEW TO 2ND PLACE @ 427.31 MPH IN CHAMPIONSHIP RACE. BURNSTINE (34) PLACED 4TH.

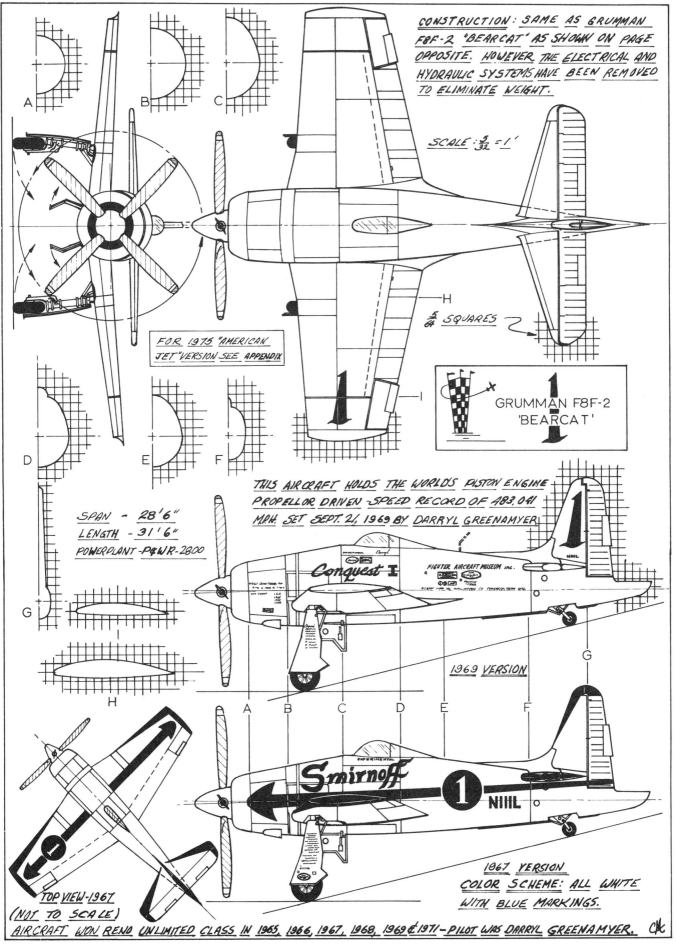

CONSTRUCTION: SAME AS GRUMMAN F8F-2 "BEARCAT" AS SHOWN ON PAGE OPPOSITE. HOWEVER THE ELECTRICAL AND HYDRAULIC SYSTEMS HAVE BEEN REMOVED TO ELIMINATE WEIGHT.

SCALE: $\frac{3}{32} = 1'$

FOR 1975 "AMERICAN JET" VERSION SEE APPENDIX

$\frac{5}{64}$ SQUARES

GRUMMAN F8F-2 'BEARCAT'

THIS AIRCRAFT HOLDS THE WORLD'S PISTON ENGINE PROPELLOR DRIVEN SPEED RECORD OF 483.041 M.P.H. SET SEPT. 21, 1969 BY DARRYL GREENAMYER.

SPAN - 28' 6"
LENGTH - 31' 6"
POWERPLANT - P&W R-2800

Conquest I

FIGHTER AIRCRAFT MUSEUM inc.

1969 VERSION

Smirnoff

N111L

1967 VERSION
COLOR SCHEME: ALL WHITE WITH BLUE MARKINGS.

TOP VIEW-1967
(NOT TO SCALE)
AIRCRAFT WON RENO UNLIMITED CLASS IN 1965, 1966, 1967, 1968, 1969 & 1971 - PILOT WAS DARRYL GREENAMYER.

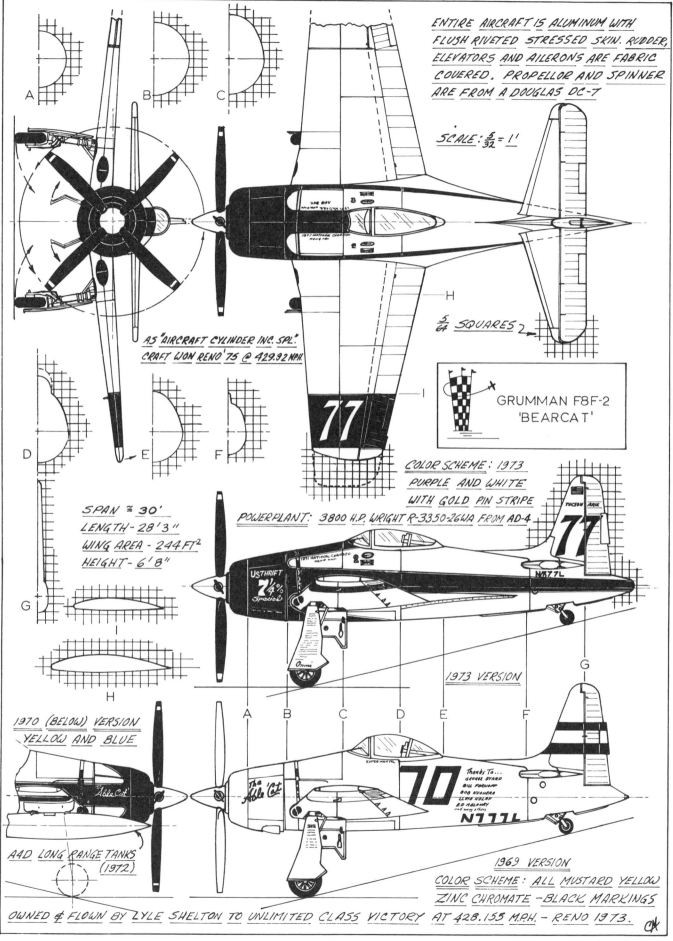

ENTIRE AIRCRAFT IS ALUMINUM WITH FLUSH RIVETED STRESSED SKIN. RUDDER, ELEVATORS AND AILERONS ARE FABRIC COVERED. PROPELLOR AND SPINNER ARE FROM A DOUGLAS DC-7

SCALE: $\frac{5}{32}$ = 1'

$\frac{5}{64}$ SQUARES

AS "AIRCRAFT CYLINDER INC. SPL." CRAFT WON RENO '75 @ 429.92 MPH.

GRUMMAN F8F-2 'BEARCAT'

COLOR SCHEME: 1973 PURPLE AND WHITE WITH GOLD PIN STRIPE

POWERPLANT: 3800 H.P. WRIGHT R-3350-26WA FROM AD-4

SPAN ≈ 30'
LENGTH - 28'3"
WING AREA - 244 FT²
HEIGHT - 6'8"

1973 VERSION

A B C D E F G

1970 (BELOW) VERSION YELLOW AND BLUE

A4D LONG RANGE TANKS (1972)

1969 VERSION
COLOR SCHEME: ALL MUSTARD YELLOW ZINC CHROMATE - BLACK MARKINGS

OWNED & FLOWN BY LYLE SHELTON TO UNLIMITED CLASS VICTORY AT 428.155 M.P.H. - RENO 1973.

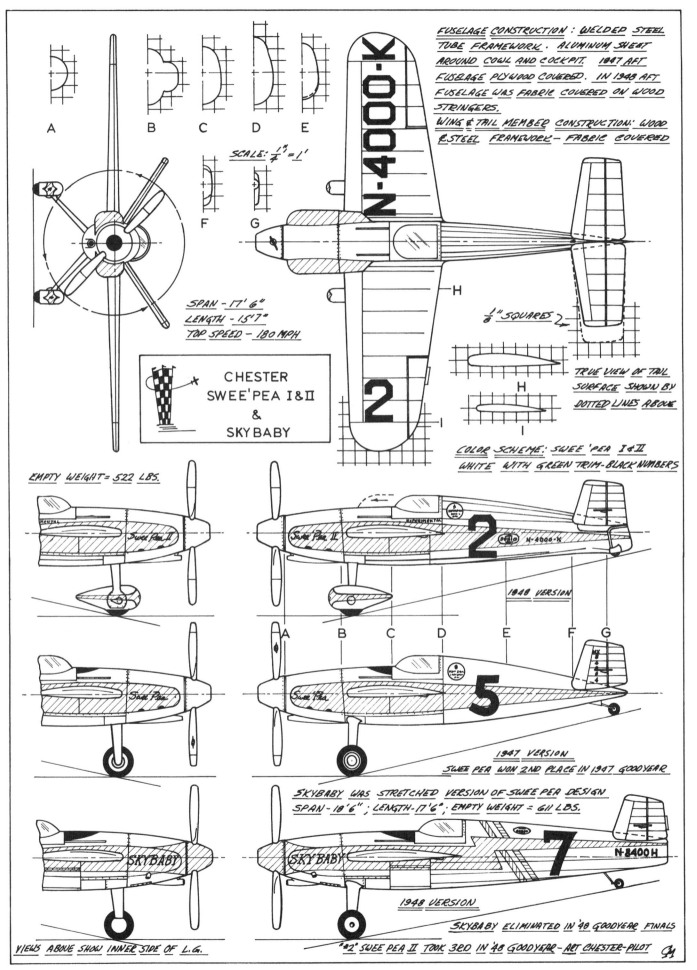

A   B   C   D   E

F   G

SCALE: $\frac{1}{4}$" = 1'

FUSELAGE CONSTRUCTION: WELDED STEEL
TUBE FRAMEWORK. ALUMINUM SHEET
AROUND COWL AND COCKPIT. 1947 AFT
FUSELAGE PLYWOOD COVERED. IN 1948 AFT
FUSELAGE WAS FABRIC COVERED ON WOOD
STRINGERS.
WING & TAIL MEMBER CONSTRUCTION: WOOD
& STEEL FRAMEWORK - FABRIC COVERED

N-4000-K

2

SPAN - 17' 6"
LENGTH - 15' 7"
TOP SPEED - 180 MPH

CHESTER
SWEE'PEA I & II
&
SKY BABY

H

$\frac{1}{8}$" SQUARES

H

I

TRUE VIEW OF TAIL
SURFACE SHOWN BY
DOTTED LINES ABOVE

COLOR SCHEME: SWEE'PEA I & II
WHITE WITH GREEN TRIM - BLACK NUMBERS

EMPTY WEIGHT = 522 LBS.

Swee Pea II

Swee Pea II

2   N-4000-K

1948 VERSION

A   B   C   D   E   F   G

Swee Pea

Swee Pea

5

1947 VERSION

SWEE PEA WON 2ND PLACE IN 1947 GOODYEAR

SKYBABY WAS STRETCHED VERSION OF SWEE PEA DESIGN
SPAN - 18' 6"; LENGTH - 17' 6"; EMPTY WEIGHT = 611 LBS.

SKYBABY

SKYBABY

7   N-8400H

1948 VERSION

SKYBABY ELIMINATED IN '48 GOODYEAR FINALS

VIEWS ABOVE SHOW INNER SIDE OF L.G.

"2" SWEE PEA II TOOK 3RD IN '48 GOODYEAR - ART CHESTER - PILOT

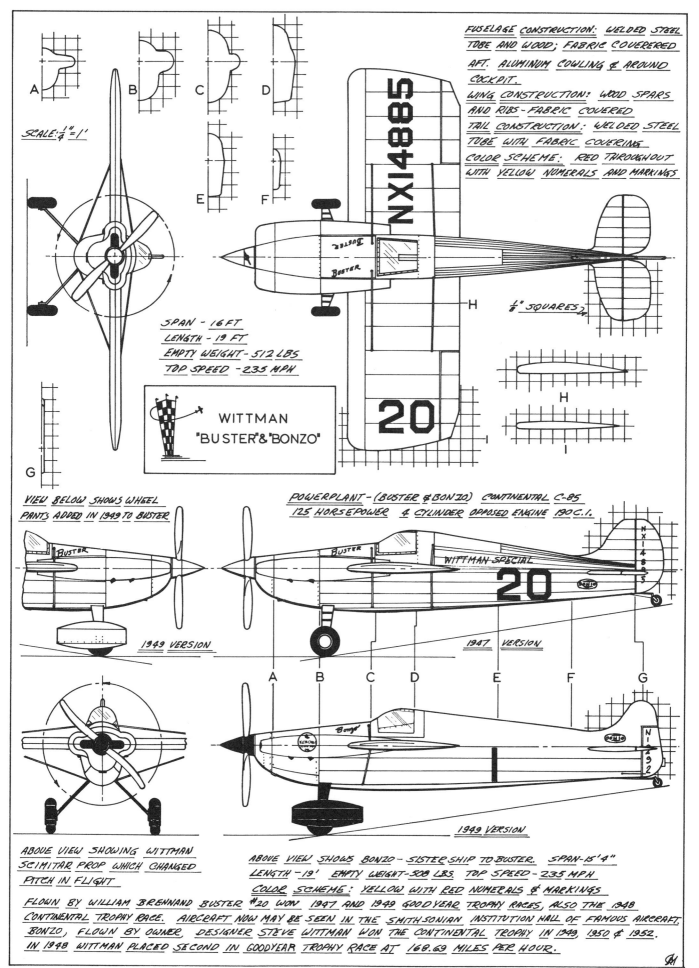

FUSELAGE CONSTRUCTION: WELDED STEEL
TUBE AND WOOD; FABRIC COUERERED
AFT. ALUMINUM COWLING & AROUND
COCKPIT.
WING CONSTRUCTION: WOOD SPARS
AND RIBS - FABRIC COUERED
TAIL CONSTRUCTION: WELDED STEEL
TUBE WITH FABRIC COUERING
COLOR SCHEME: RED THROUGHOUT
WITH YELLOW NUMERALS AND MARKINGS

SCALE: 1/4" = 1'

A B C D E F

NX14885

20

SPAN - 16 FT
LENGTH - 19 FT
EMPTY WEIGHT - 512 LBS
TOP SPEED - 235 MPH

WITTMAN
"BUSTER" & "BONZO"

1/8" SQUARES

H

I

G

VIEW BELOW SHOWS WHEEL
PANTS ADDED IN 1949 TO BUSTER

POWERPLANT - (BUSTER & BONZO) CONTINENTAL C-85
125 HORSEPOWER 4 CYLINDER OPPOSED ENGINE 190 C.I.

WITTMAN SPECIAL

20

1949 VERSION

1947 VERSION

A B C D E F G

1949 VERSION

ABOVE VIEW SHOWING WITTMAN
SCIMITAR PROP WHICH CHANGED
PITCH IN FLIGHT

ABOVE VIEW SHOWS BONZO - SISTER SHIP TO BUSTER. SPAN - 15'4"
LENGTH - 19' EMPTY WEIGHT - 508 LBS. TOP SPEED - 235 MPH
COLOR SCHEME: YELLOW WITH RED NUMERALS & MARKINGS

FLOWN BY WILLIAM BRENNAND BUSTER #20 WON 1947 AND 1949 GOODYEAR TROPHY RACES, ALSO THE 1948
CONTINENTAL TROPHY RACE. AIRCRAFT NOW MAY BE SEEN IN THE SMITHSONIAN INSTITUTION HALL OF FAMOUS AIRCRAFT.
BONZO, FLOWN BY OWNER, DESIGNER STEVE WITTMAN WON THE CONTINENTAL TROPHY IN 1949, 1950 & 1952.
IN 1948 WITTMAN PLACED SECOND IN GOODYEAR TROPHY RACE AT 168.69 MILES PER HOUR.

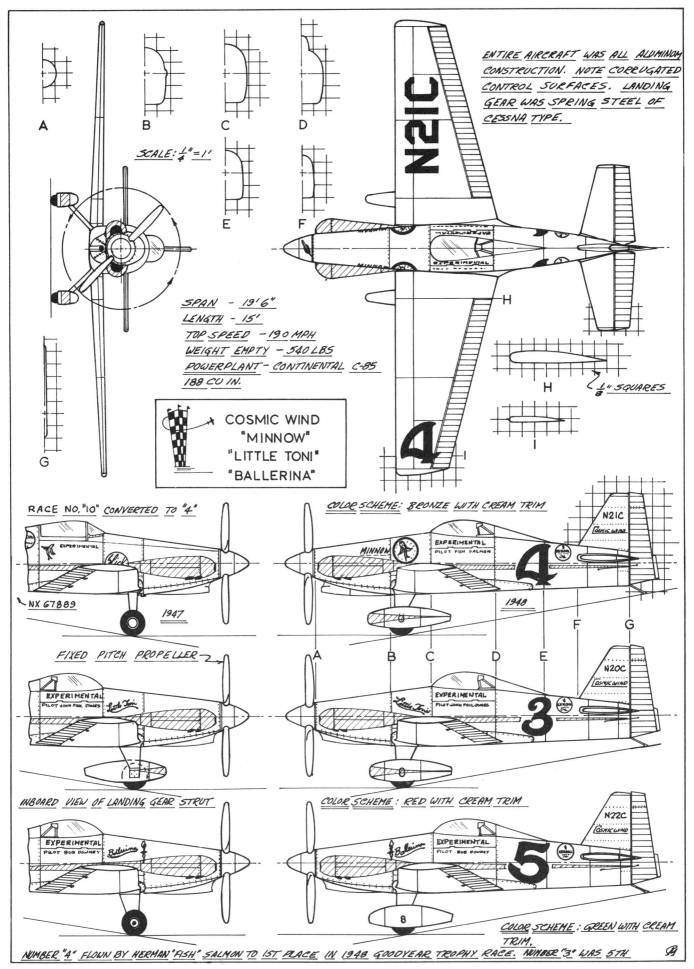

ENTIRE AIRCRAFT WAS ALL ALUMINUM
CONSTRUCTION. NOTE CORRUGATED
CONTROL SURFACES. LANDING
GEAR WAS SPRING STEEL OF
CESSNA TYPE.

SCALE: 1/4" = 1'

A B C D E F

SPAN - 19' 6"
LENGTH - 15'
TOP SPEED - 190 MPH
WEIGHT EMPTY - 540 LBS
POWERPLANT - CONTINENTAL C-85
188 CU IN.

H 1/8" SQUARES

H I

G

COSMIC WIND
"MINNOW"
"LITTLE TONI"
"BALLERINA"

RACE NO. "10" CONVERTED TO "4"

COLOR SCHEME: BRONZE WITH CREAM TRIM

NX 67889   1947

FIXED PITCH PROPELLER

INBOARD VIEW OF LANDING GEAR STRUT

COLOR SCHEME: RED WITH CREAM TRIM

COLOR SCHEME: GREEN WITH CREAM TRIM.

NUMBER "4" FLOWN BY HERMAN "FISH" SALMON TO 1ST PLACE IN 1948 GOODYEAR TROPHY RACE. NUMBER "3" WAS 5TH.

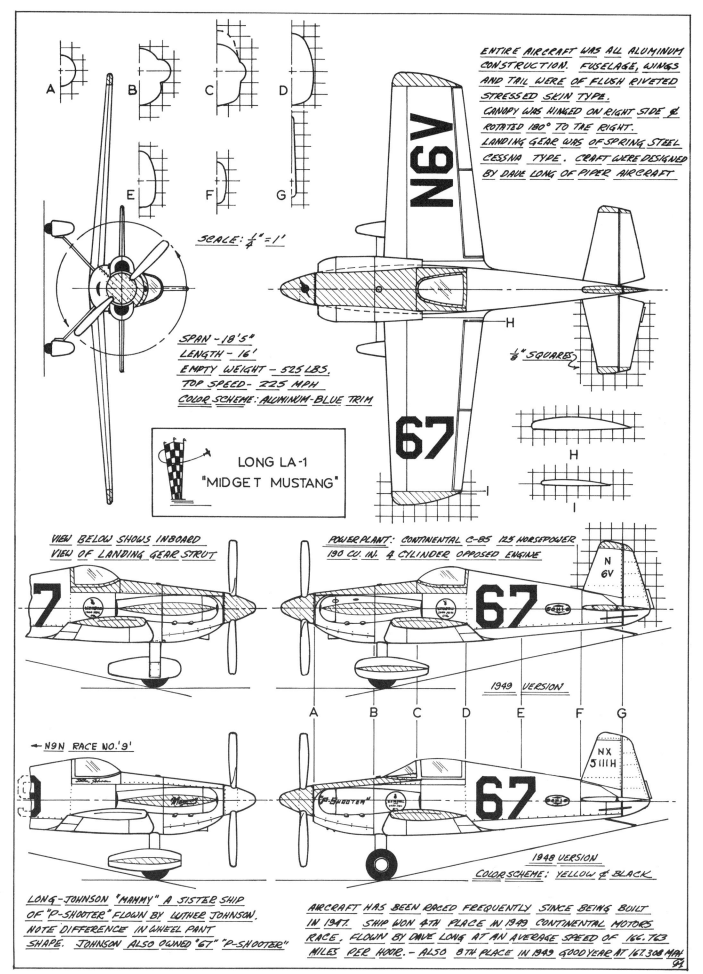

A B C D
E F G

ENTIRE AIRCRAFT WAS ALL ALUMINUM CONSTRUCTION. FUSELAGE, WINGS AND TAIL WERE OF FLUSH RIVETED STRESSED SKIN TYPE.
CANOPY WAS HINGED ON RIGHT SIDE & ROTATED 180° TO THE RIGHT.
LANDING GEAR WAS OF SPRING STEEL CESSNA TYPE. CRAFT WERE DESIGNED BY DAVE LONG OF PIPER AIRCRAFT

SCALE: 1/4" = 1'

SPAN – 18'5"
LENGTH – 16'
EMPTY WEIGHT – 525 LBS.
TOP SPEED – 225 MPH
COLOR SCHEME: ALUMINUM–BLUE TRIM

LONG LA-1 "MIDGET MUSTANG"

H
1/8" SQUARE

H
I

VIEW BELOW SHOWS INBOARD VIEW OF LANDING GEAR STRUT

POWER PLANT: CONTINENTAL C-85 125 HORSEPOWER 190 CU. IN. 4 CYLINDER OPPOSED ENGINE

N 6V

1949 VERSION

A B C D E F G

←N9N RACE NO. '9'

LONG-JOHNSON "MAMMY" A SISTER SHIP OF "P-SHOOTER" FLOWN BY LUTHER JOHNSON. NOTE DIFFERENCE IN WHEEL PANT SHAPE. JOHNSON ALSO OWNED "67" "P-SHOOTER"

NX 5111H

1948 VERSION
COLOR SCHEME: YELLOW & BLACK

AIRCRAFT HAS BEEN RACED FREQUENTLY SINCE BEING BUILT IN 1947. SHIP WON 4TH PLACE IN 1949 CONTINENTAL MOTORS RACE. FLOWN BY DAVE LONG AT AN AVERAGE SPEED OF 166.763 MILES PER HOUR. – ALSO 8TH PLACE IN 1949 GOODYEAR AT 167.308 MPH

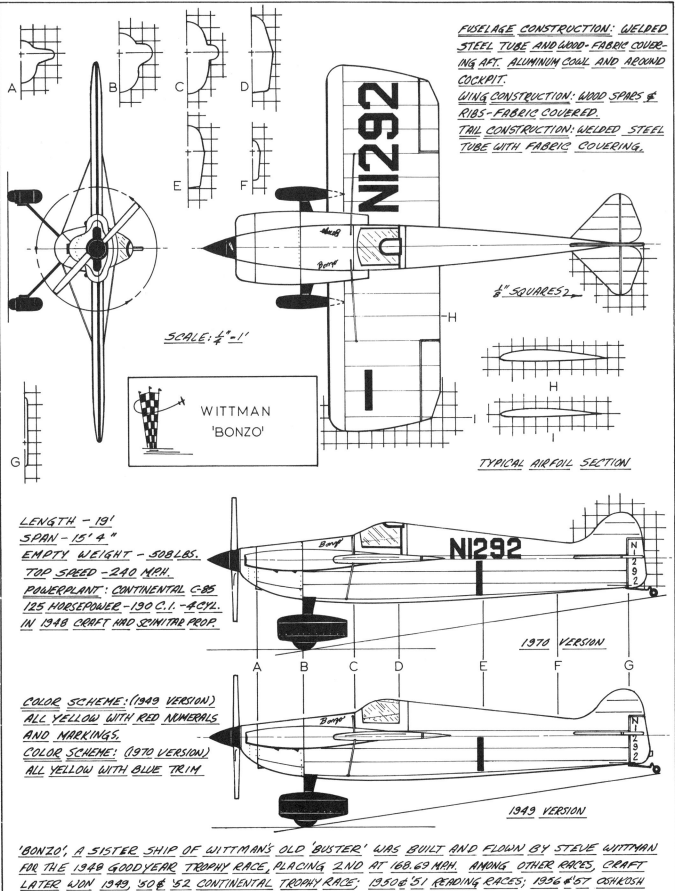

FUSELAGE CONSTRUCTION: WELDED STEEL TUBE AND WOOD-FABRIC COVERING AFT. ALUMINUM COWL AND AROUND COCKPIT.
WING CONSTRUCTION: WOOD SPARS & RIBS-FABRIC COVERED.
TAIL CONSTRUCTION: WELDED STEEL TUBE WITH FABRIC COVERING.

SCALE: ¼"=1'

⅛" SQUARES

WITTMAN 'BONZO'

TYPICAL AIRFOIL SECTION

LENGTH - 19'
SPAN - 15' 4"
EMPTY WEIGHT - 508 LBS.
TOP SPEED - 240 M.P.H.
POWERPLANT: CONTINENTAL C-85
125 HORSEPOWER - 190 C.I. - 4 CYL.
IN 1948 CRAFT HAD SCIMITAR PROP.

1970 VERSION

COLOR SCHEME: (1949 VERSION)
ALL YELLOW WITH RED NUMERALS
AND MARKINGS.
COLOR SCHEME: (1970 VERSION)
ALL YELLOW WITH BLUE TRIM

1949 VERSION

'BONZO', A SISTER SHIP OF WITTMAN'S OLD 'BUSTER' WAS BUILT AND FLOWN BY STEVE WITTMAN FOR THE 1948 GOODYEAR TROPHY RACE, PLACING 2ND AT 168.69 M.P.H. AMONG OTHER RACES, CRAFT LATER WON 1949, '50 & '52 CONTINENTAL TROPHY RACE; 1950 & '51 READING RACES; 1956 & '57 OSHKOSH RACES; 2ND IN 1964 & '66 CHAMPIONSHIP FORMULA 1 RACES AT RENO.

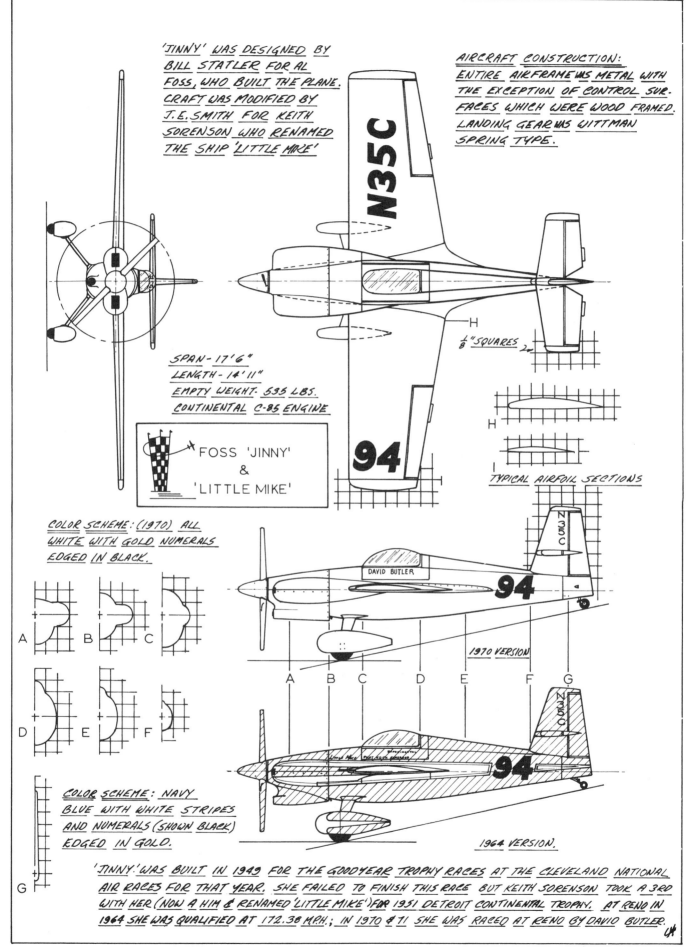

'JINNY' WAS DESIGNED BY BILL STATLER FOR AL FOSS, WHO BUILT THE PLANE. CRAFT WAS MODIFIED BY J.E. SMITH FOR KEITH SORENSON WHO RENAMED THE SHIP 'LITTLE MIKE'

AIRCRAFT CONSTRUCTION: ENTIRE AIRFRAME WS METAL WITH THE EXCEPTION OF CONTROL SURFACES WHICH WERE WOOD FRAMED. LANDING GEAR WS WITTMAN SPRING TYPE.

N35C

94

SPAN- 17' 6"
LENGTH- 14' 11"
EMPTY WEIGHT- 535 LBS.
CONTINENTAL C-85 ENGINE

FOSS 'JINNY' & 'LITTLE MIKE'

H
⅛" SQUARES

H
I
TYPICAL AIRFOIL SECTIONS

COLOR SCHEME: (1970) ALL WHITE WITH GOLD NUMERALS EDGED IN BLACK.

A   B   C

D   E   F

G

N35C
DAVID BUTLER
94
1970 VERSION

A   B   C   D   E   F   G

N35C
94
1964 VERSION.

COLOR SCHEME: NAVY BLUE WITH WHITE STRIPES AND NUMERALS (SHOWN BLACK) EDGED IN GOLD.

'JINNY' WAS BUILT IN 1949 FOR THE GOODYEAR TROPHY RACES AT THE CLEVELAND NATIONAL AIR RACES FOR THAT YEAR. SHE FAILED TO FINISH THIS RACE BUT KEITH SORENSON TOOK A 3RD WITH HER (NOW A HIM & RENAMED 'LITTLE MIKE') FOR 1951 DETROIT CONTINENTAL TROPHY. AT RENO IN 1964 SHE WAS QUALIFIED AT 172.38 M.P.H.; IN 1970 & 71 SHE WAS RACED AT RENO BY DAVID BUTLER.

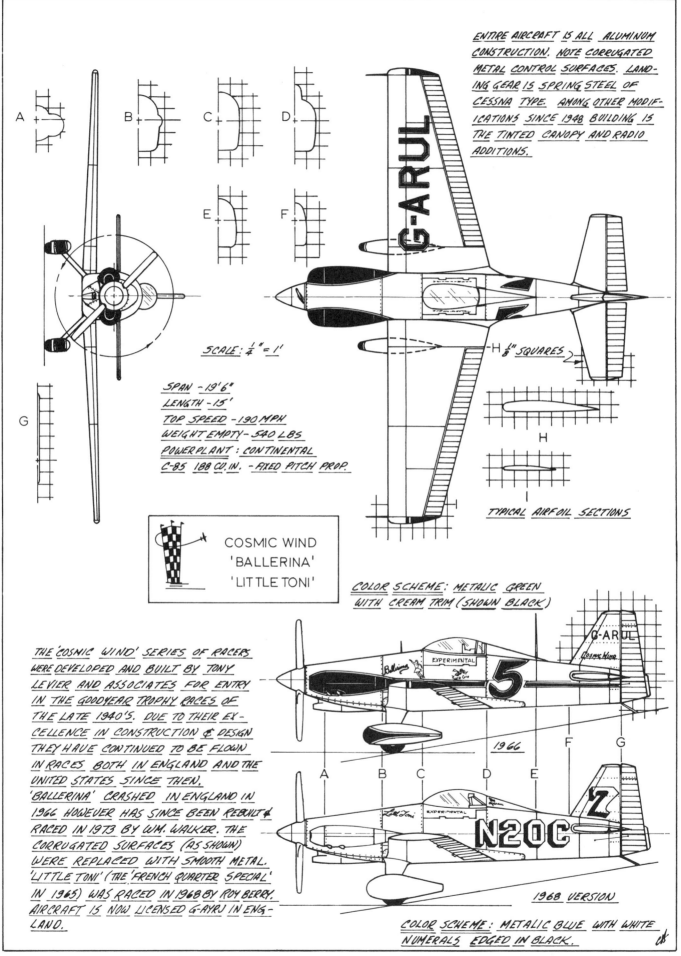

A B C D

E F

ENTIRE AIRCRAFT IS ALL ALUMINUM CONSTRUCTION. NOTE CORRUGATED METAL CONTROL SURFACES. LANDING GEAR IS SPRING STEEL OF CESSNA TYPE. AMONG OTHER MODIFICATIONS SINCE 1948 BUILDING IS THE TINTED CANOPY AND RADIO ADDITIONS.

G-ARUL

H ⅛" SQUARES

SCALE: ¼" = 1'

SPAN - 19'6"
LENGTH - 15'
TOP SPEED - 190 MPH
WEIGHT EMPTY - 540 LBS
POWER PLANT: CONTINENTAL
C-85 188 CU. IN. - FIXED PITCH PROP.

G

H

I

TYPICAL AIRFOIL SECTIONS

COSMIC WIND
'BALLERINA'
'LITTLE TONI'

THE 'COSMIC WIND' SERIES OF RACERS WERE DEVELOPED AND BUILT BY TONY LEVIER AND ASSOCIATES FOR ENTRY IN THE GOODYEAR TROPHY RACES OF THE LATE 1940'S. DUE TO THEIR EXCELLENCE IN CONSTRUCTION & DESIGN THEY HAVE CONTINUED TO BE FLOWN IN RACES BOTH IN ENGLAND AND THE UNITED STATES SINCE THEN. 'BALLERINA' CRASHED IN ENGLAND IN 1966 HOWEVER HAS SINCE BEEN REBUILT & RACED IN 1973 BY WM. WALKER. THE CORRUGATED SURFACES (AS SHOWN) WERE REPLACED WITH SMOOTH METAL. 'LITTLE TONI' (THE 'FRENCH QUARTER SPECIAL' IN 1965) WAS RACED IN 1968 BY ROY BERRY. AIRCRAFT IS NOW LICENSED G-AYRJ IN ENGLAND.

COLOR SCHEME: METALIC GREEN WITH CREAM TRIM (SHOWN BLACK)

G-ARUL

EXPERIMENTAL

Ballerina

5

1966

A B C D E F G

Little Toni

EXPERIMENTAL

N20C

Z

1968 VERSION

COLOR SCHEME: METALIC BLUE WITH WHITE NUMERALS EDGED IN BLACK.

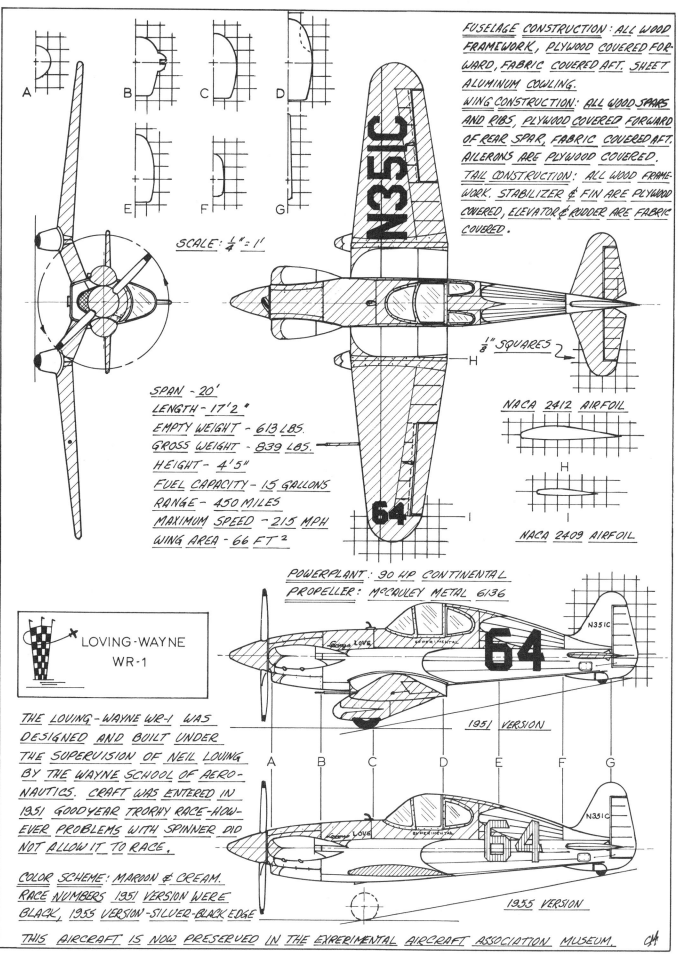

FUSELAGE CONSTRUCTION: ALL WOOD FRAMEWORK, PLYWOOD COVERED FORWARD, FABRIC COVERED AFT. SHEET ALUMINUM COWLING.

WING CONSTRUCTION: ALL WOOD SPARS AND RIBS, PLYWOOD COVERED FORWARD OF REAR SPAR, FABRIC COVERED AFT. AILERONS ARE PLYWOOD COVERED.

TAIL CONSTRUCTION: ALL WOOD FRAMEWORK. STABILIZER & FIN ARE PLYWOOD COVERED, ELEVATOR & RUDDER ARE FABRIC COVERED.

SCALE: ¼" = 1'

N351C

64

SPAN - 20'
LENGTH - 17' 2"
EMPTY WEIGHT - 613 LBS.
GROSS WEIGHT - 839 LBS.
HEIGHT - 4' 5"
FUEL CAPACITY - 15 GALLONS
RANGE - 450 MILES
MAXIMUM SPEED - 215 MPH
WING AREA - 66 FT²

⅛" SQUARES

NACA 2412 AIRFOIL

NACA 2409 AIRFOIL

POWERPLANT: 90 HP CONTINENTAL
PROPELLER: McCAULEY METAL 6136

LOVING-WAYNE
WR-1

1951 VERSION

A   B   C   D   E   F   G

THE LOVING-WAYNE WR-1 WAS DESIGNED AND BUILT UNDER THE SUPERVISION OF NEIL LOVING BY THE WAYNE SCHOOL OF AERONAUTICS. CRAFT WAS ENTERED IN 1951 GOODYEAR TROPHY RACE-HOWEVER PROBLEMS WITH SPINNER DID NOT ALLOW IT TO RACE.

COLOR SCHEME: MAROON & CREAM. RACE NUMBERS 1951 VERSION WERE BLACK, 1955 VERSION-SILVER-BLACK EDGE

1955 VERSION

THIS AIRCRAFT IS NOW PRESERVED IN THE EXPERIMENTAL AIRCRAFT ASSOCIATION MUSEUM.

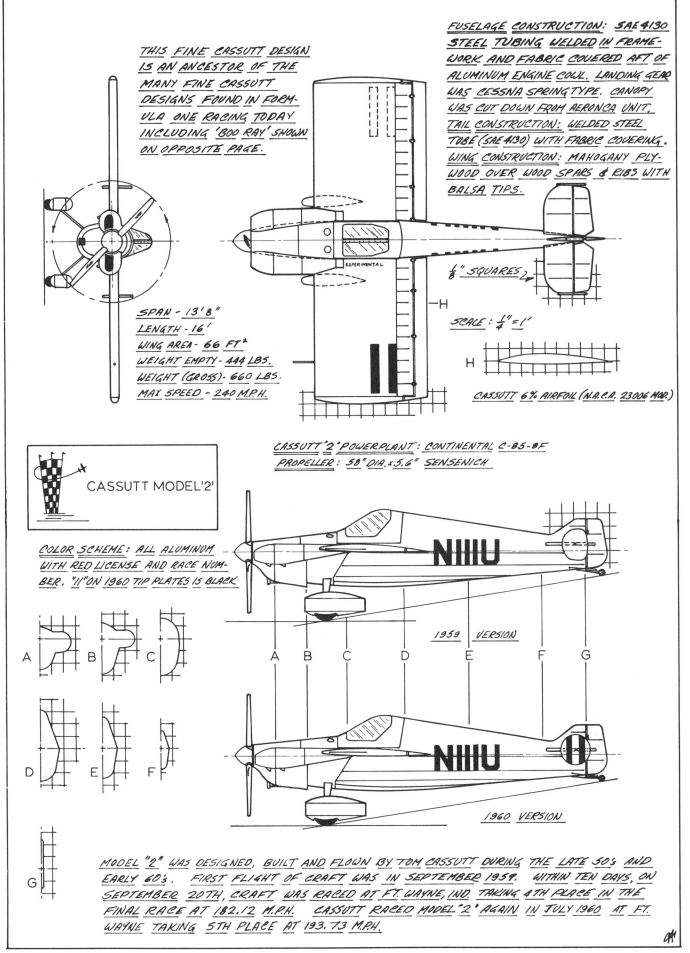

THIS FINE CASSUTT DESIGN IS AN ANCESTOR OF THE MANY FINE CASSUTT DESIGNS FOUND IN FORMULA ONE RACING TODAY INCLUDING 'BOO RAY' SHOWN ON OPPOSITE PAGE.

FUSELAGE CONSTRUCTION: SAE 4130 STEEL TUBING WELDED IN FRAMEWORK AND FABRIC COVERED AFT OF ALUMINUM ENGINE COWL. LANDING GEAR WAS CESSNA SPRINGTYPE. CANOPY WAS CUT DOWN FROM AERONCA UNIT. TAIL CONSTRUCTION: WELDED STEEL TUBE (SAE 4130) WITH FABRIC COVERING. WING CONSTRUCTION: MAHOGANY PLYWOOD OVER WOOD SPARS & RIBS WITH BALSA TIPS.

SPAN - 13' 8"
LENGTH - 16'
WING AREA - 66 FT²
WEIGHT EMPTY - 444 LBS.
WEIGHT (GROSS) - 660 LBS.
MAX. SPEED - 240 M.P.H.

EXPERIMENTAL

$\frac{1}{8}$" SQUARES

SCALE: $\frac{1}{4}$" = 1'

H

CASSUTT 6% AIRFOIL (N.A.C.A. 23006 MOD.)

CASSUTT "2" POWERPLANT: CONTINENTAL C-85-8F
PROPELLER: 58" DIA. x 5.6" SENSENICH

CASSUTT MODEL '2'

COLOR SCHEME: ALL ALUMINUM WITH RED LICENSE AND RACE NUMBER. "11" ON 1960 TIP PLATES IS BLACK

A   B   C

D   E   F

G

NIIIU

1959 VERSION

A   B   C   D   E   F   G

NIIIU

1960 VERSION

MODEL "2" WAS DESIGNED, BUILT AND FLOWN BY TOM CASSUTT DURING THE LATE 50's AND EARLY 60's. FIRST FLIGHT OF CRAFT WAS IN SEPTEMBER 1959. WITHIN TEN DAYS, ON SEPTEMBER 20TH, CRAFT WAS RACED AT FT. WAYNE, IND. TAKING 4TH PLACE IN THE FINAL RACE AT 182.12 M.P.H. CASSUTT RACED MODEL "2" AGAIN IN JULY 1960 AT FT. WAYNE TAKING 5TH PLACE AT 193.73 M.P.H.

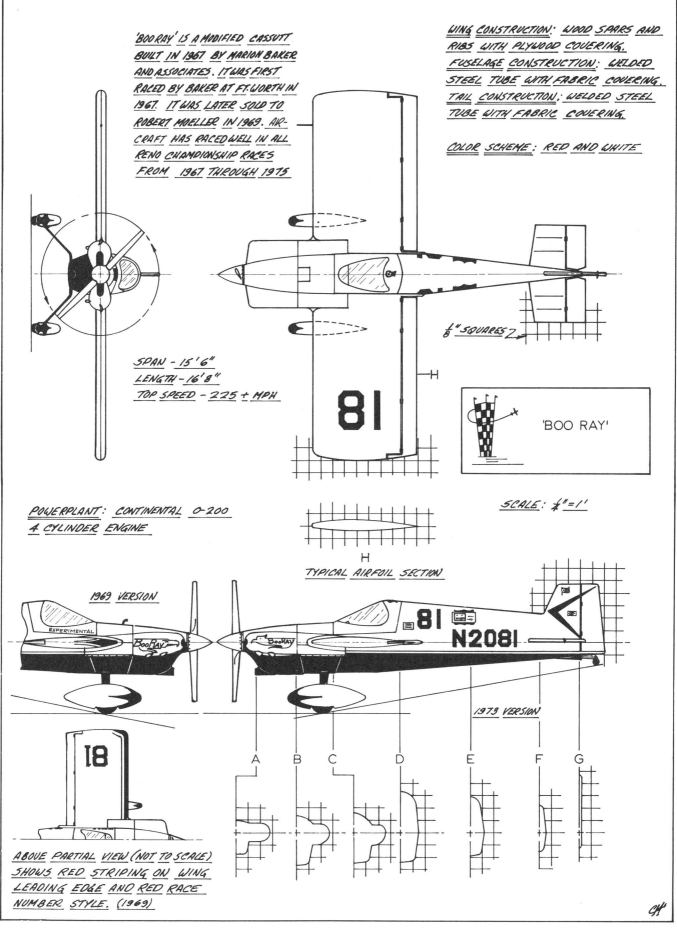

'BOO RAY' IS A MODIFIED CASSUTT BUILT IN 1967 BY MARION BAKER AND ASSOCIATES. IT WAS FIRST RACED BY BAKER AT FT. WORTH IN 1967. IT WAS LATER SOLD TO ROBERT MOELLER IN 1969. AIRCRAFT HAS RACED WELL IN ALL RENO CHAMPIONSHIP RACES FROM 1967 THROUGH 1975

WING CONSTRUCTION: WOOD SPARS AND RIBS WITH PLYWOOD COVERING. FUSELAGE CONSTRUCTION: WELDED STEEL TUBE WITH FABRIC COVERING. TAIL CONSTRUCTION: WELDED STEEL TUBE WITH FABRIC COVERING.

COLOR SCHEME: RED AND WHITE

SPAN - 15'6"
LENGTH - 16'8"
TOP SPEED - 225 + MPH

⅛" SQUARES

81

H

'BOO RAY'

SCALE: ¾"=1'

POWERPLANT: CONTINENTAL O-200 4 CYLINDER ENGINE

H

TYPICAL AIRFOIL SECTION

1969 VERSION

EXPERIMENTAL   BooRay   BooRay   81   N2081

1973 VERSION

18

ABOVE PARTIAL VIEW (NOT TO SCALE) SHOWS RED STRIPING ON WING LEADING EDGE AND RED RACE NUMBER STYLE. (1969)

A   B   C   D   E   F   G

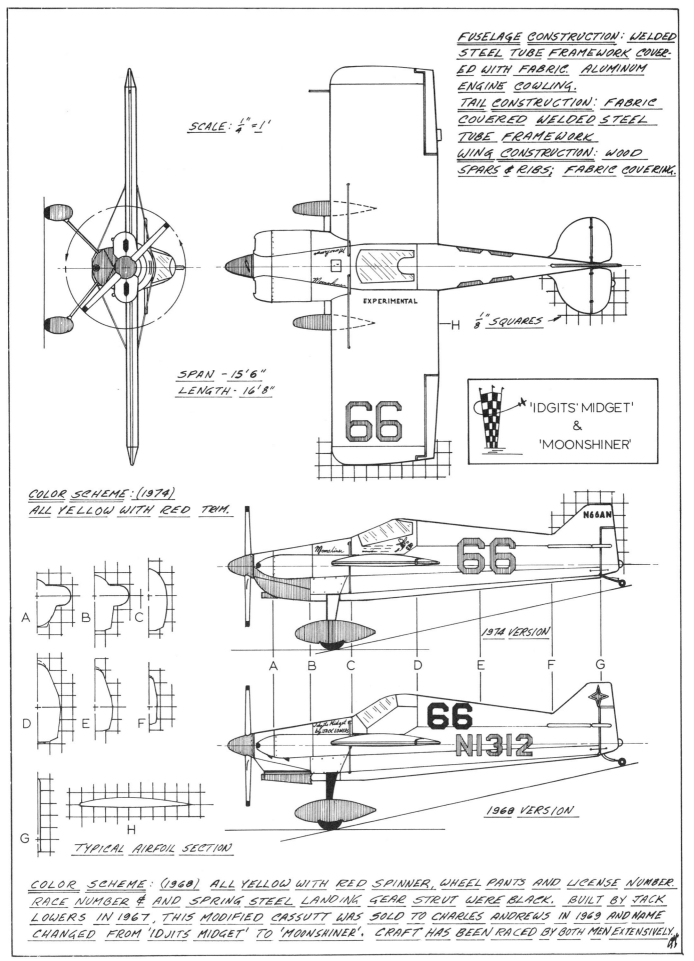

FUSELAGE CONSTRUCTION: WELDED
STEEL TUBE FRAMEWORK COVER-
ED WITH FABRIC. ALUMINUM
ENGINE COWLING.
TAIL CONSTRUCTION: FABRIC
COVERED WELDED STEEL
TUBE FRAMEWORK
WING CONSTRUCTION: WOOD
SPARS & RIBS; FABRIC COVERING.

SCALE: $\frac{1}{4}$" = 1'

EXPERIMENTAL

H $\frac{1}{8}$" SQUARES

SPAN - 15'6"
LENGTH - 16'8"

66

'IDGITS' MIDGET'
&
'MOONSHINER'

COLOR SCHEME: (1974)
ALL YELLOW WITH RED TRIM.

N66AN

66

1974 VERSION

A   B   C   D   E   F   G

A   B   C

D   E   F

G   H

TYPICAL AIRFOIL SECTION

66
N1312

1968 VERSION

COLOR SCHEME: (1968) ALL YELLOW WITH RED SPINNER, WHEEL PANTS AND LICENSE NUMBER.
RACE NUMBER & AND SPRING STEEL LANDING GEAR STRUT WERE BLACK. BUILT BY JACK
LOWERS IN 1967, THIS MODIFIED CASSUTT WAS SOLD TO CHARLES ANDREWS IN 1969 AND NAME
CHANGED FROM 'IDJITS MIDGET' TO 'MOONSHINER'. CRAFT HAS BEEN RACED BY BOTH MEN EXTENSIVELY.

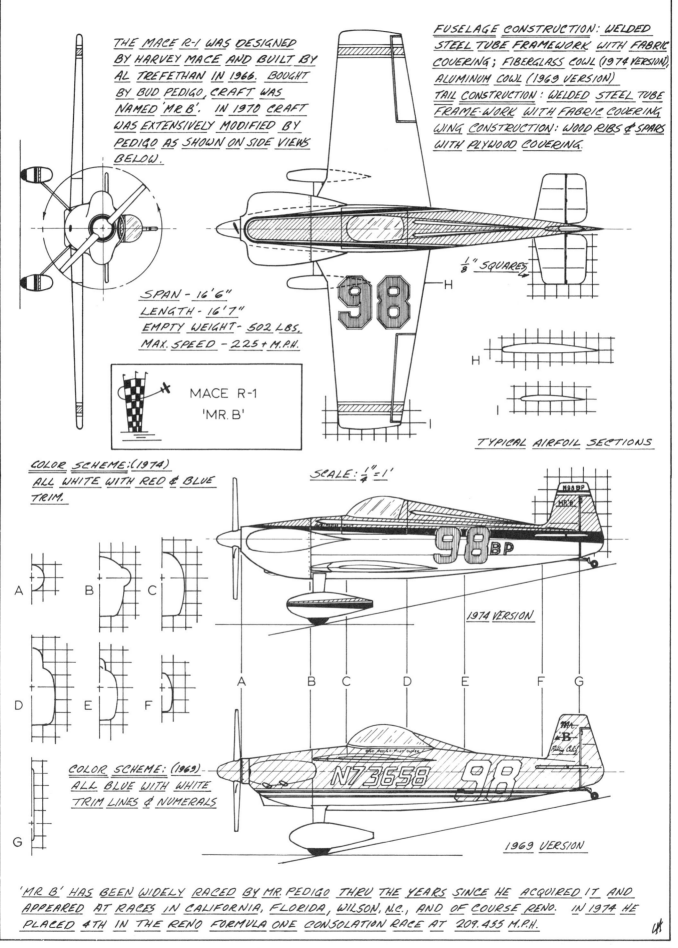

THE MACE R-1 WAS DESIGNED BY HARVEY MACE AND BUILT BY AL TREFETHAN IN 1966. BOUGHT BY BUD PEDIGO, CRAFT WAS NAMED 'MR. B'. IN 1970 CRAFT WAS EXTENSIVELY MODIFIED BY PEDIGO AS SHOWN ON SIDE VIEWS BELOW.

FUSELAGE CONSTRUCTION: WELDED STEEL TUBE FRAMEWORK WITH FABRIC COVERING; FIBERGLASS COWL (1974 VERSION), ALUMINUM COWL (1969 VERSION)
TAIL CONSTRUCTION: WELDED STEEL TUBE FRAME-WORK WITH FABRIC COVERING.
WING CONSTRUCTION: WOOD RIBS & SPARS WITH PLYWOOD COVERING.

SPAN - 16'6"
LENGTH - 16'7"
EMPTY WEIGHT - 502 LBS.
MAX. SPEED - 225 + M.P.H.

MACE R-1
'MR. B'

⅛" SQUARES

TYPICAL AIRFOIL SECTIONS

COLOR SCHEME: (1974)
ALL WHITE WITH RED & BLUE TRIM.

SCALE: ¼" = 1'

1974 VERSION

COLOR SCHEME: (1969)
ALL BLUE WITH WHITE TRIM LINES & NUMERALS

N73658

1969 VERSION

'MR. B' HAS BEEN WIDELY RACED BY MR. PEDIGO THRU THE YEARS SINCE HE ACQUIRED IT AND APPEARED AT RACES IN CALIFORNIA, FLORIDA, WILSON, N.C., AND OF COURSE RENO. IN 1974 HE PLACED 4TH IN THE RENO FORMULA ONE CONSOLATION RACE AT 209.455 M.P.H.

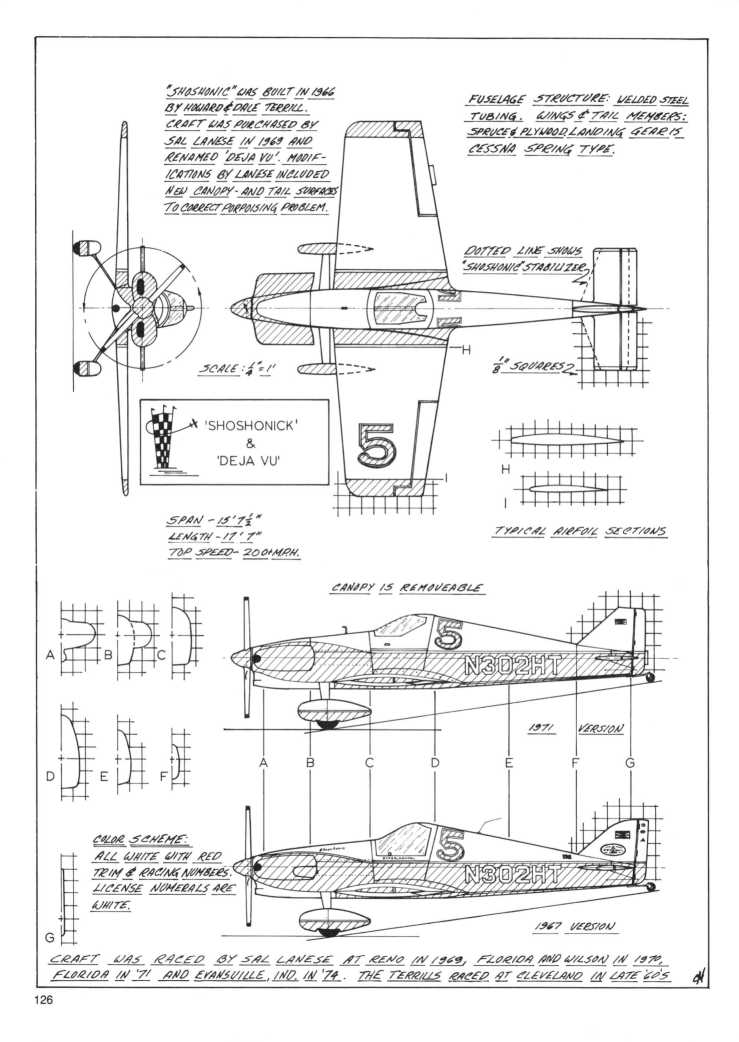

"SHOSHONIC" WAS BUILT IN 1966 BY HOWARD & DALE TERRILL. CRAFT WAS PURCHASED BY SAL LANESE IN 1969 AND RENAMED 'DEJA VU'. MODIF- ICATIONS BY LANESE INCLUDED NEW CANOPY- AND TAIL SURFACES TO CORRECT PORPOISING PROBLEM.

FUSELAGE STRUCTURE: WELDED STEEL TUBING. WINGS & TAIL MEMBERS: SPRUCE & PLYWOOD. LANDING GEAR IS CESSNA SPRING TYPE.

DOTTED LINE SHOWS "SHOSHONIC" STABILIZER

SCALE: 1/4" = 1'

1/8" SQUARES

'SHOSHONICK' & 'DEJA VU'

H

I

TYPICAL AIRFOIL SECTIONS

SPAN - 15' 7 1/2"
LENGTH - 17' 7"
TOP SPEED - 200+ M.P.H.

CANOPY IS REMOVEABLE

A   B   C

D   E   F

5

N302HT

1971 VERSION

A   B   C   D   E   F   G

COLOR SCHEME: ALL WHITE WITH RED TRIM & RACING NUMBERS. LICENSE NUMERALS ARE WHITE.

G

5

N302HT

1967 VERSION

CRAFT WAS RACED BY SAL LANESE AT RENO IN 1969, FLORIDA AND WILSON IN 1970, FLORIDA IN '71 AND EVANSVILLE, IND. IN '74. THE TERRILLS RACED AT CLEVELAND IN LATE '60'S

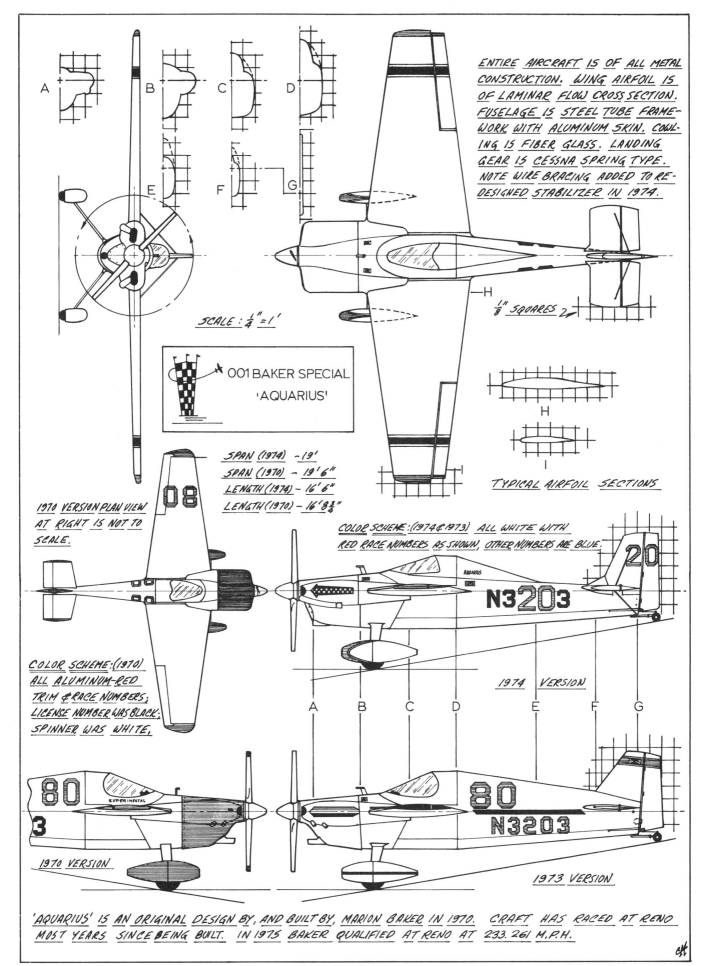

A B C D

E F G

ENTIRE AIRCRAFT IS OF ALL METAL
CONSTRUCTION. WING AIRFOIL IS
OF LAMINAR FLOW CROSS SECTION.
FUSELAGE IS STEEL TUBE FRAME-
WORK WITH ALUMINUM SKIN. COWL-
ING IS FIBER GLASS. LANDING
GEAR IS CESSNA SPRING TYPE.
NOTE WIRE BRACING ADDED TO RE-
DESIGNED STABILIZER IN 1974.

SCALE: ¼" = 1'

001 BAKER SPECIAL
'AQUARIUS'

H

⅛" SQUARES

H

I

TYPICAL AIRFOIL SECTIONS

SPAN (1974) - 19'
SPAN (1970) - 19'6"
LENGTH (1974) - 16'6"
LENGTH (1970) - 16'8¾"

1970 VERSION PLAN VIEW
AT RIGHT IS NOT TO
SCALE.

COLOR SCHEME: (1974 & 1973) ALL WHITE WITH
RED RACE NUMBERS AS SHOWN, OTHER NUMBERS ARE BLUE.

AQUARIUS

N3203

20

COLOR SCHEME: (1970)
ALL ALUMINUM-RED
TRIM & RACE NUMBERS;
LICENSE NUMBER WAS BLACK;
SPINNER WAS WHITE.

1974 VERSION

A B C D E F G

80
3
EXPERIMENTAL

80
N3203

1970 VERSION

1973 VERSION

'AQUARIUS' IS AN ORIGINAL DESIGN BY, AND BUILT BY, MARION BAKER IN 1970. CRAFT HAS RACED AT RENO
MOST YEARS SINCE BEING BUILT. IN 1975 BAKER QUALIFIED AT RENO AT 233.261 M.P.H.

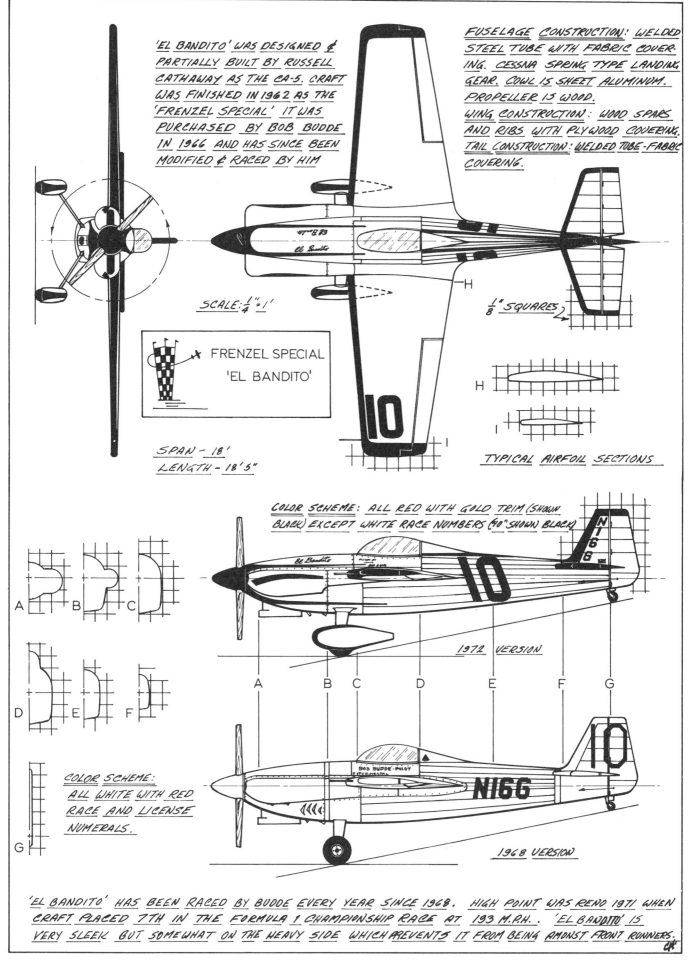

'EL BANDITO' WAS DESIGNED & PARTIALLY BUILT BY RUSSELL CATHAWAY AS THE CA-5. CRAFT WAS FINISHED IN 1962 AS THE 'FRENZEL SPECIAL' IT WAS PURCHASED BY BOB BUDDE IN 1966 AND HAS SINCE BEEN MODIFIED & RACED BY HIM

FUSELAGE CONSTRUCTION: WELDED STEEL TUBE WITH FABRIC COVERING. CESSNA SPRING TYPE LANDING GEAR. COWL IS SHEET ALUMINUM. PROPELLER IS WOOD.
WING CONSTRUCTION: WOOD SPARS AND RIBS WITH PLYWOOD COVERING.
TAIL CONSTRUCTION: WELDED TUBE-FABRIC COVERING.

SCALE: 1/4" = 1'

FRENZEL SPECIAL
'EL BANDITO'

1/8" SQUARES

H

TYPICAL AIRFOIL SECTIONS

SPAN - 18'
LENGTH - 18'5"

COLOR SCHEME: ALL RED WITH GOLD TRIM (SHOWN BLACK) EXCEPT WHITE RACE NUMBERS (40" SHOWN BLACK)

1972 VERSION

A   B   C   D   E   F   G

COLOR SCHEME: ALL WHITE WITH RED RACE AND LICENSE NUMERALS.

1968 VERSION

'EL BANDITO' HAS BEEN RACED BY BUDDE EVERY YEAR SINCE 1968. HIGH POINT WAS RENO 1971 WHEN CRAFT PLACED 7TH IN THE FORMULA 1 CHAMPIONSHIP RACE AT 193 M.P.H. 'EL BANDITO' IS VERY SLEEK BUT SOMEWHAT ON THE HEAVY SIDE WHICH PREVENTS IT FROM BEING AMONST FRONT RUNNERS.

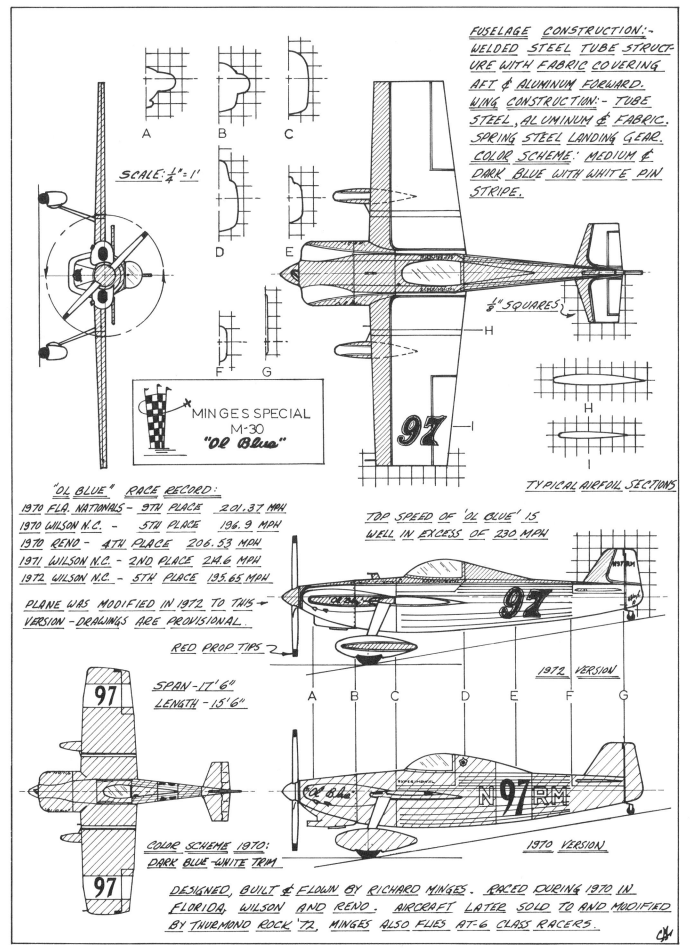

FUSELAGE CONSTRUCTION:-
WELDED STEEL TUBE STRUCT-
URE WITH FABRIC COVERING
AFT & ALUMINUM FORWARD.
WING CONSTRUCTION:- TUBE
STEEL, ALUMINUM & FABRIC.
SPRING STEEL LANDING GEAR.
COLOR SCHEME: MEDIUM &
DARK BLUE WITH WHITE PIN
STRIPE.

SCALE: $\frac{1}{4}$" = 1'

A   B   C

D   E

F   G

$\frac{1}{8}$" SQUARES

H

MINGES SPECIAL
M-30
"Ol Blue"

97

H

I

TYPICAL AIRFOIL SECTIONS

"OL BLUE" RACE RECORD:
1970 FLA. NATIONALS - 9TH PLACE   201.37 MPH
1970 WILSON N.C. -   5TH PLACE   196.9 MPH
1970 RENO -   4TH PLACE   206.53 MPH
1971 WILSON N.C. - 2ND PLACE   214.6 MPH
1972 WILSON N.C. - 5TH PLACE   195.65 MPH

PLANE WAS MODIFIED IN 1972 TO THIS →
VERSION - DRAWINGS ARE PROVISIONAL.

RED PROP TIPS

TOP SPEED OF 'OL BLUE' IS
WELL IN EXCESS OF 230 MPH

97

1972 VERSION

A   B   C   D   E   F   G

SPAN - 17' 6"
LENGTH - 15' 6"

97

97

COLOR SCHEME 1970:
DARK BLUE - WHITE TRIM

'Ol Blue   N 97 RM

1970 VERSION

DESIGNED, BUILT & FLOWN BY RICHARD MINGES. RACED DURING 1970 IN
FLORIDA, WILSON AND RENO. AIRCRAFT LATER SOLD TO AND MODIFIED
BY THURMOND ROCK '72. MINGES ALSO FLIES AT-6 CLASS RACERS.

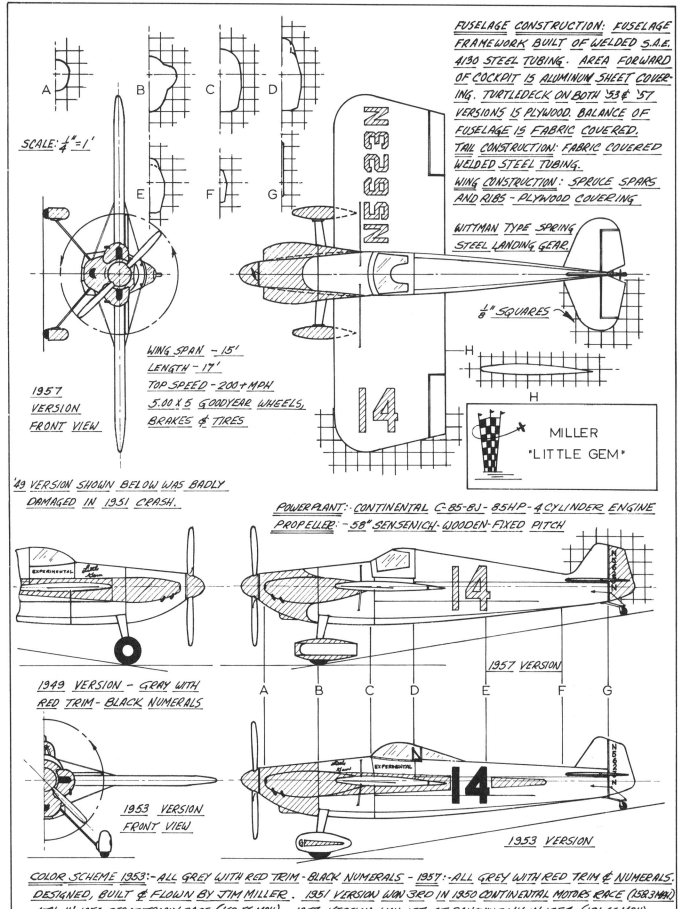

SCALE: $\frac{1}{4}$"=1'

A B C D

E F G

FUSELAGE CONSTRUCTION: FUSELAGE FRAMEWORK BUILT OF WELDED S.A.E. 4130 STEEL TUBING. AREA FORWARD OF COCKPIT IS ALUMINUM SHEET COVERING. TURTLEDECK ON BOTH '53 & '57 VERSIONS IS PLYWOOD. BALANCE OF FUSELAGE IS FABRIC COVERED.
TAIL CONSTRUCTION: FABRIC COVERED WELDED STEEL TUBING.
WING CONSTRUCTION: SPRUCE SPARS AND RIBS - PLYWOOD COVERING

WITTMAN TYPE SPRING STEEL LANDING GEAR.

$\frac{1}{8}$" SQUARES

1957 VERSION FRONT VIEW

WING SPAN - 15'
LENGTH - 17'
TOP SPEED - 200+ MPH
5.00 X 5 GOODYEAR WHEELS, BRAKES & TIRES

H

MILLER "LITTLE GEM"

'49 VERSION SHOWN BELOW WAS BADLY DAMAGED IN 1951 CRASH.

POWERPLANT: CONTINENTAL C-85-8J- 85HP- 4 CYLINDER ENGINE
PROPELLER: - 58" SENSENICH- WOODEN- FIXED PITCH

EXPERIMENTAL Little Gem

1949 VERSION - GRAY WITH RED TRIM- BLACK NUMERALS

1957 VERSION

A B C D E F G

1953 VERSION FRONT VIEW

1953 VERSION

COLOR SCHEME 1953:- ALL GREY WITH RED TRIM - BLACK NUMERALS - 1957:- ALL GREY WITH RED TRIM & NUMERALS.
DESIGNED, BUILT & FLOWN BY JIM MILLER. 1951 VERSION WON 3RD IN 1950 CONTINENTAL MOTORS RACE (158.3 MPH)
4TH IN 1950 REBAT TROPHY RACE (169.55 MPH). 1957 VERSION WON 1ST AT DANSVILLE, N.Y. IN 1954 (181.06 MPH)
AND 6TH PLACE IN 1957 FT. WAYNE, IND. RACE, (175.88 MPH). SEE NEXT PAGE FOR MORE ON THIS AIRCRAFT.

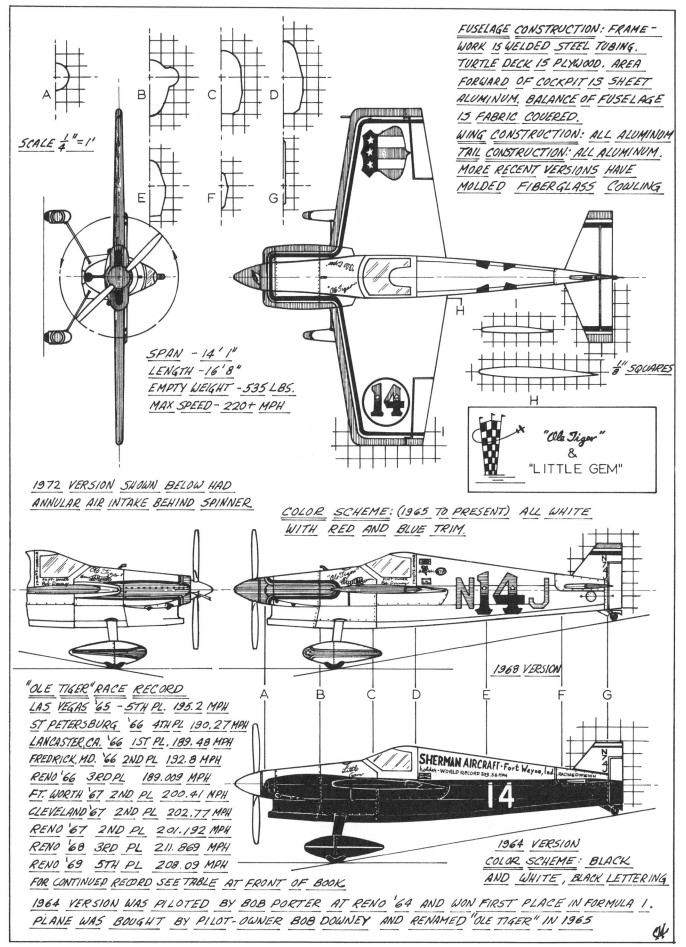

SCALE $\frac{1}{4}$" = 1'

FUSELAGE CONSTRUCTION: FRAME-
WORK IS WELDED STEEL TUBING.
TURTLE DECK IS PLYWOOD. AREA
FORWARD OF COCKPIT IS SHEET
ALUMINUM. BALANCE OF FUSELAGE
IS FABRIC COVERED.
WING CONSTRUCTION: ALL ALUMINUM
TAIL CONSTRUCTION: ALL ALUMINUM.
MORE RECENT VERSIONS HAVE
MOLDED FIBERGLASS COWLING

SPAN – 14' 1"
LENGTH – 16' 8"
EMPTY WEIGHT – 535 LBS.
MAX SPEED – 220+ MPH

$\frac{1}{8}$" SQUARES

"Ole Tiger"
&
"LITTLE GEM"

1972 VERSION SHOWN BELOW HAD
ANNULAR AIR INTAKE BEHIND SPINNER

COLOR SCHEME: (1965 TO PRESENT) ALL WHITE
WITH RED AND BLUE TRIM.

N14J

1968 VERSION

SHERMAN AIRCRAFT · Fort Wayne, Ind.
holder - WORLD RECORD 209.56 MPH
RACING DIVISION
14

"OLE TIGER" RACE RECORD
LAS VEGAS '65 – 5TH PL. 195.2 MPH
ST PETERSBURG '66 4TH PL 190.27 MPH
LANCASTER, CA. '66 1ST PL. 189.48 MPH
FREDRICK, MD. '66 2ND PL. 192.8 MPH
RENO '66 3RD PL 189.009 MPH
FT. WORTH '67 2ND PL 200.41 MPH
CLEVELAND '67 2ND PL 202.77 MPH
RENO '67 2ND PL 201.192 MPH
RENO '68 3RD PL 211.869 MPH
RENO '69 5TH PL 208.09 MPH
FOR CONTINUED RECORD SEE TABLE AT FRONT OF BOOK

1964 VERSION
COLOR SCHEME: BLACK
AND WHITE, BLACK LETTERING

1964 VERSION WAS PILOTED BY BOB PORTER AT RENO '64 AND WON FIRST PLACE IN FORMULA 1.
PLANE WAS BOUGHT BY PILOT-OWNER BOB DOWNEY AND RENAMED "OLE TIGER" IN 1965

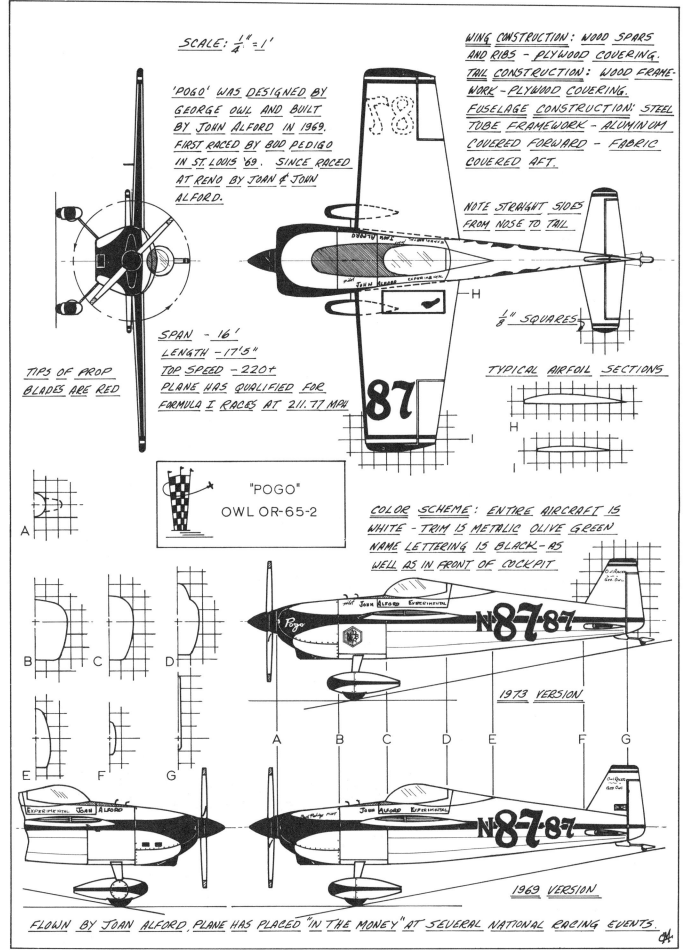

SCALE: $\frac{1}{4}'' = 1'$

'POGO' WAS DESIGNED BY GEORGE OWL AND BUILT BY JOHN ALFORD IN 1969. FIRST RACED BY BUD PEDIGO IN ST. LOUIS '69. SINCE RACED AT RENO BY JOAN & JOHN ALFORD.

WING CONSTRUCTION: WOOD SPARS AND RIBS - PLYWOOD COVERING. TAIL CONSTRUCTION: WOOD FRAMEWORK - PLYWOOD COVERING. FUSELAGE CONSTRUCTION: STEEL TUBE FRAMEWORK - ALUMINUM COVERED FORWARD - FABRIC COVERED AFT.

NOTE STRAIGHT SIDES FROM NOSE TO TAIL

$\frac{1}{8}''$ SQUARES

TIPS OF PROP BLADES ARE RED

SPAN - 16'
LENGTH - 17'5"
TOP SPEED - 220+
PLANE HAS QUALIFIED FOR FORMULA I RACES AT 211.77 MPH.

TYPICAL AIRFOIL SECTIONS

"POGO"
OWL OR-65-2

COLOR SCHEME: ENTIRE AIRCRAFT IS WHITE - TRIM IS METALIC OLIVE GREEN NAME LETTERING IS BLACK - AS WELL AS IN FRONT OF COCKPIT

1973 VERSION

1969 VERSION

FLOWN BY JOAN ALFORD, PLANE HAS PLACED "IN THE MONEY" AT SEVERAL NATIONAL RACING EVENTS.

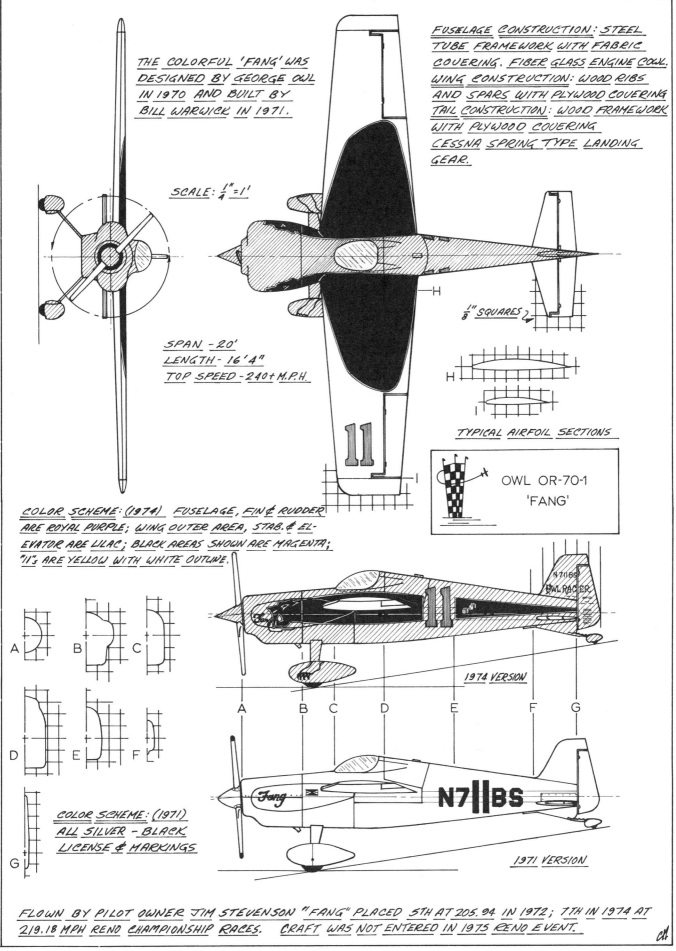

THE COLORFUL 'FANG' WAS DESIGNED BY GEORGE OWL IN 1970 AND BUILT BY BILL WARWICK IN 1971.

FUSELAGE CONSTRUCTION: STEEL TUBE FRAMEWORK WITH FABRIC COVERING. FIBER GLASS ENGINE COWL. WING CONSTRUCTION: WOOD RIBS AND SPARS WITH PLYWOOD COVERING TAIL CONSTRUCTION: WOOD FRAMEWORK WITH PLYWOOD COVERING CESSNA SPRING TYPE LANDING GEAR.

SCALE: $\frac{1}{4}"=1'$

SPAN - 20'
LENGTH - 16'4"
TOP SPEED - 240+ M.P.H.

$\frac{1}{8}"$ SQUARES

TYPICAL AIRFOIL SECTIONS

OWL OR-70-1 'FANG'

COLOR SCHEME: (1974) FUSELAGE, FIN & RUDDER ARE ROYAL PURPLE; WING OUTER AREA, STAB. & ELEVATOR ARE LILAC; BLACK AREAS SHOWN ARE MAGENTA; "11"s ARE YELLOW WITH WHITE OUTLINE.

1974 VERSION

COLOR SCHEME: (1971) ALL SILVER - BLACK LICENSE & MARKINGS

1971 VERSION

FLOWN BY PILOT OWNER JIM STEVENSON "FANG" PLACED 5TH AT 205.94 IN 1972; 7TH IN 1974 AT 219.18 MPH RENO CHAMPIONSHIP RACES. CRAFT WAS NOT ENTERED IN 1975 RENO EVENT.

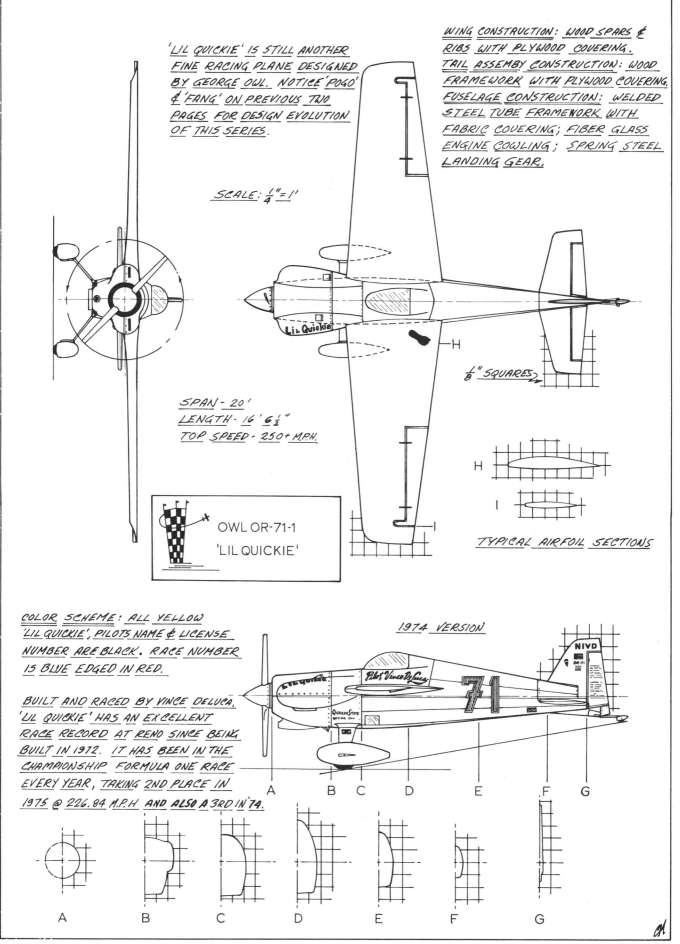

'LIL QUICKIE' IS STILL ANOTHER FINE RACING PLANE DESIGNED BY GEORGE OWL. NOTICE 'POGO' & 'FANG' ON PREVIOUS TWO PAGES FOR DESIGN EVOLUTION OF THIS SERIES.

WING CONSTRUCTION: WOOD SPARS & RIBS WITH PLYWOOD COVERING. TAIL ASSEMBY CONSTRUCTION: WOOD FRAMEWORK WITH PLYWOOD COVERING. FUSELAGE CONSTRUCTION: WELDED STEEL TUBE FRAMEWORK WITH FABRIC COVERING; FIBER GLASS ENGINE COWLING; SPRING STEEL LANDING GEAR.

SCALE: $\frac{1}{4}$" = 1'

$\frac{1}{8}$" SQUARES

SPAN - 20'
LENGTH · 16' 6$\frac{1}{2}$"
TOP SPEED · 250+ M.P.H.

H

I

TYPICAL AIRFOIL SECTIONS

OWL OR-71-1
'LIL QUICKIE'

COLOR SCHEME: ALL YELLOW 'LIL QUICKIE', PILOTS NAME & LICENSE NUMBER ARE BLACK. RACE NUMBER IS BLUE EDGED IN RED.

BUILT AND RACED BY VINCE DELUCA, 'LIL QUICKIE' HAS AN EXCELLENT RACE RECORD AT RENO SINCE BEING BUILT IN 1972. IT HAS BEEN IN THE CHAMPIONSHIP FORMULA ONE RACE EVERY YEAR, TAKING 2ND PLACE IN 1975 @ 226.84 M.P.H AND ALSO A 3RD IN '74.

1974 VERSION

A   B   C   D   E   F   G

A   B   C   D   E   F   G

134

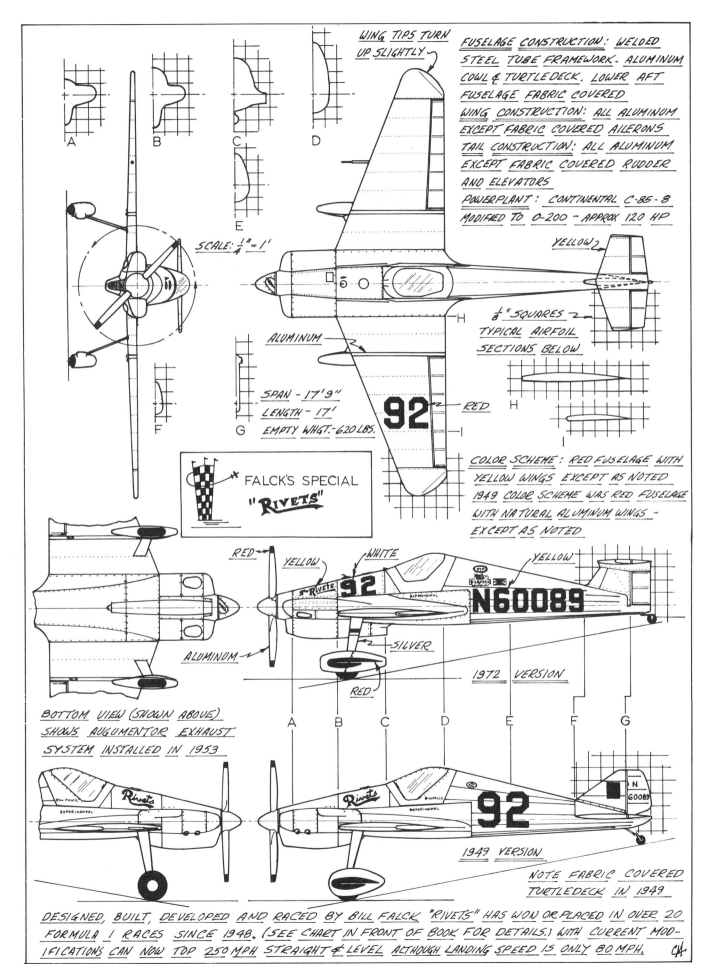

WING TIPS TURN UP SLIGHTLY

FUSELAGE CONSTRUCTION: WELDED STEEL TUBE FRAMEWORK. ALUMINUM COWL & TURTLEDECK. LOWER AFT FUSELAGE FABRIC COVERED

WING CONSTRUCTION: ALL ALUMINUM EXCEPT FABRIC COVERED AILERONS

TAIL CONSTRUCTION: ALL ALUMINUM EXCEPT FABRIC COVERED RUDDER AND ELEVATORS

POWERPLANT: CONTINENTAL C-85-8 MODIFIED TO O-200 - APPROX 120 HP

YELLOW

SCALE: 1/4" = 1'

1/8" SQUARES
TYPICAL AIRFOIL SECTIONS BELOW

ALUMINUM

H

SPAN - 17'9"
LENGTH - 17'
EMPTY WHGT.-620 LBS.

92   RED

H

I

FALCK'S SPECIAL "Rivets"

COLOR SCHEME: RED FUSELAGE WITH YELLOW WINGS EXCEPT AS NOTED 1949 COLOR SCHEME WAS RED FUSELAGE WITH NATURAL ALUMINUM WINGS - EXCEPT AS NOTED

RED   YELLOW   WHITE   YELLOW

92   N60089

ALUMINUM   SILVER

RED

1972 VERSION

BOTTOM VIEW (SHOWN ABOVE) SHOWS AUGUMENTOR EXHAUST SYSTEM INSTALLED IN 1953

A   B   C   D   E   F   G

Rivets   92   N 60089

1949 VERSION

NOTE FABRIC COVERED TURTLEDECK IN 1949

DESIGNED, BUILT, DEVELOPED AND RACED BY BILL FALCK "RIVETS" HAS WON OR PLACED IN OVER 20 FORMULA 1 RACES SINCE 1948. (SEE CHART IN FRONT OF BOOK FOR DETAILS.) WITH CURRENT MODIFICATIONS CAN NOW TOP 250 MPH STRAIGHT & LEVEL ALTHOUGH LANDING SPEED IS ONLY 80 MPH.

CA

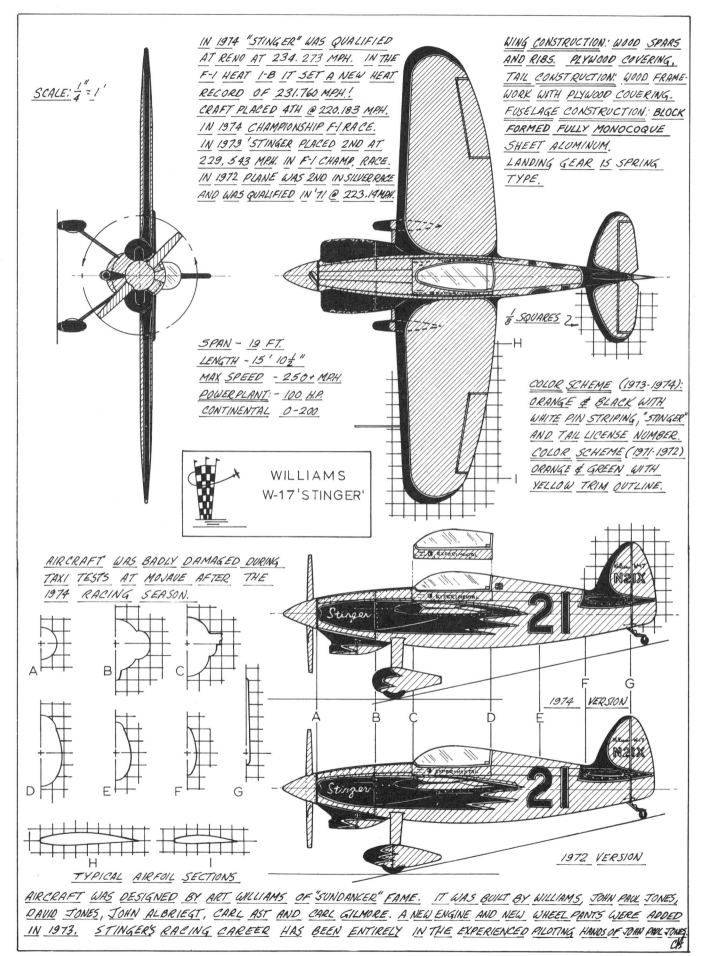

SCALE: $\frac{1}{4}'' = 1'$

IN 1974 "STINGER" WAS QUALIFIED AT RENO AT 234.273 MPH. IN THE F-1 HEAT I-B IT SET A NEW HEAT RECORD OF 231.760 MPH! CRAFT PLACED 4TH @ 220.183 MPH. IN 1974 CHAMPIONSHIP F-1 RACE. IN 1973 'STINGER PLACED 2ND AT 229.543 MPH. IN F-1 CHAMP. RACE. IN 1972 PLANE WAS 2ND IN SILVER RACE AND WAS QUALIFIED IN '71 @ 223.14 MPH.

WING CONSTRUCTION: WOOD SPARS AND RIBS. PLYWOOD COVERING. TAIL CONSTRUCTION: WOOD FRAMEWORK WITH PLYWOOD COVERING. FUSELAGE CONSTRUCTION: BLOCK FORMED FULLY MONOCOQUE SHEET ALUMINUM. LANDING GEAR IS SPRING TYPE.

SPAN - 19 FT.
LENGTH - 15' 10½"
MAX SPEED - 250+ M.P.H.
POWERPLANT: - 100 H.P.
CONTINENTAL O-200

$\frac{1}{8}$ SQUARES

WILLIAMS
W-17 'STINGER'

COLOR SCHEME (1973-1974): ORANGE & BLACK WITH WHITE PIN STRIPING, "STINGER" AND TAIL LICENSE NUMBER. COLOR SCHEME (1971-1972) ORANGE & GREEN WITH YELLOW TRIM OUTLINE.

AIRCRAFT WAS BADLY DAMAGED DURING TAXI TESTS AT MOJAVE AFTER THE 1974 RACING SEASON.

A   B   C
D   E   F   G
H   I

TYPICAL AIRFOIL SECTIONS

1974 VERSION

1972 VERSION

AIRCRAFT WAS DESIGNED BY ART WILLIAMS OF "SUNDANCER" FAME. IT WAS BUILT BY WILLIAMS, JOHN PAUL JONES, DAVID JONES, JOHN ALBRIEGT, CARL AST AND CARL GILMORE. A NEW ENGINE AND NEW WHEEL PANTS WERE ADDED IN 1973. STINGER'S RACING CAREER HAS BEEN ENTIRELY IN THE EXPERIENCED PILOTING HANDS OF JOHN PAUL JONES.

WING CONSTRUCTION: $5\frac{1}{4}$" BOX SPAR TAPERED AT TIP. RIBS ARE $\frac{1}{4}$" PLYWOOD WITH CAP STRIPS TO PROVIDE GLUING SURFACE. SKIN IS $\frac{1}{16}$" BIRCH PLYWOOD

FUSELAGE CONSTRUCTION: SEMI-MONOCOQUE WITH SIDE LONGERONS OF $\frac{3}{8}$" BOX SPARS 8" WIDE FROM TAIL POST TO INSTRUMENT PANEL TAPERED TO $5\frac{1}{2}$" AT FIREWALL.

SCALE: $\frac{1}{4}$" = 1'

FUSE. CONST. (CONT.) COVERED WITH $\frac{1}{16}$" BIRCH PLYWOOD IN STRESSED AREAS. NON-STRESSED AREAS COVERED WITH $\frac{1}{16}$" MAHOGANY PLYWOOD. COWLING IS FORMED ALUMINUM. FIBERGLASS USED FOR FUEL TANK AND TAILWHEEL SPRING. LANDING GEAR STRUTS ARE FIR AND FIBERGLASS.

TAIL ASSY.: ALL WOOD FRAME, PLY. COVERED

SPAN ~ 16'
WING AREA - 70 FT.²
LENGTH - 18' 6"
WEIGHT EMPTY - 540 LBS.
WEIGHT GROSS - 780 LBS.
MAX SPEED - 245 M.P.H.
LANDING SPEED - 65-70 M.P.H.

5.00 X 5" TIRES

MACE R-2 'SHARK'

$\frac{1}{8}$" SQUARES

AIRFOIL: SHARP NOSE 23012

POWERPLANT: CONTINENTAL O-200 4 CYLINDER OPPOSED ENGINE. 59" X 66" PITCH PROP

CANOPY - REVERSED ALFORD "OWL"
SPINNER - 2" SHORTER "MIDGET MUSTANG"

SHARK

N711HM

41

1970 VERSION

A B C D E F G

VIEW BELOW SHOWS SPACING OF RIBS & SPARS.

A B C D E F G

COLOR SCHEME: 1969 GM DARK METALIC GRAY. PALE YELLOW NUMBERS WITH $\frac{1}{2}$" WHITE EDGE. RED SHARK MOUTH AND EYE WITH BLACK TRIM. GRAY SEAM TAPE.

DESIGNED, BUILT AND FLOWN BY HARVEY MACE. PLACED SECOND IN CONSOLATION RACE AT 1970 RENO RACES AT 193.896 M.P.H.; 4TH IN '75 RENO SILVER RACE-200.5

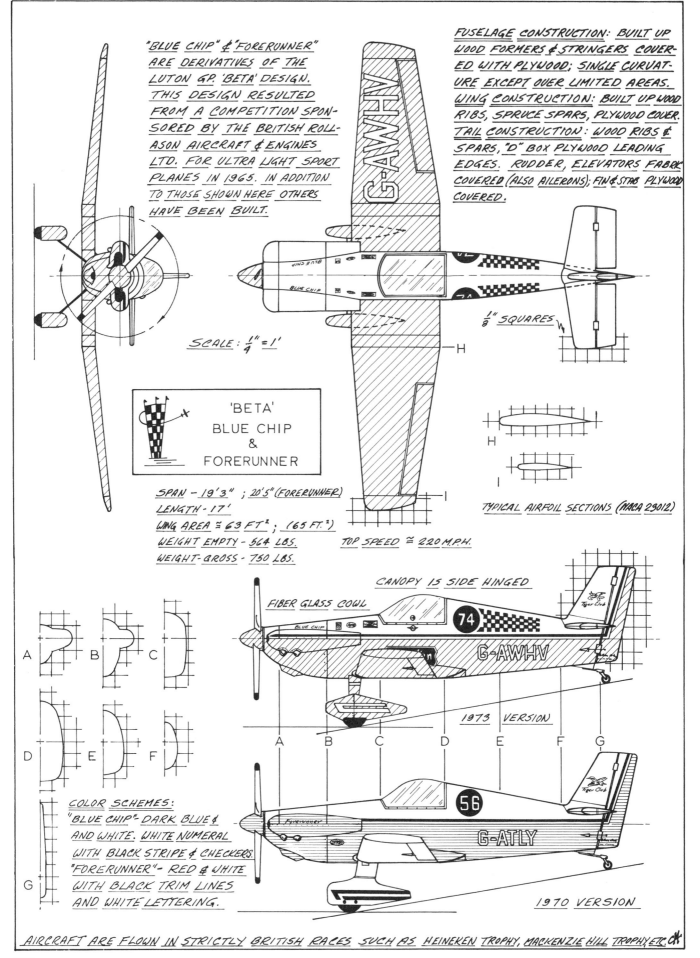

"BLUE CHIP" & "FORERUNNER" ARE DERIVATIVES OF THE LUTON GP. 'BETA' DESIGN. THIS DESIGN RESULTED FROM A COMPETITION SPONSORED BY THE BRITISH ROLL-ASON AIRCRAFT & ENGINES LTD. FOR ULTRA LIGHT SPORT PLANES IN 1965. IN ADDITION TO THOSE SHOWN HERE OTHERS HAVE BEEN BUILT.

FUSELAGE CONSTRUCTION: BUILT UP WOOD FORMERS & STRINGERS COVERED WITH PLYWOOD; SINGLE CURVATURE EXCEPT OVER LIMITED AREAS. WING CONSTRUCTION: BUILT UP WOOD RIBS, SPRUCE SPARS, PLYWOOD COVER. TAIL CONSTRUCTION: WOOD RIBS & SPARS, "D" BOX PLYWOOD LEADING EDGES. RUDDER, ELEVATORS FABRIC COVERED (ALSO AILERONS); FIN & STAB PLYWOOD COVERED.

G-AWHV

SCALE: 1/4" = 1'

⅛" SQUARES

'BETA'
BLUE CHIP
&
FORERUNNER

SPAN - 19'3" ; 20'5" (FORERUNNER)
LENGTH - 17'
WING AREA ≈ 63 FT² ; (65 FT²)
WEIGHT EMPTY - 564 LBS.
WEIGHT-GROSS - 750 LBS.

TOP SPEED ≅ 220 M.P.H.

H

I

TYPICAL AIRFOIL SECTIONS (NACA 23012)

FIBER GLASS COWL

CANOPY IS SIDE HINGED

BLUE CHIP

74

Tiger Club

G-AWHV

1973 VERSION

A   B   C   D   E   F   G

A   B   C

D   E   F

G

COLOR SCHEMES:
"BLUE CHIP" - DARK BLUE & AND WHITE. WHITE NUMERAL WITH BLACK STRIPE & CHECKERS. "FORERUNNER" - RED & WHITE WITH BLACK TRIM LINES AND WHITE LETTERING.

Forerunner

56

Tiger Club

G-ATLY

1970 VERSION

AIRCRAFT ARE FLOWN IN STRICTLY BRITISH RACES SUCH AS HEINEKEN TROPHY, MACKENZIE HILL TROPHY, ETC.

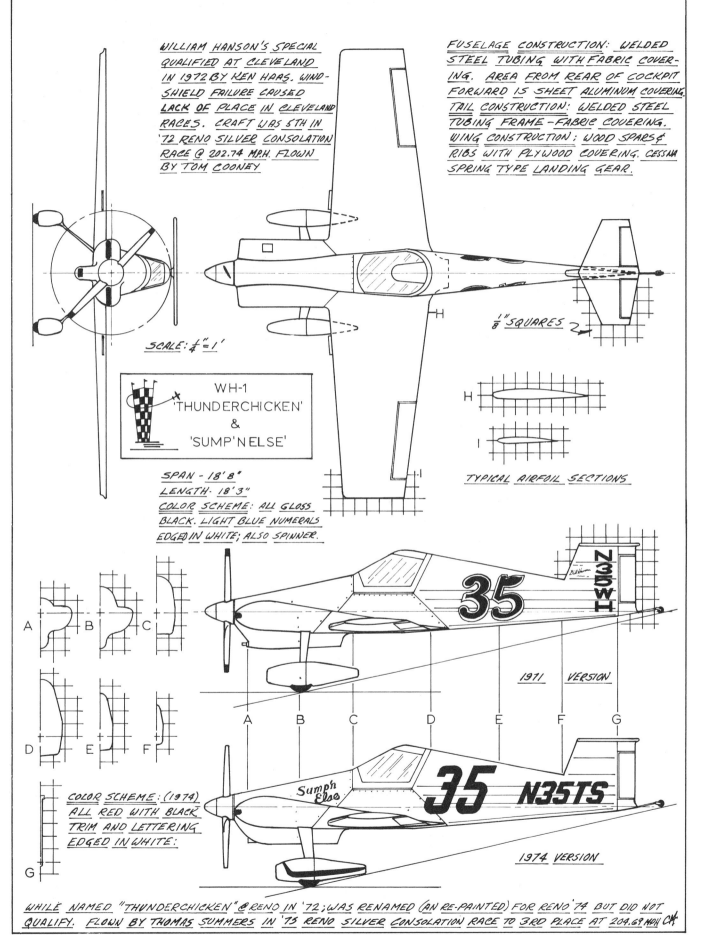

WILLIAM HANSON'S SPECIAL
QUALIFIED AT CLEVELAND
IN 1972 BY KEN HAAS. WIND-
SHIELD FAILURE CAUSED
LACK OF PLACE IN CLEVELAND
RACES. CRAFT WAS 5TH IN
'72 RENO SILVER CONSOLATION
RACE @ 202.74 M.P.H. FLOWN
BY TOM COONEY

FUSELAGE CONSTRUCTION: WELDED
STEEL TUBING WITH FABRIC COVER-
ING. AREA FROM REAR OF COCKPIT
FORWARD IS SHEET ALUMINUM COVERING.
TAIL CONSTRUCTION: WELDED STEEL
TUBING FRAME-FABRIC COVERING.
WING CONSTRUCTION: WOOD SPARS &
RIBS WITH PLYWOOD COVERING. CESSNA
SPRING TYPE LANDING GEAR.

SCALE: ¼"=1'

⅛" SQUARES

WH-1
'THUNDERCHICKEN'
&
'SUMP'N ELSE'

H

I

TYPICAL AIRFOIL SECTIONS

SPAN - 18' 8"
LENGTH - 18' 3"
COLOR SCHEME: ALL GLOSS
BLACK. LIGHT BLUE NUMERALS
EDGED IN WHITE; ALSO SPINNER.

A B C

D E F

35 N35WH
1971 VERSION

A B C D E F G

COLOR SCHEME: (1974)
ALL RED WITH BLACK
TRIM AND LETTERING
EDGED IN WHITE:

G

Sumph Else
35 N35TS
1974 VERSION

WHILE NAMED "THUNDERCHICKEN" @ RENO IN '72; WAS RENAMED (AN RE-PAINTED) FOR RENO '74 BUT DID NOT
QUALIFY. FLOWN BY THOMAS SUMMERS IN '75 RENO SILVER CONSOLATION RACE TO 3RD PLACE AT 204.69 MPH CA.

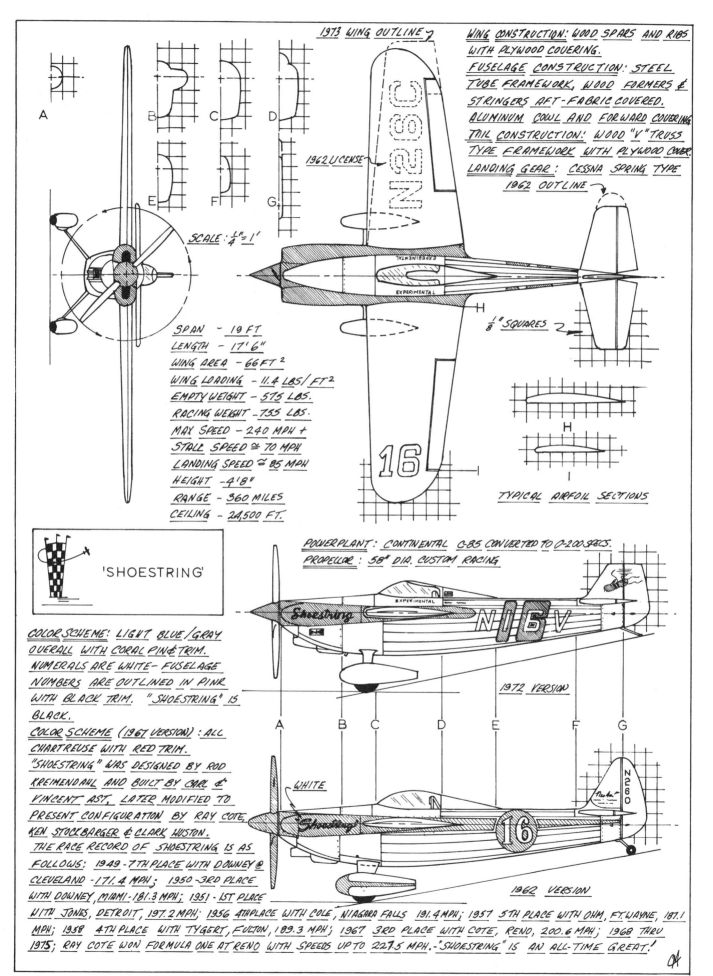

A   B   C   D   E   F   G

1973 WING OUTLINE

1962 LICENSE

SCALE: ¼" = 1'

WING CONSTRUCTION: WOOD SPARS AND RIBS WITH PLYWOOD COVERING.
FUSELAGE CONSTRUCTION: STEEL TUBE FRAMEWORK, WOOD FORMERS & STRINGERS AFT-FABRIC COVERED. ALUMINUM COWL AND FORWARD COVERING
TAIL CONSTRUCTION: WOOD "V" TRUSS TYPE FRAMEWORK WITH PLYWOOD COVER.
LANDING GEAR: CESSNA SPRING TYPE

1962 OUTLINE

⅛" SQUARES

H

TYPICAL AIRFOIL SECTIONS

SPAN - 19 FT
LENGTH - 17' 6"
WING AREA - 66 FT²
WING LOADING - 11.4 LBS/FT²
EMPTY WEIGHT - 575 LBS.
RACING WEIGHT - 755 LBS.
MAX SPEED - 240 MPH +
STALL SPEED ≅ 70 MPH
LANDING SPEED ≅ 85 MPH
HEIGHT - 4' 8"
RANGE - 360 MILES
CEILING - 24,500 FT.

'SHOESTRING'

POWERPLANT: CONTINENTAL C-85 CONVERTED TO 0-200 SPECS.
PROPELLOR: 58" DIA. CUSTOM RACING

1972 VERSION

A   B   C   D   E   F   G

COLOR SCHEME: LIGHT BLUE/GRAY OVERALL WITH CORAL PIN & TRIM. NUMERALS ARE WHITE- FUSELAGE NUMBERS ARE OUTLINED IN PINK WITH BLACK TRIM. "SHOESTRING" IS BLACK.
COLOR SCHEME (1967 VERSION): ALL CHARTREUSE WITH RED TRIM.
"SHOESTRING" WAS DESIGNED BY ROD KREIMENDAHL AND BUILT BY CARL & VINCENT AST, LATER MODIFIED TO PRESENT CONFIGURATION BY RAY COTE, KEN STOCKBARGER & CLARK HUSTON.
THE RACE RECORD OF SHOESTRING IS AS FOLLOWS: 1949 -7TH PLACE WITH DOWNEY @ CLEVELAND -171.4 MPH; 1950 -3RD PLACE WITH DOWNEY, MIAMI -181.3 MPH; 1951 -1ST PLACE WITH JONES, DETROIT, 197.2 MPH; 1956 4TH PLACE WITH COLE, NIAGARA FALLS 191.4 MPH; 1957 5TH PLACE WITH OHM, FT. WAYNE, 187.1 MPH; 1958 4TH PLACE WITH TYGERT, FULTON, 189.3 MPH; 1967 3RD PLACE WITH COTE, RENO, 200.6 MPH; 1968 THRU 1975; RAY COTE WON FORMULA ONE AT RENO WITH SPEEDS UP TO 227.5 MPH. "SHOESTRING" IS AN ALL-TIME GREAT!

WHITE

1962 VERSION

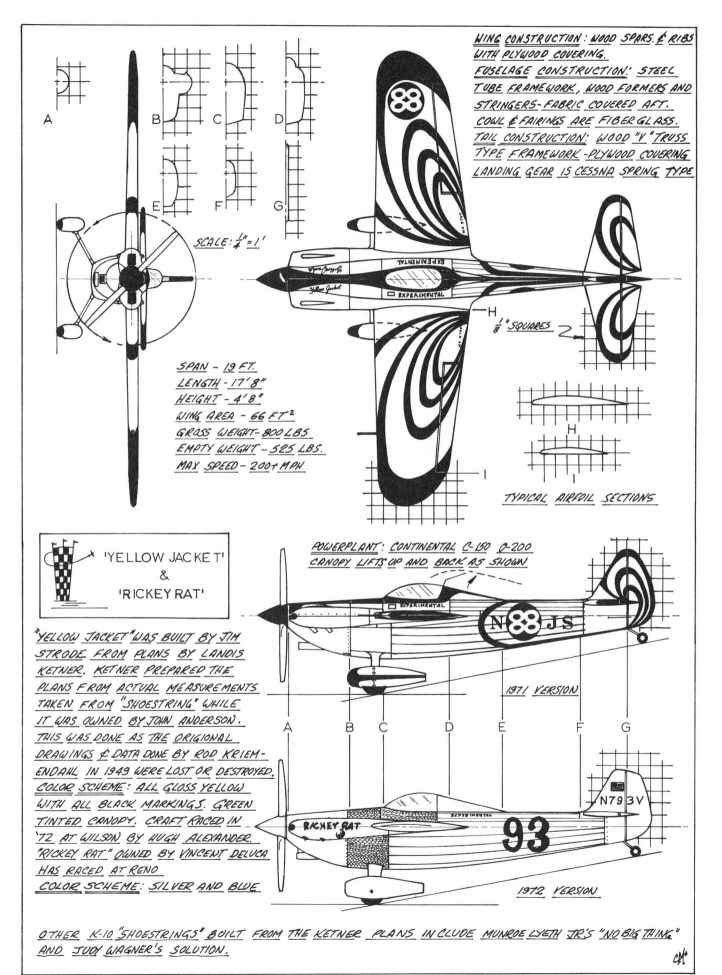

WING CONSTRUCTION: WOOD SPARS & RIBS WITH PLYWOOD COVERING.
FUSELAGE CONSTRUCTION: STEEL TUBE FRAMEWORK, WOOD FORMERS AND STRINGERS-FABRIC COVERED AFT. COWL & FAIRINGS ARE FIBER GLASS.
TAIL CONSTRUCTION: WOOD "V" TRUSS TYPE FRAMEWORK -PLYWOOD COVERING
LANDING GEAR IS CESSNA SPRING TYPE

A B C D
E F G

SCALE: $\frac{1}{4}$" = 1'

SPAN - 19 FT.
LENGTH - 17' 8"
HEIGHT - 4' 8"
WING AREA - 66 FT²
GROSS WEIGHT - 800 LBS
EMPTY WEIGHT - 525 LBS.
MAX SPEED - 200+ MPH

$\frac{1}{8}$" SQUARES

H

H

I

TYPICAL AIRFOIL SECTIONS

'YELLOW JACKET'
&
'RICKEY RAT'

POWERPLANT: CONTINENTAL C-150 O-200
CANOPY LIFTS UP AND BACK AS SHOWN

1971 VERSION

A B C D E F G

1972 VERSION

"YELLOW JACKET" WAS BUILT BY JIM STRODE. FROM PLANS BY LANDIS KETNER. KETNER PREPARED THE PLANS FROM ACTUAL MEASUREMENTS TAKEN FROM "SHOESTRING" WHILE IT WAS OWNED BY JOHN ANDERSON. THIS WAS DONE AS THE ORIGIONAL DRAWINGS & DATA DONE BY ROD KRIEMENDAHL IN 1949 WERE LOST OR DESTROYED.
COLOR SCHEME: ALL GLOSS YELLOW WITH ALL BLACK MARKINGS. GREEN TINTED CANOPY. CRAFT RACED IN '72 AT WILSON BY HUGH ALEXANDER. "RICKEY RAT" OWNED BY VINCENT DELUCA HAS RACED AT RENO
COLOR SCHEME: SILVER AND BLUE

OTHER K-10 "SHOESTRINGS" BUILT FROM THE KETNER PLANS INCLUDE MUNROE LYETH JR'S "NO BIG THING" AND JUDY WAGNER'S SOLUTION.

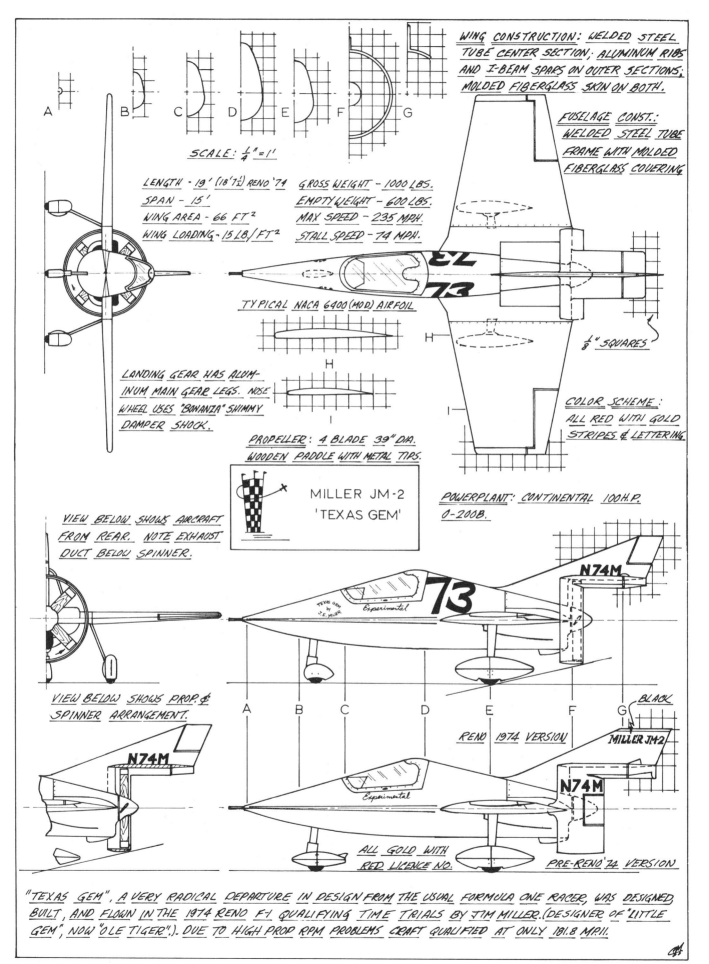

WING CONSTRUCTION: WELDED STEEL TUBE CENTER SECTION; ALUMINUM RIBS AND I-BEAM SPARS ON OUTER SECTIONS; MOLDED FIBERGLASS SKIN ON BOTH.

FUSELAGE CONST.: WELDED STEEL TUBE FRAME WITH MOLDED FIBERGLASS COVERING

A   B   C   D   E   F   G

SCALE: $\frac{1}{4}" = 1'$

LENGTH - 19' (18'7½) RENO '74
SPAN - 15'
WING AREA - 66 FT²
WING LOADING - 15 LB/FT²

GROSS WEIGHT - 1000 LBS.
EMPTY WEIGHT - 600 LBS.
MAX SPEED - 235 MPH.
STALL SPEED - 74 MPH.

TYPICAL NACA 6400 (MOD) AIRFOIL

H

$\frac{1}{8}"$ SQUARES

LANDING GEAR HAS ALUM-INUM MAIN GEAR LEGS. NOSE WHEEL USES "BONANZA" SHIMMY DAMPER SHOCK.

H

I

COLOR SCHEME: ALL RED WITH GOLD STRIPES & LETTERING

PROPELLER: 4 BLADE 39" DIA. WOODEN PADDLE WITH METAL TIPS.

MILLER JM-2 'TEXAS GEM'

POWERPLANT: CONTINENTAL 100 H.P. O-200B.

VIEW BELOW SHOWS AIRCRAFT FROM REAR. NOTE EXHAUST DUCT BELOW SPINNER.

N74M

73

Experimental

TEXAS GEM by J.E. MILLER

VIEW BELOW SHOWS PROP. & SPINNER ARRANGEMENT.

A   B   C   D   E   F   G   BLACK

RENO 1974 VERSION

MILLER JM2

N74M

ALL GOLD WITH RED LICENCE NO.

Experimental

N74M

PRE-RENO '74 VERSION

"TEXAS GEM", A VERY RADICAL DEPARTURE IN DESIGN FROM THE USUAL FORMULA ONE RACER, WAS DESIGNED, BUILT, AND FLOWN IN THE 1974 RENO F-1 QUALIFYING TIME TRIALS BY JIM MILLER.(DESIGNER OF "LITTLE GEM", NOW "OLE TIGER".). DUE TO HIGH PROP RPM PROBLEMS CRAFT QUALIFIED AT ONLY 181.8 M.P.H.

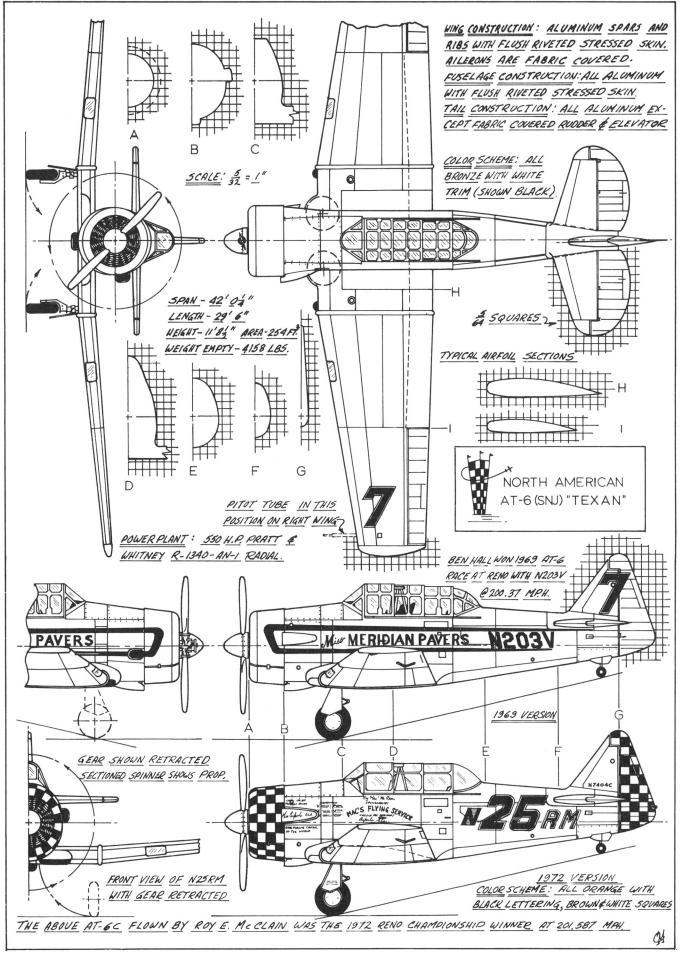

WING CONSTRUCTION: ALUMINUM SPARS AND RIBS WITH FLUSH RIVETED STRESSED SKIN. AILERONS ARE FABRIC COVERED.
FUSELAGE CONSTRUCTION: ALL ALUMINUM WITH FLUSH RIVETED STRESSED SKIN.
TAIL CONSTRUCTION: ALL ALUMINUM EXCEPT FABRIC COVERED RUDDER & ELEVATOR

COLOR SCHEME: ALL BRONZE WITH WHITE TRIM (SHOWN BLACK).

SCALE: $\frac{5}{32} = 1''$

SPAN - 42' 0$\frac{1}{4}$"
LENGTH - 29' 6"
HEIGHT - 11' 8$\frac{1}{2}$" AREA - 254 FT.
WEIGHT EMPTY - 4158 LBS.

$\frac{3}{64}$ SQUARES

TYPICAL AIRFOIL SECTIONS

PITOT TUBE IN THIS POSITION ON RIGHT WING

POWER PLANT: 550 H.P. PRATT & WHITNEY R-1340-AN-1 RADIAL.

NORTH AMERICAN AT-6 (SNJ) "TEXAN"

BEN HALL WON 1969 AT-6 RACE AT RENO WITH N203V @ 200.37 M.P.H.

PAVERS

Miss MERIDIAN PAVERS N203V

1969 VERSION

GEAR SHOWN RETRACTED
SECTIONED SPINNER SHOWS PROP.

FRONT VIEW OF N25RM WITH GEAR RETRACTED

MAC'S FLYING SERVICE

N25RM

N7404C

1972 VERSION
COLOR SCHEME: ALL ORANGE WITH BLACK LETTERING, BROWN & WHITE SQUARES

THE ABOVE AT-6C FLOWN BY ROY E. McCLAIN WAS THE 1972 RENO CHAMPIONSHIP WINNER AT 201.587 MPH

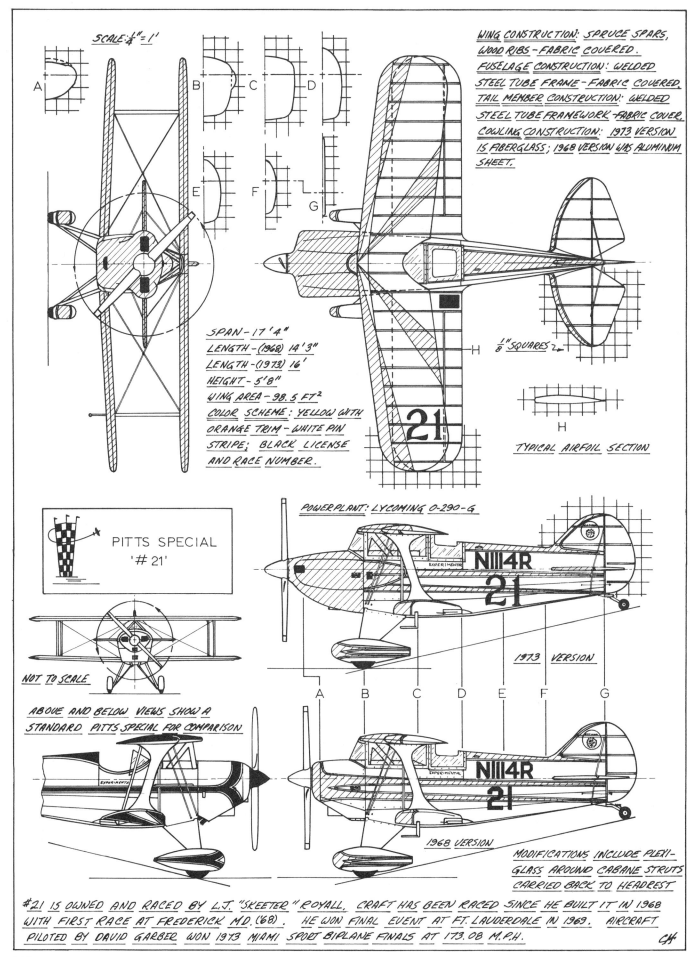

SCALE: ¼" = 1'

WING CONSTRUCTION: SPRUCE SPARS, WOOD RIBS – FABRIC COVERED.
FUSELAGE CONSTRUCTION: WELDED STEEL TUBE FRAME – FABRIC COVERED.
TAIL MEMBER CONSTRUCTION: WELDED STEEL TUBE FRAMEWORK – FABRIC COVER.
COWLING CONSTRUCTION: 1973 VERSION IS FIBERGLASS; 1968 VERSION WAS ALUMINUM SHEET.

SPAN – 17'4"
LENGTH – (1968) 14'3"
LENGTH – (1973) 16'
HEIGHT – 5'8"
WING AREA – 98.5 FT²
COLOR SCHEME: YELLOW WITH ORANGE TRIM – WHITE PIN STRIPE; BLACK LICENSE AND RACE NUMBER.

⅛" SQUARES

H

TYPICAL AIRFOIL SECTION

PITTS SPECIAL '# 21'

NOT TO SCALE

POWERPLANT: LYCOMING O-290-G

N1114R
21

1973 VERSION

A   B   C   D   E   F   G

ABOVE AND BELOW VIEWS SHOW A STANDARD PITTS SPECIAL FOR COMPARISON

N1114R
21

1968 VERSION

MODIFICATIONS INCLUDE PLEXI-GLASS AROUND CABANE STRUTS CARRIED BACK TO HEADREST

#21 IS OWNED AND RACED BY L.J. "SKEETER" ROYALL. CRAFT HAS BEEN RACED SINCE HE BUILT IT IN 1968 WITH FIRST RACE AT FREDERICK M.D. (68). HE WON FINAL EVENT AT FT. LAUDERDALE IN 1969. AIRCRAFT PILOTED BY DAVID GARBER WON 1973 MIAMI SPORT BIPLANE FINALS AT 173.08 M.P.H.

CH

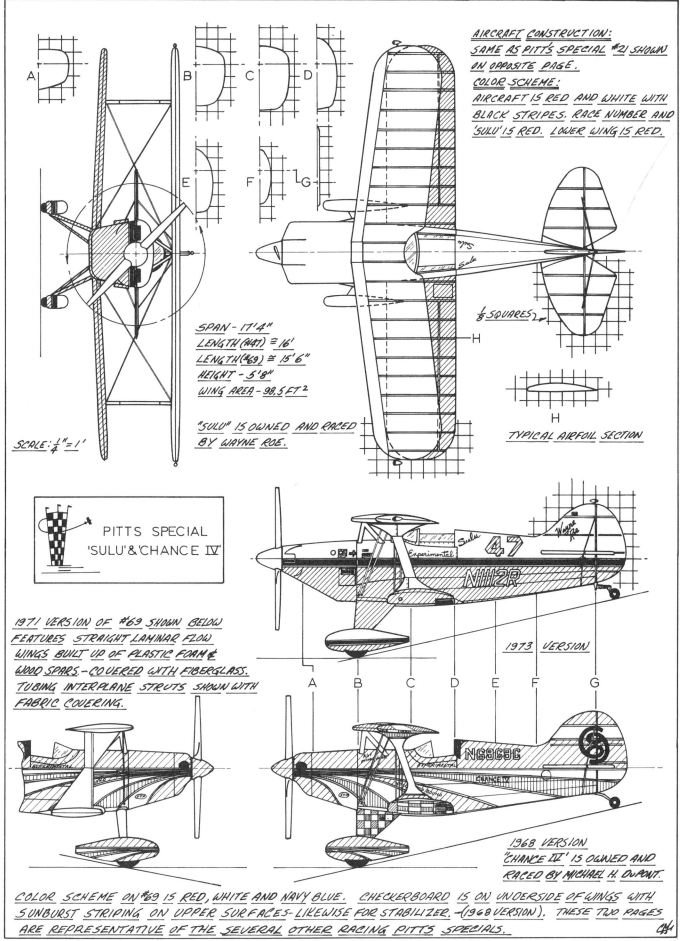

AIRCRAFT CONSTRUCTION:
SAME AS PITT'S SPECIAL #21 SHOWN
ON OPPOSITE PAGE.
COLOR SCHEME:
AIRCRAFT IS RED AND WHITE WITH
BLACK STRIPES. RACE NUMBER AND
'SULU' IS RED. LOWER WING IS RED.

A B C D

E

F G

SPAN - 17'4"
LENGTH (#47) ≅ 16'
LENGTH (#69) ≅ 15'6"
HEIGHT - 5'8"
WING AREA - 98.5 FT²

"SULU" IS OWNED AND RACED
BY WAYNE ROE.

SCALE: ¼" = 1'

⅛ SQUARES

H

H

TYPICAL AIRFOIL SECTION

PITTS SPECIAL
'SULU' & 'CHANCE IV'

1971 VERSION OF #69 SHOWN BELOW
FEATURES STRAIGHT LAMINAR FLOW
WINGS BUILT UP OF PLASTIC FOAM &
WOOD SPARS - COVERED WITH FIBERGLASS.
TUBING INTERPLANE STRUTS SHOWN WITH
FABRIC COVERING.

Experimental Sulu 47 Wayne Roe
N1112R

1973 VERSION

A B C D E F G

N6968C
CHANCE IV

1968 VERSION
"CHANCE IV" IS OWNED AND
RACED BY MICHAEL H. DUPONT.

COLOR SCHEME ON #69 IS RED, WHITE AND NAVY BLUE. CHECKERBOARD IS ON UNDERSIDE OF WINGS WITH
SUNBURST STRIPING ON UPPER SURFACES - LIKEWISE FOR STABILIZER. (1968 VERSION). THESE TWO PAGES
ARE REPRESENTATIVE OF THE SEVERAL OTHER RACING PITTS SPECIALS.

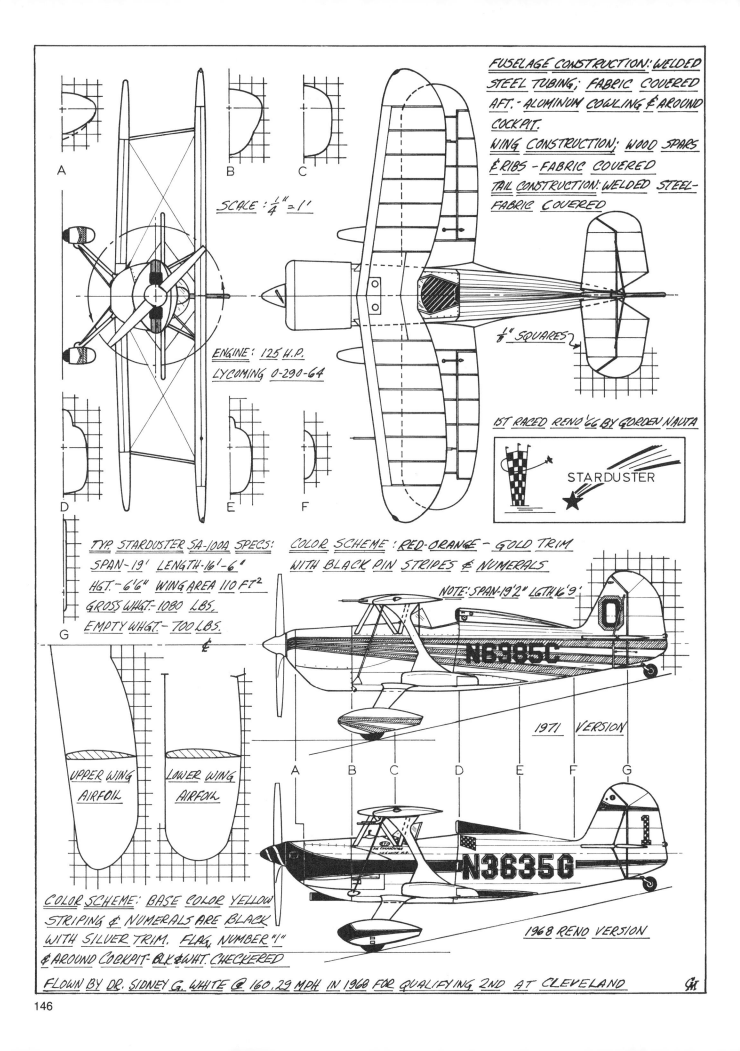

FUSELAGE CONSTRUCTION: WELDED
STEEL TUBING; FABRIC COVERED
AFT. - ALUMINUM COWLING & AROUND
COCKPIT.
WING CONSTRUCTION: WOOD SPARS
& RIBS - FABRIC COVERED
TAIL CONSTRUCTION: WELDED STEEL-
FABRIC COVERED

SCALE: $\frac{1}{4}$" = 1'

ENGINE: 125 H.P.
LYCOMING 0-290-64

$\frac{1}{8}$" SQUARES

1ST RACED RENO '66 BY GORDEN NAUTA

STARDUSTER

TYP. STARDUSTER SA-100A SPECS:
SPAN ~ 19' LENGTH ~ 16'-6"
HGT. - 6'6" WING AREA 110 FT²
GROSS WHGT. - 1080 LBS.
EMPTY WHGT. - 700 LBS.

COLOR SCHEME: RED-ORANGE - GOLD TRIM
WITH BLACK PIN STRIPES & NUMERALS

NOTE: SPAN-19'2" LGTH.16'9"

N6985C

1971 VERSION

A   B   C   D   E   F   G

UPPER WING
AIRFOIL

LOWER WING
AIRFOIL

N3635G

1968 RENO VERSION

COLOR SCHEME: BASE COLOR YELLOW
STRIPING & NUMERALS ARE BLACK
WITH SILVER TRIM. FLAG, NUMBER "1"
& AROUND COCKPIT- BLK & WHT. CHECKERED

FLOWN BY DR. SIDNEY G. WHITE @ 160.29 MPH IN 1968 FOR QUALIFYING 2ND AT CLEVELAND

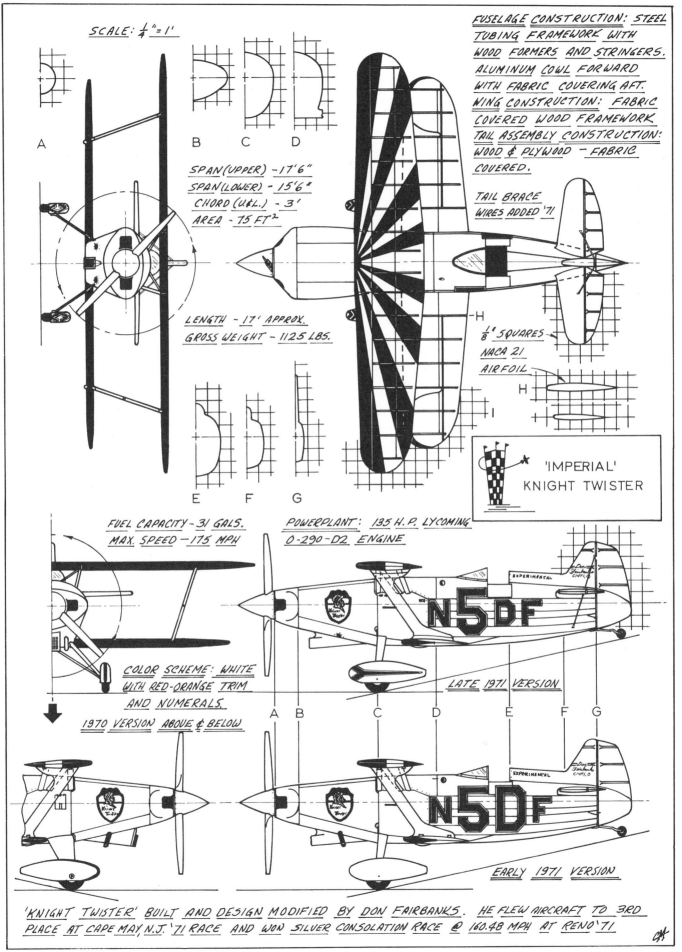

SCALE: $\frac{1}{4}$" = 1'

A   B   C   D

SPAN (UPPER) – 17'6"
SPAN (LOWER) – 15'6"
CHORD (U.&L.) – 3'
AREA – 75 FT²

LENGTH – 17' APPROX.
GROSS WEIGHT – 1125 LBS.

E   F   G

FUSELAGE CONSTRUCTION: STEEL
TUBING FRAMEWORK WITH
WOOD FORMERS AND STRINGERS.
ALUMINUM COWL FORWARD
WITH FABRIC COVERING AFT.
WING CONSTRUCTION: FABRIC
COVERED WOOD FRAMEWORK
TAIL ASSEMBLY CONSTRUCTION:
WOOD & PLYWOOD – FABRIC
COVERED.

TAIL BRACE
WIRES ADDED '71

H

$\frac{1}{8}$" SQUARES
NACA 21
AIRFOIL

H

I

'IMPERIAL'
KNIGHT TWISTER

FUEL CAPACITY – 31 GALS.
MAX. SPEED – 175 MPH

POWERPLANT: 135 H.P. LYCOMING
O-290-D2 ENGINE

N5DF

EXPERIMENTAL

LATE 1971 VERSION

COLOR SCHEME: WHITE
WITH RED-ORANGE TRIM
AND NUMERALS.

1970 VERSION ABOVE & BELOW

A   B   C   D   E   F   G

N5DF

EXPERIMENTAL

EARLY 1971 VERSION

'KNIGHT TWISTER' BUILT AND DESIGN MODIFIED BY DON FAIRBANKS. HE FLEW AIRCRAFT TO 3RD
PLACE AT CAPE MAY, N.J. '71 RACE AND WON SILVER CONSOLATION RACE @ 160.48 MPH AT RENO '71

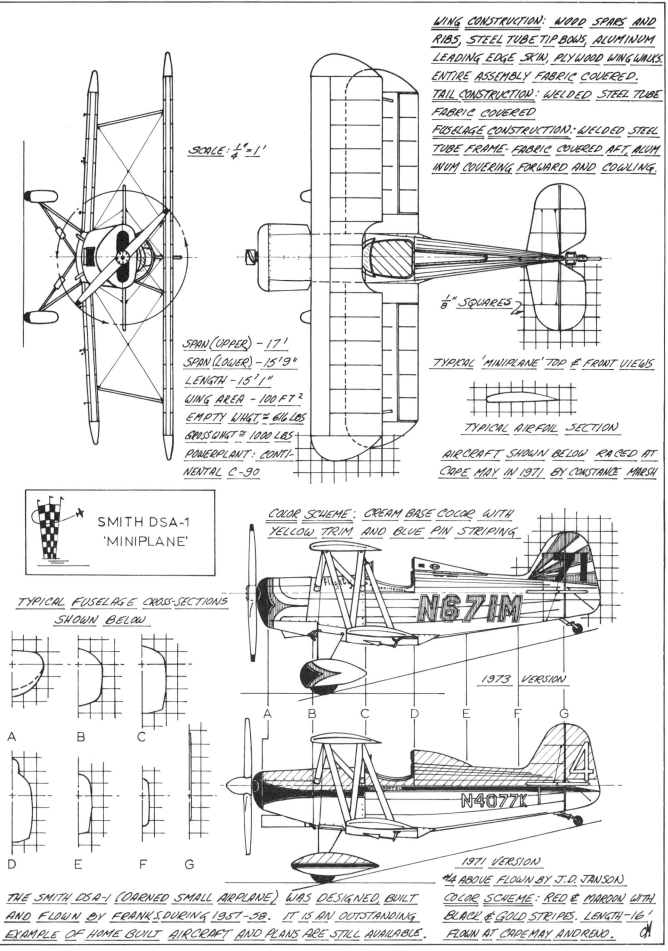

WING CONSTRUCTION: WOOD SPARS AND RIBS, STEEL TUBE TIP BOWS, ALUMINUM LEADING EDGE SKIN, PLYWOOD WINGWALKS. ENTIRE ASSEMBLY FABRIC COVERED.

TAIL CONSTRUCTION: WELDED STEEL TUBE FABRIC COVERED

FUSELAGE CONSTRUCTION: WELDED STEEL TUBE FRAME- FABRIC COVERED AFT, ALUMINUM COVERING FORWARD AND COWLING.

SCALE: $\frac{1}{4}$" = 1'

$\frac{1}{8}$" SQUARES

TYPICAL 'MINIPLANE' TOP & FRONT VIEWS

TYPICAL AIRFOIL SECTION

SPAN (UPPER) - 17'
SPAN (LOWER) - 15'9"
LENGTH - 15'1"
WING AREA - 100 FT²
EMPTY WHGT ≅ 616 LBS
GROSS WHGT ≅ 1000 LBS
POWERPLANT: CONTINENTAL C-90

AIRCRAFT SHOWN BELOW RACED AT CAPE MAY IN 1971 BY CONSTANCE MARSH

SMITH DSA-1 'MINIPLANE'

COLOR SCHEME: CREAM BASE COLOR WITH YELLOW TRIM AND BLUE PIN STRIPING

N671M

1973 VERSION

TYPICAL FUSELAGE CROSS-SECTIONS SHOWN BELOW

A B C
D E F G

N4077K

1971 VERSION
#4 ABOVE FLOWN BY J.D. JANSON
COLOR SCHEME: RED & MAROON WITH BLACK & GOLD STRIPES. LENGTH -16'
FLOWN AT CAPE MAY AND RENO.

THE SMITH DSA-1 (DARNED SMALL AIRPLANE) WAS DESIGNED, BUILT AND FLOWN BY FRANK S. DURING 1951-58. IT IS AN OUTSTANDING EXAMPLE OF HOME BUILT AIRCRAFT AND PLANS ARE STILL AVAILABLE.

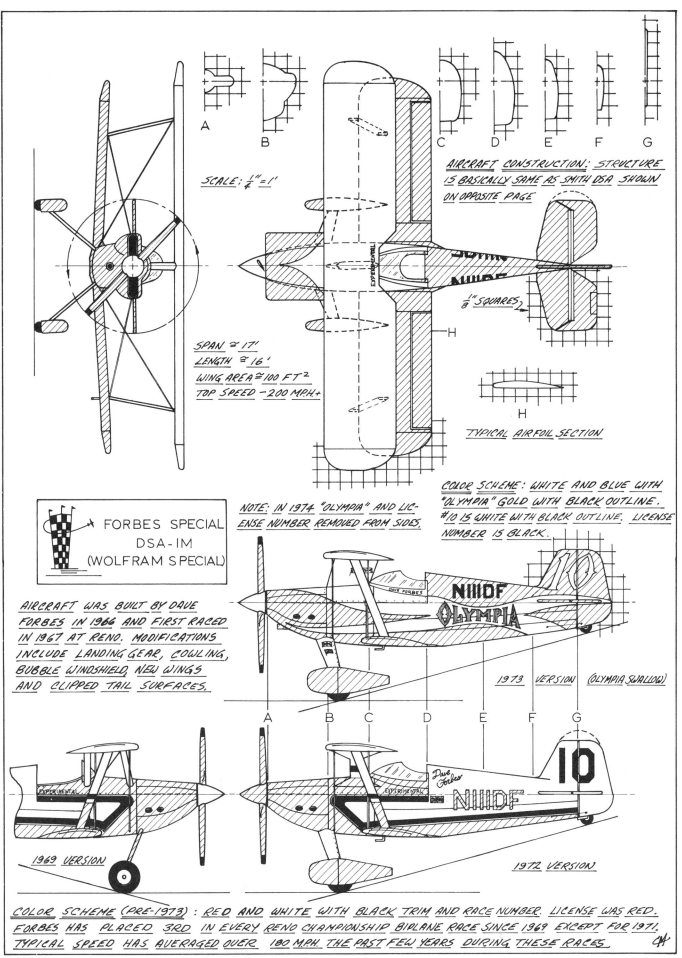

A B C D E F G

SCALE: $\frac{1}{4}'' = 1'$

AIRCRAFT CONSTRUCTION: STRUCTURE IS BASICALLY SAME AS SMITH DSA SHOWN ON OPPOSITE PAGE

SPAN ≅ 17'
LENGTH ≅ 16'
WING AREA ≅ 100 FT²
TOP SPEED — 200 M.P.H.+

$\frac{1}{8}''$ SQUARES

H

TYPICAL AIRFOIL SECTION

FORBES SPECIAL
DSA-1M
(WOLFRAM SPECIAL)

COLOR SCHEME: WHITE AND BLUE WITH "OLYMPIA" GOLD WITH BLACK OUTLINE. #10 IS WHITE WITH BLACK OUTLINE. LICENSE NUMBER IS BLACK.

NOTE: IN 1974 "OLYMPIA" AND LICENSE NUMBER REMOVED FROM SIDES.

AIRCRAFT WAS BUILT BY DAVE FORBES IN 1966 AND FIRST RACED IN 1967 AT RENO. MODIFICATIONS INCLUDE LANDING GEAR, COWLING, BUBBLE WINDSHIELD, NEW WINGS AND CLIPPED TAIL SURFACES.

N111DF
OLYMPIA

1973 VERSION (OLYMPIA SWALLOW)

A B C D E F G

1969 VERSION

10
N111DF

1972 VERSION

COLOR SCHEME (PRE-1973): RED AND WHITE WITH BLACK TRIM AND RACE NUMBER. LICENSE WAS RED. FORBES HAS PLACED 3RD IN EVERY RENO CHAMPIONSHIP BIPLANE RACE SINCE 1969 EXCEPT FOR 1971. TYPICAL SPEED HAS AVERAGED OVER 180 M.P.H. THE PAST FEW YEARS DURING THESE RACES.

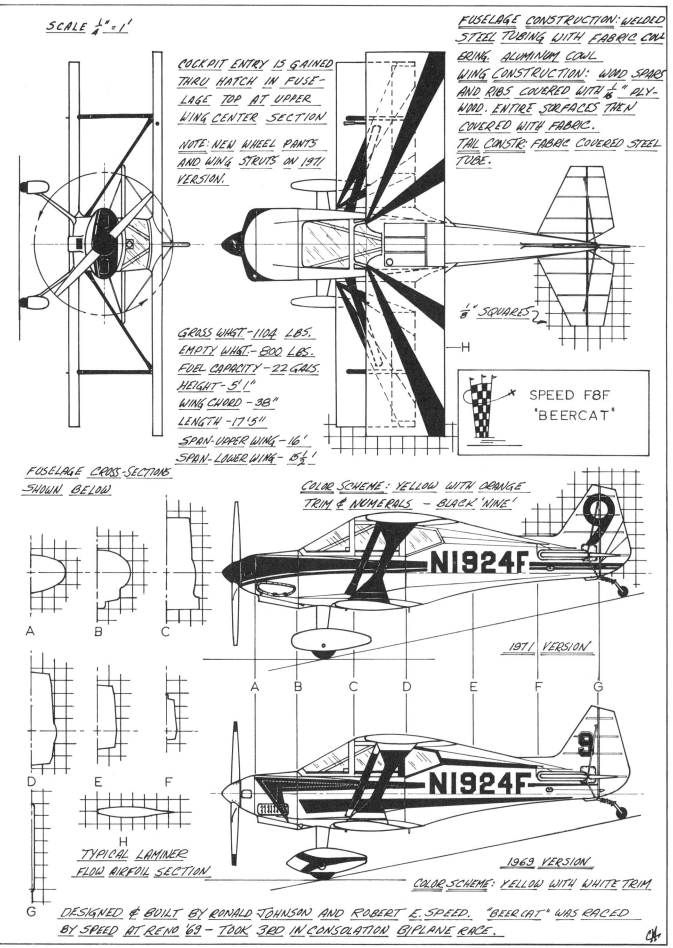

SCALE $\frac{1}{4}" = 1'$

COCKPIT ENTRY IS GAINED THRU HATCH IN FUSELAGE TOP AT UPPER WING CENTER SECTION

NOTE: NEW WHEEL PANTS AND WING STRUTS ON 1971 VERSION.

FUSELAGE CONSTRUCTION: WELDED STEEL TUBING WITH FABRIC COVERING. ALUMINUM COWL

WING CONSTRUCTION: WOOD SPARS AND RIBS COVERED WITH $\frac{1}{16}"$ PLYWOOD. ENTIRE SURFACES THEN COVERED WITH FABRIC.

TAIL CONSTR: FABRIC COVERED STEEL TUBE.

$\frac{1}{8}"$ SQUARES

H

GROSS WHGT. - 1104 LBS.
EMPTY WHGT. - 800 LBS.
FUEL CAPACITY - 22 GALS.
HEIGHT - 5' 1"
WING CHORD - 38"
LENGTH - 17' 5"
SPAN - UPPER WING - 16'
SPAN - LOWER WING - 15½'

SPEED F8F "BEERCAT"

FUSELAGE CROSS-SECTIONS SHOWN BELOW

COLOR SCHEME: YELLOW WITH ORANGE TRIM & NUMERALS - BLACK 'NINE'

N1924F

1971 VERSION

A   B   C

A   B   C   D   E   F   G

D   E   F

G

H
TYPICAL LAMINER FLOW AIRFOIL SECTION

N1924F

1969 VERSION

COLOR SCHEME: YELLOW WITH WHITE TRIM

DESIGNED & BUILT BY RONALD JOHNSON AND ROBERT E. SPEED. "BEERCAT" WAS RACED BY SPEED AT RENO '69 - TOOK 3RD IN CONSOLATION BIPLANE RACE.

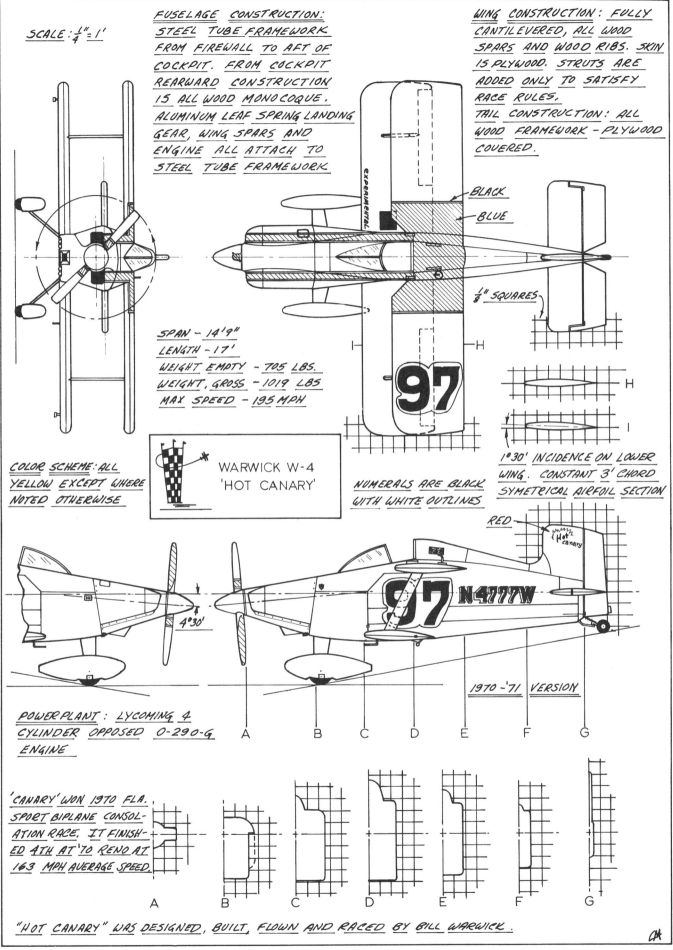

SCALE: $\frac{1}{4}$" = 1'

FUSELAGE CONSTRUCTION:
STEEL TUBE FRAMEWORK
FROM FIREWALL TO AFT OF
COCKPIT. FROM COCKPIT
REARWARD CONSTRUCTION
IS ALL WOOD MONOCOQUE.
ALUMINUM LEAF SPRING LANDING
GEAR, WING SPARS AND
ENGINE ALL ATTACH TO
STEEL TUBE FRAMEWORK

WING CONSTRUCTION: FULLY
CANTILEVERED, ALL WOOD
SPARS AND WOOD RIBS. SKIN
IS PLYWOOD. STRUTS ARE
ADDED ONLY TO SATISFY
RACE RULES.
TAIL CONSTRUCTION: ALL
WOOD FRAMEWORK - PLYWOOD
COVERED.

EXPERIMENTAL

BLACK

BLUE

$\frac{1}{8}$" SQUARES

SPAN - 14'9"
LENGTH - 17'
WEIGHT EMPTY - 705 LBS.
WEIGHT, GROSS - 1019 LBS
MAX SPEED - 195 MPH

97

H

I

1°30' INCIDENCE ON LOWER
WING. CONSTANT 3' CHORD
SYMETRICAL AIRFOIL SECTION

COLOR SCHEME: ALL
YELLOW EXCEPT WHERE
NOTED OTHERWISE

WARWICK W-4
'HOT CANARY'

NUMERALS ARE BLACK
WITH WHITE OUTLINES

RED

Hot canary

4°30'

97 N4777W

1970-'71 VERSION

A B C D E F G

POWERPLANT: LYCOMING 4
CYLINDER OPPOSED O-290-G
ENGINE

'CANARY' WON 1970 FLA.
SPORT BIPLANE CONSOL-
ATION RACE. IT FINISH-
ED 4TH AT '70 RENO AT
163 MPH AVERAGE SPEED.

A B C D E F G

"HOT CANARY" WAS DESIGNED, BUILT, FLOWN AND RACED BY BILL WARWICK.

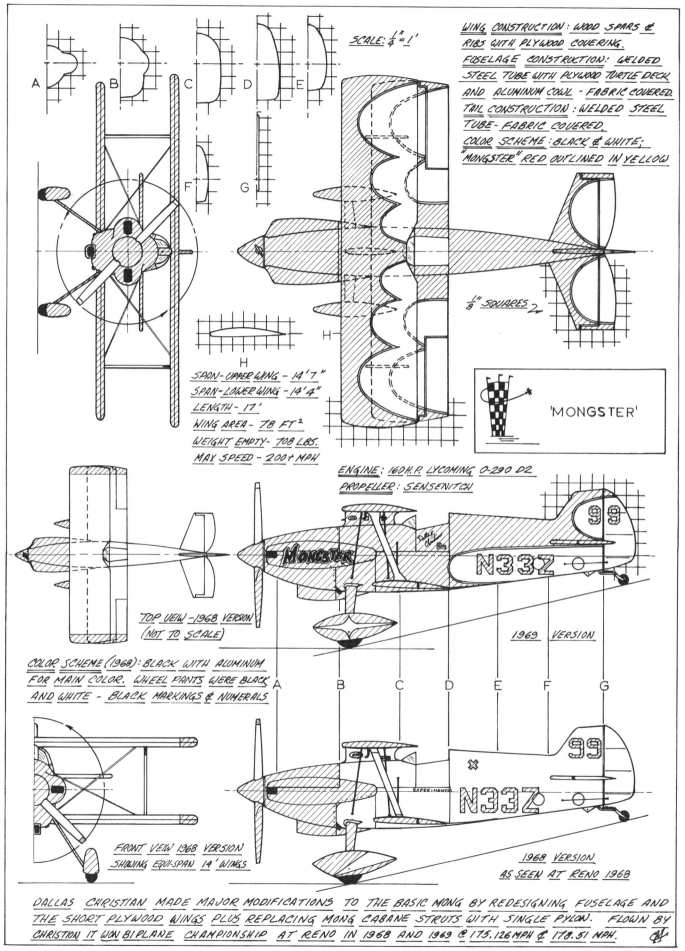

SCALE: $\frac{1}{4}$" = 1'

WING CONSTRUCTION: WOOD SPARS &
RIBS WITH PLYWOOD COVERING.
FUSELAGE CONSTRUCTION: WELDED
STEEL TUBE WITH PLYWOOD TURTLE DECK
AND ALUMINUM COWL - FABRIC COVERED.
TAIL CONSTRUCTION: WELDED STEEL
TUBE - FABRIC COVERED.
COLOR SCHEME: BLACK & WHITE;
"MONGSTER" RED OUTLINED IN YELLOW

$\frac{1}{8}$" SQUARES

SPAN - UPPER WING - 14'7"
SPAN - LOWER WING - 14'4"
LENGTH - 17'
WING AREA - 78 FT²
WEIGHT EMPTY - 708 LBS.
MAX SPEED - 200+ MPH

'MONGSTER'

ENGINE: 160 H.P. LYCOMING O-290 D2
PROPELLER: SENSENITCH

TOP VEIW - 1968 VERSION
(NOT TO SCALE)

1969 VERSION

COLOR SCHEME (1968): BLACK WITH ALUMINUM
FOR MAIN COLOR. WHEEL PANTS WERE BLACK
AND WHITE - BLACK MARKINGS & NUMERALS

A   B   C   D   E   F   G

FRONT VEIW 1968 VERSION
SHOWING EQUI-SPAN 14' WINGS

1968 VERSION
AS SEEN AT RENO 1968

DALLAS CHRISTIAN MADE MAJOR MODIFICATIONS TO THE BASIC MONG BY REDESIGNING FUSELAGE AND
THE SHORT PLYWOOD WINGS PLUS REPLACING MONG CABANE STRUTS WITH SINGLE PYLON. FLOWN BY
CHRISTON IT WON BIPLANE CHAMPIONSHIP AT RENO IN 1968 AND 1969 @ 175.126 MPH & 178.51 MPH.

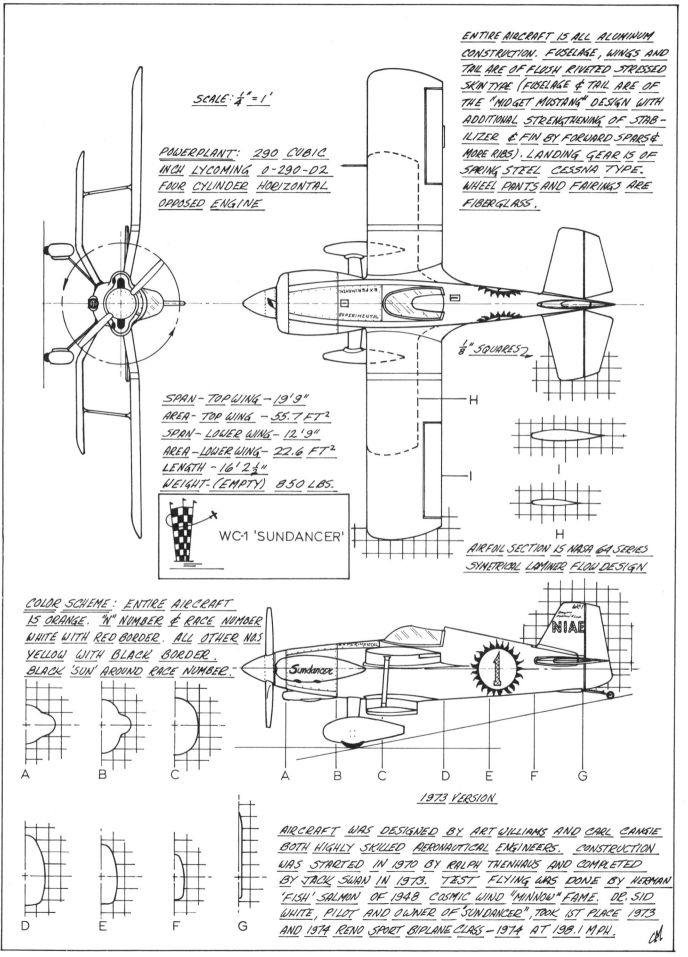

SCALE: $\frac{1}{4}" = 1'$

POWERPLANT: 290 CUBIC INCH LYCOMING O-290-D2 FOUR CYLINDER HORIZONTAL OPPOSED ENGINE

ENTIRE AIRCRAFT IS ALL ALUMINUM CONSTRUCTION. FUSELAGE, WINGS AND TAIL ARE OF FLUSH RIVETED STRESSED SKIN TYPE. (FUSELAGE & TAIL ARE OF THE "MIDGET MUSTANG" DESIGN WITH ADDITIONAL STRENGTHENING OF STABILIZER & FIN BY FORWARD SPARS & MORE RIBS). LANDING GEAR IS OF SPRING STEEL CESSNA TYPE. WHEEL PANTS AND FAIRINGS ARE FIBERGLASS.

SPAN - TOP WING - 19'9"
AREA - TOP WING - 55.7 FT²
SPAN - LOWER WING - 12'9"
AREA - LOWER WING - 22.6 FT²
LENGTH - 16'2½"
WEIGHT - (EMPTY) 850 LBS.

$\frac{1}{8}"$ SQUARES

WC-1 'SUNDANCER'

AIRFOIL SECTION IS NASA 64 SERIES SYMETRICAL LAMINER FLOW DESIGN

COLOR SCHEME: ENTIRE AIRCRAFT IS ORANGE. "N" NUMBER & RACE NUMBER WHITE WITH RED BORDER. ALL OTHER NOS YELLOW WITH BLACK BORDER. BLACK 'SUN' AROUND RACE NUMBER.

A   B   C

A B C   D   E   F   G

D   E   F   G

1973 VERSION

AIRCRAFT WAS DESIGNED BY ART WILLIAMS AND CARL CANGIE BOTH HIGHLY SKILLED AERONAUTICAL ENGINEERS. CONSTRUCTION WAS STARTED IN 1970 BY RALPH THENHAUS AND COMPLETED BY JACK SWAN IN 1973. TEST FLYING WAS DONE BY HERMAN 'FISH' SALMON OF 1948 COSMIC WIND "MINNOW" FAME. DR. SID WHITE, PILOT AND OWNER OF "SUNDANCER", TOOK 1ST PLACE 1973 AND 1974 RENO SPORT BIPLANE CLASS - 1974 AT 198.1 M.P.H.

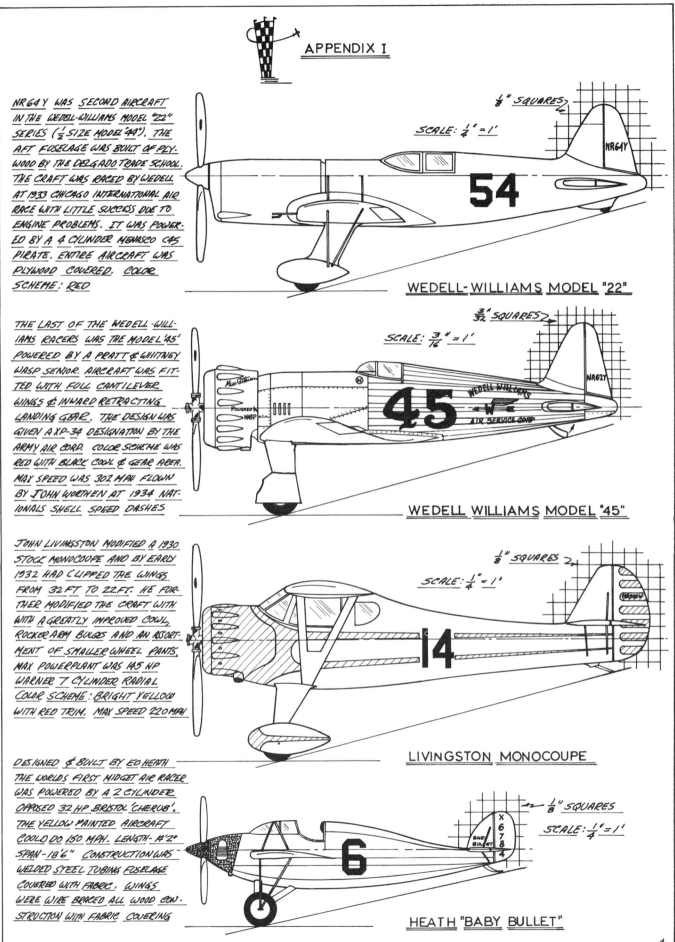

APPENDIX I

NR64Y WAS SECOND AIRCRAFT IN THE WEDELL-WILLIAMS MODEL "22" SERIES (½ SIZE MODEL "44"). THE AFT FUSELAGE WAS BUILT OF PLYWOOD BY THE DELGADO TRADE SCHOOL. THE CRAFT WAS RACED BY WEDELL AT 1933 CHICAGO INTERNATIONAL AIR RACE WITH LITTLE SUCCESS DUE TO ENGINE PROBLEMS. IT WAS POWERED BY A 4 CYLINDER MENASCO C45 PIRATE. ENTIRE AIRCRAFT WAS PLYWOOD COVERED. COLOR SCHEME: RED

⅛" SQUARES
SCALE: ¼" = 1'

WEDELL-WILLIAMS MODEL "22"

THE LAST OF THE WEDELL-WILLIAMS RACERS WAS THE MODEL "45" POWERED BY A PRATT & WHITNEY WASP SENIOR. AIRCRAFT WAS FITTED WITH FULL CANTILEVER WINGS & INWARD RETRACTING LANDING GEAR. THE DESIGN WAS GIVEN A XP-34 DESIGNATION BY THE ARMY AIR CORP. COLOR SCHEME WAS RED WITH BLACK COWL & GEAR AREA. MAX SPEED WAS 302 MPH FLOWN BY JOHN WORTHEN AT 1934 NATIONALS SHELL SPEED DASHES

3/32" SQUARES
SCALE: 3/16" = 1'

WEDELL WILLIAMS MODEL "45"

JOHN LIVINGSTON MODIFIED A 1930 STOCK MONOCOUPE AND BY EARLY 1932 HAD CLIPPED THE WINGS FROM 32 FT TO 22 FT. HE FURTHER MODIFIED THE CRAFT WITH WITH A GREATLY IMPROVED COWL, ROCKER ARM BULGES AND AN ASSORTMENT OF SMALLER WHEEL PANTS. MAX POWERPLANT WAS 145 HP WARNER 7 CYLINDER RADIAL COLOR SCHEME: BRIGHT YELLOW WITH RED TRIM. MAX SPEED 220 MPH

⅛" SQUARES
SCALE: ¼" = 1'

LIVINGSTON MONOCOUPE

DESIGNED & BUILT BY ED HEATH THE WORLDS FIRST MIDGET AIR RACER WAS POWERED BY A 2 CYLINDER OPPOSED 32 HP BRISTOL 'CHERUB'. THE YELLOW PAINTED AIRCRAFT COULD DO 150 MPH. LENGTH- 14'2" SPAN- 18'6" CONSTRUCTION WAS WELDED STEEL TUBING FUSELAGE COVERED WITH FABRIC. WINGS WERE WIRE BRACED ALL WOOD CONSTRUCTION WITH FABRIC COVERING

⅛" SQUARES
SCALE: ¼" = 1'

HEATH "BABY BULLET"

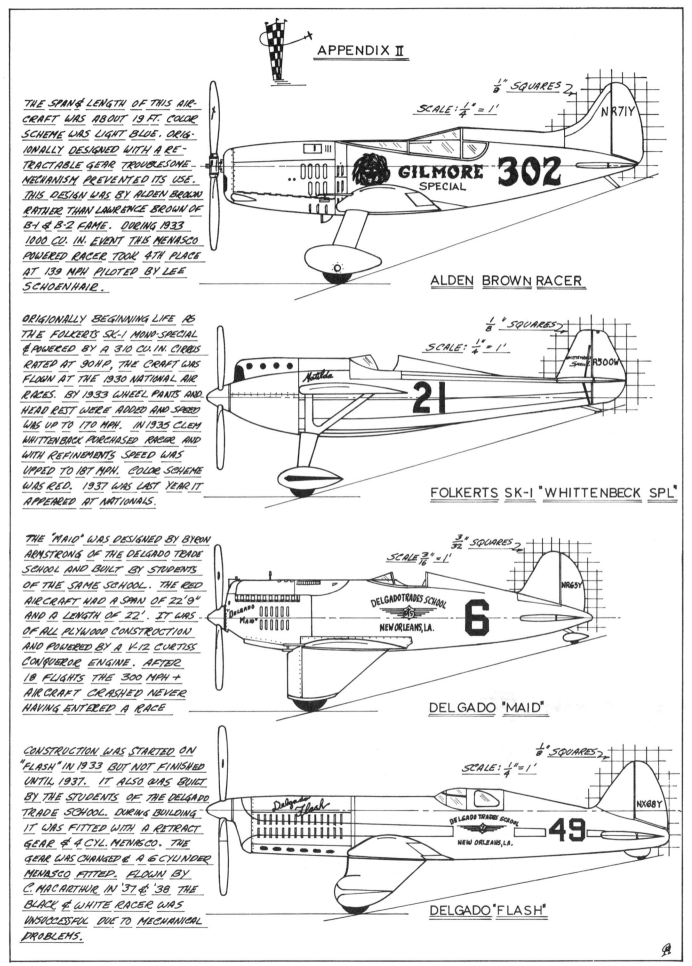

APPENDIX II

THE SPAN & LENGTH OF THIS AIR-
CRAFT WAS ABOUT 19 FT. COLOR
SCHEME WAS LIGHT BLUE. ORIG-
IONALLY DESIGNED WITH A RE-
TRACTABLE GEAR TROUBLESOME
MECHANISM PREVENTED ITS USE.
THIS DESIGN WAS BY ALDEN BROWN
RATHER THAN LAWRENCE BROWN OF
B-1 & B-2 FAME. DURING 1933
1000 CU. IN. EVENT THIS MENASCO
POWERED RACER TOOK 4TH PLACE
AT 139 MPH PILOTED BY LEE
SCHOENHAIR.

⅛" SQUARES
SCALE: ¼" = 1'
NR71Y
GILMORE SPECIAL 302

ALDEN BROWN RACER

ORIGIONALLY BEGINNING LIFE AS
THE FOLKERTS SK-1 MONO-SPECIAL
& POWERED BY A 310 CU. IN. CIRRUS
RATED AT 90 HP, THE CRAFT WAS
FLOWN AT THE 1930 NATIONAL AIR
RACES. BY 1933 WHEEL PANTS AND
HEAD REST WERE ADDED AND SPEED
WAS UP TO 170 MPH. IN 1935 CLEM
WHITTENBACK PORCHASED RACER AND
WITH REFINEMENTS SPEED WAS
UPPED TO 187 MPH. COLOR SCHEME
WAS RED. 1937 WAS LAST YEAR IT
APPEARED AT NATIONALS.

⅛" SQUARES
SCALE: ¼" = 1'
R300W
Matilda 21

FOLKERTS SK-1 "WHITTENBECK SPL"

THE "MAID" WAS DESIGNED BY BYRON
ARMSTRONG OF THE DELGADO TRADE
SCHOOL AND BUILT BY STUDENTS
OF THE SAME SCHOOL. THE RED
AIRCRAFT HAD A SPAN OF 22'9"
AND A LENGTH OF 22'. IT WAS
OF ALL PLYWOOD CONSTRUCTION
AND POWERED BY A V-12 CURTISS
CONQUEROR ENGINE. AFTER
18 FLIGHTS THE 300 MPH +
AIRCRAFT CRASHED NEVER
HAVING ENTERED A RACE

³⁄₃₂" SQUARES
SCALE ³⁄₁₆" = 1'
NR65Y
"Delgado Maid" DELGADO TRADES SCHOOL
NEW ORLEANS, LA. 6

DELGADO "MAID"

CONSTRUCTION WAS STARTED ON
"FLASH" IN 1933 BUT NOT FINISHED
UNTIL 1937. IT ALSO WAS BUILT
BY THE STUDENTS OF THE DELGADO
TRADE SCHOOL. DURING BUILDING
IT WAS FITTED WITH A RETRACT
GEAR & 4 CYL. MENASCO. THE
GEAR WAS CHANGED & A 6 CYLINDER
MENASCO FITTED. FLOWN BY
C. MACARTHUR IN '37 & '38 THE
BLACK & WHITE RACER WAS
UNSUCCESSFUL DUE TO MECHANICAL
PROBLEMS.

⅛" SQUARES
SCALE: ¼" = 1'
NX68Y
Delgado Flash DELGADO TRADES SCHOOL
NEW ORLEANS, LA. 49

DELGADO "FLASH"

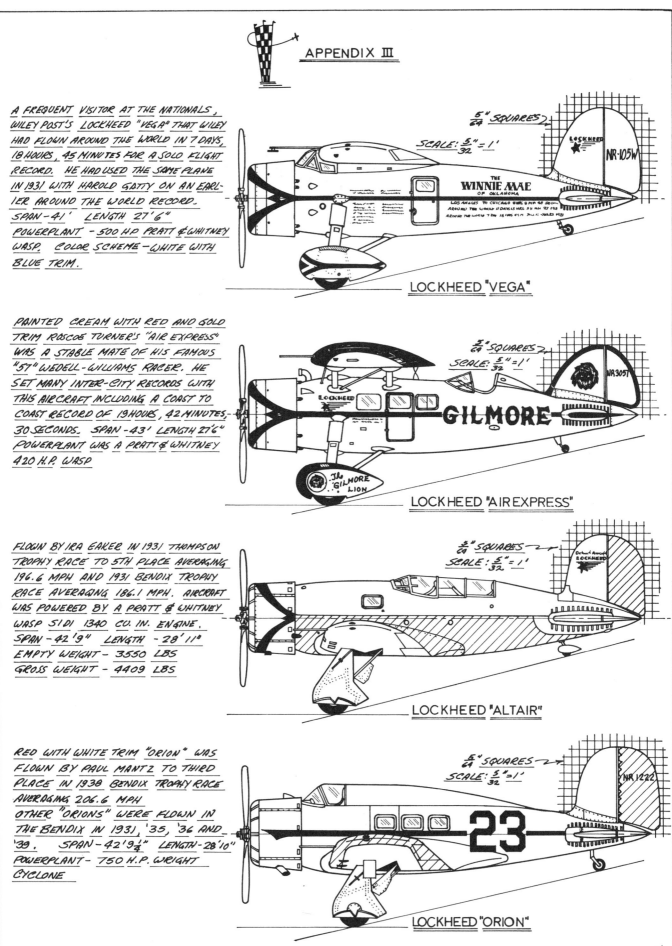

APPENDIX III

A FREQUENT VISITOR AT THE NATIONALS, WILEY POST'S LOCKHEED "VEGA" THAT WILEY HAD FLOWN AROUND THE WORLD IN 7 DAYS, 18 HOURS, 45 MINUTES FOR A SOLO FLIGHT RECORD. HE HAD USED THE SAME PLANE IN 1931 WITH HAROLD GATTY ON AN EARLIER AROUND THE WORLD RECORD. SPAN - 41' LENGTH 27'6" POWERPLANT - 500 H.P. PRATT & WHITNEY WASP. COLOR SCHEME - WHITE WITH BLUE TRIM.

LOCKHEED "VEGA"

PAINTED CREAM WITH RED AND GOLD TRIM ROSCOE TURNER'S "AIR EXPRESS" WAS A STABLE MATE OF HIS FAMOUS "57" WEDELL-WILLIAMS RACER. HE SET MANY INTER-CITY RECORDS WITH THIS AIRCRAFT INCLUDING A COAST TO COAST RECORD OF 19 HOURS, 42 MINUTES, 30 SECONDS. SPAN - 43' LENGTH 27'6" POWERPLANT WAS A PRATT & WHITNEY 420 H.P. WASP

LOCKHEED "AIR EXPRESS"

FLOWN BY IRA EAKER IN 1931 THOMPSON TROPHY RACE TO 5TH PLACE AVERAGING 196.6 MPH AND 1931 BENDIX TROPHY RACE AVERAGING 186.1 MPH. AIRCRAFT WAS POWERED BY A PRATT & WHITNEY WASP SIDI 1340 CU. IN. ENGINE. SPAN - 42'9" LENGTH - 28'11" EMPTY WEIGHT - 3550 LBS GROSS WEIGHT - 4409 LBS

LOCKHEED "ALTAIR"

RED WITH WHITE TRIM "ORION" WAS FLOWN BY PAUL MANTZ TO THIRD PLACE IN 1938 BENDIX TROPHY RACE AVERAGING 206.6 MPH OTHER "ORIONS" WERE FLOWN IN THE BENDIX IN 1931, '35, '36 AND '39. SPAN - 42'9¼" LENGTH - 28'10" POWERPLANT - 750 H.P. WRIGHT CYCLONE

LOCKHEED "ORION"

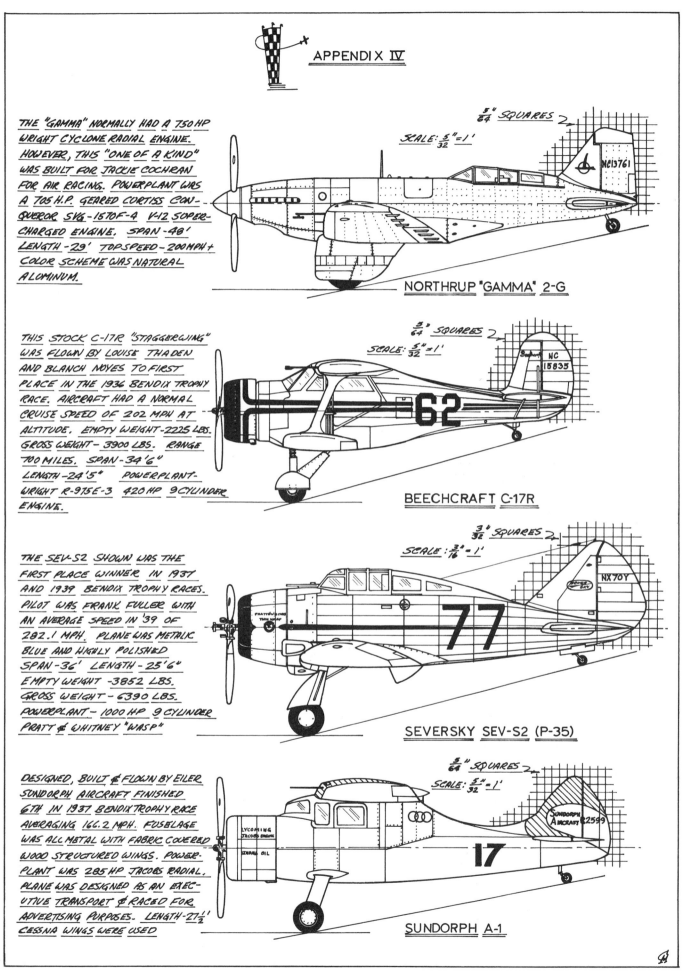

APPENDIX IV

THE "GAMMA" NORMALLY HAD A 750 HP WRIGHT CYCLONE RADIAL ENGINE. HOWEVER, THIS "ONE OF A KIND" WAS BUILT FOR JACKIE COCHRAN FOR AIR RACING. POWERPLANT WAS A 705 H.P. GEARED CURTISS CONQUEROR SVG-1570F-4 V-12 SUPERCHARGED ENGINE. SPAN-48' LENGTH-29' TOP SPEED-200 MPH+ COLOR SCHEME WAS NATURAL ALUMINUM.

⁵⁄₆₄" SQUARES
SCALE: ⁵⁄₃₂" = 1'
NC13761

NORTHRUP "GAMMA" 2-G

THIS STOCK C-17R "STAGGERWING" WAS FLOWN BY LOUISE THADEN AND BLANCH NOYES TO FIRST PLACE IN THE 1936 BENDIX TROPHY RACE. AIRCRAFT HAD A NORMAL CRUISE SPEED OF 202 MPH AT ALTITUDE. EMPTY WEIGHT-2225 LBS. GROSS WEIGHT - 3900 LBS. RANGE 700 MILES. SPAN-34'6" LENGTH -24'5" POWERPLANT-WRIGHT R-975E-3 420 HP 9 CYLINDER ENGINE.

⁵⁄₆₄" SQUARES
SCALE: ⁵⁄₃₂" = 1'
Beechcraft NC 15835
62

BEECHCRAFT C-17R

THE SEV-S2 SHOWN WAS THE FIRST PLACE WINNER IN 1937 AND 1939 BENDIX TROPHY RACES. PILOT WAS FRANK FULLER WITH AN AVERAGE SPEED IN '39 OF 282.1 MPH. PLANE WAS METALIC BLUE AND HIGHLY POLISHED SPAN-36' LENGTH - 25'6" EMPTY WEIGHT -3852 LBS. GROSS WEIGHT - 6390 LBS. POWERPLANT - 1000 HP 9 CYLINDER PRATT & WHITNEY "WASP"

³⁄₃₂" SQUARES
SCALE: ³⁄₁₆" = 1'
NX70Y
77

SEVERSKY SEV-S2 (P-35)

DESIGNED, BUILT & FLOWN BY EILER SUNDORPH AIRCRAFT FINISHED 6TH IN 1937 BENDIX TROPHY RACE AVERAGING 166.2 MPH. FUSELAGE WAS ALL METAL WITH FABRIC COVERED WOOD STRUCTURED WINGS. POWERPLANT WAS 285 HP JACOBS RADIAL. PLANE WAS DESIGNED AS AN EXECUTIVE TRANSPORT & RACED FOR ADVERTISING PURPOSES. LENGTH-27½' CESSNA WINGS WERE USED

⁵⁄₆₄" SQUARES
SCALE: ⁵⁄₃₂" = 1'
Sundorph Aircraft NC2599
17

SUNDORPH A-1

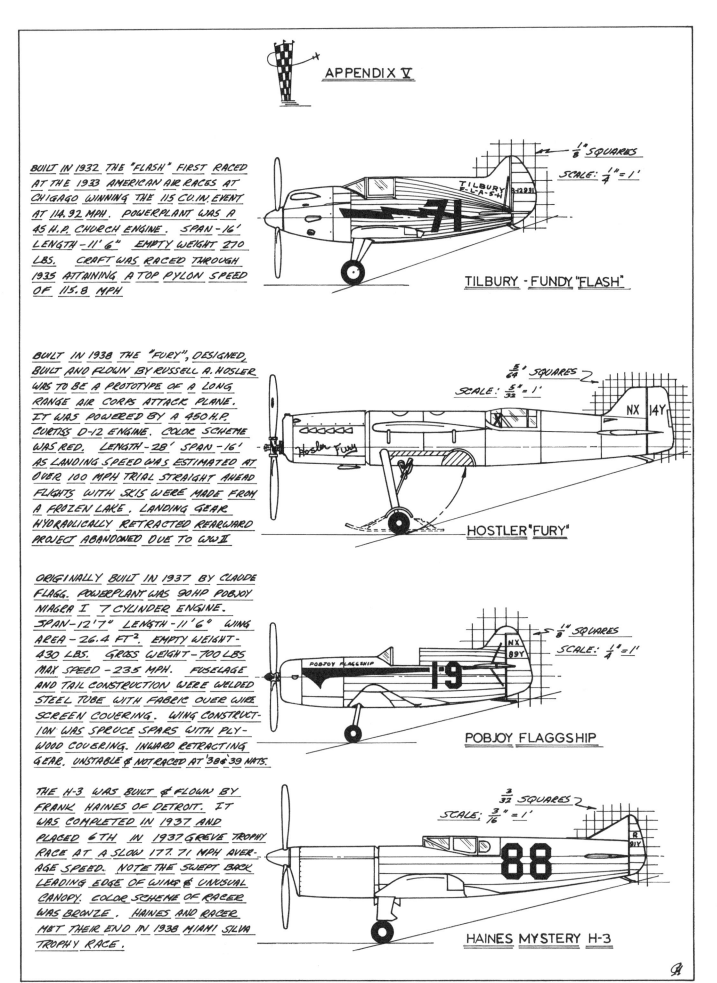

BUILT IN 1932 THE "FLASH" FIRST RACED AT THE 1933 AMERICAN AIR RACES AT CHIGAGO WINNING THE 115 CU.IN. EVENT AT 114.92 MPH. POWERPLANT WAS A 45 H.P. CHURCH ENGINE. SPAN - 16' LENGTH - 11' 6" EMPTY WEIGHT 270 LBS. CRAFT WAS RACED THROUGH 1935 ATTAINING A TOP PYLON SPEED OF 115.8 MPH

⅛" SQUARES
SCALE: ¼" = 1'

TILBURY - FUNDY "FLASH"

BUILT IN 1938 THE "FURY", DESIGNED, BUILT AND FLOWN BY RUSSELL A. HOSLER WAS TO BE A PROTOTYPE OF A LONG RANGE AIR CORPS ATTACK PLANE. IT WAS POWERED BY A 450 H.P. CURTISS D-12 ENGINE. COLOR SCHEME WAS RED. LENGTH - 28' SPAN - 16' AS LANDING SPEED WAS ESTIMATED AT OVER 100 MPH TRIAL STRAIGHT AHEAD FLIGHTS WITH SKIS WERE MADE FROM A FROZEN LAKE. LANDING GEAR HYDRAULICALLY RETRACTED REARWARD PROJECT ABANDONED DUE TO GW II

⁵⁄₆₄' SQUARES
SCALE: ⁵⁄₃₂" = 1'

HOSTLER "FURY"

ORIGINALLY BUILT IN 1937 BY CLAUDE FLAGG. POWERPLANT WAS 90 HP POBJOY NIAGRA I 7 CYLINDER ENGINE. SPAN - 12' 7" LENGTH - 11' 6" WING AREA - 26.4 FT². EMPTY WEIGHT - 430 LBS. GROSS WEIGHT - 700 LBS MAX SPEED - 235 MPH. FUSELAGE AND TAIL CONSTRUCTION WERE WELDED STEEL TUBE WITH FABRIC OVER WIRE SCREEN COVERING. WING CONSTRUCT-ION WAS SPRUCE SPARS WITH PLY-WOOD COVERING. INWARD RETRACTING GEAR. UNSTABLE & NOT RACED AT '38 & '39 NATS.

⅛" SQUARES
SCALE: ¼" = 1'

POBJOY FLAGGSHIP

THE H-3 WAS BUILT & FLOWN BY FRANK HAINES OF DETROIT. IT WAS COMPLETED IN 1937 AND PLACED 6TH IN 1937 GREVE TROPHY RACE AT A SLOW 177.71 MPH AVER-AGE SPEED. NOTE THE SWEPT BACK LEADING EDGE OF WING & UNUSUAL CANOPY. COLOR SCHEME OF RACER WAS BRONZE. HAINES AND RACER MET THEIR END IN 1938 MIAMI SILVA TROPHY RACE.

²⁄₃₂ SQUARES
SCALE: ³⁄₁₆" = 1'

HAINES MYSTERY H-3

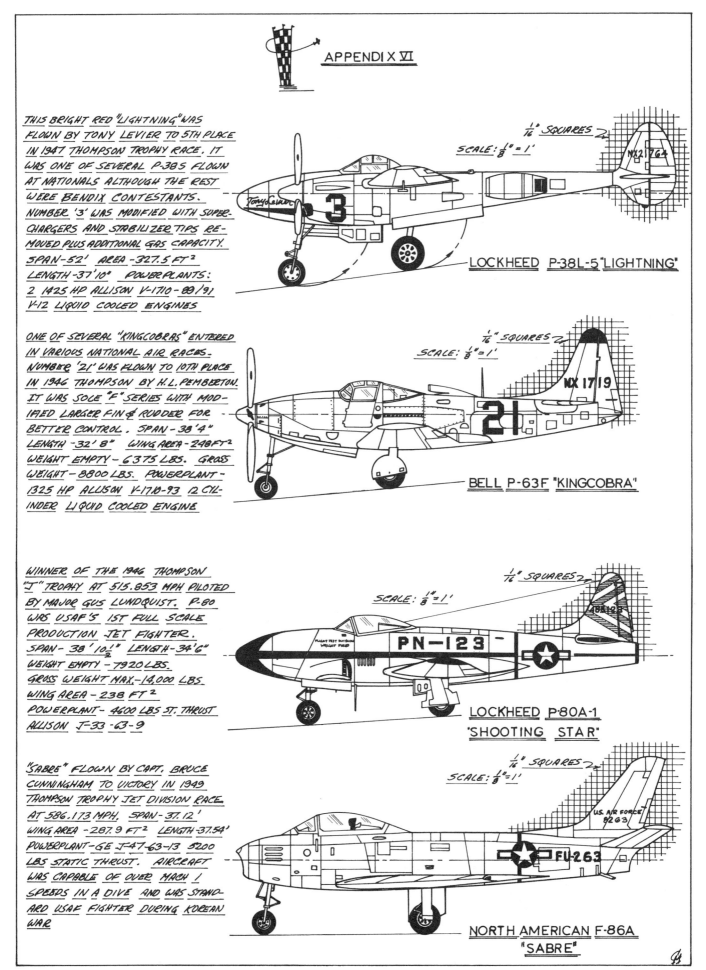

APPENDIX VI

THIS BRIGHT RED "LIGHTNING" WAS FLOWN BY TONY LEVIER TO 5TH PLACE IN 1947 THOMPSON TROPHY RACE. IT WAS ONE OF SEVERAL P-38S FLOWN AT NATIONALS ALTHOUGH THE REST WERE BENDIX CONTESTANTS. NUMBER '3' WAS MODIFIED WITH SUPER-CHARGERS AND STABILIZER TIPS RE-MOVED PLUS ADDITIONAL GAS CAPACITY. SPAN - 52' AREA - 327.5 FT² LENGTH - 37'10" POWERPLANTS: 2 1425 HP ALLISON V-1710-89/91 V-12 LIQUID COOLED ENGINES

¹⁄₁₆" SQUARES
SCALE: ⅛" = 1'
NX21764

LOCKHEED P-38L-5 "LIGHTNING"

ONE OF SEVERAL "KINGCOBRAS" ENTERED IN VARIOUS NATIONAL AIR RACES. NUMBER '21' WAS FLOWN TO 10TH PLACE IN 1946 THOMPSON BY H.L. PEMBERTON. IT WAS SOLE "F" SERIES WITH MOD-IFIED LARGER FIN & RUDDER FOR BETTER CONTROL. SPAN - 38'4" LENGTH - 32'8" WING AREA - 248 FT² WEIGHT EMPTY - 6375 LBS. GROSS WEIGHT - 8800 LBS. POWERPLANT - 1325 HP ALLISON V-1710-93 12 CYL-INDER LIQUID COOLED ENGINE.

¹⁄₁₆" SQUARES
SCALE: ⅛" = 1'
NX1719

BELL P-63F "KINGCOBRA"

WINNER OF THE 1946 THOMPSON "J" TROPHY AT 515.853 MPH PILOTED BY MAJOR GUS LUNDQUIST. P-80 WAS USAF'S 1ST FULL SCALE PRODUCTION JET FIGHTER. SPAN - 38'10½" LENGTH - 34'6" WEIGHT EMPTY - 7920 LBS. GROSS WEIGHT MAX - 14,000 LBS. WING AREA - 238 FT² POWERPLANT - 4600 LBS ST. THRUST ALLISON J-33-63-9

¹⁄₁₆" SQUARES
SCALE: ⅛" = 1'
48A123
PN-123

LOCKHEED P-80A-1 "SHOOTING STAR"

"SABRE" FLOWN BY CAPT. BRUCE CUNNINGHAM TO VICTORY IN 1949 THOMPSON TROPHY JET DIVISION RACE AT 586.173 MPH. SPAN - 37.12' WING AREA - 287.9 FT² LENGTH - 37.54' POWERPLANT - GE J-47-63-13 5200 LBS STATIC THRUST. AIRCRAFT WAS CAPABLE OF OVER MACH 1 SPEEDS IN A DIVE AND WAS STAND-ARD USAF FIGHTER DURING KOREAN WAR

¹⁄₁₆" SQUARES
SCALE: ⅛" = 1'
U.S. AIR FORCE 8263
FU-263

NORTH AMERICAN F-86A "SABRE"

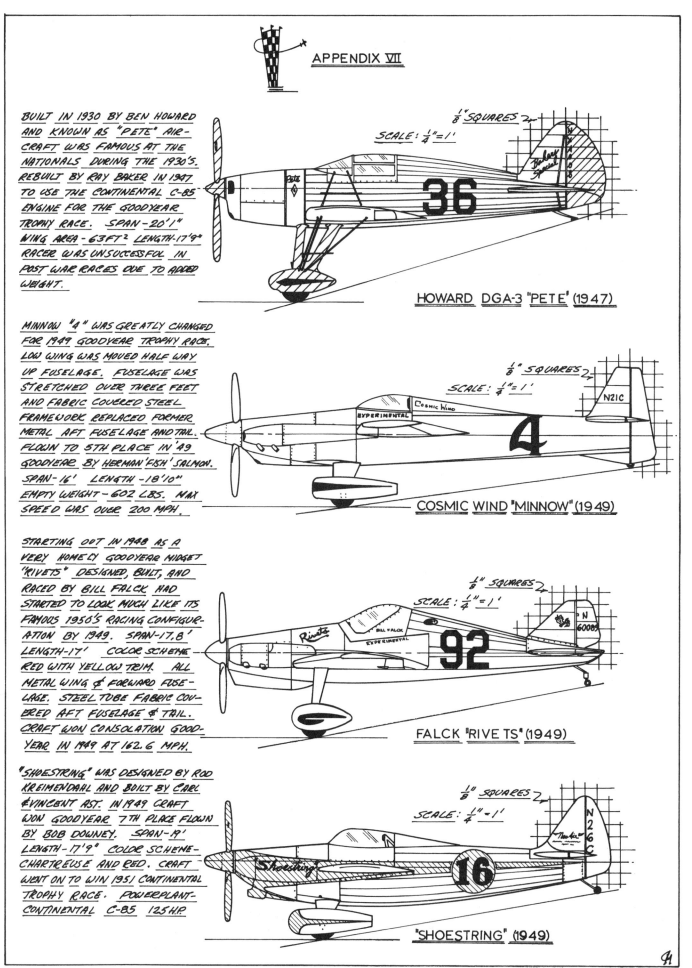

APPENDIX VII

BUILT IN 1930 BY BEN HOWARD AND KNOWN AS "PETE" AIR-CRAFT WAS FAMOUS AT THE NATIONALS DURING THE 1930'S. REBUILT BY RAY BAKER IN 1947 TO USE THE CONTINENTAL C-85 ENGINE FOR THE GOODYEAR TROPHY RACE. SPAN-20'1" WING AREA-63 FT² LENGTH-17'9" RACER WAS UNSUCCESSFUL IN POST WAR RACES DUE TO ADDED WEIGHT.

$\frac{1}{8}$" SQUARES
SCALE: $\frac{1}{4}$"=1'

HOWARD DGA-3 "PETE" (1947)

MINNOW "4" WAS GREATLY CHANGED FOR 1949 GOODYEAR TROPHY RACE. LOW WING WAS MOVED HALF WAY UP FUSELAGE. FUSELAGE WAS STRETCHED OVER THREE FEET AND FABRIC COVERED STEEL FRAMEWORK REPLACED FORMER METAL AFT FUSELAGE AND TAIL. FLOWN TO 5TH PLACE IN '49 GOODYEAR BY HERMAN 'FISH' SALMON. SPAN-16' LENGTH -18'10" EMPTY WEIGHT - 602 LBS. MAX SPEED WAS OVER 200 MPH.

$\frac{1}{8}$" SQUARES
SCALE: $\frac{1}{4}$"=1'

COSMIC WIND "MINNOW" (1949)

STARTING OUT IN 1948 AS A VERY HOMELY GOODYEAR MIDGET "RIVETS" DESIGNED, BUILT, AND RACED BY BILL FALCK HAD STARTED TO LOOK MUCH LIKE ITS FAMOUS 1950'S RACING CONFIGUR-ATION BY 1949. SPAN-17.8' LENGTH-17' COLOR SCHEME RED WITH YELLOW TRIM. ALL METAL WING & FORWARD FUSE-LAGE. STEEL TUBE FABRIC COV-ERED AFT FUSELAGE & TAIL. CRAFT WON CONSOLATION GOOD-YEAR IN 1949 AT 162.6 MPH.

$\frac{1}{8}$" SQUARES
SCALE: $\frac{1}{4}$"=1'

FALCK "RIVETS" (1949)

"SHOESTRING" WAS DESIGNED BY ROD KREIMENDAHL AND BUILT BY CARL & VINCENT AST. IN 1949 CRAFT WON GOODYEAR 7TH PLACE FLOWN BY BOB DOWNEY. SPAN-19' LENGTH-17'9" COLOR SCHEME-CHARTREUSE AND RED. CRAFT WENT ON TO WIN 1951 CONTINENTAL TROPHY RACE. POWERPLANT-CONTINENTAL C-85 125 H.P.

$\frac{1}{8}$" SQUARES
SCALE: $\frac{1}{4}$"=1'

"SHOESTRING" (1949)

'GOTCHA' IS PAINTED ORANGE WITH BLACK AND WHITE TRIM. FLOWN BY PATRICK J. PALMER TO 3RD PLACE IN '73 RENO CHAMPIONSHIP RACE AT 203.822 M.P.H. - TOOK 1ST IN CALIFORNIA AIR CLASSIC AT 219.891 M.P.H. IN '73. CRAFT PLACED 2ND IN '72 RENO SILVER CONSOLATION RACE AT 197.20 M.P.H. AT RENO '71. PALMER PLACED 3RD IN AT-6 SILVER CONSOLATION RACE AT 196.19 M.P.H.; CRAFT TOOK RENO '75 RACE AT 207.19 M.P.H.

NORTH AMERICAN SNJ-5 "GOTCHA"

'SKY PRINTS SPECIAL' IS RED WITH WHITE LETTERING. SPINNER IS POLISHED ALUMINUM. JOHN MOSBY TOOK 1ST IN HAROLD NEUMAN CLASSIC @ 207.69 M.P.H.-MIAMI '73. FLOWN BY JACK LOWERS AT RENO '73 TO 1ST IN CONSOLATION RACE AT 212.390 M.P.H. IN 1972 MOSBY TOOK 1ST IN QUALIFYING TRIALS AT 210.526 M.P.H. & 2ND IN AT-6 CHAMPIONSHIP RACE @ 201.305 M.P.H.

NORTH AMERICAN AT-6C "MISS BEHAVIN"

SCALE: 5/32 = 1'

5/64 SQUARES

THE AIRCRAFT AT RIGHT HAS BEIGE-YELLOW WINGS AND STABILIZER. FUSELAGE IS GLOSSY OLIVE DRAB, BLACK AND WHITE CHECKERBOARD ON COWL, WHITE WHEELS & SPINNER, RED, WHITE & BLUE RUDDER, BLUE BAND AROUND FUSELAGE WITH WHITE STARS AND BORDER. QUALIFIED AT RENO '71 IN 3RD PLACE AT 204.16 MPH BY RICHARD SYKES.

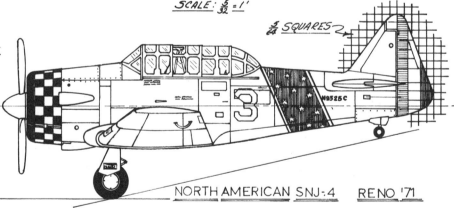

NORTH AMERICAN SNJ-4   RENO '71

THIS MARK II IS PAINTED A HIGH GLOSS DARK GREEN. RACE NUMBERS AND AREA AROUND CROSS ARE WHITE. BAND AROUND FUSELAGE IS YELLOW. CROSS & CHEVERONS ARE BLACK. FLOWN BY CALVIN CONROY TO 5TH PLACE IN HAROLD NEUMAN SPEED CLASSIC AT 196.01 M.P.H.-MIAMI '73. OWNER E.J. MODES FLEW CRAFT TO 5TH AT RENO AT-6 CONSOLATION RACE RENO '73 @ 199.692 M.P.H.

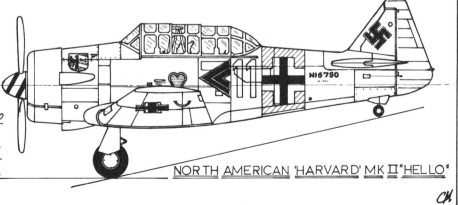

NORTH AMERICAN 'HARVARD' MK II "HELLO"

CM

APPENDIX IX

THIS AIRCRAFT IS THE WELL KNOWN UNLIMITED PACE PLANE SEEN AT MAJOR AIR RACES SUCH AS RENO, MOJAVE & MIAMI. PILOTED BY THE WORLD RENOWNED AEROBATIC PILOT BOB HOOVER OF ROCKWELL INTERNATIONAL "SHRIKE COMMANDER" & F-86 STUNT FAME, WHILE NOT AN AIR RACER, THIS YELLOW AND BLACK P-51, BECAUSE OF ITS YEARS SERVING AIR RACING IS INCLUDED HERE.

NORTH AMERICAN P-51D 'MUSTANG'

THE COLOR SCHEME OF THIS AIRCRAFT ALMOST DEFIES DESCRIPTION. THE AREAS OF CHECKERBOARD ARE RED & YELLOW, BLACK BANDS SURROUND THE STAR & BAR INSIGNIA WHICH IS LIGHT BLUE. SHARK MOUTH IS RED & WHITE. BALANCE OF TRIM IS BLACK & YELLOW AS SHOWN. AIRCRAFT IS OWNED & FLOWN BY KEN BURNSTINE. DUE TO SEVERAL TECHNICALITIES IT WON THE '74 RENO RACE AT ONLY 381.482 M.P.H.

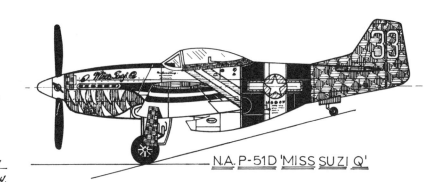

N.A. P-51D 'MISS SUZI Q'

CLIFF CUMMINS OWNS AND RACES "MISS CANDACE". THIS 'MUSTANG' HAS CLIPPED WINGS, MODIFIED OIL COOLER ON FUSELAGE BOTTOM AND GREATLY REDUCED CANOPY. STRIPES ON TAIL ARE RED. NAME OF AIRCRAFT IS WHITE TRIMMED IN YELLOW & BLACK. NUMBER "69" IS BLACK - YELLOW BORDER. CUMMINS FLEW AIRCRAFT TO 2ND PLACE AT RENO '73 @ 417.016 M.P.H.

SCALE: 1/8" = 1'

1/16" SQUARES

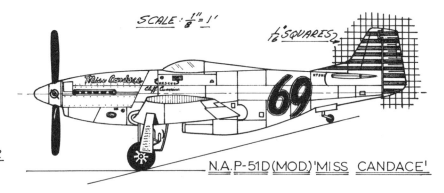

N.A. P-51D (MOD) 'MISS CANDACE'

EDWARD WEINER FLEW THIS YELLOW & BLACK CHECKERBOARD AIRCRAFT CROSS COUNTRY IN THE HAROLDS CLUB TRANSCONTINENTAL TROPHY DASH FROM MILWAUKEE TO RENO IN 1968. CRAFT WON RACE AT AN AVERAGE SPEED OF 361.141 M.P.H. #14 & 'BARDAHL' WERE BLACK WITH WHITE TRIM. LANDING GEAR, WHEEL WELLS WERE WHITE. ROLLS ROYCE MERLIN V-1650-7 DELIVERED 1700 H.P. - MAX SPEED WAS 450 M.P.H.

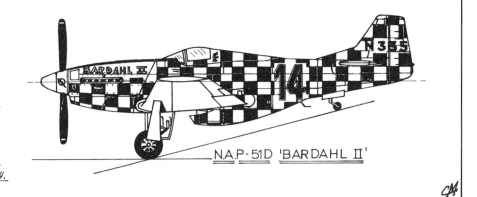

N.A. P-51D 'BARDAHL II'

APPENDIX X

MIRA J. SLOVAK'S "MR. MENNEN" ARRIVED AT RENO IN 1972 TOO LATE TO QUALIFY FOR THE UNLIMITED EVENT. HOWEVER THE FLASHY 'COBRA' WAS A REAL CROWD PLEASER FROM AN APPEARANCE STANDPOINT. CRAFT WAS ALL WHITE WITH GREEN STRIPES & MARKINGS EDGED IN GOLD. 12 CYLINDER ALLISON ENGINE CAN PUT OUT 2200 H.P., SPAN IS 34 FT., LENGTH IS 30'2". LICENSE NUMBER IS N40A.

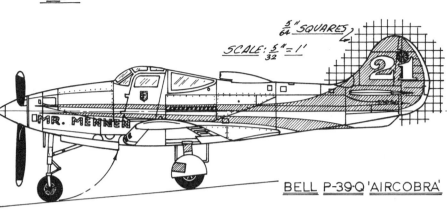

SCALE: $\frac{5}{32}$" = 1'

$\frac{5}{64}$" SQUARES

BELL P-39-Q 'AIRCOBRA'

JOHN R. SANDBERG'S FLAMING RED 'COBRA' HAS A POLISHED CHROME PLATED SPINNER, WHITE LETTERING WITH BLACK TRIM AND BLACK 'TIPSY MISS'. AIRCRAFT HAS HAD POOR LUCK AT RENO & MOJAVE DUE TO MECHANICAL PROBLEMS. WINGS HAVE BEEN CLIPPED, AIRSCOOP ENLARGED, EXHAUST MODIFIED AND WING FILLETS ENLARGED. ALLISON ENGINE PUTS OUT 2300+ H.P.

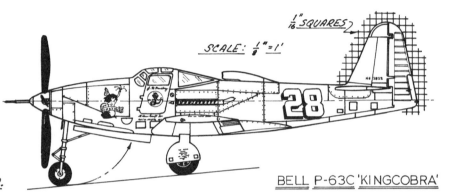

SCALE: $\frac{1}{8}$" = 1'

$\frac{1}{16}$" SQUARES

BELL P-63C 'KINGCOBRA'

A MOST UNUSUAL ENTRY IN THE RENO UNLIMITED CATAGORY, THIS 'JUG' PLACED 4TH IN THE '74 UNLIMITED MEDALLION RACE PILOTED BY MARVIN "LEFTY" GARDNER. AIRCRAFT IS LIGHT GRAY WITH YELLOW & BLACK CHECKERED COWLING. DIMENSIONS ARE: SPAN-40'9$\frac{3}{8}$"; LENGTH-36'1$\frac{3}{4}$"; HEIGHT-14'7"; WING AREA-300 FT². POWERPLANT IS 2535 H.P. P&W R-2800-59.

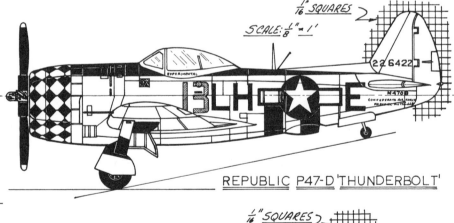

SCALE: $\frac{1}{8}$" = 1'

$\frac{1}{16}$" SQUARES

REPUBLIC P47-D 'THUNDERBOLT'

THIS 'CORSAIR' DONE IN THE MARKINGS OF VMF-312 U.S.M.C., CVE-115 BAIROKO, KOREA, FEB. 1952 IS PILOTED BY ROBERT E. GUILFORD. CRAFT TOOK 6TH PLACE IN '74 RENO UNLIMITED MEDALLION RACE. COLOR IS NAVY BLUE WITH RED & WHITE CHECKERED COWL. ALL LETTERING IS WHITE. SPAN-41'; LENGTH-34$\frac{1}{2}$'; HEIGHT-13'; WING AREA-314 FT². POWERPLANT IS 2100 H.P. P&W 2800-18W.

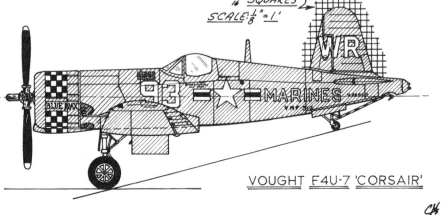

SCALE: $\frac{1}{8}$" = 1'

$\frac{1}{16}$" SQUARES

VOUGHT F4U-7 'CORSAIR'

THE T-33 IS A STRETCHED ADAPT-
ATION OF THE LOCKHEED F-80C
'SHOOTING STAR' TO ALLOW FOR A SEC-
OND SEAT. THE LATE LEROY PENHALL,
OWNER OF 'FIGHTER IMPORTS', OBTAINED
T-33 & F-86 JETS FROM CANADA FOR
MODIFICATION & RESALE IN U.S. RED
AND YELLOW CRAFT AT RIGHT WAS FLOWN
IN JET RACE AT MOJAVE '74 & '75.
SPAN - 38' 10½"; LENGTH - 37' 9"; HEIGHT -
11' 8"; WING AREA - 237 FT²; MAX SPEED - 580 MPH.

1/16" SQUARES
SCALE: 1/8" = 1'

N6633D

CANADAIR T-33 'SILVER STAR'

'SABRE' SHOWN IS ALL WHITE WITH
RED STRIPE. LEADING EDGE OF
VERTICAL FIN IS POLISHED ALUMINUM.
'FIGHTER IMPORTS' TRADE MARK IS
BLUE AND LICENSE NUMBER IS GOLD.
F-86 & T-33 ABOVE WERE BUILT
BY CANADAIR LTD. SPAN - 37' 1";
LENGTH - 37' 6"; HEIGHT - 14' 7";
WING AREA - 287.9 FT². MAX SPEED -
680 M.P.H. CRAFT COMPETED IN
MOJAVE JET RACES.

1/16" SQUARES
SCALE: 1/8" = 1'

N8686D

CANADAIR F-86 (CL-13B) 'SABRE'

LLOYD A. HAMILTON OWNS THIS HAWKER
SEA FURY II. 1972 COLOR SCHEME
SHOWN IS DARK GREEN WITH YELLOW
FUSELAGE & TAIL STRIPE. LICENCE
AND RACING NUMERALS WERE WHITE.
CRAFT WAS LATER CHANGED TO SEA-
FOAM GREEN WITH ROYAL AUSTRALIAN
NAVY MARKINGS. HAMILTON PLACED
THIRD IN HEAT 2-A IN 1972 UN-
LIMITED CONTEST AT RENO.

1/16" SQUARES
SCALE: 1/8" = 1'

15

N588

HAWKER 'SEA FURY II'

CRAFT APPEARED AT RENO IN 1969
FLOWN BY WALTER OHLRICH. IT
BORE A RED #10 RACING NUMBER ON
THE FIN. THE SPINNER WAS ALTERNATE
RED, WHITE & BLUE QUARTERS, COWL
WAS RED WITH WHITE STRIPE IN CEN-
TER. STRIPING ON WHITE FUSELAGE
WAS BLUE. PLANE WAS NAMED 'MISS
PRISS'. JOHN A. HERLIHY NOW OWNS
PLANE (RENAMED 'SWEET P') AND HAD
STRIPPED PAINT FOR '1974 RENO RACE.

5/64" SQUARES
SCALE: 5/32" = 1'

N7827C

GRUMMAN F8F-2
'BEARCAT'

CLEMENS F. FISCHER HAS MADE HIS 'MONG SPORT' INTO 'SUPER MONG' BY CHANGING WINGS TO LAMINAR FLOW FIBERGLASS COVERED ALUMINUM FRAMED ONES THAT ARE ONLY $2\frac{7}{32}$" THICK. ALSO HE HAS ADDED A CLOSE FITTING COWL. AIRCRAFT IS ALL WHITE WITH BLACK LICENSE, BLACK & GREEN "8" AND GREEN TRIM. FISCHER HAS FLOWN IN EVERY CHAMPIONSHIP RENO BIPLANE RACE SINCE 1965. HE CAME IN THIRD IN 1968, HIS BEST RACE.

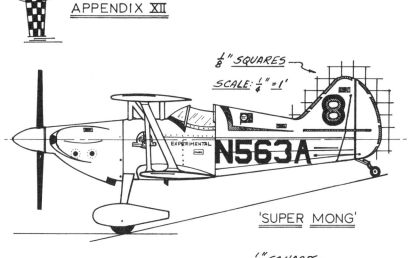

$\frac{1}{8}$" SQUARES
SCALE: $\frac{1}{4}$" = 1'

'SUPER MONG'

WILLIAM NAGEL BUILT "MONG GOOSE" AND HAS POWERED IT WITH A KIT BUILT FRANKLIN 4 CYLINDER ENGINE. COLOR SCHEME IS ALL WHITE BASE COLOR. RACE NUMBERS AND LICENSE NUMBERS ARE RED-ORANGE, INNER STRIPES ON FUSELAGE SIDES, WHEEL PANTS, WING & STAB. ARE RED ORANGE WITH DARK BLUE OUTLINE. 'MONG GOOSE' IS DARK BLUE. LENGTH = 15'8½"; SPAN = 12'1". PLANE SO FAR HAS BEEN SLOW DUE TO ENGINE.

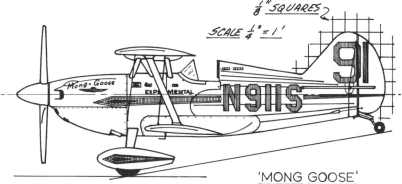

$\frac{1}{8}$" SQUARES
SCALE $\frac{1}{4}$" = 1'

'MONG GOOSE'

'J.L. SEAGULL' WAS DESIGNED AND BUILT BY RIM KAMSKAS. FLOWN BY CURRENT OWNER J.O. HALL AIRCRAFT WON 2ND PLACE IN RENO BIPLANE CHAMPIONSHIP RACE IN 1972 AT 180.04 M.P.H.. FANCY PAINT SCHEME WAS DESIGNED BY ARTIST KEN THOMS. CRAFT IS ALL WHITE WITH GOLD GULLS; VARIOUS SHADES OF BLUE ON LOWER FUSELAGE & PANTS CREATE WAVE EFFECT.

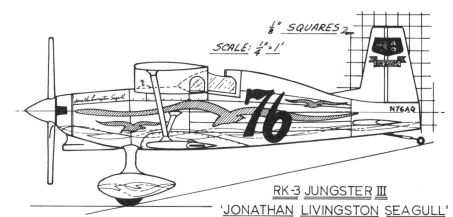

$\frac{1}{8}$" SQUARES
SCALE: $\frac{1}{4}$" = 1'

RK-3 JUNGSTER III
'JONATHAN LIVINGSTON SEAGULL'

EARL HOFFMAN HAS FLOWN "SUSIE BEE", AN ORIGINAL DESIGN BUILT BY GENE SALINA IN 1967, IN THE RENO CHAMP. BIPLANE RACE EVERY YEAR SINCE 1969 EXCEPT 1972. COLOR SCHEME IS WHITE WITH BLACK TRIM & GOLD PIN STRIPE. WING IS FABRIC COVERED WOOD; SPAN 15'5". FUSELAGE IS FABRIC COVERED STEEL TUBE FRAMEWORK. LENGTH IS 15'2". LYCOMING O-290-G ENG.

$\frac{1}{8}$" SQUARES
SCALE: $\frac{1}{4}$" = 1'

'SUSIE BEE'

THE OWL RACER OR-65-2 "YELLOW
PERIL" HAS A SPECIAL WING DE-
SIGNED BY OWNER, BUILDER, PILOT,
RALPH WISE. SPAN IS 20'5"; CHORD
AT ROOT IS 50" AND 25" AT TIPS.
COLOR SCHEME IS YELLOW WITH
MAROON TRIM & POLISHED ALUMINUM
SPINNER. CRAFT TOOK IST IN '72 F-1 MED-
ALLION RACE (RENO) AT 195.181 MPH.
PLANE WAS SOLD TO JERRY HIBBARD
AND HAS SINCE CRASHED & BURNED.

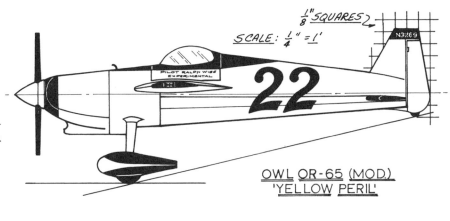

⅛" SQUARES
SCALE: ¼" = 1'

OWL OR-65 (MOD.)
'YELLOW PERIL'

JUDITH WAGNER BUILT THIS SHOE-
STRING IV FROM KETNER PLANS IN
1971. NAMED "WAGNER SOLUTION"
AIRCRAFT IS PAINTED A HIGH
GLOSS BRIGHT ORANGE. MODIFIC-
ATIONS INCLUDE CLIPPED RUDDER &
FIN, ADDED DORSAL FIN AND CLEAN-
ED UP CARB. INTAKE. POWERPLANT
IS O-200 CONTINENTAL. SHE PLACED
5TH IN FORMULA ONE HEAT 1-A IN
1973 AT 210.117 M.P.H.

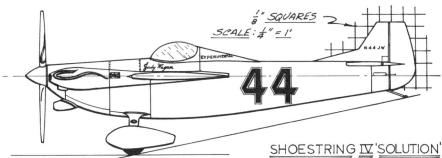

⅛" SQUARES
SCALE: ¼" = 1'

SHOESTRING IV 'SOLUTION'

BUILT BY MUNROE LYETH, JR. "NOBIG-
THING" IS A SHOESTRING K-10 FROM
KETNER PLANS. COLOR SCHEME IS
RED WITH WHITE NAME & RACE NUM-
BER. #24 HAS BLACK OUTLINE.
OTHER LETTERING IS BLACK ON
WHITE BACKGROUNDS. PLANE WAS
BUILT IN '72 AND PLACED 6TH IN
HEAT 1-A AT RENO '72. AIRCRAFT
WAS RACED AT MIAMI IN 1973.

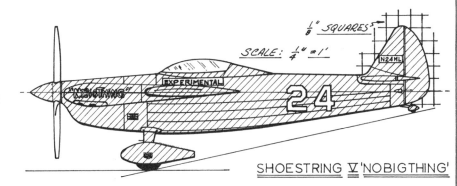

⅛" SQUARES
SCALE: ¼" = 1'

SHOESTRING V 'NOBIGTHING'

ERNEST PROSCH DESIGNED & BUILT
"LOKI" FOR 1973 SEASON. EXCEPT
FOR FIBERGLASS WHEEL PANTS
AND WING FILLETS CRAFT IS ALL
METAL. COLOR SCHEME IS ALL
WHITE WITH RED-ORANGE SPINNER,
STRIPES, LICENSE NO. AND FLYING
SURFACE TIPS. RACING NO. AND
"LOKI" ARE BLACK. SPAN-17'10¼";
LENGTH-19'10½". RACED AT RENO
IN '73 & '74 BY ROBERT REINSETH.

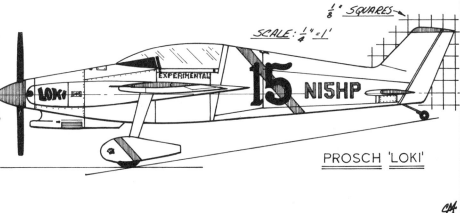

⅛" SQUARES
SCALE: ¼" = 1'

PROSCH 'LOKI'

'SCARAB', A CASSUTT III, WAS BUILT IN 1967 BY BOB GREIGER AND RACED AT FREDERICK MD. & RENO IN 1968. OWNED BY THE ERIE-SCARAB RACING ASSOCIATION OF CLEVELAND, CRAFT WAS FLOWN BY SAL LANESE. COLOR SCHEME WAS RED WITH BLACK AND WHITE TRIM. LICENSE NUMBER AND 'EXPERIMENTAL' WERE GOLD. SPAN = 15' LENGTH = 16'3" WOOD WING; STEEL TUBE & FABRIC FUSELAGE & TAIL.

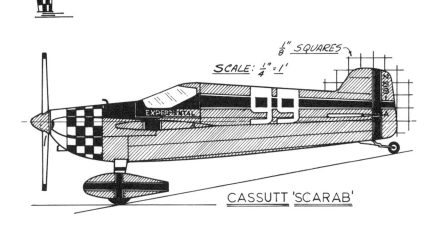

SCALE: $\frac{1}{4}" = 1'$
$\frac{1}{8}"$ SQUARES

CASSUTT 'SCARAB'

FUSELAGE OF 'MOTHER HOLLIDAY' IS CASSUTT FITTED WITH 'RIVETS' STYLE CANOPY. WING WAS DESIGNED BY OWNER, BUILDER, PILOT NICK JONES. COLOR SCHEME IS BLUE & WHITE FUSELAGE AND TAIL; RACE AND LICENSE NUMBER ARE GOLD – OTHER MARKING BLACK. WINGS ARE NATURAL MAHOGANY FINISH. LENGTH = 15'; SPAN = 15' WHEEL PANTS HAVE CLAM-SHELL DOORS.

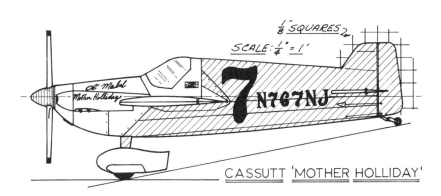

SCALE: $\frac{1}{4}" = 1'$
$\frac{1}{8}"$ SQUARES

CASSUTT 'MOTHER HOLLIDAY'

"SNOOPY", A CASSUTT II, WAS BUILT IN 1967 BY JIM WILSON AND RACED BY HIM AT CLEVELAND & MIAMI. PLANE IS PAINTED LAVENDER MIST WITH WHITE SPINNER & RACE NUMBER; BLACK & WHITE CHECKERBOARD ON CONTROL SURFACES; BLACK LICENSE NUMBER. SPAN = 14'10½" LENGTH = 16'8". CRAFT SOLD TO JOHN THOMSON IN '70; RENAMED 'DIXIE REBEL'.

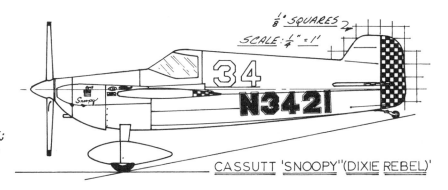

SCALE: $\frac{1}{4}" = 1'$
$\frac{1}{8}"$ SQUARES

CASSUTT 'SNOOPY' (DIXIE REBEL)

JIM WILSON BUILT "PLUM CRAZY" WITH A SPECIAL SELF DESIGNED THIN TAPERED WING FOR WHICH HE SELLS PLANS. SPAN = 18' LENGTH = 17'4". COLOR SCHEME IS PLUM FUSELAGE & PANTS; WHITE 'APPLE CHEEKS' AND RACE NUMBER. WINGS AND STABILIZER ARE WHITE. WILSON PLACED 4TH IN 1972 & 1973 IN RENO CHAMPIONSHIP FORMULA ONE RACES.

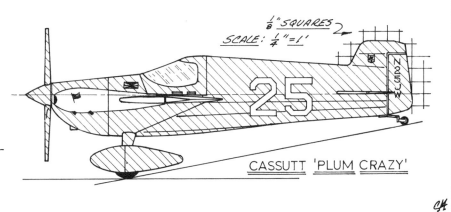

SCALE: $\frac{1}{4}" = 1'$
$\frac{1}{8}"$ SQUARES

CASSUTT 'PLUM CRAZY'

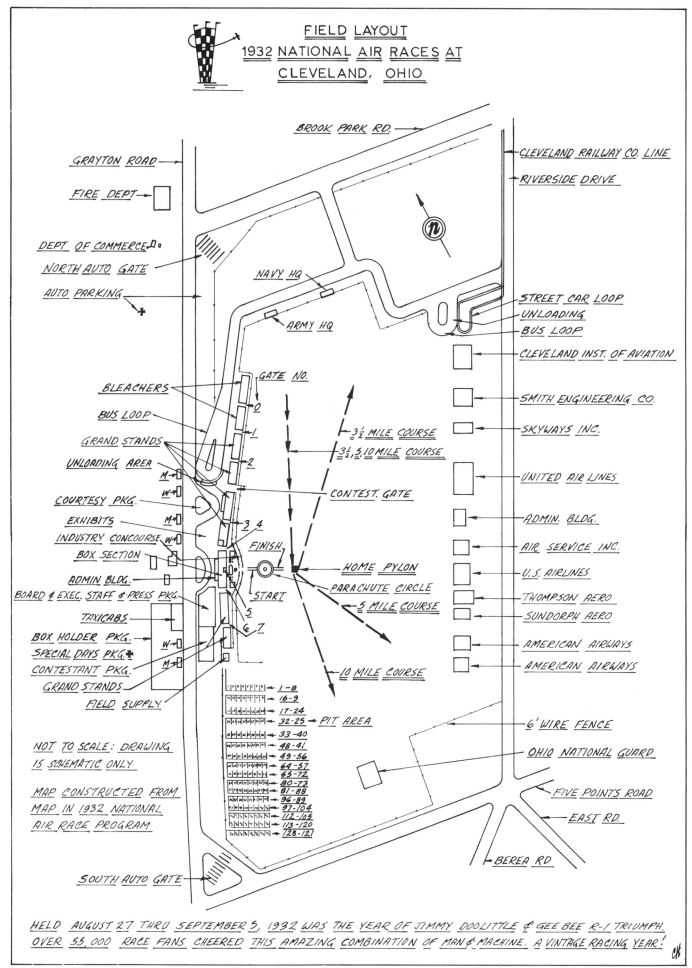

FIELD LAYOUT
1932 NATIONAL AIR RACES AT
CLEVELAND, OHIO

BROOK PARK RD.

GRAYTON ROAD

FIRE DEPT

DEPT OF COMMERCE
NORTH AUTO GATE

AUTO PARKING

CLEVELAND RAILWAY CO. LINE

RIVERSIDE DRIVE

NAVY HQ

ARMY HQ

STREET CAR LOOP
UNLOADING
BUS LOOP

CLEVELAND INST. OF AVIATION

GATE NO.

BLEACHERS

BUS LOOP

GRAND STANDS

UNLOADING AREA

COURTESY PKG.

EXHIBITS

INDUSTRY CONCOURSE

BOX SECTION

ADMIN BLDG.

BOARD & EXEC. STAFF & PRESS PKG.

TAXICABS

BOX HOLDER PKG.

SPECIAL DAYS PKG.

CONTESTANT PKG.

GRAND STANDS

FIELD SUPPLY

0

1

2

3 4

5

6 7

3½ MILE COURSE
3½, 5, 10 MILE COURSE

CONTEST. GATE

FINISH

START

HOME PYLON
PARACHUTE CIRCLE
5 MILE COURSE

10 MILE COURSE

SMITH ENGINEERING CO.

SKYWAYS INC.

UNITED AIR LINES

ADMIN. BLDG.

AIR SERVICE INC.

U.S. AIRLINES

THOMPSON AERO

SUNDORPH AERO

AMERICAN AIRWAYS

AMERICAN AIRWAYS

1-8
16-9
17-24
32-25 ← PIT AREA
48-41
49-56
64-57
65-72
80-73
81-88
96-89
97-104
112-105
113-120
128-121

NOT TO SCALE: DRAWING
IS SCHEMATIC ONLY

MAP CONSTRUCTED FROM
MAP IN 1932 NATIONAL
AIR RACE PROGRAM

6' WIRE FENCE

OHIO NATIONAL GUARD

FIVE POINTS ROAD

EAST RD.

BEREA RD

SOUTH AUTO GATE

HELD AUGUST 27 THRU SEPTEMBER 5, 1932 WAS THE YEAR OF JIMMY DOOLITTLE & GEE BEE R-1 TRIUMPH.
OVER 55,000 RACE FANS CHEERED THIS AMAZING COMBINATION OF MAN & MACHINE. A VINTAGE RACING YEAR!

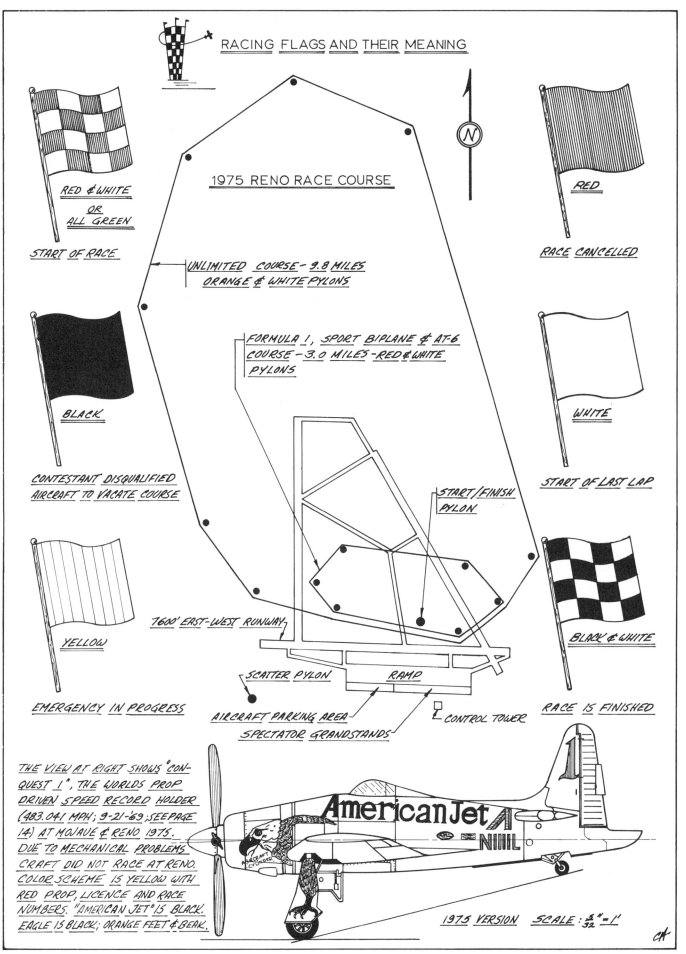

RACING FLAGS AND THEIR MEANING

RED & WHITE
OR
ALL GREEN

START OF RACE

1975 RENO RACE COURSE

RED

RACE CANCELLED

UNLIMITED COURSE - 9.8 MILES
ORANGE & WHITE PYLONS

FORMULA 1, SPORT BIPLANE & AT-6
COURSE - 3.0 MILES - RED & WHITE
PYLONS

BLACK

CONTESTANT DISQUALIFIED
AIRCRAFT TO VACATE COURSE

WHITE

START OF LAST LAP

START/FINISH
PYLON

YELLOW

EMERGENCY IN PROGRESS

1600' EAST-WEST RUNWAY

SCATTER PYLON   RAMP

CONTROL TOWER

AIRCRAFT PARKING AREA
SPECTATOR GRANDSTANDS

BLACK & WHITE

RACE IS FINISHED

THE VIEW AT RIGHT SHOWS "CON-
QUEST 1", THE WORLDS PROP
DRIVEN SPEED RECORD HOLDER
(483.041 MPH; 9-21-'69; SEE PAGE
14) AT MOJAVE & RENO 1975.
DUE TO MECHANICAL PROBLEMS
CRAFT DID NOT RACE AT RENO.
COLOR SCHEME IS YELLOW WITH
RED PROP, LICENCE AND RACE
NUMBERS. "AMERICAN JET" IS BLACK.
EAGLE IS BLACK; ORANGE FEET & BEAK.

American Jet
N111L

1975 VERSION   SCALE: $\frac{3}{32}$" = 1'

CA

TABLE OF ENTRIES IN MAJOR AIR RACES

JAMES GORDON BENNETT CUP

Year	Pilot	Aircraft	Speed
1909	Curtiss	Golden Flyer	47.6
	Bleriot	Bleriot XI	46.8
	Latham	Antoinette	42.5
	Lefebvre	Wright	37.7
	Cockburn	Earman	—
1910	Grahame-White	Bleriot XI bis	61.0
	Moisant	Bleriot XI	31.5
	Ogilvie	Wright C	29.4
	Latham	Antoinette	17.8
	Leblanc	Bleriot	—
	Drexel	Bleriot XI	—
	Radley	Bleriot XI bis	—
	Brookins	Baby Wright	—
1911	Weyman	Nieuport	78.0
	Leblanc	Bleriot	75.8
	Nieuport	Nieuport	75.1
	Ogilvie	Baby Wright	53.3
	Chevalier	Nieuport	—
	Hamel	Bleriot	—
1912	Vedrines	Deperdussin	105.5
	Provost	Deperdussin	103.8
	Frey	Hanriot	—
1913	Provost	Deperdussin	124.5
	Vedrines	Bleriot XI	123.0
	Gilbert	Deperdussin	119.5
	Crombez	Deperdussin	106.9
1920	Sadi-Lecointe	Nieuport	168.5
	deRomanet	Spad	113.5
	Kirch	Nieuport	—
	Raynham	Martinsyde	—
	Schroeder	Verville Packard	—
	Rinehart	Dayton Wright	—
	Rohles	Curtiss Texas Wildcat	—

SCHNEIDER TROPHY RACE

Year	Pilot	Aircraft	Speed
1913	Provost	Deperdussin	45.7
	Weyman	Nieuport	—
1914	Pixton	Sopwith Tabloid	86.5
	Burri	F.B.A.	62.0
1920	Bologna	Savoia S-12	107.2
1921	Briganti	Macchi M-7	117.9
	Zanetti	Macchi M-19	—
1921	Briganti	Macchi M-7	117.9
	Zanetti	Macchi M-19	—
1922	Baird	Sea Lion III	145.7
	Passaleva	Savoia S-51	143.5
	Zanetti	Macchi M-17	133.0
	Corniglio	Macchi M-7	90.6
1922	Baird	Sea Lion III	145.7
	Passaleva	Savoia S-51	143.5
	Zanetti	Macchi M-17	133.0
	Corniglio	Macchi M-7	90.6
1923	Rittenhouse	Curtiss R-3	177.4
	Irvine	Curtiss R-3	173.5
	Baird	Sea Lion III	157.2
	Hurel	Cams 38	—
	Wead	Wright NW-2	—
1923	Webster	Nieuport	168.5
	Worsley	Spad	113.5
	Guazzetti	Nieuport	—
	Raynham	Martinsyde	—
	Kinkead	Verville Packard	—
	deBernardi	Dayton Wright	—
1925	Doolittle	Curtiss R3C-2	232.6
	Broad	Gloster III	199.2
	deBriganti	Macchi M-33	168.4
	Cuddihy	Curtiss R3C-2	—
	Ofstie	Curtiss R3C-2	—
	Baird	Supermarine S-4	—
1926	deBernardi	Macchi M-39	246.5
	Schilt	Curtiss R3C-2	231.3
	Bacula	Macchi M-39	218.0
	Tomlinson	Curtiss F6C-1	136.9
	Cuddihy	Curtiss R3C-4	—
1927	Webster	Supermarine S-5	281.6
	Worsley	Supermarine S-5	273.1
	Guazzetti	Macchi M-52	—
	Kinkead	Gloster IV B	—
	deBernardi	Macchi M-52	—

SCHNEIDER TROPHY RACE (CONTINUED)

Year	Pilot	Aircraft	Speed
1929	Waghorn	Supermarine S-6	328.6
	DalMolin	Macchi M-52R	284.2
	Grieg	Supermarine S-5	282.1
	Atcherly	Supermarine S-6	—
	Cadringer	Macchi M-67	—
	Monti	Macchi M-67	—
1931	Boothman	Supermarine S-6B	340.1

PULITZER TROPHY RACE

Year	Pilot	Aircraft	Speed
1920	Mosely	Verville Packard	156.5
	Hartney	Thomas Morse MB-3	148.0
	Acosta	SVA A-1	134.5
	Streett	Orewco "D"	133.0
	Laurents	Vought VE-7	125.0
	Roullot	DeHaviland DH-4	124.0
	Taylor	SVA-9	117.0
	Kirby	SE-5A	116.7
	Colt	Morane-Saulnier	95.0
	Bradley	Leoning Special	150.0
1921	Acosta	Curtiss R-1	176.7
	Coombs	Curtiss Cox	170.3
	Macready	Thomas Morse MB-6	160.7
	Bertaud	Ansaldo Balilla	149.8
	Hartney	Thomas Morse MB-7	—
	Curran	SVA-9	—
1922	Maughan	Curtiss R-6	205.8
	Maitland	Curtiss R-6	198.8
	Brow	Curtiss R-2	193.2
	Williams	Curtiss R-1	188.0
	Barksdale	Verville Sperry R-3	181.0
	Mosely	Verville Packard R-1	179.0
	Johnson	Verville Sperry R-3	178.0
	Whitehead	Leoning R-4	170.2
	Schulz	Leoning R-4	160.9
1923	Williams	Curtiss R2C-1	243.7
	Brow	Curtiss R2C-1	241.8
	Sanderson	Wright F2W	230.1
	Callaway	Wright F2W	230.0
	Miller	Curtiss R-6	218.9
	Corkill	Curtiss R-6	216.5
	Pearson	Verville Sperry R-3	—
1924	Mills	Verville Sperry R-3	215.7
	Brookley	Curtiss R-6	214.7
	Stoner	Curtiss PW-8A	167.9
	Skeel	Curtiss R-6	—
1925	Bettis	Curtiss R3C-1	248.9
	Williams	Curtiss R3C-1	241.7
	Dawson	Curtiss P-1	169.9
	Norton	Curtiss PW-8	168.8
	Cook	Curtiss PW-8	167.4
	Cuddihy	Curtiss PW-8	—

NATIONAL AIR RACES 1926-1928

Year	Pilot	Aircraft	Speed
1926	Cuddihy	Boeing FB-3	180.5
	Elliott	Curtiss P-2	178.6
	Hoyt	Curtiss P-2	170.9
	Nutt	Curtiss P-2	170.8
	McCormick	Curtiss P-2	169.6
	Barner	Boeing FB-3	163.6
	Sanderson	Boeing FB-3	163.4
	Ballard	Curtiss P-1	159.3
	McKiernan	Curtiss P-1	—
1927	Batten	Curtiss XP-6A	201.2
	Lyon	Curtiss XP-6A	189.6
	Jeter	Boeing FB-5	176.9
	Regan	Boeing FB-5	175.9
	Bogan	Boeing FB-5	172.9
	Beverly	Boeing PW-9C	169.7
	Rogers	Curtiss F6C-4	161.5
	Cornelius	Curtiss P-1B	161.5
	Woodring	Curtiss P-1B	159.2
	Malloy	Curtiss P-1B	—
1928	Jeter	Boeing XF4B-1	172.3
	Cruise	Boeing F2B-1	159.9
	Harrigan	Boeing F2B-1	151.6
	Burroughs	Boeing F2B-1	150.3
	Crommelin	Boeing F2B-1	149.8
	Williamson	Boeing F2B-1	146.0

THOMPSON TROPHY RACE

Year	Pilot	Aircraft	Speed
1929	Davis	Travel Air Model R	194.9
	Breene	Curtiss Hawk P-3A	186.8
	Turner	Lockheed "Vega"	163.8
1930	Holman	Laird "Solution"	201.9
	Haizlip	Travel Air Model R	199.8
	Howard	Howard "Pete"	162.8
	Adams	Travel Air Biplane	142.6
1931	Bayles	Gee Bee Model Z	236.2
	Wedell	Wedell-Williams "44"	228.0
	Jackson	Laird "Solution"	211.2
	Hall	Gee Bee Model Y	201.3
	Eaker	Lockheed Altair	196.8
	Howard	Howard "Pete"	163.6
	Ong	Laird Speedwing	153.0
	Doolittle	Laird "Super Solution"	—
1932	Doolittle	Gee Bee R-1	252.7
	Wedell	Wedell-Williams "44"	242.5
	Turner	Wedell-Williams "57"	233.0
	Haizlip	Wedell-Williams "92"	231.3
	Gehlbach	Gee Bee R-2	222.1
	Hall	Hall "Bulldog"	215.6
	Ong	Howard "Ike"	191.1
1933	Wedell	Wedell-Williams "44"	237.9
	Gehlbach	Wedell-Williams "92"	224.9
	Minor	Howard "Mike"	199.9
	Hague	Keith-Rider R-2	183.2
	Granville	Gee Bee Model Y	173.1
1934	Turner	Wedell-Williams "57"	248.1
	Minor	Brown B-2	214.9
	Worthen	Wedell-Williams "45"	208.4
	Neumann	Howard "Ike"	207.1
	Rae	Keith-Rider R-1	205.4
	Chester	Chester "Jeep"	191.6
1935	Neumann	Howard "Mr. Mulligan"	220.2
	Wittman	Wittman "Bonzo"	218.7
	Rae	Keith-Rider R-1	213.9
	Jacobson	Howard "Mike"	209.1
	Miles	Seversky SEV-3	193.6
	McKeen	Brown B-2	188.9
	Turner	Wedell-Williams "57"	—
1936	Detroyat	Caudron C-460	264.3
	Ortman	Keith Rider R-3	248.0
	Rae	Keith Rider R-4	236.6
	Neumann	Folkerts "Toots"	233.1
	McKeen	Brown B-2	230.5
	Crosby	Crosby Special CR-3	226.1
1937	Kling	Folkerts "Jupiter"	256.9
	Ortman	Marcoux Bromberg R-3	256.8
	Turner	Laird-Turner LTR-14	253.8
	Sinclair	Seversky SEV-S2	252.4
	Wittman	Wittman "Bonzo"	250.1
	Moore	Seversky SEV-S2	238.4
	Gotch	Schoenfeldt "Firecracker"	217.8
1938	Turner	Laird-Turner LTR-14	283.4
	Ortman	Marcoux Bromberg R-3	269.7
	Wittman	Wittman "Bonzo"	259.1
	Wade	HM-1 (Time Flies)	249.8
	Mackey	Wedell-Williams "57"	249.6
	Jacobson	Keith-Rider "8 Ball"	214.5
1939	Turner	Laird-Turner LTR-14	282.5
	LeVier	Schoenfeldt "Firecracker"	272.5
	Ortman	Marcoux Bromberg R-3	254.4
	Crosby	Crosby Special CR-4	244.5
	Wittman	Wittman "Bonzo"	241.3
	Mackey	Wedell-Williams "57"	232.9
1946	Johnston	P-39Q "Aircobra"	373.9
	LeVier	P-38L-5 "Lightning"	370.1
	Ortman	P-51D-30 "Mustang"	367.6
	Raymond	P-51D "Mustang"	364.6
	Swanson	P-51D "Mustang"	362.1
	Cleland	F-2G-1 "Corsair"	357.5
	Edmundson	P-51D "Mustang"	354.4
	Wittman	P-63C-5 "Kingcobra"	341.2
	Lilly	P-63A "Kingcobra"	328.2
	Pemberton	P-63F "Kingcobra"	304.4
1947	Cleland	F-2G-1 "Corsair"	396.1
	Becker	F-2G-1 "Corsair"	390.1
	Demming	P-39Q "Aircobra"	389.8
	Beville	P-51D "Mustang"	360.8
	LeVier	P-38L-5 "Lightning"	357.5
	Bour	P-63A "Kingcobra"	327.3
1948	Johnson	P-51D "Mustang"	383.8
	Raymond	P-51D "Mustang"	365.2
	Newhall	P-63C-5 "Kingcobra"	313.6
	Brown	P-39Q "Aircobra"	392.4
1949	Cleland	F-2G-1 "Corsair"	397.1
	Puckett	F-2G-1 "Corsair"	393.5
	McKillen	F-2G-1 "Corsair"	387.6
	Beville	P-51D "Mustang"	381.2
	Tucker	P-63C-5 "Kingcobra"	378.3
	Hagerstrom	P-51D "Mustang"	372.7
	Newhall	P-51K "Mustang"	372.3
	Hannon	P-51A "Mustang"	300.4
	Johnson	P-51D "Mustang"	—
	Odom	P-51C "Mustang"	—

BENDIX TROPHY RACE

Year	Pilot	Aircraft	Speed
1931	Doolittle	Laird "Super Solution"	223.0
	Johnson	Lockheed "Orion"	198.8
	Blevins	Lockheed "Orion"	189.0
	Eacker	Lockheed Altair	186.1
1932	Haizlip	Wedell-Williams "92"	245.0
	Wedell	Wedell-Williams "44"	232.0
	Turner	Wedell-Williams "57"	226.0
	Gehlback	Gee Bee R-2	210.0
	Vance	Vance Flying Wing	—
1933	Turner	Wedell-Williams "57"	214.8
	Wedell	Wedell-Williams "44"	209.2
	Boardman	Gee Bee R-1	—
	Thaw	Gee Bee R-2	—
	Gehlbach	Wedell-Williams "92"	—
	Earhart	Lockheed "Vega"	—
1934	Davis	Wedell-Williams "44"	216.2
	Worthen	Wedell-Williams "92"	203.2
	Gehlbach	Gee Bee "QED"	—
1935	Neumann-Howard	Howard "Mr. Mulligan"	238.7
	Turner	Wedell-Williams "57"	238.5
	Thaw	Northrup "Gamma"	201.9
	Hunt	Lockheed "Orion"	174.8
1936	Thaden-Noyes	Beech C-17	165.3
	Ingalls	Lockheed "Orion"	157.5
	Bulick	Vultee V1A-1	156.5
	Pomeroy	Douglas DC-2	151.5
	Earhart	Lockheed "Electra"	148.7
	Howard-Wife	Howard "Mr. Mulligan"	—
	Jacobson	Northrup "Gamma"	—
	Miles	Gee Bee "QED"	—
1937	Fuller	Seversky SEV-S2 (P-35)	258.2
	Ortman	Marcoux Bromberg R-3	224.8
	Cochran	Beech "Staggerwing"	194.7
	Sinclair	Seversky SEV-S2	184.9
	Burcham	Lockheed 12	184.5
	Sundorph	Sundorph A-1	166.2
	Perlick	Beech "Staggerwing" A17F	—
	Mackey	Wedell-Williams "44"	—
1938	Cochran	Seversky SEV-S2	249.7
	Fuller	Seversky SEV-S2	238.6
	Mantz	Lockheed "Orion"	206.6
	Constant	Beech "Staggerwing"	199.3
	Hadley	Beech "Staggerwing"	181.8
	LaJatte	Spartan 7W	177.4
	Armistead	Gee Bee "QED"	—
	Perlick	Beech A-17F	—
	Cordova	Bellanca Trimotor	—
1939	Fuller	Seversky SEV-S2	282.1
	Bussy	Bellanca Trimotor	244.5
	Mantz	Lockheed "Orion"	234.9
	Constant	Beech "Staggerwing"	231.4
	Davis	Spartan 7W	196.8
	Maycock	Beech "Staggerwing"	187.2
1946	Mantz	P-51C "Mustang"	435.5
	Cochran	P-51B "Mustang"	420.9
	Mayson	P-51C "Mustang"	408.2
	Eddy	P-51D "Mustang"	373.3
	Harp	P-38 "Lightning"	370.4
	Husted	A-26C "Invader"	367.9
	Tucker	P-63C-5 "Kingcobra"	367.1
1947	Mantz	P-51C "Mustang"	460.4
	DeBona	P-51D "Mustang"	458.2
	Lunken	P-51D "Mustang"	408.7
	Gimbel	P-51B "Mustang"	404.1
	Eddy	P-51D "Mustang"	376.5
	Mayson	P-51C "Mustang"	376.1
	Whitton	FG-1 "Corsair"	320.0
1948	Mantz	P-51C "Mustang"	448.0
	Carney	P-51C "Mustang"	446.1
	Cochran	P-51B "Mustang"	445.8
	Lunken	P-51D "Mustang"	441.6
	Stallings	DH "Mosquito"	341.1
	DeBona	P-51C "Mustang"	—
1949	DeBona	P-51C "Mustang"	470.1
	Reaver	P-51C "Mustang"	450.2
	Salmon	P-51C "Mustang"	449.2
	Bussart	DH "Mosquito"	343.8
	Cameron	B-26C "Invader"	—
	Perron	AT-12	—

GREVE TROPHY RACE

Year	Pilot	Aircraft	Speed
1934	Minor	Brown B-2	213.3
	Neumann	Howard "Ike"	211.6
	Rae	Keith-Rider R-1	211.0
	Miles	Miles & Atwood Spl.	206.2
	Chester	Chester "Jeep"	203.4
1935	Neumann	Howard "Mike"	212.7
	Rae	Keith-Rider R-1	210.1
	McKeen	Brown B-2	206.4
	Chester	Chester "Jeep"	199.1
	Miles	Miles & Atwood Spl.	189.6
	Wittman	"Chief Oshkosh"	189.4
	Elmendorf	Wedell-Williams "22"	175.1
1936	Detroyat	Caudron C-460	247.3
	Neumann	Folkerts "Toots"	225.9
	Chester	Chester "Jeep"	224.7
	Kling	Keith-Rider "Suzy"	218.3
	Jacobson	Howard "Mike"	214.4
	Rae	Keith-Rider R-1	212.3
	McKeen	Brown B-2	204.5
	Miles	Miles & Atwood Spl.	—

GREVE TROPHY RACE (CONTINUED)

Year	Pilot	Aircraft	Speed
1937	Kling	Folkerts SK-3	232.27
	Wittman	"Chief Oshkosh"	231.99
	Gotch	Schoenfeld-Rider R-4	231.59
	Rae	Folkerts SK4	224.19
	McKeen	Brown B-2	223.64
	Haines	Haines H-3	177.71
	McArthur	Delgado "Flash"	—
1938	LeVier	Schoenfeld-Rider R-4	250.9
	Chester	Chester "Goon"	250.4
	Jacobson	Rider R-6 "8 Ball"	218.2
	Ortman	Marcoux-Bromberg-Jackrabbit	192.5
	Crosby	Crosby CR-4	—
	Dory	Bushey-McGrew	—
1939	Chester	Chester "Goon"	263.4
	LeVier	Schoenfeld-Rider R-4	—
	Crosby	Crosby CR-4	—
	Williams	Brown B-2	—

GOODYEAR TROPHY RACE

Year	Pilot	Aircraft	Speed
1947	Brennand	Wittman "Buster"	165.9
	Penrose	"Chester Swee Pea"	165.4
	Salmon	Cosmic Wind "Special"	158.8
	LeVier	Cosmic Wind "Little Toni"	157.9
	Siem	"Loose Siem"	151.3
	Robinson	Modified Brown B-1	143.9
1948	Salmon	Cosmic Wind "Minnow"	169.7
	Wittman	Wittman Special	168.9
	Chester	Chester "Swee Pea II"	168.2
	Brennand	Wittman "Buster"	167.1
	Robinson	Cosmic Wind "Little Toni"	165.1
	Quigley	Pitts Special	164.9
	Downey	Cosmic Wind "Ballerina"	161.5
	LeFevers	Falcon Special	156.6
1949	Brennand	Wittman "Buster"	177.3
	Sorenson	"Deerfly"	176.7
	Wittman	Wittman "Bonzo"	176.2
	Ast	Cosmic Wind "Ballerina"	176.0
	Salmon	Cosmic Wind "Minnow"	175.7
	Mone	Williams "Estrellita"	175.0
	Downey	Mercury Air	171.4
	Johnson	Long LA-1	167.3
	Kistler	Kistler Special	153.4
	Foss	"Jinny"	—

CHAMPIONSHIP RACE RESULTS: RENO

UNLIMITED

Year	Pilot	Aircraft	#	Speed
1964	Love	North American P-51D	8	381.96
	Slovak	Grumman F8F-2	80	355.52
	Lacy	North American P-51D	64	354.74
	Hall	North American P-51D	2	344.45
	Ohlrich	Grumman F8F-2	10	343.43
	Weiner	North American P-51D	14	282.72
	Greenamyer	Grumman F8F-2	1	351.88
1965	Greenamyer	Grumman F8F-2	1	375.10
	Lyford	North American P-51D	8	368.57
	Lacy	North American P-51D	64	356.97
	Slovak	Grumman F8F-2	80	356.00
	Ohlrich	Grumman F8F-2	10	333.22
	Shelton	North American P-51D	12	331.99
1966	Greenamyer	Grumman F8F-2	1	396.22
	Hall	North American P-51D	2	372.70
	Lacy	North American P-51D	64	360.63
	Adams	North American P-51D	9	—
	Weaver	North American P-51D	15	—
	Lyford	North American P-51D	8	—
1967	Greenamyer	Grumman F8F-2	1	392.62
	Weiner	North American P-51D	45	373.71
	Lacy	North American P-51D	64	363.21
	Hall	North American P-51D	5	363.07
	Loening	North American P-51D	2	359.87
	Lyford	North American P-51D	8	—
1968	Greenamyer	Grumman F8F-2	1	388.65
	Hall	North American P-51D	5	386.85
	Lacy	North American P-51D	64	388.12
	Ohlrich	Grumman F8F-2	10	344.30
	Weiner	North American P-51D	49	—
	Loening	North American P-51D	2	—
1969	Greenamyer	Grumman F8F-2	1	412.63
	Hall	North American P-51D	5	377.23
	Lacy	North American P-51D	64	371.70
	Cummins	North American P-51D	69	358.84
	Shelton	Grumman F8F-2	70	356.37
	Balz	Grumman F8F-1	7	318.29

UNLIMITED (CONTINUED)

Year	Pilot	Aircraft	#	Speed
1970	Lacy	North American P-51D	64	387.34
	Loening	North American P-51D	2	376.69
	Penhall	North American P-51D	81	373.82
	Keefe	North American P-51D	11	371.55
	Balz	Grumman F8F-1	7	334.43
	Greenamyer	Grumman F8F-2	1	297.06
	Shelton	Grumman F8F-2	77	—
1973	Shelton	Grumman F8F-2	77	428.16
	Cummins	North American P-51D	69	417.08
	Wright	North American P-51D	5	407.50
	Sliker	Grumman F8F-2	4	381.60
	Keefe	North American P-51D	11	359.27
	Love	North American P-51D	97	—
	Fountain	Grumman F8F-2	24	—
1976	Gardner	North American P-51D	25	379.62
	Greenamyer	North American P-51D	1	366.36
	Keefe	North American P-51D	11	326.77
	Leeward	North American P-51D	9	302.99
	Whittington	North American P-51D	09	—
	Klabo	North American P-51D	85	—
	McClain	North American RB-51	5	—
	Crocker	North American P-51D	6	—
1979	Crocker	"Sumthin' Else"	6	422.30
	Hinton	"Red Baron"	5	415.97
	Putman	"Ciuchetton"	86	399.91
	Klabo	"Fat Cat"	85	387.00
	Hamilton	"Baby Gorilla"	16	343.72
1982	Hevle	"Dago Red"	4	405.09
	Klabo	"Fat Cat"	85	386.48
	Williams	"No Name Lady"	86	386.09
	Hinton	"Bud Light Special"	1	362.50
	Destefani	"Mangia-Pane"	72	354.86
	Dilley	"Lou IV"	19	349.91
1985	Hinton	Super Corsair	1	438.19
	Anderson	"Dreadnought"	8	429.43
	Brickert	"Dago Red"	4	426.85
	Hamilton	"Furias"	15	411.95
1971	Greenamyer	Grumman F8F-2	1	413.99
	Shelton	Grumman F8F-2	77	413.07
	Cooper	Hawker "Sea Fury"	87	412.58
	Balz	North American P-51D	5	412.10
	Penhall	North American P-51D	81	385.57
	Keefe	North American P-51D	11	—
	Loening	North American P-51D	2	—
1974	Burnstine	North American P-51D	33	381.48
	Henderson	North American P-51D	25	372.03
	Wright	North American P-51D	66	340.24
	Herlihy	Grumman F8F-2	20	320.25
	Shelton	Grumman F8F-2	77	—
	Love	North American P-51D	97	—
	McClain	North American P-51D	5	—
1977	Greenamyer	North American RB-51	5	430.70
	Whittington	North American P-51D	09	425.70
	Cummins	North American P-51D	69	424.36
	Klabo	North American P-51D	85	407.92
	Putman	North American P-51D	86	389.08
	McClain	North American P-51D	17	383.49
	Gardner	North American P-51D	25	374.67
1980	McClain	"Jeannie"	69	433.01
	Crocker	"Sumthin' Else"	6	429.78
	Whittington	"Precious Metal"	9	404.70
	Putman	"Ciuchetton"	86	397.81
	Whittington	"GeGe II"	4	358.45
1983	Anderson	"Dreadnought"	8	425.24
	Whittington	"Precious Metal"	9	414.65
	Crocker	"Sumthin' Else"	6	394.60
	Destefani	"Mangia-Pane"	72	384.36
1986	Brickert	"Dreadnought"	8	434.49
	Hamilton	"Furias"	15	429.37
	Destefani	"Strega"	7	416.88
	Preston	"Dago Red"	4	413.85
	Penny	"Rare Bear"	77	407.57
	Kelley	"Lou IV"	19	367.56
1972	Balz	North American P-51D	5	416.16
	Shelton	Grumman F8F-2	77	404.70
	Keefe	North American P-51D	11	398.53
	Lacy	North American P-51D	64	341.89
	Mitchem	Goodyear FG-10	94	341.99
	Baillie	Fury II	0	340.83
	Laidley	Grumman F8F-2	1	—
1975	Shelton	Grumman F8F-2	77	429.92
	McClain	North American P-51D	5	427.31
	Sliker	Grumman F8F-2	4	381.97
	Burnstine	North American P-51D	34	—
	Klabo	North American P-51D	85	—
	Cummins	North American P-51D	69	—
	Levitz	North American P-51D	81	—
1978	Hinton	North American RB-51	5	415.46
	Whittington	North American P-51D	09	414.77
	Putman	North American P-51D	86	396.21
	Keefe	North American P-51D	11	374.69
	Smith	North American P-51D	4	370.39
	Hamilton	Hawker "Sea Fury"	16	342.14
	Wright	North American P-51D	20	—
1981	Holm	"Jeannie"	69	431.29
	Crocker	"Sumthin' Else"	6	419.37
	Hevle	"Mangia-Pane"	72	388.14
	Klabo	"Fat Cat"	85	379.29
	Martin	"Ridge Runner"	7	364.42
	Hamilton	"Baby Gorilla"	16	357.50
1984	Holm	"Stiletto"	84	437.62
	Crocker	"Sumthin' Else"	6	431.15
	Hinton	Super Corsair	1	413.69
	Leeward	Leeward Air Ranch Spec.	44	407.41
	Levitz	"Tipsy Too"	28	385.59
	Granley	"Miss America"	11	384.39
1987	Destefani	"Strega"	7	452.56
	Brickert	"Dreadnought"	8	449.75
	Preston	"Dago Red"	4	439.46
	Maloney	Super Corsair	1	416.91
	Williams	"Pegasus"	55	386.89
	Levitz	"Miss Ashley"	38	375.82

UNLIMITED (CONTINUED)

Year	Pilot	Aircraft	#	Speed
1988	Shelton	"Rare Bear"	77	456.82
	Brickert	"Dreadnought"	8	451.20
	Hinton	"Tsunami"	18	429.95
	Putman	"Georgia Mae"	69	408.29
	Hamilton	"Furias"	15	403.63
	Maloney	Super Corsair	1	368.13
1991	Shelton	"Rare Bear"	77	481.62
	Destefani	"Strega"	7	478.68
	Holm	"Tsunami"	18	478.14
	Yancey	"Perestroika"	101	428.29
	Sanders	"Dreadnought"	8	426.51
	Rheinschild	"Risky Business"	45	423.50
	Maloney	"All Coast"	1	406.42
	Pardue	"Fury"	66	357.67

Year	Pilot	Aircraft	#	Speed
1989	Shelton	"Rare Bear"	77	450.91
	Brickert	"Dreadnought"	8	427.87
	Maloney	All Coast Super Corsair	1	406.27
	Yancey	"Yak II"	101	406.05
	Hinton	"Tsunami"	18	385.75
	Price	"Dago Red"	4	384.32
	Crocker	"Sumthin' Else"	6	358.89
1992	Destefani	"Strega"	7	450.84
	Sanders	"Dreadnought"	8	442.50
	Yancey	"Peristroika"	101	433.56
	Jackson	"Stiletto"	84	426.22
	Rupp	"Old Crow"	5	424.24
	Eldridge	Coast Super Corsair	1	420.80
	Levitz	"Miss Ashley"	38	378.34

Year	Pilot	Aircraft	#	Speed
1990	Rheinschild	"Risky Business"	45	415.53
	Levitz	"Miss Ashley"	38	407.21
	Cutshall	"E2S"	91	380.30
	Gardner	"Thunderbird"	25	376.88
	Baker	"Sky Fury"	711	372.12
	Janes	"Cottonmouth"	20	371.84
	Stephens	"Baby Gorilla"	16	369.33
1993	Destefani	"Strega"	7	455.38
	Sanders	"Dreadnought"	8	450.62
	Yancey	"Yak II"	101	439.54
	Rheinschild	"Risky Business"	45	436.94
	Eldridge	Coast Super Corsair	1	418.66
	Pardue	"Seafury"	66	406.71
	Speer	"Deja Vu"	56	399.87

FORMULA I

Year	Pilot	Aircraft	#	Speed
1964	Porter	Miller "Little Gem"	14	193.44
	Wittman	Wittman "Bonzo"	1	187.42
	Scholl	"Miss San Bernardino"	31	171.76
	Downey	"Miss Cosmic Wind"	6	166.57
	Quarton	Cagsutt-Quarton	19	162.86
1967	Falck	"Rivets"	92	202.70
	Downey	Miller "Ole Tiger"	14	201.19
	Cote	"Shoestring"	16	200.56
	Stover	"Miss San Bernardino"	31	191.08
	Baker	Baker "Boo Ray"	81	183.89
	Wilson	Wilson "Snoopy"	34	—
1970	Cote	"Shoestring"	16	220.07
	Falck	"Rivets"	92	215.96
	Moeller	"Boo Ray"	81	210.84
	Minges	"Ol' Blue"	97	206.53
	Downey	"Ole Tiger"	14	206.14
	Jones	"Mother Holliday"	7	205.42
	Berry	"Little Toni"	3	199.91

Year	Pilot	Aircraft	#	Speed
1965	Porter	"Deerfly"	39	202.14
	Falck	"Rivets"	92	196.19
	Downey	Miller "Ole Tiger"	14	194.44
	Scholl	"Miss San Bernardino"	31	190.06
	Townsend	"French Quarter Special"	7	184.40
	Stead	"Miss Cosmic Wind"	6	—
1968	Cote	"Shoestring"	16	214.61
	Falck	"Rivets"	92	212.36
	Downey	"Ole Tiger"	14	211.87
	Baker	"Boo Ray"	81	198.44
	Berry	"Little Toni"	7	197.59
	Jella	"Little Bit"	2	187.09
1971	Cote	"Shoestring"	16	224.14
	Falck	"Rivets"	92	220.30
	Downey	"Ole Tiger"	14	219.25
	Wilson	"Plum Crazy"	25	212.46
	Jones	"Mother Holliday"	7	210.73
	Thomson	"Dixie Rebel"	34	207.03
	Budde	"El Bandito"	10	193.00
	Moeller	"Boo Ray"	81	—

Year	Pilot	Aircraft	#	Speed
1966	Falck	"Rivets"	92	193.10
	Wittman	"Bonzo"	1	191.90
	Downey	Miller "Ole Tiger"	14	189.01
	Scholl	"Miss San Bernardino"	31	185.25
	Berry	"Miss Dallas"	97	174.45
	Cote	"Shoestring"	16	—
1969	Cote	"Shoestring"	16	214.61
	Falck	"Rivets"	92	212.36
	Downey	"Ole Tiger"	14	211.87
	Baker	"Boo Ray"	81	198.44
	Pedigo	"Pogo"	87	198.44
	Jones	"Mother Holliday"	7	198.44
	Berry	"Little Toni"	3	197.59
	Jella	"Little Bit"	2	187.0
1972	Cote	"Shoestring"	16	223.95
	Moeller	"Boo Ray"	81	220.97
	Downey	"Ole Tiger"	14	212.91
	Wilson	"Plum Crazy"	25	210.47
	Stevenson	"Fan"	11	205.91
	DeLuca	"Lil' Quickie"	71	205.76
	Beck	"Pogo"	87	203.92
	Falck	"Rivets"	92	—

FORMULA I (CONTINUED)

Year	Pilot	Aircraft	#	Speed
1973	Cote	"Shoestring"	16	231.26
	Jones (J.P.)	"Stinger"	21	229.54
	Moeller	"Boo Ray"	81	225.38
	Falck	"Rivets"	92	224.16
	DeLuca	"Lil' Quickie"	71	219.60
	Beck	"Knat"	18	214.63
	Jones	"Mother Holliday"	7	211.27
	Wilson	"Plum Crazy"	25	207.21
1974	Cote	"Shoestring"	16	235.42
	Moeller	"Boo Ray"	81	226.24
	DeLuca	"Lil' Quickie"	71	222.68
	Jones (J.P.)	"Stinger"	21	220.18
	Jones	"Mother Holliday"	7	220.13
	Falck	"Rivets"	92	219.68
	Stevenson	"Fang"	11	219.18
	Downey	"Ole Tiger"	14	209.71
1975	Cote	"Shoestring"	16	227.46
	DeLuca	"Lil' Quickie"	71	226.84
	Falck	"Rivets"	92	222.41
	Moeller	"Boo Ray"	81	221.09
	Wofford	"Proud Bird"	9	218.98
	Jones	"Mother Holliday"	7	218.09
	Wagner	"Wagner Solution"	44	217.96
	Baker	"Aquarius"	20	214.71
1976	DeLuca	"Lil' Quickie"	71	228.75
	Downey	"Falcon"	28	222.39
	Falck	"Rivets"	92	221.65
	Wagner	"Wagner Solution"	44	220.46
	Moeller	"Boo Ray"	81	219.74
	Tuttle	"Pegasus"	95	215.41
	Budde	"Okie Streaker"	19	204.40
	Stevenson	"Fang"	11	196.59
1977	Parker	"Top Turkey"	93	226.12
	Wagner	"Wagner Solution"	44	217.52
	Wilson	"Aloha"	71	217.41
	Wofford	"Schultz-Lemire"	9	216.92
	Reinseth	"Pole Cat"	6	216.65
	Summers	"Hansen Special"	35	202.96
	Eskildsen	"Kistler Special"	31	170.72
1978		Championship Race cancelled due to high winds.		
1979	Parker	"Wild Turkey"	3	240.09
	Cote	"Shoestring/Circus, Circus"	16	236.01
	Wagner	"Wagner Solution"	44	232.51
	Wentworth	"Fang"	11	225.47
	Wise	"Wise Owl"	7	225.38
	Wilson	"Aloha"	71	221.63
1980	Parker	"American Special"	3	249.07
	Cote	"Shoestring/Circus, Circus"	16	242.96
	Wagner	"Wagner Solution"	44	238.79
	Moeller	"Boo Ray"	81	232.54
	Drew	"Fang"	11	229.84
	Downey	"Falcon"	28	225.78
	Anspach	"Polecat"	93	225.72
1981	Cote	"Shoestring"	16	232.13
	Wagner	"Wagner Solution"	44	221.87
	Fogg	"Aloha"	1	221.51
	Jensen	"Penguin"	25	217.30
	Miller	"Texas Gem"	73	216.02
	Dowd	"Illusion"	5	211.56
	Summers	"Sump'n Else"	35	208.62
1982	Sharp	"Aero Magic"	43	224.52
	Fogg	"Aloha"	1	223.90
	Dowd	"Illusion"	5	222.87
	Miller	"Texas Gem"	73	—
	Jensen	"Penguin"	25	—
	Wentworth	"Flexi-Flyer"	69	—
	Wise	"Wise Owl"	7	—
1983	Wentworth	"Flexi-Flyer"	69	239.02
	Thompson	"Empire Strikes Back"	71	224.85
	Dowd	"Illusion"	5	224.18
	Cote	"Judy's Turn"	44	223.88
	Sharp	"Aero Magic"	43	222.11
	Fogg	"Aloha"	1	220.21
	Miller	"Texas Gem"	73	192.19
1984	Cote	"Judy"	44	236.07
	Aslett	"Flexi-Flyer"	69	235.34
	Sharp	"Aero Magic"	43	233.81
	Dowd	"Illusion"	5	229.90
	Miller	"Texas Gem"	73	224.68
	Fogg	"Aloha"	4	216.69
	Beck	"Miss U.S.A."	18	—
1985	Cote	"Judy"	44	229.09
	Aslett	"Lil Thumper"	69	226.35
	Miller	"Texas Gem"	73	220.70
	Sawyer	"Lucy P"	74	215.50
	Drew	"Alouetta"	2	212.21
	Summers	"Sump'n Else"	35	196.26
	Harris	"Gold Fever"	25	—
1986	Sharp	"Aero Magic"	43	229.61
	Drew	"Friberg Special"	2	222.41
	Miller	"Texas Gem"	73	221.39
	Sawyer	"Lucy P"	74	219.65
	Fogg	"Aloha"	4	217.99
	Harris	"Gold Fever"	25	205.45
	Slayton	"Stinger"	21	199.92
1987	Preston	"Sitting Duck"	44	232.99
	Sharp	"Aero Magic"	43	227.11
	Miller	"Pushy Cat"	14	224.13
	Hubler	"Aloha"	4	220.67
	Harris	"Gold Fever"	25	216.82
	Drew	"Friberg Special"	2	214.51
	Roberson	"Puffin"	73	206.54

FORMULA I (CONTINUED)

Year	Pilot	Aircraft	#	Speed
1988	Preston	"Sitting Duck"	44	240.75
	Sharp	"Aero Magic"	43	234.67
	Morris	"Sahara"	33	230.31
	Drew	"Friberg Special"	2	227.62
	Roberson	"Puffin"	73	222.07
	Dowd	"Super Spook"	77	220.23
	Miller	"Pushy Cat"	14	—
1991	Sharp	"Nemesis"	3	245.26
	Miller	"Pushy Cat"	14	242.21
	Bumford	"Bummer's Bullet"	55	241.59
	Porter	"Sitting Duck"	44	240.99
	Beck	"Miss Reno"	69	230.83
	Gray	"F/X"	96	224.57
	Drew	"Alouette"	2	216.56

Year	Pilot	Aircraft	#	Speed
1989	Cote	"Alley Cat"	4	231.25
	Miller	"Pushy Cat"	14	229.95
	Morris	"Sahara"	33	219.25
	Porter	"Aero Magic"	43	212.00
	Kirol	"Super Shock"	77	211.15
	Slayton	"Stinger"	21	207.84
	Sharp	"Blue Streak"	96	—
1992	Sharp	"Nemesis"	3	238.18
	Porter	"Sitting Duck"	44	232.31
	Miller	"Pushy Cat"	14	231.01
	Bumford	"Bummer's Bullet"	55	227.79
	Bohannon	"Pushy Galore"	89	225.29
	Channing	"Miss Reno"	69	216.02
	Hubler	"Mariah"	95	215.44

Year	Pilot	Aircraft	#	Speed
1990	Miller	"Pushy Cat"	14	237.41
	Porter	"Sitting Duck"	44	237.08
	Bumford	"Bummer's Bullet"	55	233.85
	Cote	"Alley Cat"	4	230.04
	Beck	"Miss Reno"	69	225.02
	Gray	"F/X"	96	224.23
	Gray	"Areo Magic"	43	217.78
1993	Sharp	"Nemesis"	3	246.85
	Rossi	"Chico Puro"	63	233.86
	Miller	"Pushy Cat"	14	233.55
	Ippolito	"Alley Cat"	4	227.68
	Hauptman	"Judy"	44	227.11
	Hubler	"Mariah"	95	225.11
	Channing	"Miss Reno"	69	220.69

SPORT BIPLANE

Year	Pilot	Aircraft	#	Speed
1964	Parsons	Knight Twister	—	144.57
	Shannon	Knight Twister	—	143.41
	Nagel	Knight Twister	—	131.50
	Boland	Starduster	—	130.63
	Rechenmacher	EAA Special	—	120.44
1967	Boland	Mong Sport	3	151.64
	White	Starduster	1	151.31
	McIntire	Pitts Special	17	151.29
	Christian	Mong Sport	99	147.69
	Fischer	Mong Sport	8	146.72
	Smith	Mong Special	26	133.46
1970	Boland	Mong Sport	3	177.45
	Christian	"Mongster"	99	168.49
	Forbes	DSA Miniplane	10	163.67
	Warwick	"Hot Canary"	97	163.27
	Hoffman	"Susie Bee"	44	151.61
	Garber	Pitts Special	18	141.45
	Fischer	Mong Sport	8	156.01

Year	Pilot	Aircraft	#	Speed
1965	Boland	Mong Sport	3	148.68
	Parsons	Knight Twister	11	146.06
	Rechenmacher	EAA Biplane	22	118.81
	Ormsbee	DSA Miniplane	5	117.42
	Fischer	Starduster	7	115.43
	White	Starduster	1	91.49
1968	Christian	"Mongster"	99	175.13
	Boland	Mong Sport	3	171.18
	Fischer	Mong Sport	8	155.15
	White	Starduster	1	153.13
	Swinn	Pitts Special	37	148.37
	Smith	Mong Sport	26	143.90
1971	Boland	Mong Sport	3	181.67
	Deschamps	"Sorceress"	89	175.29
	Christian	"Mongster"	99	173.84
	Forbes	DSA Forbes-Wolfram	10	169.08
	Warwick	"Hot Canary"	97	167.96
	Hoffman	"Susie Bee"	44	164.60
	Fischer	Mong Sport	8	160.68
	Hall	Jungster III	76	—

Year	Pilot	Aircraft	#	Speed
1966	Wickliffe	"Dollar Special"	11	147.72
	White	Starduster	1	144.72
	McIntire	Pitts Special	17	144.67
	Boland	Mong Sport	3	148.42
	Harendeen	Pitts Special	37	133.06
	Fischer	Mong Sport	8	127.10
1969	Christian	"Mongster"	99	184.02
	Boland	Mong Sport	3	183.49
	Forbes	DSA Miniplane	10	159.29
	Hoffman	"Suzie Bee"	44	157.89
	Fischer	Mong Sport	8	157.66
	Coons	Starduster	13	156.48
	Schulte	Starduster	45	153.32
	DuPont	Pitts Special	69	153.28
1972	Beck	"Sorceress"	89	189.72
	Hall	"Jonathan L. Seagull"	76	180.04
	Forbes	"Forbes Special"	10	178.03
	Fischer	"Super Mong"	8	167.75
	Boland	"Gone Mong"	3	184.89
	Christian	"Mongster"	99	—
	Warwick	"Hot Canary"	97	—
	Thomas	"Miss Q"	7	—

SPORT BIPLANE (CONTINUED)

1973

Pilot	Aircraft	#	Speed
White	"Sundancer"	1	194.95
Beck	"Sorceress"	89	184.62
Forbes	"Olympia Swallow"	10	184.50
Boland	"Gone Mong"	3	178.81
Fairbanks	"White Knight"	5	168.88
Hoffman	"Suzie Bee"	44	166.03
Fischer	"Super Mong"	8	161.01
Janson	DSA Miniplane	4	147.82

1974

Pilot	Aircraft	#	Speed
White	"Sundancer"	1	198.17
Beck	"Sorceress"	89	191.53
Forbes	Forbes Special	10	182.97
Fairbanks	"White Knight"	5	170.18
Hoffman	"Suzie Bee"	44	168.98
Raven	"Spirit of '76"	76	159.20
Fischer	"Super Mong"	8	157.78
Janson	DSA Miniplane	4	149.15

1975

Pilot	Aircraft	#	Speed
Beck	"Sorceress"	89	198.99
White	"Sundancer"	1	196.41
Forbes	"Cobra"	2	177.67
Fairbanks	"White Knight"	5	171.02
Hoffman	"Suzie Bee"	44	171.02
Wrolstad	"Super Chick"	14	168.16
Fischer	"Super Mong"	8	163.64
Clark	Mong Sport	46	143.28

1976

Pilot	Aircraft	#	Speed
Beck	"Sorceress"	89	202.15
Hines	"Sundancer"	1	198.44
Forbes	"Cobra"	2	178.22
Fairbanks	"White Knight"	5	177.38
Aberle	Mong Sport	32	168.82
Fischer	"Super Mong"	8	163.17
Allen	Pitts Special	42	139.35
Brown	"Washoe Zephyr"	90	139.22

No Biplane Class races at Reno during 1977, 1978, 1979.

1980

Pilot	Aircraft	#	Speed
Hines	"Sundancer"	1	206.62
Kramer	"Cobra"	22	177.05
Fairbanks	"White Knight"	5	176.38
Brown	"Tonapah Low"	00	172.93
Smith	"Taste of Honey"	6	172.17
Grieshaber	"Mongster"	99	164.63
Wentworth	"Super Chic"	14	155.40
Beck	"Sorceress"	89	210.73

1981

Pilot	Aircraft	#	Speed
Hines	"Sundancer"	1	209.44
Kramer	"Cobra"	22	187.13
Mortensen	"Amsoil/Rutan Special"	3	181.13
Aberle	"Two Bits"	25	174.41
Allen	"Tonapah Low"	00	170.98
Morss	"Mongster"	99	170.28
Kempf	"Check 6"	26	143.70
Brown	"Scarlet"	29	143.61

1982

Pilot	Aircraft	#	Speed
Hines	"Sundancer"	1	209.40
Mortensen	"Amsoil/Rutan Racer"	3	209.21
Beck	"Sorceress"	89	206.29
Aberle	"Two Bits"	25	196.46

1983

Pilot	Aircraft	#	Speed
Hines	"Sundancer"	1	217.60
Beck	"Sorceress"	89	202.35
Kramer	"Cobra"	22	186.40

1984

Pilot	Aircraft	#	Speed
Beck	"Miss Tahoe"	00	189.97
Fairbanks	"White Knight"	5	185.35
Hugo	"Taste of Honey"	6	165.49
Marrocola	"Snaggle Tooth Sal"	35	148.55
Allen	"Red Baron"	1	139.98

1985

Pilot	Aircraft	#	Speed
Beck	"Miss Lake Tahoe"	00	195.62
Fairbanks	"White Knight"	5	177.67
Mortensen	"Pacific Flyer"	91	175.48
Hugo	"Taste of Honey"	6	162.49
Schulte	"Pits 'N Pieces"	42	144.70
Penketh	"Passion Pitts"	4	143.84

1986

Pilot	Aircraft	#	Speed
Preston	"Miss Lake Tahoe"	00	192.67
Fairbanks	"White Knight"	5	166.17
Hugo	"A Taste of Honey"	6	165.97
Selvidge	"Slick"	2	164.78
Meyer	"Chuck"	111	161.42
Brown	"Scarlet"	29	156.40
Stubbs	"Casey"	30	154.91
Penketh	"Passion Pitts"	4	150.93

1987

Pilot	Aircraft	#	Speed
Aberle	"Long Gone Mong"	31	196.47
Fairbanks	"White Knight"	5	179.28
Allen	"Southern Air Transport"	21	178.24
Morss	"Amsoil Pacific Flyer"	91	176.36
Meyer	"Chuck"	111	169.73
Selvidge	"Slick"	2	169.11
Kempf	"Bully Bee"	11	164.64
Penketh	"Passion Pitts"	4	158.41

1988

Pilot	Aircraft	#	Speed
Preston	"Top Cat"	00	205.92
Aberle	"Long Gone Mong"	31	203.98
Penketh	"My Pitts"	1	179.89
Paquin	"Buzz Job"	90	179.70
Fairbanks	"White Knight"	5	176.47
Allen	"Southern Air Transport"	21	175.52
Selvidge	"Slick"	2	167.64
Lister	"Little Red Baron"	77	162.49

1989

Pilot	Aircraft	#	Speed
Aberle	"Wanna Play II"	40	196.14
Maxwell	"Legal Eagle"	69	185.65
Mortenson	"Amsoil Pacific Flyer"	91	184.70
Paquin	"Buzz Job"	90	179.77
Penketh	"My Pitts"	1	176.70
Harris	"Sonoma Red"	62	168.83
Ferguson	"Let The Good Times Roll"	20	164.59
Penketh	"Passion Pitts"	4	159.51

1990

Pilot	Aircraft	#	Speed
Mortensen	"Amsoil Pacific Flyer"	91	192.28
Maxwell	"Legal Eagle"	69	184.76
Paquin	"Buzz Job"	90	180.46
Penketh	"My Pitts"	1	175.78
Morse	—	111	173.09
Detsch	"Uno"	55	172.50
Ferguson	"Let The Good Times Roll"	20	165.85

SPORT BIPLANE (CONTINUED)

Year	Pilot	Aircraft	#	Speed
1991	Ueno	"Sumari"	18	195.27
	Way	"Magic"	27	183.84
	Allen	"Legal Eagle"	69	180.23
	Smith	"Glass Slipper"	88	177.73
	Stubbs	"Caseu"	30	171.69
	Penketh	"My Pitts"	1	169.21
	Enefer	"Thunder Chicken"	10	167.45
	Harris	"Sonoma Red"	62	164.04
1992	Smith	"Glass Slipper"	88	193.89
	Allen	"Legal Eagle"	69	192.10
	Johnson	"Twerpster"	40	191.90
	Way	"Magic"	27	181.35
	Stubbs	"Patty Anne"	30	177.78
	Penketh	"My Pitts"	1	176.64
	Blackwood	"Blacked Out"	111	168.27
	Pacquin	"Buzz Job"	90	164.11
1993	Nelson	"Full Tilt Boogie"	40	208.47
	Cox	"Wild Thing"	33	202.49
	Allen	"Legal Eagle"	69	193.68
	Smith	"Glass Slipper"	88	190.64
	Way	"Magic"	27	182.32
	Stubbs	"Patty Anne"	30	178.57
	Pacquin	"Buzz Job"	90	180.42
	Brown	"Tonopah Low II"	00	168.39

AT-6 (SNJ)

Year	Pilot	Aircraft	#	Speed
1968	Otzen	SNJ-5	1	181.32
	Sykes	SNJ-4	3	181.25
	Livingston	SNJ-5	9	180.98
	Williams	SNJ-4	5	174.43
	Baker	SNJ-5	6	174.09
	Keefe	SNJ-5	11	169.71
1969	Hall	Mk. II	7	190.90
	Minges	AT-6D	96	182.13
	Philippi	SNJ-5	4	179.89
	Snyder	SNJ-5	99	179.22
	McKinney	AT-6D	22	176.76
	Malaspina	AT-6G	14	176.26
1970				
1971	Mitchem	AT-6C	94	205.85
	Palmer	SNJ-5	9	195.71
	Turnbull	SNJ-5	72	189.14
	Barrett	LSNJ-5	10	188.21
	Kostelnik	AT-6G	47	158.20
	Phillippi	SNJ-5	4	—
1972	McClain	AT-6C	25	201.59
	Mosby	AT-6C	44	201.31
	Turnbull	SNJ-5	72	197.04
	Metcalf	Mk. IV	88	188.85
	Suacci	AT-6D	69	—
	Phillippi	SNJ-5	4	—
1973	Turnbull	SNJ-5	72	206.60
	Mott	SNJ-5	42	204.35
	Palmer	SNJ-5	9	203.82
	Suacci	AT-6D	69	202.25
	Wilson	SNJ-5	10	200.09
	Early	SNJ-5	70	197.71
1974	Palmer	AT-6F	9	211.35
	McClain	SNJ-4	5	207.84
	Mott	SNJ-5	42	206.01
	Buehn	SNJ-4	43	202.91
	Wilson	SNJ-5	10	202.53
1975	Palmer	AT-6F	9	207.17
	Buehn	SNJ-4	43	202.34
	Wells	SNJ-5	9	202.25
	Rina	SNJ-6	73	200.09
	McClain	SNJ-4	5	197.85
	Turnbull	SNJ-5	72	196.95
1976	Palmer	AT-6F	99	210.68
	Rina	SNJ-6	73	208.95
	Mosby	Mk. II	44	206.85
	Landry	SNJ-6	98	206.75
	Sykes	AT-6C	3	202.63
	DeWalt	AT-6	74	199.08
1977	Twombly	T-6	41	209.66
	Palmer	T-6F	99	209.51
	Rina	SNJ-6	73	206.16
	Mott	SNJ-5	42	204.40
	Beck	SNJ-4	2	202.82
	DeWalt	AT-6	74	200.88
1978	Rina	"Miss Everything"	73	205.71
	Twombly	"Spooled Up"	41	203.39
	Sykes	"Two Five Charles"	3	201.79
	Mott	"Mis-Chief"	42	198.75
	Palmer	"Gotcha"	99	190.54

No AT-6 (SNJ) Races at Reno in 1979 & 1980.

Year	Pilot	Aircraft	#	Speed
1981	Mosby	"Miss Behavin"	44	222.78
	Rina	"Miss Everything"	73	222.49
	Beck	"Cal. Med-Fly"	2	220.27
	Sykes	"Two Five Charles"	3	219.35
	McDonald	"Big Red"	5	217.94
	Goss	"Warlock"	75	214.65
1982	Twombly	"Miss Behavin"	44	214.90
	Rina	"Miss Everything"	73	213.85
	Goss	"Warlock"	75	213.55
	Beck	"Cal. Med-Fly"	2	208.65
	Buehn	"Ruthie"	39	206.92
	Gist	"Texas Red"	68	206.45
1983	Sykes	"The Mystery Ship"	14	225.94
	Rina	"Miss Everything"	73	223.16
	Buehn	"Angel's Desire"	3	222.87
	Mott	"Mis-Chief"	42	220.38
	Gist	"Texas Red"	68	217.24
	Catalano	"Nuthin' Fancy"	94	216.23

AT-6 (SNJ) (CONTINUED)

Year	Pilot	Aircraft	#	Speed
1984	Rina	"Miss Everything"	73	217.26
	Buehn	"Thunderbolt"	18	217.12
	Mott	"Mis-Chief"	42	216.94
	Catalano	"Nuthin' Fancy"	94	214.17
	Goss	"Warlock"	75	213.22
	Gist	"Texas Red"	68	209.47
1987	Van Fossen	"Miss TNT"	27	226.36
	Mott	"Mischief"	42	224.78
	Goss	"Warlock"	75	223.50
	Difani	"Thunderbolt"	18	219.22
	Hutchins	"Silver Baby"	1	217.73
	Bruce	"Dash One"	4	225.66
1990	Dwelle	"Tinkertoy"	7	229.26
	Goss	"Warlock"	75	226.78
	Van Fossen	"Miss TNT"	27	223.35
	Macy	"Six Cat"	6	222.26
	McNeely	—	90	220.75
	Difani	"Thunderbolt"	18	217.49
1993	Van Fossen	"Miss TNT"	27	226.89
	Hartung	"Boomer"	89	223.01
	Hutchins	"Mystical Power"	21	222.59
	Goss	"Warlock"	75	221.81
	Twombly	-	41	218.96
	Difani	"Thunderbolt"	18	212.19

Year	Pilot	Aircraft	#	Speed
1985	Difani	"Thunderbolt"	18	213.89
	Goss	"Warlock"	75	213.68
	Rina	"Miss Everything"	73	210.84
	Gist	"Texas Red"	68	209.07
	Van Fossen	"Miss TNT"	27	208.83
	Mott	"Mis-Chief"	42	191.03
1988	Van Fossen	"Miss TNT"	27	229.76
	Dwelle	"Tinkertoy"	7	227.94
	Difani	"Thunderbolt"	18	220.82
	Bruce	"Dash One"	4	220.48
	Twombly	"Miss Behavin"	44	218.50
	Goss	"Warlock"	75	213.71
1991	Van Fossen	"Miss TNT"	27	227.03
	Goss	"Warlock"	75	221.69
	Day	"Catch 22"	22	220.70
	Macy	"Six Cat"	6	217.51
	Hutchins	"Mystical Power"	21	215.71
	Difani	"Thunderbolt"	18	209.48

Year	Pilot	Aircraft	#	Speed
1986	Van Fossen	"Miss TNT"	27	223.45
	Heale	"Lickety Split"	9	221.39
	De Fani	"Thunderbolt"	18	220.25
	Redding	"After You"	88	216.27
	Rina	"Miss Everything"	73	215.69
	Goss	"Warlock"	75	213.50
1989	Dwelle	"Tinkertoy"	7	222.33
	Van Fossen	"Miss TNT"	27	221.12
	Goss	"Warlock"	75	218.43
	Difani	"Thunderbolt"	18	213.43
	Macy	"Six Cat"	6	212.49
	Foley	"Miss Behavin'"	44	208.94
1992	Van Fossen	"Miss TNT"	27	234.77
	Goss	"Warlock"	75	228.35
	Hartung	"Boomer"	89	227.29
	Macy	"Six Cat"	6	225.69
	Bruce	"Slo Thunder"	4	225.22
	Hutchins	"Mystical Power"	21	215.28